WING DING

WING DING

Lt. Col Gene T. Carson USA (Ret)

Copyright © 2000 by Lt. Col Gene T. Carson USA (Ret).

Library of Congress Number:		00-193417
ISBN #:	Hardcover	0-7388-5688-6
	Softcover	0-7388-5689-4

All rights reserved. No part of this book may be reproduced or transmitted in any form or by any means, electronic or mechanical, including photocopying, recording, or by any information storage and retrieval system, without permission in writing from the copyright owner.

This is a true story. In some cases names, characters and incidents have been altered to preclude any resemblance to any persons, living or dead, events or locales to the extent necessary to make such a resemblance entirely coincidental.

This book was printed in the United States of America.

To order additional copies of this book, contact:
Xlibris Corporation
1-888-7-XLIBRIS
www.Xlibris.com
Orders@Xlibris.com

Contents

FOREWORD 9
PREFACE 13

1 15
2 20
3 24
4 29
5 37
6 40
7 44
8 50
9 59
10 71
11 74
12 88
13 94
14 97
15 99
16 107
17 111
18 115
19 117
20 122
21 126
22 130
23 135
24 137
25 140

26	144
13	149
27	152
28	156
29	160
30	163
31	166
32	169
33	174
34	178
35	182
36	187
37	190
ACKNOWEDGMENTS	198
EPILOGUE	201

FOREWORD

What a golden opportunity it is to be asked to introduce my twin brother and his story. He has written a book of an era gone by; it tells of a brief time in our history. It is a book about those who lived and shared during a brief but intense air war and for those who want to know about the era. My brother, Gene, recalls moments of terror, relief, elation and exhaustion often in the same paragraph as he relates his experiences as a tail gunner and a flight engineer of a heavy bomber flying over Germany in World War II.

It is fitting for me to dwell a moment on the man and a bit about his boyhood fascination with aviation which I too shared. Much of our fascination was whetted and brought to an edge by reading pulp magazines of the old Streets and Smith variety. Our heroes were G-8 and his Aces, Bull Martin and Nippy Weston as they battled against the Hun over the skies of the Western Front. We built 'rubber-band-powered' Spads and German Fokkers launching them from the third floor attic window. Often the Fokkers would be set ablaze to make sure G-8 and his men were winning the battle.

We were about 10 years old when we experienced a real airplane ride. A cousin of our Mother owned a small flying service. During the County Fair at Leighton, Pennsylvania we managed to get a sight seeing ride in his Waco biplane. From then on we were hooked, our feet never belonged on the ground.

As you read this book you will see more than words. You will undoubtedly note how my brother, Gene, demonstrated a ready imagination as he made his transition from the kitchen to the airplane. He paved his road to success by taking full advantage of existing opportunities, many of his own making. Whenever the Army Air Corps left the door ajar, Gene, always the consummate opportunist entered in a flash.

Gene's ability to manage opportunities existed during our childhood. He could talk me into anything and often did. I recall nearly being electrocuted when he unscrewed a light bulb and had me insert a horseshoe magnet into the bare socket. "To recharge the magnet," he said. His inquisitiveness also managed to heat up the world when, while seated on the throne, he used a strike-anywhere match on the toilet seat. The toilet seat of ancient manufacture was covered with celluloid, a highly flammable material. Why he was not equally torched could only be attributed to his consistent ability to escape his manufactured situations.

Growing up with my twin brother was a lesson in living, never dull and never a doubt he would be there if I needed him. At about age ten I suffered a broken leg in a sledding accident and he managed to pull me over some very sizable hills for a five-mile trip to safety. His deed always comes to mind when I see the picture of a boy helping his brother with the statement, "He is not heavy, he is my brother." These words define my brother Gene in every respect.

On the night of Victory in Europe we managed to meet in London. I had been released from POW status in Germany where I had heard many tales about a 'second tour gunner' called "Wing Ding" and his exploits. Many of the less than fortunate associates of my brother who joined me as POW's thought I was my brother, Gene. Knowing my brother, I had no trouble believing their stories.

When I was shot down my situation was reported as killed in action. Gene, having completed his combat tour, was safe in the United States. He volunteered to return to Europe to fly another tour either to avenge me or to look for me. We finally met on Victory in Europe Day at the Rainbow Corners USO Club, Piccadilly Circus, London, through the kind assistance of Adele Astaire, Gene's good friend and a grand lady. Adele, the sister of none other than Fred Astaire spent many hours of volunteer service at the USO. I came home. Gene, satisfied by our reunion, went to North Africa.

I remained in the Air Force. Gene went to the Army and became a paratrooper. Our travels and military service put us in touch in Japan, Korea, and Vietnam. We stood together in Texas and saluted the casket of my son 1st.Lt.John Harvey Carson, a Marine Company Commander, who had fallen in Vietnam. After we laid John Harvey to rest we tended to the business at hand, serving our country. We went to Vietnam; it seemed only proper to do our tours.

I hope you enjoy the book. Gene has written it from his heart. It is truthful and honest with humor and tragedy. As he says, "It was a nasty business we were in." I am honored to have this chance to briefly introduce a brother I love. He proved himself to be a great warrior and a fine gentleman.

John W. Carson
Lt. Col. USAF (Ret.)

S/Sgt. John W. Carson

PREFACE

I was a tail gunner and flight engineer on a B-17 Flying Fortress. I flew out of England with the 8th US Army Air Corps from 1943 to 1945. My twin brother, John W. Carson was flying with the 15th Air Corps out of Italy. On December 20, 1943 he was reported killed in action when the "Eager Beaver", a B-17 on which he was flying as radio operator, suffered a direct hit from flak while in the vicinity of Athens, Greece. He was on his 28th combat mission.

I went to Mitchell Field, Long Island, New York when my overseas tour of duty had been completed. Around the end of February 1944, I was in New York City attending a Wings Club dinner at the Waldorf Astoria Hotel where I was being honored as a recipient of the Distinguished Flying Cross. During the evening I was offered an opportunity to make a telephone call to my mother. She informed me of the report of my brother's death. My reaction to the news was disbelief. I told her I did not believe the report and promised to find John. Not wanting to rain on the parade, I told no one during the evening. The next day was different. It marked the start of my search for my brother. Nothing else mattered. Each day I had a goal to be one step closer to my return to Europe, back into harm's way. My love for my brother and my promise to our mother was of first priority.

This story is dedicated to those who flew and to the ground crews who made the flying possible, to those who survived and to the many others who did not. It is also dedicated to another group; those who lost loved ones in the great air war and to the men and women who today wonder what it was like for their fathers, brothers, grandfathers and uncles to fly during the world's greatest air war.

I write so those who were never there will have an opportunity to know and understand what took place. But most of all, I write because it was real and it happened. It happened long ago and soon there will be no one left to write about it except those who were not there, and they will never be able to tell it like it was.

1
THE GREAT AIR WAR

I no longer hear the roar of the engines, the chatter of the guns and the savage bursting of the flak. The smell of cordite and the fumes of gasoline no longer curl into my nostrils. The great air war of World War II is history. However, there are nights and there are days I find myself reliving moments of a now historic era. The memory returns as if a realistic dream and once again I find myself a member of a B-17 crew. My eyes search the sky for the Luftwaffe; flak rattles our B-17. I see aircraft fall, both theirs and ours. Too few parachutes dot the sky. I slowly come to the realization, I am here and it is now. The records of the 8th Air Force list more than 47,000 casualties with over 26,000 deaths.

There were short missions and long missions. But there never was an easy mission. Each mission however short or long was filled with danger from the onset to the end. The final bell tolled for those involved in on-ground explosions, crashes on take-off, the all too frequent mid-air collisions, crashes during flight and crashes on landing. In some cases death came from friendly fire and errant bombs dropped from one of our own aircraft flying at a higher altitude onto one of our aircraft at a lower altitude.

A bomber's crew, although a team, was largely dependent on the skills of its pilot and copilot. When it came to ordinary airplane handling skills, there were great pilots and mediocre pilots. But the pilot who could hold a bomber in tight formation while flying into flak thick enough to walk on was without question a great pilot. And so too were those pilots who held steady in face of the Luftwaffe's unrelenting, vicious and intense fighter attacks as they came ripping head on through the bomber's formation with machine guns and cannon blazing. It took courage and self-discipline for a pilot to hold the aircraft in formation under such circumstances. Not all pilots had such courage. For the bomber pilots such courage and self-discipline were mandatory prerequisites.

How do I know of these things? I was there; I flew with fellow aircrew members and with some of those great and courageous pilots. Only twice was it my misfortune to share the cockpit as a flight engineer when the pilot or copilot failed to measure up. In both cases the man in the other seat demonstrated the superb skill and courage necessary to save both aircraft and crew.

During my first tour, while flying as a tail gunner, it was my good fortune to fly with pilot Otis C. Ingebritsen and copilot Edward J. Meginnies, men of skill and courage. Both were second lieutenants and not long out of flight school and B-17 training. Otis Ingebritsen, known as 'Dingle' had recently taken over the crew at Dyersburg, Tennessee after the original pilot had been killed in a crash while flying with a friend. He keenly felt the pressure of being new to the crew. However his professional approach tended to give others confidence. I never heard him raise his voice. Ed Meginnies, known as 'Mac' was a reluctant B-17 copilot. He had been trained as a fighter pilot and resented being thrust into the cockpit of the B-17. However, he put his dream aside and became part of the team. His moves in the cockpit were sure and positive; it was as if he had become a part of the airplane.

Our crew was assigned to the 560th Squadron of the 388th Bomb Group. We started and nearly completed our tour as a crew. Soon after our first mission we changed flight engineers. Sergeant Harold L. Pepper left our crew and was replaced by Technical Sergeant Charles "Chuck" Allred. On January 5, 1944 our bombardier, Michael J. Chaklos was killed when a piece of flak penetrated an artery in his groin. His loss, so near the end of our tour, had a deep impact on the crew. Suddenly, a friend was gone. Today, Mike is at peace in the cemetery at Madingley, England.

The odds were stacked against completing a tour; 450 combat-crews passed through the 388th Bomb Group during the war. Of these 141 crews failed to make it. Some were killed in crashes; some were killed on missions. Others were prisoners of war and in rare cases some had evaded capture. Records also indicate during its first 100 missions the 388th Bomb Group lost 83 crews. The Group's next 206 missions had a loss of 58 crews.

One period, October 8, 1943 through October 14, 1943 is indelibly and forever stamped into my mind. During those four days the 8th Air Force suffered a loss of approximately 142 heavy bombers, a total of 1,420 officers and men. It was as if the brass residing in higher headquarters had found a need to make a point by castrating the ability of the Germans to continue waging war. We were the pawns used in a great effort by the disciples of strategic bombing to prove their point. Today as I reflect on history I give little thought to what was correct. I only appraise my own good fortune. For surely, I went to the circus and I was allowed to see the elephant and come home to tell about it.

For those of us who flew against the pilots of the Luftwaffe and the superb antiaircraft gunners of the Third Reich, the clock ticks on as our final days draw ever closer. But we have memories, memories enough to tell a thousand tales. Tales not unlike what you read here. There are tales of skill, courage, and daring, memories of trying to survive as well as memories of fun times between the flying and the dying. Combat airmen lived and died in a much cleaner environment than did the ground combat soldier; at the end of a mission, if fortunate, we returned to a hot meal and a clean bed. We had no foxholes or bunkers in which to take shelter. There was only the thin skin of our airplane to protect us, a skin you could punch a hole in with a screwdriver. If our thin-skinned airplane suffered battle damage the crew might be fortunate and have sufficient time to enjoy the option of a parachute jump into enemy territory. But such a jump almost always meant prison camp and possible death. A successfully completed mission found some of us, like Pavlov's dog, waiting for a calming shot of whisky at the de-briefing room.

Sometimes it took more than one drink and sympathetic intelligence personnel quietly violated regulations.

We named our aircraft after ladies, places, animals, people, and things. We drank a lot of warm beer, learned to drink tea, danced the hokey-pokey and courted the ladies of the land. We experienced the warmth and friendship of the British people, enjoyed the wonders the country had to offer and invented a few new wonders of our own as we took in the friendly sights and nights of Piccadilly Circus as spectators and participants. There was the Windmill Theater. It never closed, and the friendly Rainbow Corner Club near Piccadilly Circus where Fred Astaire's sister Adele worked tirelessly as a volunteer.

We lived a good life between missions. But on most mission days we awoke to the predawn dampness with full knowledge of what was to come. We were about to face a formidable enemy. As I reflect back I know I was scared and with good reason. We were up against some of the world's finest fighter pilots and extremely accurate antiaircraft fire. Each mission was flown with full awareness it could be a final mission. There was no certainty of a tomorrow and like many others I lived for today.

People speak of courage. I am not really sure about courage. Under moments of stress when it seems as if there are only seconds left to live strange things take place. Who can give you courage or train you to know exactly what to do when a burst of flak punches a softball size hole in the windshield and fragments spray throughout the cockpit area? Who can prepare you to do what is necessary when severed oxygen and hydraulic lines ignite with unbelievable intensity next to a box of flares? I'm still not sure it's courage when you conquer intense pain from wounds and continue to fight for survival. Such are not moments calling for courage; they are moments demanding action. There is no time for courage.

The need for courage comes the next day. It comes the day after you have returned to your barracks where you found the empty bunks already stripped of personal effects and property. There is no trace of the personal effects of the prior occupants. You endure a long and lonely night of bad dreams and sleep fitfully with interrupting thoughts. You know you are going again at dawn; it is then when there will be a need for courage.

Breakfast at the mess hall usually consisted of an abomination known as powdered eggs, a type of canned meat known as Spam and "SOS", a dish consisting of gravy and any kind of meat the cook could find, spread on toast. It was commonly known by the rather vulgar title as, "shit on a shingle".

Fear is controllable, but sometimes there is an excessive need to use the latrine. It is also possible for your mind to cause your body to revolt and your breakfast may not set well leading to a painful knot in the area of the solar plexus. You manage to burp; there is some relief. The pain continues, but now you feel better and participate in some of the pre-briefing pseudo-bravado banter exchanged by those in the room.

You are in your seat when the briefing officer pulls the curtain aside to show a long red line indicating the route to the target. You listen intently as you are told what to expect on the way to the target, over the target, and on the way home. This is when there is a time for a silent prayer. It is also a time to search deep to find your courage.

2
THE BOY WHO WENT TO WAR

I cannot write the story unless I introduce you to the boy who went to war. It is almost unbelievable, but the calendar indicates on January 4, 2000 more than three-quarters of a century had passed since I first saw the light of day. I look back with few regrets.

However, my body bears the scars of earlier eras and feels the pain of Purple Hearts, some not too well done parachute jumps and more than a few youthful indiscretions. The story I am about to relate took place a long time ago, long before many of you were born.

It was 1938. My twin brother, John and I were thirteen years old when we were accepted as students at the Hershey Industrial School, Hershey, Pennsylvania. In those days the school was known as 'HIS'. It was a school for white orphan and half-orphan boys.

Acceptance was based on the needs of an applicant's family and a student's qualification as determined by testing. We were excited with the news we had been accepted. It was at Hershey I learned to milk a cow, chop corn, harvest fields of grain, make hay, cut the early morning asparagus and look at the rear end of a pair of mules moving from one end of a field to the other.

The environment of the school was structured to teach ethics, high morals and integrity. Today the school still teaches ethics, high morals and integrity, but it has a different name and to some extent different philosophies. It is now called the Milton S. Hershey School.

It has assets in excess of $5 billion and accepts boys and girls of all races. Unfortunately modern labor laws preclude having students perform the farm work which instilled in us the work ethic.

John and I shared a room at a farm unit known as Arcadia. It covered more than 350 acres of land, had a herd of about thirty Holstein cows, some horses and mules. Meals were served family style and the food was of the best quality. The students at Arcadia ranged in age from thirteen to seventeen.

The environment was ideal. However, like any new venture, there was the trauma of change and the pain of homesickness. We were leaving our real home and moving into a more disciplined environment where standing was determined by a pecking order.

I learned about pecking order my first night at the home. We were sitting in study hall with about twenty other boys. Without warning something crashed onto the right side of my face. I was on the floor, sitting on my rear, looking up. Blood streamed from my split lip and nose. Standing over me was an older student; Robert is enough of a name. In his hands he held a volume of the World Book. Robert struck me without warning or reason. When I asked him why, he said, " To teach you your place." I said nothing more. I licked the blood from my lip and sniffed to stop my nose from bleeding. I had learned my place. But in my heart I made a vow. I would get even.

A word of caution is in order here. No one should draw a conclusion from one such experience. To the contrary the school was a wonderful place. I would have to say my time at Hershey represented some of the finest and most formative years of my life.

One of the main goals of the school was to prepare students for a vocational trade of their choice. My brother John elected to take auto mechanic training and I decided to learn the bakery trade. This resulted in my being transferred from the farm called Arcadia to a unit known as Oakleigh, located on the outskirts of Hershey. My bakery training took place in a new model bakery with the finest equipment. Milton M. Hunchberger, a long time professional baker, was our instructor. I recall his words, "Gene you are a fine baker, but unless you change your attitude you will not live to see your twenty-fifth birthday." Mr. Hunchberger was not always right.

Next door to the bakery, in the same building, was a small candy shop where all sorts of candies were made. Mr. Hershey was a frequent visitor to our shops. Our training programs called for two weeks in the shop and two weeks in class. John's auto-mechanics classroom was located in the shop section of the main high school building high on the hill overlooking the city of Hershey.

The bakery was located in Hershey at one end of the Ice Arena next to Hershey Park. The sports arena, ice arena swimming pool and ballroom were all within spitting distance. In those days I had a trumpet and was taking lessons much to the frustration of the music teacher. I would often slip out of the bakery and go to the ballroom to listen to the big bands during their rehearsal. All of the great names played there. Among some of the well known playing Hershey were the Dorseys, Benny Goodman, Glen Miller and a host of others. They were all willing to sign a boy's autograph book, but I found Glen Miller to the friendliest of all.

The other diversions were the sports arena where the midget cars roared around the quarter mile track to the delight of the racing fans and the ice area where the hockey team Hershey Bears held forth. I doubt if there could have been a more exciting environment for a teen-age boy.

My route to and from the home where I lived with twenty-five other boys took me through the park and past the zoo. One of my games was to annoy a huge European Red Deer when he was in rut. The monster would come crashing into the fence as I teased him. If the fence had ever given way I would not be here to write these words.

My other interest was to be expected of a maturing youth. In the summer the park filled with pretty young female visitors. I think I was about fifteen when these visitors became more interesting than the European Red Deer.

Her name, like so many others, has long since been forgotten. But she came from Philadelphia and was of Italian descent. She was a gorgeous creature and she captured my heart. It was from her I received my first electrifying kiss and came to a realization; girls had soft and curvaceous bodies. Then like the leaves of autumn on the maple tree my youthful teacher disappeared back into the depths of the city from whence she came. I was heartbroken for several days.

To this day one of my early misdeeds comes back in my memory to haunt me. A man named Charlie worked in the candy shop as an instructor. He must have been fifty or so years old. One day I accidentally dropped a large steel sheet pan. The pan struck the tile floor with a tremendous crash. Charlie jumped and cursed me for making the noise. He claimed World War I had given him bad nerves. I thought it funny and frequently dropped a sheet pan just to see Charlie jump and hear him swear. If Charlie were alive today I would fall on my knees and beg his forgiveness, because now, after three wars, I understand why Charlie jumped. I too have found I do not care for unexpected loud noises. Unfortunately, for Charlie my awareness came too late.

At the end of about three and a half years of school I was an accomplished baker capable of taking my place in any commercial firm at a journeyman level. The school's program allowed students to take pre-graduation employment several months prior to graduation. I was offered a job as the dough man at the Pennway Bakery in Annville, Pennsylvania only about an hour's drive from Hershey. As dough man it was my responsibility to mix the bread dough and have it ready for final production each day. The work was done late in the afternoon and early morning.

At first I enjoyed the work and fulfilled my responsibilities at the bakery without difficulty. But soon after our June high school graduation I found my thoughts were constantly about my brother John who was already in military service. I too felt a need to serve our country. Come with me now and share those memories and stories of another time and place.

3
HOT DOG FRANK'S

Across from the Pennway Bakery on Main Street was a small restaurant built in the style of the diners so popular in those days; a cash register was located to the left near the front of a long counter. Aligned along the counter was a row of stools. On the right side, against the wall, there were a number of booths. The cuisine was for the most part fast food, sandwiches, hamburgers and hot dogs. The owner, a Greek immigrant known only as Frank, called his restaurant "Hot Dog Frank's". It was a favorite between class gathering place for students at Lebanon Valley College. Frank became somewhat of a surrogate father figure to his young customers. In his feigned gruffness there was always a word of advice and a friendly ear listening to problems.

While not at work at the bakery, I was a steady customer at Frank's. Probably, because I had been fatherless since I was one year old, Frank became a person to whom I turned for advice and counsel while devouring hot dogs smothered with sauerkraut, onions, and mustard. The beverage of choice, at a nickel a cup was Frank's black coffee. Frank had his own philosophy on how to run a successful business. It was simple; never let anyone else touch the cash register. Frank made it a point to collect and ring up every sale. He called it "the Greek system".

Just after midnight on November 6, 1942, I stood for the last time on the floor of the bakery. The war had been going on for almost a year and we did not seem to be winning. I felt a need to serve my country and thoughts of enlisting had often crossed my mind. However, the owner of Pennway Bakery, Harry Hunter, was quick to point out the need for bakers and claimed they were essential. I had come to the conclusion I was only essential to Harry Hunter.

The aroma of freshly baked bread filled the air as the final loaf started its rounds through the huge oven. I looked around the bakery and thought of my twin brother, John, now in the Army Air Corps, training to be a radio operator on a bomber crew. John had been in service for about five months, having left the day after our high school graduation. I recalled how mother cried when John told her he had enlisted and was leaving for service the next day. I also thought about the reason for her concern.

Our father, Thomas W. Carson, originally from Beckley, West Virginia, died from the after effects of phosgene gas poisoning suffered during World War I. His early death at about age 27, left our mother, Esther H. Carson, with twin boys only one year old. Mother never remarried. Every day she took time to look at our father's picture hung on the wall above the fireplace mantle. She often told us, "Your father always said he never wanted you boys to be soldiers." She cried on high school graduation night when John told her of his enlistment as she had undoubtedly cried when Tom Carson died. Again, her tears were to no avail. The country was at war. My twin brother John had heard the bugle call. Now I too was hearing the echo of the bugle.

I removed my apron and took one last look around the bakery; according to the clock on the wall it was nearly midnight. I decided to walk over to Hot Dog Frank's. I wanted to talk to Frank and was sure he would be alone because it was closing time. As I entered Frank greeted me, saying, "Hey it's closing time."

I responded, "I know Frank but I need to talk." I barely had time to sit down before Frank placed a hot dog, and a cup of coffee in front of me. "I want to talk with you," were magic words to Frank who though a good listener was also a dispenser of volumes of sage advice.

"What's your problem?" Frank asked.

"Frank, you know my twin brother is in the Air Corps. I am thinking of enlisting too," I said.

Frank asked, "What's keeping you? Are you really going to go or are you going to let Harry Hunter talk you out of it?"

"No Frank, I made up my mind," I replied.

Frank paused for a moment while wiping the counter, lifted his head and slowly let his eyes meet mine. "When are you going?" he asked.

"Today, this morning Frank, I'm going to catch the early bus."

Frank nodded his head in agreement and said, "Then you should go." He continued with a caution, "You better not tell Harry Hunter though, he'll try to talk you out of going,"

Frank came out from behind the counter and refused to accept payment. He embraced me in much the same way European men embrace their fellow men and muttered, "Come back boy, come back." I felt a lump rising in my throat and started to hurry out of the door.

"Wait," Frank growled. He went to his cash register, removed something and thrust it into my jacket pocket and pushed me out of his restaurant. I did not look back. The emotion of the moment had taken over. I did not want Frank to see the tears in my eyes.

I left Hot Dog Franks and walked toward the old bridge across Swatara Creek. On arriving at the bridge I moved with care down the slippery narrow path to the edge of the stream. There was, in those days, and may still be, a large flat rock under the bridge over Swatara Creek. I spent some of my last hours as a civilian sitting on the large flat rock. The gentle gurgle of the rippling stream and the peace and quiet of early morning had lulled me into a tranquil mood. Time came to a standstill; my thoughts seemed to have ceased. The sound of splashing water brought me back to the here and now.

In the dim light it was possible to see swirls in the shallow water as a large trout chased minnows in search of a meal. An eerie shadow accompanied by the soft rustle of wings swept under the bridge not ten feet from where I sat. It was a large barn owl also in search of food. The owl swerved, swooped low near the edge of the stream. It grabbed something and with a few flaps of its great wings magically moved across the stream to gracefully land on a branch of the huge Elm tree on the far bank.

As I watched the owl the chill of the early November morning became noticeable; frost was beginning to form. A pink glow in the eastern sky announced the arrival of a new day.

I got up from my seat on the rock and slowly walked back to my bedroom above the Pennway Bakery. The grass and the now slightly frozen ground crunched under each footstep. Back in my room I wrote a brief note to Harry Hunter, apologized for my unannounced departure and asked him to give my clothes to the Salvation Army. I packed a small bag with a change of socks, underwear, toothbrush, my rarely used razor, locked the door and left. On my way out I slid the room key and note under Harry Hunter's office door. I thought of my mother and hoped she would not be too distressed when she learned of my enlistment.

The day had barely started when the bus to Harrisburg, Pennsylvania arrived. I climbed on, paid my fare and moved to the rear to sit in silence. I put my hand in the pocket of my jacket and pulled out money. Hot Dog Frank had given me $20! After such a generous gift I knew I had to pass the physical and be accepted. I could never go back and face Frank as a failure. I had a strange feeling as if a door had closed and another door was about to open. I prayed I would measure up to whatever challenges might be ahead.

Thomas W. Carson our father

4
THE BUGLE BLOWS

The processing station at Harrisburg was the epitome of military efficiency and offered cultural shocks for which I was unprepared. First, we were weighed and measured, then our eyes, ears and nostrils were checked. The examination room was filled with naked men; their bodies were of all shapes and sizes. I had seen naked males before in high school during showers at the gym. This was different. Some of the men were twice my age and twice my size. I was embarrassed and intimidated by my nakedness.

I shuffled along from station to station until I was in front of a doctor seated on a stool. The examination became more personal. "Turn your head to the right and cough," the doctor directed as he probed my groin in the area of my testicles. He continued, "Turn your head to the left and cough." The doctor's next command was even more personal. "Turn around, bend over and spread your cheeks," he said and continued to examine me. The probing was unpleasant, but my grimace was more from embarrassment than discomfort. He asked a few brief questions which I promptly answered. Then apparently satisfied there was no evidence of a disqualifying physical problem or a social disease, he dismissed me with a wave of his hand. I was elated. I had passed my physical!

Someone gave the order, "Everyone get dressed and move into the next room." I hurried to comply. The entire procedure was accompanied by intense feelings of a need to do everything properly and as quickly as possible. The group, about fifty in number, moved into a large room without chairs. As we left the physical exam room a second group was entering. My thoughts were reminiscent of a visit I once made to a slaughterhouse. Little did I then know or understand the accuracy of my ominous observation. The new room was sparsely decorated. It had two prominent features; the American flag and a lieutenant with shoes shined to a high gloss. The brass on his uniform sparkled in the lights.

The lieutenant directed the group to line up and ordered, "Take one step forward, raise your right hand and repeat after me." I do not remember his exact words. But I do remember hearing him say, "Welcome, you are in the army now. Everyone outside and get on the buses." Everyone left the room and boarded the buses under the careful supervision of uniformed personnel. Our destination was to New Cumberland Station, a short distance from Harrisburg.

New Cumberland was our first introduction to the United States Army. All of us, new recruits, still in our civilian attire, were hustled off the buses to a constant officious barking of orders from an assortment of nondescript low ranking non-commissioned officers. It was as if someone had turned on a switch. We were suddenly subjected to the control of those who seemed to delight in exercising authority. Again there was an urgent feeling of the importance to quickly comply with orders lest some fearful calamity take place. Everyone fell out to march. We marched, albeit with great awkwardness, to where the uniforms were to be issued. The first item issued was a duffel bag. As we moved through the line each man announced his size to the clerk. The clerk in turn would issue the item based on what size he, the clerk, thought was appropriate. When it came to getting fitted for shoes it was different. Feet seemed to be considered a primary source of travel for a soldier and the fitting of shoes received more careful attention.

Somewhere during all of these procedures each man was assigned a serial number and dog tags were issued. Along with the serial number came strict orders to remember the serial number or there would be no food or pay. Dog tags were to be worn at all times. Someone noticed a difference in serial numbers. A draftee's number was not the same as the serial number assigned to a volunteer. Volunteers immediately assumed a superior attitude. Surely a volunteer was in the Army because they wanted to serve their country. The draftees were there because they had no choice.

My first few days in the service were especially difficult. Until then the only person I ever shared a room with was my twin brother. Now there were fifty to sixty men in the barracks; cots were only a few feet apart, everything each man owned was in a duffel bag hanging on his bunk. Cigarette smoke hung like a huge cloud throughout the room. Sleep was elusive and the night seemed to drag. The silence of the night was frequently interrupted by the sound of snores, coughing and someone releasing a window-rattling fart accompanied by a series of raucous laughter and comments. Sleep, when it finally came, was of short duration. It ended with a banging of trash can lids, the shrill of a whistle and shouts of, "Everybody up, off and on; off your ass and on your feet!"

The latrine, spotlessly clean, but humbling, continued to provide a crude introduction to military life. About a dozen toilets were lined up in a row along one wall. Partitions were nonexistent. Latrine etiquette required a quick flush follow each bowel movement. Needless to say, not everyone practiced such a fastidious routine. Along another wall there was a trough, about fifteen to twenty feet in length. It served as a community urinal. For sure, privacy had no part in the life of the enlisted soldier. Wash basins were in the same room along yet another wall. Each man lined up and took his turn to shave and perform necessary ablutions. The time allotted to shave and brush one's teeth was limited. Fortunately my beard did not yet require the daily attention of a razor. Proper etiquette at the wash basin required the user rinse the basin when done; again, the manners of some men were far better than the manners of others.

Our stay at New Cumberland lasted three days; long enough to get shots, sore arms, see a few training films, learn important army do's and don'ts and stumble around in a pitiful effort at close order drill. Then with duffel bags slung over shoulders it was onto a train. Our luxury train consisted of coach cars left over from the 1920 era. The cars, long ago retired, had been pressed back into service as troop transports. No one told us recruits where we were going or when we would get there. We were not allowed to get off the troop train until it arrived at the final destination. Rumors ran rampant. Someone knew someone who knew exactly where the train was going, when it would get there and what would take place after it got there. In truth no one knew anything.

"Jesus," muttered Bill Gleason from Middletown, "at least they could tell us where we are going." Someone responded, "What difference would it make if you knew where you were going? You would still be going there." Harry Gaspar, a draftee from Harrisburg said, "I think we are going to Florida. They are training troops there."

The trip to wherever took more than three days. There were no accommodations for sleeping. It was either sleep sitting up or on the floor in the aisle. Some of the older men quickly took over an area and engaged in a nonstop poker game. Tempers flared as the old coal burning locomotive chugged, stopped, waited, and chugged on. Stops were for other trains to pass and for coal and water. Soot permeated everything; nostrils, pores and clothing. Approximately three days after departing from New Cumberland the train stopped outside of Jacksonville, Florida for coal and water.

"I told you guys we were going to Miami Beach for training," boasted a guy who had been dubbed "Oracle" because he seemed to know everything. Late the next day the train did arrive in the Miami area. The sun was shining, the weather was warm and no one objected to leaving the train. We traveled by bus to our next destination, the 38th Street Hotel, at Miami Beach. The hotel was like an oasis in the middle of a desert. Semi private rooms, showers, good food, and the warmth of Florida during the winter. We felt like tourists on a vacation of thirty days while the army converted us from civilian to soldier. The daily routine rarely varied. It was lectures, close order drill, more lectures, training films, the rifle range and training films. We soon learned to march in unison while singing ribald songs to keep cadence.

I had been at the hotel for about three weeks and was in the orderly room one evening, hammering away at about thirty-five words a minute on the office typewriter. The First Sergeant came in and asked, "What are you doing?" I expected him to berate me for being in the orderly room. I honestly told him, "Writing a letter home." The next day I was called out of formation and assigned to the orderly room. My basic training had ended. I was placed on special duty as a typist. Overnight I became a part of the detachment and moved out of the section of the hotel where the trainees were quartered. In my ignorance of military procedures I was of the opinion my new inside connections would in some way enable me to fulfill my desire to fly.

My new status entitled me to a weekend pass. Although my pass was limited to fifty miles I planned to stretch it and visit my mother who was living at Fort Myers, approximately 140 miles north via the Tamiami Trail, through the Everglades. Friday evening I caught the city bus and rode to the outskirts of Miami. Across the street from the last bus stop there was a small diner. It reminded me of Hot Dog Frank's. Be it nostalgia or hunger, I decided to go in and get something to eat before starting my trip to Fort Myers.

Immediately upon entering the diner I noticed the occupants were all civilians. I came to the conclusion because regulations prohibited the wear of civilian clothing by military personnel. All occupants were in civilian attire. Another thing struck me as strange; there were no women in the diner, only men. However their friendly welcome and many invitations to come and join them eased my apprehensions. I smiled and opted to sit alone at the counter. Almost immediately a rather robust individual got up from one of the booths and joined me. He placed a friendly hand on my shoulder and introduced himself and offered to pay for my food.

His greeting was warm and friendly, "Hi, soldier, my name is Bill, your money isn't any good here. I am buying. What would you like to have?"

Bill's friendly offer surprised me. I thanked him and ordered a cheeseburger, fries and a Coke. He asked me what I was doing this far out of the city and where I was going. When I told him my destination was Ft. Myers to visit my mother he gave a low whistle.

"Do you know it is 140 miles across the Everglades," Bill asked and added, "How do you plan to go there?"

"I am going to hitch-hike up the Tamiami Trail," was my response.

"How would you like a ride?" Bill asked and offered to take me there if I would ride with him on the buddy seat of his Harley-Davidson.

"Sounds good to me," I told him and proceeded to eat my cheeseburger and fries. I quickly finished eating and Bill suggested we should get started. As we left I thought some of the comments made by other customers were unusual.

"Hey you got a good one Bill," and "Be good to the soldier Bill."

We walked outside; Bill wasted no time. He kick-started his bike and directed me to get on the buddy seat behind him. We headed north on the Tamiami Trail, destination Fort Myers. We rode up the highway for about fifteen minutes. I looked back; down the Tamiami Trail, the lights of Miami were only a glow in the sky.

Without comment, Bill brought the Harley to a stop on the side of the highway. He told me to get off so he could check something. I dismounted. His next move was unexpected. He tried to kiss me and touched me in a way I could not misunderstand. His intentions were clear. He was interested in some sort of a sexual encounter. Despite having gone to an all-boy school I had never before experienced or even heard of two males having such a relationship. For certain, someone had omitted an essential part of my education. My heart was pounding. There was no doubt in my mind. Bill was not going to take me to Fort Myers. I was confused and scared. My mind was racing, filled with thoughts of how to escape from my predicament.

"Wait," I told Bill, "You are being so good to take me home, I think I should tell you something."

"What is it?" Bill asked.

I replied, "Well, I think I am all right, but I have to take shots for two more weeks."

My good friend Bill stepped back. There was no further conversation other than his cursing. He fired up his bike, spun it around and headed for Miami. The once friendly Bill and his motorcycle were quickly disappearing. What moments earlier had been a promised ride to Fort Myers was now only the sound of a Harley Davidson moving ever farther away with tail-lights fast fading in the direction of Miami.

I stood there for a moment, laughing as I watched Bill disappear. I congratulated myself for quick thinking. Then I evaluated my situation. I was alone, 10 miles away from civilization, with Everglades on all sides. I still had about 130 miles remaining on my journey to Ft. Myers.

I decided to walk until someone came along and gave me a ride. I'd taken only 30 or 40 steps on my journey when a sound reached my ears; it was a new sound, one I had never heard before. Despite the newness of the sound my mind identified it in a flash, rattlesnake! At first I stood still. Then ever so slowly, I started to back away from the sound. I had moved not more than 10 steps to my rear when I heard, for the second time in my life, another rattlesnake. Or had the first one circled around me? I froze in place and tried to decide what to do. The rattlesnakes did not attack but the Everglades mosquitoes did. They had found a free meal. I remained in the middle of the highway, swatting mosquitoes for what seemed hours. I was no longer certain my trip to Fort Myers was such a good idea.

Then out of the darkness, from the direction of Miami, I saw the lights of a vehicle and heard the whine of tires on the macadam roadway. I firmly planted myself in the middle of the Tamiami Trail. The driver had a choice. Either run me down or stop and pick me up. He stopped. It was a bread truck making a delivery to Fort Myers. When he asked me how I had gotten so far out on the Tamiami Trail I told him I had been walking hoping for a ride. The trip to Fort Myers was uneventful. I slept most of the way. We arrived at about five o'clock in the morning. My mother was, of course, happy to see me. She insisted I let her take me back to Miami Beach. I agreed only after I was sure she had enough gasoline ration stamps to afford the trip. She remained in Miami a few days and used her ever-present portable Singer Sewing Machine to alter my uniforms. By the time she returned to Ft. Myers she had me looking like a real soldier and had earned a goodly sum tailoring the uniforms of other basic trainees.

5
LIFE IN THE KITCHEN

Basic training for my group was nearly complete. I was busy typing personnel records and awaiting for my orders to aerial gunnery school. My patience had grown thin. I did not want to spend the war on Miami Beach typing personnel records.

"Hey Carson," the First Sergeant said, "you are going to Buckley Field, Colorado." I was excited. At last I was going to a real air base. My joy, however, was to have a short life. The orders to Buckley Field were orders to Cooks and Bakers School.

"Cooks and Bakers School," I howled. "I don't want to be a cook. I want to fly. This has to be a mistake," I protested. "I put in for aerial gunnery school." It was no mistake. The army had decided. I was going to be a cook! I was about to leave sunny Florida and head for Denver, Colorado in the middle of winter. I complained, begged and objected without success. I was soon on a train headed for Denver, Colorado.

My second day in class at the school did not go well. A S/Sgt. Fitzgerald was in the process of teaching a class on baking. I knew his presentation was incorrect. I made a mistake. I stood up and told him he was wrong. Surprise! Neither the Army Air Corps nor S/Sgt Fitzgerald had an interest in what I thought. My daring to express my thoughts resulted in a quick assignment to determine how well I could scrub pans and mop the floor. I spent the next three days scrubbing, mopping and thinking about methods of getting out of the kitchen.

At the end of my third day I was called into the office of the lieutenant in charge. He proceeded to lecture me on my poor attitude and advise me of the availability of the stockade for malfeasant students. I replied, "Sir, I don't know the meaning of malfeasant. But I do know S/Sgt Fitzgerald doesn't know enough about baking to teach other people how to bake." The next afternoon I was called to the lieutenant's office again. The mess sergeant, S/Sgt Fitzgerald and a couple of other instructors were there. The lieutenant asked me where I learned to bake. I told him about my training at Hershey and my experience at the Pennway bakery. My fate was sealed. Almost all of my time from then on was spent teaching the instructors and the students the art of baking. I never learned the first thing about cooking.

I had very little interest in how the Army Air Corps would feed the troops. I was not happy; I wanted to fly. However, my flying at Buckley Field was limited to flying around the kitchen and into Denver at every opportunity. Most impressive and longest lasting in my memory was the intense cold of Colorado and a telephone operator.

The notice on the bulletin board announced a dance at the Service Club. Harry Wallace, one of the other students, talked me into going. "Some of the girls are really attractive," he said as he and several others prepared to go. We caught the base bus and on arrival at the Service Club received a warm welcome from the hostesses. Harry was right; some of them were attractive. I was standing around trying to decide whether or not to stay when a lady wearing a tag marked, "My name is Millie" approached me. "Why aren't you dancing?" she asked. I laughed and told her, "I have two left feet." She immediately took my arm and led me to the dance floor and found out I did indeed have two left feet. She suggested we sit down and talk; I readily agreed. Millie explained she was one of the chaperons for a Denver hostess club. We talked for a while and she asked, "Do you ever come into Denver?" "No," I responded, "I don't know anyone there." Millie told me she was a telephone operator and gave me a number where I could reach her if I ever came to town. I thanked her and put it out of my mind.

I was off duty the weekend following the dance and decided to give Millie a call. She seemed happy to hear from me and told me how to find her house. I stopped at the Base Exchange and bought a box of Whitman's Samplers and followed instructions. Millie met me at the door and acted as if the box of candy was the greatest gift in the world. I soon learned she was a spinster, nearly twice my age and a senior supervisor at the Denver telephone company. Millie was adamant; she insisted I stay and have dinner with her. She opened a bottle of wine she had been saving "for a special occasion," she said.

After dinner we sat in front of the fireplace and drank the last of the wine. The evening turned both romantic and a little late. Millie suggested I stay overnight. "You are welcome to use the guest room," she said. I showered and went to bed. I woke up aware of someone in the room. It was Millie. "I wanted to be sure you had enough blankets," she said. However, it ended up with Millie not the blankets providing a welcome respite from the bite of Colorado's winter winds. Sunday morning Millie asked me to go to church with her. We went to church where Millie introduced me as her nephew from back east. I continued my regular visits to "Aunt Millie" until mid March when my time at Cooks and Bakers School came to an end.

I graduated from Cooks and Bakers School. But I had a narrow escape. The school authorities at Buckley Field decided to keep me as the baking instructor. Fortunately they had a priority requirement to send a cook to Hamilton Field, California and were unable to keep me at Buckley Field. I was promoted to Corporal and transferred to Hamilton Field.

I was excited to get orders assigning me to Hamilton Field, California. "Now," I thought, "there will be a chance to fly." Millie was not so pleased, in fact she was heartbroken. I suggested she come with me. However, her maturity and good judgment prevailed. We had a tearful farewell at the train station. I promised to remember the many things she taught me and tenderly kissed my "Aunt" Millie goodbye. She complained, "I will never find another one like you. Who will keep me warm at night?" I again suggested she come to California. But Millie told me she loved me too much to make such a mistake.

6
HAMILTON FIELD

Filled with anticipation I proceeded to Hamilton Field without delay. On arrival I made my way to the squadron orderly room. The stench of cigar smoke permeated the area. The origin of the foul odor was soon apparent. As I entered the orderly room I noted a cloud of cigar smoke. The smoke seemed to be dispersed by vibrations from the gravel voice of First Sergeant James Welch. "Are you Carson," he asked. "I am Carson," I said as I eyeballed the body of the man with the bear of a voice. He could not have been more than five feet tall. Yet, something about his manner demanded respect.

Not wanting to waste time I told First Sergeant James Welch of my desire to fly. He leaned back in his chair, rolled his cigar around in his mouth and grunted. Then he leaned forward and fumigated the area with his cigar smoke, laughed and said, "Get the flying crap out of your head kid. You are a cook; your place is in the kitchen."

About a week after my arrival at Hamilton Field on a cold and rainy predawn March morning I had my first taste of combat. The air raid alarm sounded at about 0300 hours. Everyone was required to draw a weapon and ammunition and head for the defense perimeter located somewhere in the hills surrounding the base. There would be no Pearl Harbor here!

Believing an attack was immanent I was excited and eager to respond. I quickly put my raincoat on over my skivvies and slipped on shoes without socks. Someone thrust a rifle with ammunition into my hands and told me where to go. I donned a steel helmet and headed for the hills. On arrival I found a pre-dug foxhole filled with water.

On a cold and wet March 1943 morning I prepared to die from hypothermia or be slaughtered by invading Japanese. The Japanese failed to materialize. I was freezing and had to run in place to keep warm. To make matters worse I could not recall the password. In my panic and the excitement of the impending "invasion" the password had fled from my mind. I was compelled to remain on the hill, cold and wet, until daylight. I firmly believed I would be shot as an invader unless I could produce the password. The lesson of the day was not wasted. I had learned to dress properly and never forget the password.

It did not take long to discover San Francisco was a wonderful city with abundant opportunities for recreation. However, most of the city recreation cost far more than I could afford and much of the free stuff appeared to be like my experience with Bill, in the Everglades. I was not inclined to such relationships. Therefore, to supplement my income I found part time work as a short-order cook in the Staff NCO Club. Things were going well. I baked a birthday cake for Captain Harris, my squadron commander, and discovered the flight line.

It was at the flight line I found my major source of recreation without putting a demand on my wallet. Various pilots were always coming and going. Most of them were willing to take along a passenger. However there was a problem. Most of the aircraft did not carry spare parachutes and regulations required each passenger to have a parachute. A solution to this problem was unexpectedly offered.

One of the regular customers at the short order bar of the Staff NCO Club was a Staff Sergeant Thomas from flight line supply. He overheard me telling one of the other cooks about my problem. Sgt. Thomas called me aside and offered me a deal. He would "lend" me the necessary equipment. My side of the deal was I in turn would present him with "courtesy" short orders and draft beer. My desire to fly took precedence over all the honesty my grandfather had ever tried to instill in me. I gave Sergeant Thomas the key to my locker. The next morning all of the essential equipment was in my locker. A pair of goggles, a helmet, A-2 jacket, flight suit and a seat pack parachute. I had no difficulty in convincing myself the use of the equipment was within the scope of regulations. I am not sure how I rationalized giving the away the club's beer and food in exchange for the equipment.

Although a cook, I was quickly transformed into the most realistic fake aircrew member in the United States Army Air Corps. My duties in the kitchen became an acceptable chore. Those duties were the price I had to pay in order to fly.

My trips took me all over the Northwest and various parts of California. I flew to the Mojave desert area where I was able to visit my twin brother, John, a Staff Sergeant and a genuine air crew member. We shared a wonderful evening. John protected my ego and his friends never knew his brother was a cook. Every opportunity found me at the flight line off on unauthorized flights around the country. These were often enhanced when a friendly pilot allowed me to get a little "stick time".

Unfortunately the aerial joy riding proved to be my undoing. On numerous occasions my return ride back to Hamilton Field failed to materialize in time for me to report for duty on my kitchen shift. Time and time again mess sergeant, Master Sergeant Murray chewed me out on each absence and warned me about joy riding. "Carson," he said, "You're a damn good cook and you can make sergeant if you just stop the screwing around with those airplanes." I could not stop. The need to fly was too great.

It has often been said, "If you take a pitcher to the well too often it will be broken." My pitcher broke on a ride back from a short trip. We were south of Monterey and east of Carmel, California at about 4,000 feet in an AT6. The engine started to run rough; it coughed, emitted smoke and lost power. The pilot looked back. I erroneously interpreted it as a signal to jump. When he banked hard to the right, the canopy was already open; I went out. There was no initial sensation of falling, just quiet. After a drop of a few hundred feet, while falling face down in a spread eagle position, I pulled the ripcord. The opening shock was not unpleasant. I could see the canopy billow out above me. To the side at a lower level I saw the plane with flaps and wheels down headed for a meadow. My parachute had a slight oscillation. Below I could see the lush carpet of grass. My parachute continued to oscillate. I was swinging like the pendulum on a grandfather clock. Contact with the ground came as a thud while I was at about ten degrees from perpendicular. The lush carpet of grass was a myth. Underneath the surface was as hard as a paved street. The shock of landing was painful. I was badly bruised and hurting. Off to one side I could see the airplane. The pilot had successfully landed before I hit the ground.

My return to Hamilton Field was in a military police vehicle, destination, to the office of my Squadron Commander. First Sergeant Welch, chewing on his ever-present cigar greeted me at the door of the orderly room. "Carson, you look like shit. This time your ass is grass," he snarled. He then told Captain Harris, "Carson is here, Captain." "Send him in," bellowed the Captain. I entered, saluted and squeaked out my name and stood there, at rigid attention, trying my best not to shake. As I recall my appearance and presentation fell far short of being the epitome of a proper soldier. The "old man" was having none of it. He was talking court martial on charges of AWOL, wrongful possession of government equipment and a host of other violations for which I could be locked up. He wanted to know how I came into possession of aviator's equipment. I told him it had been left in my locker by mistake and all I did was use it. The First Sergeant interrupted, "Bull shit, you're lying!" He continued, "Captain this cook has been flying all over the place. The Mess Sergeant tells me he has been late for work about a dozen times." No doubt, the Captain knew I was lying, but I was not about to admit it and he was not going to force the issue. He ordered, "No more flying. You are restricted to the base until I decide what to do with you." I returned to the kitchen, crushed, awaiting further action. I was hoping he might favorably remember his birthday cake.

7
WING DING

Word of my experience spread around the squadron. Some one hung the nickname "Wing Ding" on me. I continued to cook and work my spare time job while waiting for my bruises to heal. I was sweating out the expected loss of my corporal stripes. About two weeks later I was told to report to the orderly room. First Sergeant Welch greeted me with his usual cloud of cigar smoke and said, "Carson, I don't want any eight balls in my outfit. I wanted the Old Man to bust your ass. Instead he is shipping you out. Your restriction is lifted." "Where am I going?" I asked. It was then I learned my next duty station would be MacDill Field, Florida without loss of stripes.

Someone told me there was a gunnery school at MacDill. In an instant my thoughts and plans turned from the kitchen to the air. While waiting for my travel orders I made one more trip into San Francisco where I committed a deed I would live to regret. Five dollars paid for a tattoo. I sat in stoic silence as the tattoo needle hummed and buzzed. Blood mixed with various colors of ink and seeped to the surface of my upper arm. Slowly but surely my new nickname, "Wing Ding" was emblazoned on my arm.

With the fresh tattoo on my arm still healing, I packed my B-4 bag, a gift from Staff Sergeant Thomas in appreciation of my silence. There was one more mission to accomplish before I left Hamilton Field. The latrine for the orderly room was at the end of the barracks next to the orderly room. In front of one of the urinals was a small box. Everyone knew this box was not to be moved. It was there so First Sergeant Welch could stand high enough to use the urinal. I checked with care to make sure my taxi was waiting and there was no one else in the barracks. Once I was sure the area was clear of other persons and my taxi was standing by, I smashed the box. Within a moment the evil deed was done. I hoped the first sergeant would not have to take a leak until I was long gone. I headed for the San Francisco Rail Transportation Office. I was on my way to Tampa, Florida.

This time there were no 1920 era railway coach cars. Transportation was via Pullman complete with porter, dining car and waiters. It was almost more than a country boy could tolerate. Such opulence was totally unexpected. But it paled in comparison to what was coming.

Sergeant William R. Barnes was already comfortably settled in the roomette of the last car of the Pullman. I soon learned he had been in service less than a year. He was on his way to Chicago to attend radio school. We were sitting in our room, waiting for the train to depart when we heard the sound of girls talking and laughing. We poked our heads out of our room looking for the source of the sound. To our amazement and pleasure the other occupants of our Pullman were all young ladies, about forty in number. They were on their way to Hunter College in New York to become WAVES. Bill Barnes and Gene Carson wasted no time in working out a schedule to allow us to share the roomette with maximum personal privacy.

The trip from the West to the East Coast of the country was made with minimal sleep. I now appreciated "Aunt Millie" and her wisdom. I shared the moments of the trip with Naomi, a beautiful girl of Mexican ancestry. We were madly in love and spent our time in either the roomette or on the observation platform of the last car.

Bill Barnes was scheduled to leave the train in Chicago. I was scheduled to change trains in Chicago and go from Chicago to Tampa, Florida. Bill Barnes detrained as scheduled. But, an appropriate monetary donation on my part convinced a friendly porter of the need for two young lovers to remain together for the longest possible time. My journey to Florida was by way of New York and from Chicago on I had the roomette to myself. When we arrived in New York I said goodbye to Naomi. We made promises of an enduring and everlasting love. I never heard from her again.

During our great trip the ladies on the train had treated Sergeant William R. Barnes and Corporal Eugene T. Carson like the experienced veterans we were. Bill Barnes had almost one year of military service and I had five months. But, the potential WAVES had none and I could see no reason to tell them of my limited combat experience. I was sure they would not be interested in my defense of Hamilton Field against a mythical enemy on a cold, wet March morning while attired in skivvies and a raincoat. The train ride was a train ride of train rides; a train ride to remember. I spent the trip from New York to Tampa, Florida recovering from a state of near exhaustion.

My assignment to MacDill Field was cause for excitement. I found I had joined a squadron flying the B-26 Martin Marauder. In addition there was an aerial gunnery school in operation at MacDill. I was certain I would be able to fly. Unfortunately the military did not see it my way. I again found my flying limited to the kitchen.

Uncured by my previous experiences, I was like a hound dog on trail. The flight line was soon located and I immediately resumed my practice of wangling rides with various pilots as they flew training flights up and down the coast. I managed to have myself assigned as a cook on the night shift. With my days free I boldly reported to the Gunnery School and attended every class I could sneak into. I quickly found the skeet range and spent hours blasting away. My skill at the skeet range became well known and I was soon making more money shooting competitive skeet than my military pay. A few goodies from the mess hall bought me all the practice shooting time my shoulder could tolerate. My schedule in the kitchen was carefully planned to preclude any conflict with gunnery school and my shooting activities.

Everything went well until one afternoon a pilot erred in judgment and crash-landed his B-26. The question of why Corporal

Carson, a cook, was on the flight became an item of interest. I was again ordered to stay away from the flight line and the gunnery school.

I had no difficulty in obeying the order restricting me from the flight line. The next day my squadron was transferred to Myrtle Beach, South Carolina. I was on my way, off on another train ride. This time there was no Pullman car and there were no attractive young ladies. I rode in the mess car as one of the cooks.

I had enough! Upon arriving at Myrtle Beach I made up my mind. I was going to fly and nothing was going to stop me. I sat down and carefully wrote a letter to the President of the United States.

"Dear President Roosevelt,

I am a widow as the result of my husband dying from phosgene gas poisoning suffered during World War I. I have twin boys. One of them S/Sgt. John W. Carson is serving at Rapid City, South Dakota as a member of a bomber crew. My other son is at Myrtle Beach, South Carolina. It would give me great peace of mind if my sons could serve together. Please send Eugene T. Carson to the same unit as his brother so they can fly together."

Most respectfully yours,
Esther H. Carson."

Of course "Mother's letter" did not inform the President the other son was a cook. I also made sure there was no return address on her letter. I saw no need for anyone to bother Mother with petty details. Approximately two weeks after I had mailed "Mother's letter" I was told to report to the orderly room, "The Captain wants to see you," the messenger said. I left the kitchen and made my way to the orderly room and reported to the First Sergeant. He immediately ushered me into the Captain's office. I saluted and stated my name.

The Captain politely invited me to sit down and asked me if I would like something to drink. Being interested in getting to the point of our impending conversation, I declined. Then he said, "Carson, I don't know whom you know or who knows you, but you have Presidential Orders sending you to Rapid City, South Dakota, without delay by the first available transportation." I sat there with a dumbfounded look on my face. When the Captain asked me what I knew about the orders I told him I had no idea of the why or wherefore. The Captain then commented, "This is very unusual." I felt an inner relief when he dismissed me from his office.

The next day I was again riding in a Pullman, this time alone, on my way to Rapid City, South Dakota. The first leg of my trip took me as far as Chicago where I was supposed to change trains and continue on to Omaha, Nebraska and then to Rapid City. Chicago was swarming with attractive and interesting young girls. It did not take me long to decide to spend a couple of extra days enjoying the city. Those few days soon became more than three weeks and I was almost out of money.

Technically absent without leave, and nearly broke, I boldly made my way to Fifth Army Headquarters and went to see a finance officer to get a partial-pay. In those days each soldier was issued a small temporary pay book folded to about the size of a pack of book matches. I presented my pay book and found my initial contact was met with coolness. However, when I presented my Special Orders, the lieutenant's attitude changed. I received prompt attention and a partial-pay of $50.

I said goodbye to a really nice student nurse named Pauline, and a girl named Beverly who was planning on going to medical school. Both young ladies were the beneficiaries of all the lessons I had learned from "Aunt" Millie. They in turn did their part in broadening my education. Sadly, I said goodbye, boarded the train and headed west.

During a slight waiting period in Omaha, Nebraska the military police stationed at the Rail Transportation Office made a routine check of my orders. They had never seen a corporal traveling on Presidential Special Orders before and eyed my special orders with some suspicion. I played my game to the hilt and refused to tell them why I was traveling on such unusual orders. In truth, there was very little I could have told them. For sure I was not about to discuss secret information such as "Mother's" personal correspondence with the President of the United States. After careful examination of my orders they were still not satisfied. But when one of them noticed a pay record dated a day before from Fifth Army Headquarters they backed off. Fortunately, they paid no attention to the nearly thirty days it had taken me to travel from Myrtle Beach to Omaha. I decided it was time to count my blessings and be on my way.

It was dark when the train departed Omaha on the way west. I walked back to the observation platform of the last Pullman car and watched the lights as we passed by. I was alone and deep in thought. My thought was I would still be a cook when I arrived at Rapid City. My past experience convinced me they would not let me fly. I would remain in the kitchen, a cook. Such a prospect was unacceptable. I took my orders out of my pocket, reviewed them in the dim light. I read each line with care, searching for anything alluding to my status as a cook. Seeing no such disclosure, I left the observation platform, returned to my baggage, removed my service record and went back to the observation platform. Once there I used my Zippo lighter and proceeded to burn my service record page by page. I watched the charred pieces blow away into the night like a thousand fireflies. When the destruction was complete I swallowed hard at the boldness of my actions. I was about to adopt a new life and hoped it would get out of the kitchen and not into the stockade.

8
THE REPLACEMENT

When I reported for duty at Rapid City, South Dakota the clerk asked for my records. I told him, "The gunnery school is sending them." Thoughts of being discovered never left my mind. But, I had made my bed and now as my grandfather used to say, "had to sleep in it". Not being assigned to a crew, I was given temporary duty in the orderly room as a clerk typist. When my twin brother saw me he shook his head in disbelief of what to him was an impropriety. Again, much to the credit of his brotherly love for me he never told anyone. However, I suspected he was embarrassed over my actions. I barely had time to meet his wife, a Chicago girl, the former Dorothy Sphinkas before he and his crew departed. Other than a few moments at Grand Island, I did not see him again until the end of the war. Two weeks later I was sent to Grand Island, Nebraska as a replacement aircrew member. I could almost feel my wings growing! I was going to fly!

There were no duties to perform at Grand Island. I had only to watch the assignment board in case of a crew assignment. While waiting I either prowled the flight line, looking through the B-17s or spent time in the armament section where I repeatedly took apart and assembled the fifty-caliber machine gun used on the B-17. My time during the evening hours was spent dating a nice young lady named Virginia.

On Virginia's eighteenth birthday, at her suggestion, I bought a pint bottle of blackberry brandy to celebrate. While seeking a place of seclusion we walked out to the golf course and became romantically involved. After a few drinks Virginia became a most sensual creature. I offered no objections.

Later, while I was walking Virginia home, a deputy Sheriff pulled up along side of us in a Ford coupe. He turned his spotlight on us and asked us where we had been. I told him we had been sitting on the golf course. Then he saw the grass stains on my knees and elbows. He ordered us to get into his car. Virginia sat between us. The deputy noticed Virginia had been drinking and asked her age. When she replied, "Eighteen, today is my birthday," the deputy accused me of statutory rape and read me the riot act about it being a felony to furnish liquor to a minor for immoral purposes. I had genuine visions of going to jail.

Virginia began to cry; she became ill, turned her head toward the deputy and threw up on his lap. It was a mess. Perhaps it was the blackberry brandy I had consumed or maybe it was my sense of humor. Suddenly my apprehension disappeared. There was the deputy with hamburger, fries and blackberry brandy all over his lap. The odor inside the deputy's small coupe was enough to gag a maggot . . . My sense of humor kicked into high gear; I laughed. "She puked on your lap," I said. The deputy, a man with a limited sense of humor did not comprehend my levity. He stopped the car, said something about damn aircrews and ordered, "Get your ass out of my car." Virginia started to follow. The deputy told her, "You stay, I'm taking you home." She called me the next day to tell me she had gotten home without trouble but was thinking it might be a good idea if we were to get married. I promised to discuss the subject with her and we made a date for later in the week.

I checked the assignment board the next day and learned I now belonged to 2nd Lt. Otis C. Ingebritsen's crew as a tail gunner. Upon receiving the information my first act was a trip to the Post Exchange. I bought a pair of aircrew member wings. When I returned from the Post Exchange I found Lt. Ingebritsen and other members of the crew waiting for me. It may have been paranoia, but I felt there was immediate suspicion and apprehension on the part of the crew as they gave me the eye. Lt. Ingebritsen asked me,

"What do they call you?" "Wing Ding," I replied and immediately regretted my response.

Fortunately nothing more was said and I was sent to supply to draw the necessary equipment. Before I could again date or call Virginia we were gone, on a train headed for Patrick Henry, a staging area at Newport News, Virginia. We waited there, restricted to the base for about two weeks and then shipped out with other B-17 crews on board one of the most miserable ships imaginable. Bunks were crowded above each other, four or five in a vertical space where there should have been one. The food was barely edible and what went down remained down with difficulty. Rather than go below decks to our assigned quarters I elected to sleep on deck. I was constantly searching the sea for signs of submarines. There were no submarines and therefore no torpedoes. We arrived in Liverpool, England without incident.

The other enlisted members of the crew had been together for most of their training. Other than myself only Lt. Ingebritsen was new to the crew. He had replaced the crew's original pilot who had been killed in a crash while flying with another pilot. I was the latest addition to the crew. With the exception of the flight engineer who was a buck sergeant, they were all staff sergeants. They were constantly pressing me for information as to why I was only a corporal. I kept my silence. There was nothing I could tell them. However, my initial welcome was not exactly with open arms. I could sense and feel their suspicion about the stranger on the crew. "Who is this guy with the nickname of Wing Ding and why is he only a corporal? Who was this screw-up? Had he been reduced or was he not worthy of promotion?"

Two things helped to change their attitude. We went to the skeet range and I easily shot several near perfect rounds; everyone wants a gunner who can shoot. Later in the day outside the enlisted service club a couple of guys ganged up on our ball turret gunner, Stanley Gajewski. Stan was not doing well at all. He might have been the world's greatest ball turret gunner, but after having a few beers he was doing a crummy job of fighting. In short order he was down and out of it. I could fight. Fighting was my bag. I had been earning money, $25 under the table, for each fight at smokers during my last few months of high school and five months prior to entering service. I enjoyed the fights almost as much as I enjoyed the under-the-table money. Stan needed help. I stepped in, all one hundred forty pounds of me, and took on both of them. It did not take much. I kicked one guy in the family jewels and cranked a couple of good right hands into the midsection of the other guy. The fight ended almost as fast as it had started. The next day I found I had "joined" the crew. Charlie Grannis the right waist gunner, was the oldest enlisted man on the crew. He made the announcement, "Fellows, we have a tail gunner!" No one ever questioned me again.

Special Orders No. 205, Headquarters 12th Replacement Control Depot, dated: September 9,1943 listed crew No. 60 as:

2nd Lt. Otis C. Ingebritsen, pilot
2nd Lt. Edward J. Meginnies, co-pilot
2nd Lt. Rensler L. Pomeroy, navigator
2nd Lt. Michael J. Chaklos, bombardier
Sgt. Harold L. Pepper, flight engineer
S/Sgt. Hubert H Windham, waist gunner
S/Sgt. William D. Pross, radio operator
S/Sgt. Charles J. Grannis, waist gunner
S/Sgt. Stanley F. Gajewski, ball turret
Cpl. Eugene T. Carson, tail gunner

Standing L/R Hubert Windham (wg) Otis Ingebritsen (p) Ed Meginnies (sp) Charlie Grannis (wg) Charles Alfred (fe) Rensler Pomeroy (n) Bill Pross (r) Kneeling Gene Carson (tg) Stanley Gajewski (bt) 560th Sqd., 388th BG

We were assigned to the 385th Bomb Group as a crew and trucked to our new unit. It was well after sundown when we arrived at our destination. Pleased to be at the end of our journey we climbed down from the truck only to be told to get back on board. There had been a change to our orders; we were being assigned to the 388th Bomb Group, 560th Squadron.

We were off again on another truck ride to a place known as Knettishall, home of the 388th Bomb Group. Shortly after entering our new barracks we learned the reason for the change of orders. The 388th had flown its first mission on July 17, 1943. In less than two months they had suffered a loss of twenty-three crews, 230 men either killed, missing in action, or prisoners of war. A few had managed to evade capture. We were the new cannon fodder.

In my mind there flashed a picture of the day I took my physical to come into the Army. I saw the second group enter the room as we walked out of it. Just like animals entering the slaughterhouse. I quickly turned off the picture.

It would be nice if I could say we were welcomed replacements. Such was not the case. The older crews treated us with indifference. Someone made a suggestion we not get too comfortable and implied we might not be around very long. We were to soon learn the reason for the apparent unfriendly attitude. We were taking the place of their friends who had been shot down and they were not interested in making new friends. It hurts to lose friends.

We received a basic orientation including some of the things to do and things not to do. Such as don't shoot at your escort when and if you had an escort. I think we flew five practice missions prior to our first combat mission. Being unfamiliar with high altitude flying I did not know how to dress and watched the others with care.

Our first combat mission was set for September 26, 1943. During the interim I was promoted from Corporal to Staff Sergeant. The crew helped me wet down my new stripes. Somehow we all made it back to the barracks where we continued the celebration despite the protests of other occupants. My illustrious military career had now covered a span of about eleven months. The bunk tag was still swinging, but I was flying. I had successfully jumped from the frying pan into the fire. A fire with the potential of getting hotter each day as it was took me farther and farther from the kitchen.

There are two very lonely places on a B-17; the positions of tail gunner and ball turret gunner. Both positions were cramped and both were cold. In the tail the gunner was on his knees, a great position if there was a need for prayer, which was often. There wasn't much room to move around, only enough space to put a pair of spare gun barrels and a couple of extra boxes of ammunition and a parachute. On the right side of the aircraft if you are looking forward, between the gun position and the tail wheel, there was a small escape door to be used in the event of an emergency.

In the ball turret there was even less mobility. The ball turret gunner rode in a fetal position, peering out of a circular window between his feet. His guns were mounted along side of his head.

The average ball turret gunner was small, but very few were small enough to carry a chest pack into the turret. However most ball turret gunners wore a parachute harness while inside the turret. If it became necessary to bail out the gunner would turn the turret until the guns pointed to a downward position. He could then exit into the waist area, snap on his parachute chest pack and bail out through the waist door. In the event of an emergency the ball turret gunner's escape could depend on assistance from the waist gunners. On our crew Stan Gajewski knew such assistance would be available from waist gunners Pop Grannis or Windy Windham. If they could have built someone to ball turret size specifications, Stan would have fit the mold. He was of the right size and he had the ability to ride in a cooped up position for long hours and he could shoot. He never complained. On more than one mission he came out with the cheeks of both buttocks frost bitten. But he never missed a mission

In the event of a fighter attack, reliable gunners in the tail and the ball turret could mean life or death to a bomber crew. Luftwaffe pilots would take bold chances to put the tail gunner out of action. With the tail gunner out of action they could press their attack with a great chance of success. Many of the dedicated ball turret gunners claimed the ball turret was one of the safest positions on the B-17. I never thought so. The ball turret was too claustrophobic and cramped for me. Records indicate a rather high casualty rate for both tail gunners and ball turret gunners. The ball turret was a smoother ride than the tail. In rough air tail gunners needed to have a strong resistance to airsickness.

Left and right waist gunners added to the protection against fighters moving in from the left or right side to place fire on the engines. We had Charlie "Pop" Grannis, a former barnstormer and air show parachute jumper covering the right side. He was all business and had a habit of repeatedly checking his equipment. Hubert Windham was a quiet country boy from Mississippi. Most of the time "Windy" had very little to say. He never allowed his face to reveal his thoughts until the day he shot down a fighter. The fighter seemed to have lost air speed and for a moment pulled up alongside our B-17. "Windy" reacted in a flash and blew him out of the sky. With a kill in the bag "Windy" turned his attention to the pilot. He expressed satisfaction when he watched the German's parachute open.

Bill Pross was not one of the world's best shots. But he was an outstanding radio operator. I always had my doubts about the ability of radio operators to effectively use the radio room gun. The common expression was they could only hit the tail and their own antenna.

The engineer Sgt. Harold L. Pepper had been a buck sergeant, a lower grade than anyone else on the crew except for me; however he too was promoted to S/Sgt. prior to flying his first combat mission. He only flew a few missions with the crew before they noticed he was not functioning as part of the team. The other enlisted members of the crew objected to him remaining on the crew and complained to Dingle, our pilot. Being new to the crew I was not included in the crew's protest. However I was quick to note the immediate replacement of S/Sgt. Harold L. Peters as our engineer. I was determined not to be replaced.

Our copilot Ed Megginies was a frustrated fighter pilot. He detested being stuck on a B-17. However, he performed his duties flawlessly. In the nose our navigator Rensler Pomery was the epitome of propriety and dignity. He was meticulous in everything he did. His partner in the nose, bombardier Mike Chaklos was the only man we lost in combat. Ironically the loss of Mike Chaklos took place on a mission where we had flak of comparatively light density.

All of those who flew, no matter what their position, had bail out procedures etched into their mind to the point where the procedure would have been automatic. It could be no other way. There was no time allocated for decision making. A successful exit and survival frequently became a matter of seconds. It was either exit or become trapped in place by centrifugal force. A moments delay, a pause in acting could result in a terrifying ride to certain death in a rapidly disintegrating airplane.

S/Sgt Gene Carson

9
COMBAT!

On September 26, 1943, Second Lieutenant Otis Ingebritsen and crew prepared to fly their first combat mission. It was the 388th Bomb Group's 24th combat mission. Immediately after lunch we proceeded to the Briefing Room and watched intently as the curtain was pulled back. There was a sigh of relief throughout the room as the old hands recognized the target. We were going to hit an airfield at Rheims/Champagne, located approximately fifty miles west and slightly north of Paris. The briefing officer noted the rather late take-off time of 1445 hours and reported the mission would last only five hours from take-off to landing. Antiaircraft fire was predicted as light and fighters were not expected. Nevertheless there were butterflies in my stomach.

We were trucked to our parked B-17 where we, as a crew of ten nervous and scared individuals, followed a ritual destined to become our routine. Pilots, Lieutenants Ingebritsen and Meginnies, along with the Ground Crew Chief, Master Sergeant Paul Irelan and our Flight Engineer Pepper carefully checked the airplane. Our navigator, Lieutenant Pomeroy, nervously went over his maps and charts; bombardier Lieutenant Chaklos repeatedly checked the bomb load, the racks and his bombsight. In the radio room Bill Pross attended to his radio and made sure he had all the necessary frequencies. Gun barrels were inserted; ammunition was checked. Each member of the crew was busy, doing and redoing, anything to keep the mind occupied. Waist gunners, "Windy" Windham and "Pop" Grannis repeatedly checked their guns while Stan Gajewski gave the ball turret a final power check.

I crawled into the tail, knelt in position and shot down a couple of imaginary fighters just to make sure I had the procedure properly established in my mind. This would be a big day for me. It would be my first high altitude flight.

With preliminaries out of the way attention was turned to the blue, electric heated suits, a type of heated long underwear made of material much like an electric blanket. These blue bunny suits were worn under our sheepskin lined flying gear and were effective in keeping us warm when in good working order. I carefully watched the others and as unobtrusively as possible emulated their actions.

However there was one final necessary act to be performed before climbing aboard. We all moved off to the side of the aircraft and in almost comic routine emptied our bladders. The lack of adequate facilities onboard the aircraft and the fact we might be otherwise occupied during a moment of need was reason enough for this somewhat odd preflight procedure.

Our ground crew chief, M/Sgt. Irelan gave us one final word. "Bring my airplane back," he said and then stood by with fire extinguisher in hand as one by one the engines coughed, smoked and roared. Each was checked at full power. This was important. The failure of an engine at take-off was always an emergency. Failure of an engine during take-off with a full load of bombs could exceed the emergency category with disastrous results. A green flare arched over the field. Our first combat mission had started!

2nd Lt. Otis Ingebritsen felt a deep sense of responsibility as he moved his B-17F off the hardstand and out onto the taxi perimeter. Countless times before he had followed identical take-off procedures. But this time it was no drill. Practice time was over; this was real! On board was a full load of bombs; he was about to fly his first combat mission. He was the pilot, the airplane commander; the onus of command weighed heavily. The fate of the crew and the aircraft belonged to Otis Ingebritsen. It was not something he could share.

On September 26, 1943 in the cockpit there was formed an unbreakable bond. No words other than those of the checklist needed to be uttered. The momentary meeting of eyes of pilot and the copilot said more than either man could have vocalized. It was a look of understanding. It spoke volumes in its silence. They were exchanging their loyalty and faith in each other. Together they would fly and together they would survive. The 388th Bomb Group had already lost twenty-three crews during its first two months of operation. Ingebritsen and Meginnies were determined not to become crew number twenty-four.

The march of B-17's along the perimeter took on the appearance of clumsy creatures creeping in trail toward the runway. Take-off was in timed intervals with a brief pause at the runway for a final power check then line up, tail wheel locked and down the runway. Lift off came at about 110 to 115 miles per hour. With wheels up the once clumsy ground bound creature became a thing of elegance and beauty. The climb continued; the aircraft circled and became part of a formation. Oxygen masks went on at between 8,000 and 10,000 feet. The group tightened up the formation. Far below, the English countryside appeared to be a painting. The coastal area and the English Channel came into view. The B-17's slowly continued their climb to 23,000 feet. Within the airplane the tension and fear in the heart and mind of each untried warrior was concealed by an outward and disciplined calm.

Flight

A formation of B-17's flying in a clear blue sky is a thing of beauty. But even a thing of beauty can have a flip side. It was also a formation of flying machines, each with a cargo of death, destruction and ten men. Ten men far from home flying in the hostile environment of high altitude and sub zero temperatures over equally hostile territory, waiting for an opportunity to deliver their cargo of death and destruction.

Otis Ingebritsen, known to the crew as Dingle gave the order, "Test fire all guns and keep a sharp look out for fighters." The ship shuddered as weapons were given a warm-up burst. Ten pair of eyes nervously searched the sky for distant telltale dots of Luftwaffe fighters as the formation of bombers, marked by condensation trails, progressed across the sky unmolested.

At high altitude personal warmth and oxygen become matters of major concern. The blue electrically heated suit worn under the sheep skin lined leather clothing was wonderful when it worked. But it had a nasty habit of burning out and giving the wearer the equivalent of a "hot-foot" at whatever location the short circuit might be located. The hapless victim would immediately disconnect the electrical plug and pull the material of the suit away from the body at the burnout location. The remainder of the ride would then be without heat. Oxygen at high altitude is a basic and essential need if life is to be sustained; therefore care had to be taken to ensure the mask fitted properly and the connection was firmly in place. It was possible for the hose of the mask to become disconnected with fatal results.

When the formation crossed into France slightly below the Belgium border sporadic flak began to make its appearance. The flak increased in density as we neared the target area and appeared in black bursts. Each burst spread out and appeared to be an octopus shaped figure. When red flame was visible in the center it was too close for comfort and offered its own sound effects. The impact on the airplane came as a dull thump, or sharp crack, depending on the nearness of the burst to the airplane. The sound was not unlike gravel thrown against a tin building. The proximity of the airplane to each burst determined the aircraft's reaction. The nearer the burst the greater the bounce and reaction of the airplane. There was no place to hide; no place to go to seek protection from the shards of metal spewing from each explosion. We were exposed targets.

As the formation turned and started the bomb run the flak could be counted on to intensify. When the bombardier announced, "Bomb bay doors are open," there was an increased feeling of vulnerability. This was closely followed by a psychological feeling of relief when the bombardier called out "Bombs away," a call which was further accented by a significant surge of the bomber as it was relieved of the extra weight. On this particular mission, old hands reported the flak as meager. However, sixteen of the twenty-one aircraft suffered flak damage. Luftwaffe fighters, as predicted, failed to show. The trip home was uneventful. It was a good day for a new crew. Unfortunately it did not tell us what was in store in the future. We were scheduled to be up early the next morning.

There was no need to awaken me on the morning of September 27th. I was awake, lying in my bunk wondering where we were going. I rolled out and stumbled to the latrine. I wanted to get there early to avoid the crowd. Having a bowel movement while sitting next to another person was extremely alien to me. I quickly finished my morning routine and headed to the mess hall. I was hungry and ate a hearty breakfast of square (powdered) eggs, accompanied with SOS and Spam. I washed it down with several cups of black coffee and thought of my last cup of coffee at Hot Dog Frank's. I wondered what Frank would say if he could see me now.

At the briefing the target was identified as the port area of Emden, Germany. We would approach the target via the North Sea and bomb from about 25,000 feet. Cold is not a good description of temperatures at 25,000 feet; it is colder than cold. Take-off was at 0730 hours and there was much to be done in a relatively short time. Guns and equipment had to be checked. Time passed quickly and we were soon rolling down the runway, seasoned combat veterans of one mission about to fly our second.

The tail of a B-17 provides minimal opportunity for conversation other than to respond to the oxygen and other mandatory checks. Being of a gregarious and loquacious nature I needed a little more social interaction than what was afforded in the tail gun position. In order to compensate I devised my own significant greeting to let the rest of the crew know all was well in the tail. Although ungifted in music I had learned to whistle the first few notes of Chopin's Funeral March. It was our second mission; we were at about 22,000 feet and the coast of England was disappearing behind us. I whistled the first few notes of the dirge. The response from the cockpit was immediate. Copilot Ed Megginies instinctively knew who did it. He yelped, "Wing Ding, this is serious business, knock it off. I don't want to hear the funeral march." Lt. Meginnies heard it again. He heard it almost every mission and he squawked every time he heard it. I ceased whistling after Mike Chaklos was killed. Somehow it seemed to be inappropriate.

There were twenty-three aircraft in our formation when we took off to fly our second mission. Seven of those aborted the mission for various mechanical reasons leaving us with only sixteen aircraft. The 96th Bomb Group was flying as the low group. Our bombardier, Mike Chaklos reported clouds over the target plus ground haze and an effective smoke screen. Flak was meager and we had P-47 fighter escort to and from the target. However, they would only be able to engage the Luftwaffe for a limited time because of their relatively low fuel capacity. Mike reported the bomb bay doors were open and in about thirty seconds gave the words, "Bombs away". The plane gave the usual lurch as it discharged the cargo of bombs. We were at about 26,000 feet. Bill Pross, our radio operator, reported the bomb bay as empty. I breathed a sigh of relief and noticed discomfort in my lower intestines.

My hearty breakfast had turned into a belly full of gas. The pain became intense. The more the pain increased the more I regretted my gluttonous breakfast. However my problems were soon replaced. Despite our fighter escort twenty-five to thirty members of the Luftwaffe made their appearance. Although most of the attacks were directed at the low group of the 96th, we had our share.

A single Me109 came down in a curving attack on our tail. I gave him a short burst. At the time I was wearing a steel infantry helmet, without a liner, over my issue leather helmet. The vibration of my guns caused the steel helmet to jiggle down over my eyes. I could not see! I shoved the steel helmet up, clear of my eyes and fired another short burst. The steel helmet again jiggled down over my eyes. This time I grabbed it and tossed it to my rear. Then my guns jammed. I had no choice; I lifted the only piece of armor plate in the tail, dove under and cleared my guns. It must have been a healthy move because at the same time all of the accumulated gas in my intestines was released in one long blast. I remember hoping I had not crapped in my pants. Luckily it was all gas.

Whether it was the nerves of first battle or a full bladder from the extra cups of coffee, I don't know. But I had to urinate. I mean I had to urinate now, not later! Fighters or no fighters, immediate action was required or I was going to pee in my pants. There was no way I wanted to sit around in wet pants with a shorted out electrical suit and frozen urine. I could not bring myself to urinate on the floor of the tail gun section. Fortunately a lull in the action allowed time to recover my discarded helmet. I reached to my rear and found my helmet and then began the arduous procedure of trying to locate my penis buried under layers of clothing. I finally found it, shriveled though it was from the intense cold. I began the process of extraction. I dug it out from beneath the multiple layers of clothing and cautiously exposed this most important item of personal equipment to the forty degrees below zero temperature. I proceeded to piddle in my steel pot. There was no splashing of the urine. Every drop froze immediately.

"Bandit at six o'clock high," Bill Pross, our radio operator calmly stated over the intercom and added, "Get him Wing Ding." It was either another Me109 or the same one returning. He was making a diving approach on our tail. I could not stop peeing any more than I could have flown without wings. Having grown up a country boy in areas where there were severe winters I knew well the consequences of having bare skin touch metal. Whatever part touched would immediately become frozen and attached. It sure as hell was not going to be what little bit was left of my foreskin. I held myself with one hand and fired with the other. Tracers streaked into the fighter's left wing. He peeled off and I piddled in peace. Having finished, I tucked everything inside of my flying gear and mumbled some incoherent nonsense. Suddenly I felt faint and dizzy. A glance to my side revealed the problem. My oxygen hose had somehow disconnected. I fumbled with the connection and while bordering on the edge of passing out managed the reconnection. I immediately recovered.

I heard the chatter of what I presumed to be the top turret guns and saw a departing fighter as he moved from our front to our rear announcing his arrival by decorating the sky with what looked like Christmas tree lights as he used his cannon. He disappeared in seconds. But not before putting three holes in our vertical stabilizer not far from where I was perched. Each hit echoed with a quick thump. It was over almost as quickly as it had taken place. I sat there awed at what had transpired. I responded to the oxygen check and continued to search the sky. Our escort was now all around us. I noticed my helmet contained a block of yellow ice.

Satisfied we were out of danger, I suddenly felt tired. I tried to relax as I continued to scan the sky for tell tale dots. My thoughts drifted back to boyhood days at Woodland Road, Mt. Pocono, Pennsylvania to a time when I was about eight years old. The month was late July or early August. Grandfather's cider barrel sat on a frame under a tree. There was a spigot on the bottom of the barrel and a cork on top. A hose ran from the cork to a gallon jug of water sitting along side of the barrel. We all knew the importance of keeping the end of the hose fully submerged. If air had entered the fermenting apple juice Grandfather would have had vinegar, not cider. I knew it was forbidden to touch the cider barrel. But thirst and temptation ruled the day. I took a soft drink bottle and filled it with cool hard cider. I drank it.

The impact of hard cider on my juvenile system was almost instantaneous. My head began to spin, I felt my bowels rumble and wisely headed up the hill for the outhouse. I was only halfway there when the enemy struck. Our Rhode Island Red rooster descended on my back. He flogged me mercilessly; I fell down and yelled for help. Grandmother came running, stick in hand. She took one look and recognized my problem. I had lost control of my bowels and had thrown up. "Why, you've been in your grandfather's cider barrel!" she said. She took me by the scruff of my neck to behind the house where the outside well pump was located. There she stripped me of my clothing and pumped cold well water on me. Something brought me back to the here and now. I shivered, opened my eyes and found my electric suit was unplugged.

I looked down and saw the coast of England. We were rapidly descending. In about thirty minutes I heard Stan Gajewski report the wheels were down. Dingle, (Otis Ingebritsen) our pilot greased the bird on the runway and we taxied to our hardstand. Only twenty-three missions remained. I was looking forward to a shot of whisky at debriefing. We were told we would not fly another mission for at least three days. But we were required to spend a major part of those three days reviewing aircraft recognition patterns. Someone had taken a shot at one of our P47 escorts.

October 1st the word came down. There would be a briefing at 1000 hours October 2nd. Take-off was scheduled for 1300 hours. We were relieved not to be rousted out during the wee hours of the morning. Rumor had it we would be flying on a short mission. A milk run as someone put it. Already I was beginning to feel like a veteran, ready to take on the entire Luftwaffe if necessary. Fortunately, for once in my life I kept my opinions to myself.

At the briefing we learned our target was a return to the port area of Emden. The route would be out over the North Sea and across the West Frisian Islands. Occupied Netherlands would be on our right as we turned in toward Emden in the vicinity of the East Frisian Islands and prepared to make our bomb run. The North Sea had already been marked in my mind as an evil place. Down in the North Sea by parachute would be death from hypothermia; a ditching would require extreme skill on the part of the entire crew in order to survive. It was not one of my favorite places.

Fighter escort was promised to and from the target area. However, as before they would not have much time remaining if they were to engage in combat. The distance from their base in England to Emden came close to stretching the fighters' productive time in the sky.

For me there was one major variation in my preflight routine. I paid attention to what I ate and to how much I ate. Otherwise my preflight routine did not vary from our previous two missions. Co-pilot Ed Meginnies, was heard to say, "I just want to get through this and go home to eat Mom's apple pie." Otis Ingebritsen, "Dingle" as always appeared to be as solid as a rock. Lord knows what turmoil must have been boiling inside of his head. Mike Chaklos, our bombardier seemed a little tense as he went over his equipment. Rensler Pomeroy, the navigator and the oldest officer on the crew was, as usual, all business. He was a man of true dignity.

We were up to about 23,000 feet when Dingle gave the order to test fire the guns. For a brief moment the ship shuddered with the vibration of our fifties. "Short bursts only, don't waste anything," he ordered. I decided it was time to whistle. There was no delay in Mac's response, "Damn it, Wing Ding, I told you no more!" Someone laughed and Dingle ordered us to knock it off and pay attention.

We were tagged onto the 96th Bomb Group. They were flying as the lead and high group. As we approached the target things were screwed up. Some of the aircraft of the lead group started to drop bombs three and four at a time. Our group dropped its bombs and then noted the 96th was making a second bomb run. Procedure required the formation to stay together. Mike reported seeing only their lead plane and four others drop bombs during the second pass over the target.

For one of our crews the second bomb run was expensive. Although the flak over the target had been meager, Lt. Felece's aircraft was hit by flak during the second run. He feathered his number one engine and then fire broke out in number two. They were last seen leaving the formation. All were reported killed. Flak may have been meager, but not for the Felece crew. They were flying their fourth mission.

As we again crossed the Frisian Islands on our way home there were a few more bursts of flak. The Luftwaffe never appeared. Dingle set us down at Knettishall, our home base, at approximately 1900 hours. We now had only twenty-two missions remaining. At the debriefing the mission was determined not the success it should have been. The analysis was the target had not been hit.

Starting with our fourth mission we had a new engineer. The enlisted members of the crew expressed dissatisfaction with the performance of our engineer and Technical Sergeant Charles "Chuck" Allred joined the crew. October 4th found us scheduled to go to Frankfurt. Take-off was about 0730 hours. Therefore we were up well before dawn and Dingle had the dubious pleasure of a misty morning take-off.

Out of the twenty-six aircraft taking off carrying incendiary bombs, eight turned back because of either mechanical problems with the airplane or a physical problem of a crewmember. We were flying with only eighteen aircraft. The standard joke was, "Every time they mention briefing my sinus starts to seeping." However, a severe sinus problem was no joking matter at high altitude. We were again following the 96th Bomb Group. After-action reports indicated we bombed not Frankfurt, but a town named Saarbrucken located ninety-five miles south of Frankfurt. Our route home was over the European coast between Calais and Dunkerque. Flak was minimal and we landed at our base at 1430 hours. Again the Luftwaffe had failed to show. Copilot Ed Meginnies complained, "Damn it Wing Ding, it is bad enough without you whistling the funeral march."

My mind was made up. I wanted to move to where the airplane was being flown. I was tired of looking where we had been. I wanted to see where we were going. There was only one way. I had to become a flight engineer, a position for which I had absolutely no training. I went to see our ground crew chief, M/Sgt. Irelan and asked for his help. He told me to come and see him whenever I could and he would teach me. I think at the time he looked at me as an extra pair of hands to help out with the dirty part of the maintenance. I had been helping him for about a week when he told me he had something for me. Paul Irelan handed me a three-ring binder. It was clearly stamped RESTRICTED. I opened the binder and found it was a technical manual for the B-17G. "This came out of one of the hanger queens," he said, making reference to a no longer airworthy bomber now being used for spare parts.

I treasured the manual and from then on spent hours reading the thick volume. Each day M/Sgt Irelan would quiz me on what I had learned. He was a patient and thoughtful man. His pride and joy was his B-17. No one ever lavished more care on an airplane. I recall his insistence on having us leave "his" airplane as clean and neat as it was when he "loaned" it to us each day.

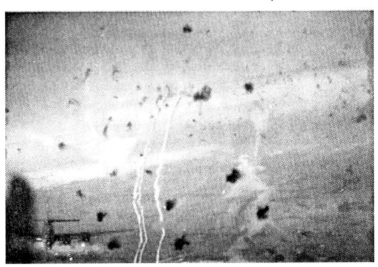

Tailgunner's view

10
HOW ARE THINGS IN AFRICA

Mail call brought a welcomed letter from my twin brother, John who was flying as a tail gunner with the 96th Squadron, 2nd Bomb Group, of the 15th Air Force. He wrote:

"Dear Bud,

The flight from the United States was uneventful, but exciting. We buzzed Milwaukee, Wisconsin the home of our navigator, Jack Drummond and went to Bangor, Maine, then on to Newfoundland. What a desolate country this is! We had to wait for favorable weather and winds then we departed for Preswick, Scotland. Morale was high as we left Scotland for Casablanca and on to our new station near Tunis.

Our base leaves much to be desired. We live in tents and use slit trenches for latrines. Every now and then there is great joy when the portable shower unit shows up. I have been to Tunis. We explored the city and found some places with good meals. But you cannot be sure of what you are eating. We even unearthed an ice cream store. However, the medics quickly put it off-limits for sanitary reasons. Someone said they were using camel milk.

One of our favorite off-duty recreations had been roaming around the old German ammo dumps. We took the live 88 rounds, propped them up against a bush and detonated them with a well-aimed rifle shot. The other day we laid a trail of powder to a dump and tossed a match into it. Our game was nearly a disaster; we barely made it to safety. I decided to end such foolishness. Sort of reminded me of when we were kids and set off the railroad torpedoes and dynamite caps. It is a wonder we were not blinded or did not lose our fingers.

As a new crew we were assigned to fly with experienced pilots prior to flying with our own pilots. We were on the same airplane we flew over from the States, Julie A, but we had the operations officer, Captain Patrick Train as pilot. Our first mission caused me to wonder about the wisdom of deciding to get into this business. We went up along the coast of France. The fighters, FW190s and Me109s lined up on our tail. I think I went blind with fear, or maybe I was so damned busy I could not recall a thing. It sure took the shine and glamour off of my wings in a hurry. We were constantly running into flak and both the Me109s and FW 190s kept hitting us. They are great adversaries. I found myself really busy on the bomb runs. I was either trying to keep the fighters out at a safe distance or praying.

Things I have learned are don't waste ammunition; carry extra ammunition and spare gun barrels; shoot in short bursts and shoot to kill.

There is a rumor we will be moving from Tunis up to Italy soon. I hope so. The living conditions in this area are miserable. Take care and be careful,

Bud."

A second letter dated September 16, 1943 arrived soon after the first one.

"Dear Bud,

Things were rough yesterday. We lost Julie A, the airplane we brought from the states. We were again flying with Captain Train. We made two trips, one in the morning and again in the afternoon in support of the troops taking the beaches at Salerno. We were elated because these were going to be what you call milk runs.

The morning was no problem. On the afternoon mission we were twenty or thirty minutes from the beach when we lost our number four engine. Captain Train elected to increase power and stay with the formation.

All went well until our return trip. As we arrived at the coast of North Africa we lost power in our number three engine. This left us without power on the right side. At the time we lost the second engine we were over a B-26 base and probably should have landed, but Captain Train decided he could make it to our home base. All went well until we were on our final approach. It was nearly dark. We were cleared for immediate landing.

Then came the unexpected; someone cut us off. We had to go around to avoid a collision with the other aircraft. The situation was still under control until we lost engine number two. There was no way we could continue to fly on one engine. I had moved from the tail to the radio room. When I looked out all I could see was the lights in those adobe buildings getting closer each second. The crew from up front had joined us in the radio room and assumed crash positions. Captain Train managed to belly land going up the side of a hill. It doesn't take much to persuade men to move quickly to get out of a crashed aircraft. Eight of us exited through the radio room hatch. The pilot and copilot, both big men, squeezed out of the side cockpit windows just as engine number three burst into flames. Our engineer, looking out for his airplane, as he always did, reentered through the waist door, obtained a fire extinguisher and put out the fire. No one was injured but Julie A was now only fit for spare parts. I guess sometimes even a milk run can be dangerous.

Take care, hope you are enjoying London,
Bud"

11
A BIG WEEK

October 8, 1943 was the start of what was to be known as a "Big Week". The word was the 8th Air Force would make a maximum effort. The late briefing and take-off was to our liking. Someone noted the red line on the briefing map was growing longer with each mission. We where headed for Bremen, Germany. Our route would take us out over the North Sea across the East Frisian Islands where we could count on being used for target practice by the antiaircraft gunners and then past Wilhelmshaven and down to Bremen. Our group was selected to lead the parade for the 45th Air Division with the 96th Bomb Group tacked on as the low group.

The briefing officer advised there would be moderate fighter opposition and intense flak. He was partially correct. Just prior to the target area about thirty-five FW 190s came up to greet us. They pressed their attack until we entered the target area; there we encountered the heaviest concentration of flak we had seen to date. We were savagely hammered by what seemed to be never ending explosions of antiaircraft fire, accompanied by sounds much like someone throwing gravel against a tin building. My hand was on my parachute as I bounced around inside the tail. There was no place to go, no where to hide. There was only one choice. Sit there and take it. I waited, almost impatiently, expecting any second for our airplane to become a ball of fire and black smoke. It did not. We flew on.

We had a new antiaircraft defense system and were using it for the first time. A hole had been cut on the left side of the radio room and a chute installed. Inside the radio room were boxes of aluminum foil. The radio operator was supposed to disperse the foil to throw off the enemy radar system. As we approached the target area there was a half-hearted dispensing of the foil. Then as the flak intensified the foil started coming out of the chute like a stream of water. Despite our predicament, I had to laugh. Whether or not the foil was effective was immaterial. It gave the radio operators something to do other than sit there and be shot at.

We put twenty-one aircraft over the target and twenty-one aircraft came home with flak damage. The Luftwaffe also paid a price; three of their fighters were confirmed shot down. Our route home was much the same as our route in. The lonely gunners on the East Frisians had their usual target practice. My dislike for them increased in proportion to their apparent increase in accuracy. We all well knew any kind of a serious hit while heading back to England would have meant ditching in the North Sea, a procedure with poor survival odds. The remainder of our trip home was uneventful. Dingle eased us down in his usual style at about 1740 hours. We returned home veterans of five missions. We were alerted to be ready to fly again the next day.

The charge of quarters rousted us out around 0330 hours October 9th. Even at breakfast the word was out. We were headed for a long ride. Rumors were put to bed shortly after daybreak during the briefing. A low gasp filled the room as the curtain drew back. The red line seemed to go on forever out across the North Sea, over Denmark then the Baltic Sea along the northeast coast of Germany to the Gulf of Danzig and on to the port city of Gydnia. Lord, what a long ride! We would be carrying a maximum fuel load of 2,780 gallons.

During our ride out to the airplane the usual chatter was noticeably absent. The length of the mission and its proximity to Berlin was heavy on our minds. Following the usual preflight routine we were soon airborne. This time there was no circling. We headed directly out over the North Sea for the coast of Denmark, climbing all the way.

As we crossed the Danish coast the flak, although not intense was unusually accurate. This same accuracy was repeated again along the German coast. As we turned into the Gulf of Danzig a heavy smoke screen began to appear over the target area. The lead bombardier found an opening and released the bombs. Three direct hits were reported on the liner Stuttgart with others falling in the dock area. We headed for home. On our return trip we encountered more flak over Denmark. Everyone gave a sigh of relief as it ceased.

I was relaxing in the tail, eating a frozen Milky Way candy bar when trouble became apparent. To our rear there appeared a formation of aircraft. I knew they could not be escorts and called out, "Bandits at six o'clock". All hell broke loose. The Luftwaffe was everywhere; about thirty-five or more twin and single engine and single engine aircraft pressed the attack with vigor. I fired short bursts, trying to be accurate. My guns worked perfectly without jamming. I thought I scored hits on several of the fighters attacking from the rear of our formation.

Below our position the leader of the low squadron, Lt. Nagorka in Iza Angel was in serious trouble. The right wing was on fire and they were going down. Only six chutes came out before the airplane blew up. Trouble continued and Lt. Kinney in Gynida left the formation with fire in the #3 engine. Then the action ended as if someone had waved a magic wand. The fighters were gone. It was almost 1830 hours when we returned home. We had been in the air for ten hours. I was looking forward to my shot of whisky and the evening meal.

On landing we received the bad news. We were going again the next day. But there was good news. Take-off would not be early. I whistled my dirge for Ed Meginnies as we left the debriefing tent. He complained and shook his fist at me. I cautioned him, "Sir, you are not allowed to threaten an enlisted man." Ed laughed, put his arm around my shoulder and said, "Wing Ding this stuff really scares me. All I want to do is get home and eat Mom's apple pie." I again whistled for him. He took a swing and deliberately missed.

Ground crews often worked through the night to repair the

damage and get us ready to go again. Their ability to affect repairs overnight under what were nearly impossible conditions was amazing. They never let us down. They were there waiting long before it was time to take-off and they were there long after we returned from a mission. In short the ground crews were incredible. There was nothing quite so sad as watching a ground crew pick up their equipment and move reluctantly away from the hardstand when their airplane failed to return.

October 10, 1943 started out as a rather relaxed Sunday. Briefing was not scheduled until 0930 hours. But when we got there none of us liked what we saw. We were going to Munster as the lead of 2nd Combat Wing of the 1st Air Task Force. Flying with us would be the 96th, 385th and 390th Bomb Groups. Our route would cross the Dutch coast and the Zuider Zee north of Amsterdam and then angle down toward Munster. We were told, "Some fighter opposition is expected." Take-off was scheduled for near noon.

Trouble started early. Both our lead aircraft with Colonel David and our deputy lead aircraft with Colonel Satterwhite were forced to abort the mission for mechanical reasons. The lead was passed to the 96th Bomb Group and the 388th moved to take over the low Group.

"Some fighter opposition is expected," turned out to be an understatement. The opposition started at the target when we were jumped by a mixed bag of Luftwaffe fighters. The Me210's were hanging back, just out of range, sending rockets and cannon fire into our formation. I lined my sights on a Me210 and said to myself, "Got him" as I saw the smoke belch. Seconds later I realized not only had I not "got him" but he had fired two rockets arching toward our B-17. Fortunately, either my annoying fire or his aiming error caused the rockets to fall short of our formation and explode. Grandmother would have washed my mouth out had she heard my expression at the sight of the rockets. "Holy shit," followed by other socially unacceptable language escaped my mouth as I watched in disbelief.

Lt. Williams from the 562nd Squadron of our Group was hit by flak just after bombs away and left the formation. The Luftwaffe moved in for the kill. Sensing the futility of trying to survive, Williams must have hit the alarm bell. There was no hesitation. The entire crew bailed out. A tough way to go as they were on their seventeenth mission, eight short of the magic twenty-five missions needed to complete a tour.

The 390th took a real beating. They lost eight aircraft. Only sixteen parachutes out of what should have been eighty were observed. Two airplanes went down with either wing or engine fires. Rockets hit two more and one of those collided with an adjacent B-17 in a fiery explosion. Bodies and parts of the two airplanes blew everywhere. It was hard to watch. No matter where I looked there were either fighters or B-17s going down; the 96th lost one and the 385th lost two aircraft. We enjoyed a brief respite from the fighter attacks as we crossed "Happy Valley" an area at the north end of the Ruhr Valley where we experienced more heavy and accurate flak. Then the Luftwaffe returned and hammered away until our arrival back at the Zuider Zee. We landed at 1703 hours. All of our seventeen returning aircraft had suffered battle damage. I had my shot of whisky at the debriefing and put my gear away.

On learning we were not flying the next day I wrote to my twin brother in Tunis, North Africa and a letter to my mother. I told our mother I was the squadron cook and how John was flying in a relatively safe part of North Africa

Monday, October 11, 1943 started out as a quiet day. The sun kept threatening to make an appearance and I purchased a necessary item of transportation. As a bicycle it did not look much like what we had at home. The brakes were on the handlebars and it came equipped with a very uncomfortable seat. But, it beat walking.

Just before dusk I peddled my way to the local pub, not far outside of the main gate. When I walked in I was politely greeted and as I looked around the pub noticed a dart game in progress. There were no other Americans. Most of the patrons were well past middle age. I sidled up to the bar and quietly ordered a beer. It arrived in what appeared to be a large mug. As I put my money on the bar someone asked, "Yank, you flying from the base?" I nodded my head while taking my first sip of beer. I was about to make a comment about how warm it seemed to be when my money was pushed back towards me by an attractive woman. "This one's on me Yank," she said as she raised her own glass and uttered, "Cheers." I wisely withheld my comment about warm beer and soon found myself engaged in a game of darts. I lost.

Quite a few beers later, I decided to return to Knettishall. I said goodnight and prepared to ride off in the dark. I started in what I thought was the general direction of the base. I fell off my bicycle. Probably the result of my having consumed too much English beer. I heard a voice ask, "Are you alright Yank?" It was the woman from the bar who had paid for my first beer. She had followed me outside and asked me if I knew which way to go. I told her I was not sure. She offered to help me. As we walked she asked me if I was flying in the morning. I must have told her no and kept on pushing my bicycle. I was in no shape to ride.

I woke up to the smell of real fried eggs and tried to decide where I was. It was 0840 hours; my clothes including my skivvies, were neatly folded on top of a chair next to the bed. I soon learned my benefactor's name was Barbara. She was in her late thirties, a widow without children. Her husband had been a sergeant in the RAF. She looked at me, smiled and said, "My, you are a young one aren't you!" She then served me breakfast and sent me on my way with a caution, "Cheers, take care."

It was 1030 hours on Tuesday when I passed the military police at the main gate and headed for my barracks. Fortunately we had the day off. I changed clothes and went to the armament shack to inspect and hand load ammunition. Then I checked and oiled my guns. They had become an important part of my life.

I rode out on the flight line to where our airplane was parked. We had been assigned a new B-17G and the chin turret had already been painted in a replica of the famed Flying Tiger's motif. We had named her Tiger Girl. I walked around the tail, found several different colors of paint and proceeded to paint a large target on the left side of the fuselage near the tail gunner's position. I then wrote in large letters, "Shoot Here Jerry". I stood back and admired my handiwork, climbed on my bicycle and returned to the barracks. No truer ever were the words: "Idle hands soon find trouble."

Tuesday, October 12th was a typical English day; it was misty, not much sun and idle time. I found myself wishing we were flying. No sooner had my thoughts settled in than our engineer, Chuck Allred, told me we were flying a practice mission at 1400 hours. A practice mission meant doing everything we would do for a real mission except carry bombs. Guns and ammunition had to be on board and in position. We could not take a chance and fly without protection. Take-off was at exactly 1410 hours. We formed up and flew for two hours and returned to base. The sun was approaching the horizon as we touched down. I decided to forego the beer, the dart game and the possibility of fresh eggs in the morning. I went back to the barracks and met two new crews who were coming in as replacements. They had a lot of questions and I tried to be nice and answer them. I did not want to give anyone the welcome we had received. Also, I wanted to write a couple of letters, one to my mother and one to my brother.

Wednesday, October 13th I got up and went to the armament shack and again checked my ammunition and weapons. As I was leaving the shack to go out to our airplane the ground maintenance officer collared me. He ranted and raved about my desecration of government property by painting a target on the side of our airplane. We had a few words and I let my mouth overload my ass. I told him to go screw himself. He insisted I was going to clean the target off the airplane and I told him I would do so when he started to fly as a tail gunner and had the paintings taken off all the other aircraft. He presented his case to Dingle to no avail. The "artwork" remained and I never heard another word about it.

I was outside of our hut, working on my bicycle. It was in my mind to make a trip to the pub; Chuck Allred must have read my mind. He approached me and cautioned, "Wing Ding, don't go anyplace tonight. We are getting up early tomorrow. They are loading extra fuel." Chuck was right. We were up early. I looked at the crummy weather and thought the mission would be scrubbed. We had the usual breakfast of square eggs, Spam and SOS. I ate with caution. Being shot at was bad enough, but being in discomfort while being shot at did not make much sense. The word in the mess was the mission was going to be a long one. The answer came from the horse's mouth when the briefing room curtain was pulled back.

Schweinfurt! "Oh, Jesus no, not again," came from the back of the room. "Holy Mother of God, this is my last mission," came yet from another corner. The line stretched on and on deep into the heartland of Germany. "This is a very important mission," the briefing officer droned. "Germany's ball bearing works must be destroyed." He continued to deliver his message of what we could expect. He assured us we would have fighter escort almost to the border of Germany and they would pick us up again as we returned. However, we would be without fighter escort for over four hundred miles. There was minimal talking. Everyone knew it was going to be a rough ride. We were scheduled to put up twenty-two aircraft and be the low group of the lead Combat Wing of the 2nd Air Task Force. The 96th Bomb Group would furnish the lead and high groups.

The day started off poorly. There was a crash on take-off. Lt. Swift, pilot of Hard Luck, had almost reached flying speed when his No. 3 engine caught fire. Smoke came from the tires as he hit the brakes. A crash was eminent. Lt. Swift ordered, "wheels up." The copilot responded and the take-off of Hard Luck became a controlled crash. With its full compliment of crew, bombs and fuel Hard Luck skidded onward with sparks flying. It came to a stop just short of a wooded area. The crew miraculously escaped their burning aircraft without injury. Take-off for the group was delayed until safety procedures could be applied. All aircraft were then diverted to another runway and the area cleared in anticipation of the explosion. When it came it was spectacular.

The formation climbed up through the cloud cover. We were in clear skies and out over the English Channel. However, with one take-off crash and five aborts for mechanical failure we were quickly reduced to a formation of sixteen aircraft. I think we had been in the air about forty-five minutes before I sensed a problem. I was busy checking my gear and test firing my guns. Something did not seem right. It was not. My parachute was missing. In my mind I visualized my parachute bag sitting on the ground at the hardstand! We were now 23,000 feet and over one hundred miles from our base.

I sat at my gun position trying to decide what to do. I knew if I reported my parachute as missing Dingle would turn back, probably abort the mission. It is not possible to describe my thoughts. Terror would be a grossly inadequate description. I could not bring myself to tell the crew. All I could do was hope for the best. I am sure I sneaked a few quick prayers in for good measure. I felt weak and afraid. Then I heard a female voice clearly state, "Trust me." I quickly checked my oxygen to be sure I was not suffering from anoxia. My connection was in place. A sense of calm came over me.

What would I do if we were hit and the crew had to bail? My plan was probably ridiculous but it was the only plan I could think of. I would try to make it to the cockpit and fly the crippled bird back to England or crash land. Good plan or not, there were no options. My basic thought was a simple, "Oh Jesus!"

We crossed Belgium, and near the German border our fighter escort gave us a final apologetic waggle of wings and turned back. The Luftwaffe arrived on the scene moments later. Obviously they had been waiting in the wings for our escort to depart. The Luftwaffe attack came with unbelievable ferocity. They outnumbered us at five to one or more. I watched in amazement as they lined up and barrel rolled through the other formations with guns blazing. I could only assume they were doing the same to our group as fighter after fighter went streaking past the tail. They offered no opportunity for even a quick shot. Others, JU88's lagged behind our formation, out of the effective range of our guns and lobbed rockets into the formation. Again and again I watched the Luftwaffe line up on other groups and fly head on wing tip to wing tip. Their courage was unquestionable. They came in six at a time; diving and turning in attempts to draw fire while another fighter tried to make the kill. From the beginning of the first fighter attacks the Luftwaffe stayed with us. Long before we arrived over the target the sky was filled with a host of bombers and fighters going down in flames. Some were falling out of control with crews pinned in by centrifugal force and still others were exploding with bodies and debris falling through the formations.

Parachutes were everywhere. Many were engulfed in flames and seemed to melt as the canopy blossomed over the jumper leaving him to become a free falling body. B-17s and Luftwaffe aircraft were going down and exploding. The ground below was marked with blazing debris and the black smoke from the rubble of aircraft wreckage. Through some miracle all sixteen of our aircraft made it to the target. The scene was one of carnage beyond imagination. It was strangely not frightening; the intensity of the action left no time for alarm. However, despite my calmness I was satisfied the end was near.

As we started our bomb run the fighter attacks eased and intense flak took over. To our rear and off to one side a B-17 took a direct hit. A wing came off and the airplane went into a flat spin. Although I knew my plea was without meaning and could not be heard, I found myself urging the crew to get out. There were no parachutes. Within ten to fifteen seconds after the initial hit the bomber was converted from what had been an airplane into thousands of particles as it exploded.

We dropped our bombs and turned for home. The intercom was a constant chatter as the crew called out Luftwaffe fighter locations. I knelt in silence. I had nothing to say. My tail guns were doing my talking in short nasty bursts. No one had to tell me there were bandits at six o'clock and there was no need for me to report their presence. The Luftwaffe was all around us. I was up to my rear end in empty shell casings. We were being mauled. I watched the decimation of the formations below and around us. I could not see how we were going to make it home. There was however a strange calmness and a feeling of someone was watching over me.

When we reached the Belgium border I searched the sky for sign of our fighter escort. They were not to be seen. Our escort was weathered in, still on the ground in England. The Luftwaffe continued to have a field day. Shell casing piled deeper at every gun position. All gun positions were complaining about being short of ammunition. Although I had quietly carried extra boxes on board before take-off each of my guns had fewer than one hundred rounds per gun remaining. Almost every round had been needed.

As we left the coast of Europe the Luftwaffe disappeared. I bent forward, rested my head on the window and began to shake and cry uncontrollably. I stopped long enough to take a deep breath and say, "Thank you God." I could not tell to this day from where came the voice with the words, "Trust me." But in my heart I knew I had not been alone in the tail. I regained my composure and my courage returned. I whistled and Ed Meginnies responded. "Damn you Wing Ding, I am going to tape your mouth shut." No one else on the crew said anything. They were happy to be alive. We peeled off and landed at 1830 hours. The ground never looked better. Three of our sixteen aircraft were forced to land at other locations.

As I climbed out of Tiger Girl, M/Sgt. Paul Irelan our ground crew chief announced to everyone, "Wing Ding forgot his parachute." Dingle asked me if I had known it was on the ground. I answered, "Yes sir." He looked at me, shook his head and walked away, saying, "Now I know why they call you Wing Ding." Chuck Allred, our engineer commented, "Wing Ding, you're either crazy as hell or you've got balls."

Wing Ding

At the debriefing I tried to convince the intelligence officer of a need for a second shot of whisky. When one of the crew told him I had flown the mission without a parachute, I was quickly given the requested second shot and asked if I wanted another. I shook my head, no. The whisky burned all the way to the bottom of my empty stomach. I was yet a little on the shaky side. The word was it would take at least three days to bring the Group's aircraft up to operational standards.

After cleaning up and storing my gear I headed for the shower. As usual there was no hot water. I quickly soaped my body and rinsed, got dressed, hopped on my bicycle and headed for the pub. I thought, after surviving what I had just been through I should have a beer. When I walked in the door someone called out, "Barbara your Yank is back." "I thought you might have been done in," she said. "You look a little shaky Yank, was it a bad one?" someone asked. I took a long sip of beer and nodded my head. "You blokes should fly at night," an old pensioner advised. He then added, "Jerry can't find you then."

One beer later I left the pub with Barbara and still later made my way back to the base. Overhead I could hear the droning of engines and saw spotlights spearing the sky. I collapsed on my bunk and fell asleep with my clothes on. When I woke up it was around midnight; I was shivering. The fire in the stove nearest my bunk was out. I pulled a blanket over my clothes and slept past breakfast.

I rode my bicycle out to the hardstand to look at Tiger Girl. I crawled into the tail gun position and sat there for perhaps thirty or more minutes. I was afraid to tell anyone about hearing a voice. If I did they would surely send me to the Flight Surgeon for treatment. I shared time with the ground crew and examined the patches they had put on to cover our battle damage. Satisfied, I moved forward and sat in the copilot's seat and re-flew the mission in comfort.

Tiger Girl

12
THE GOOSE AND OTHER THINGS

As I was about to enter my barracks I heard the unmistakable sound of a honking goose. I looked and saw someone coming toward me with a large white goose under-arm. I recognized Jimmy Barnes another tail gunner. "Jimmy, what in the hell are you doing with a goose?" I asked. "Gonna eat him, WingDing," he said. "I'm sick of eating mess hall junk, canned meat and powdered eggs."

At first I did not believe him. But when he got his knife out his intentions became clear. Fortunately those of us who were country boys knew enough to take the goose outside for the decapitation ceremony. The goose, honking in protest, died hard; blood squirted everywhere. The now headless goose twitched and kicked his last.

Once the goose was dead and dry plucked the question of cooking came up. Being the only one with any real cooking experience I was tempted to volunteer for the job. I decided against volunteering. I was out of the kitchen and I was going to stay out of the kitchen. One of the gunners was dispatched to the mess hall with instructions to come back with the largest frying pan he could find.

The goose was cut up and prepared for cooking. Chopped goose would be a good description. Smokey, the waist gunner who had been sent to the mess hall returned with a large pan and one of the cooks. The cook brought half a dozen nice size real potatoes plus salt and pepper. We agreed to let him share in our feast in exchange for his expertise. The stove was stoked to full blast. Our chopped goose soon became frying goose. The aroma had us all drooling.

However, we were soon to learn the drool-producing aroma of the cooking goose was an illusion. When it came time to eat the goose we found the old gander was as tough and chewy as a piece of shoe leather. Only those with strong molars were qualified to chew the old bird. Our age brackets so qualified us and before sunset there was nothing left except bones. A crewman quipped, "The goose was cooked."

Rather early on the morning of October 16th we had visitors. A British constable, accompanied by a farmer came to our barracks. The officer apologized for bothering us and explained the purpose of his visit. He was looking for a family pet; a large white goose. Jimmy was the first to speak. "No goose around here," he said. I could not help but notice how his quick denial brought forth more than a little interest from our Sherlock Holmes type visitor. "You gents don't mind if I just look around a bit?" he asked. Of course no one objected.

Sherlock was not on the case long before he spied a few feathers in a corner of the barracks. He picked them up and with meticulous care put them into an envelope. He soon found other evidence when he strode outside to the decapitation site. "I say gents, the goose must have been visiting here," he said wryly and fixed us with a stern gaze. We could see he was not buying our story. But we were staying with it. How could we tell them we had killed and eaten a family pet? Then, as they were about to leave the constable glanced above the door. There, on the outside, above the door, spread out like a huge fan were the wings of the late goose.

The farmer's eyes followed those of the constable. He stared at the wings. For a moment he was silent, then he spoke, "Oh, I say lads, you know, the goose, his name was Oliver, he was a family pet." I think we were truly ashamed of our act. A helmet quickly made its appearance and was passed around. Eager eaters became eager donors. The farmer left with enough money to buy a dozen geese. He was smiling at our generosity and telling the constable he had no hard feelings. The case was closed.

It was too late for breakfast so I went directly to the armament shack and worked on my guns. I replaced my old gun barrels with new ones and spent the several hours checking the ammunition I would be using the next time we flew.

The notice on the bulletin board indicated a group of ladies, members of the WAAC (Women's Army Auxiliary Corps) from 8th Air Force headquarters would be touring the base and visiting the service club. Stan Gajewski, our ball turret gunner decided to go and see what real American speaking girls looked like. Having enjoyed a good service club experience while at Denver I was in favor of having a look see. Chuck Allred told us not to waste our time. "Bunch of bats. You can't do any good with any one from the WAAC," he said. Perhaps I was still remembering my train ride from San Francisco with the soon to be WAVE candidates. Chuck's admonitions were ignored. Stan and I showered; put on our best "Class A" uniforms and peddled our bikes to the service club. The band was playing and there were about twenty members of the WAAC there. I quickly noted they were under what appeared to be control or supervision of the more mature members of their outfit.

One young lady in particular interested me. She was a beautiful girl, younger than most of the others. She stood out like a bright star. Her name was Genevieve Marie; she came from a dairy farm in Minnesota. I spent the evening talking with her. I was captivated. She was clean, wholesome and as fresh as the early morning dew. I fell in love. I had to see her again. But how could it be arranged?

Since we were still standing down on October 17th I decided to find out how to travel from Knettishall to Pine Tree, the headquarters where Genevieve was stationed and make it back in time to fly. I worked out a deal with the sergeant who drove the message center Jeep to and from Pine Tree. He agreed I could ride with him as a passenger on his trips to and from the headquarters. The courier Jeep would leave our base at about 1730 hours and start back at about 2230 hours. The schedule was like clockwork. I could rest on the return trip by sleeping. The safety belt would keep me from falling out of the Jeep.

Needless to say, my first unannounced visit was a genuine surprise to Genevieve. However, I was well received and it soon became obvious Genevieve felt the same way. Our instant love seemed to be glowing and growing. I tenderly gave her a goodnight kiss on the cheek and caught the courier Jeep back to Knettishall in time to get ready for a mission.

The 388th was to provide 22 aircraft for the mission of October 18th to Duren, Germany. This would be my ninth mission. Take-off time was scheduled for 1043 hours. The group would form and leave the English coast at approximately 1400 hours. We were to bomb from 29.000 feet, it was cold beyond description. Con trails marked our position in the sky. Eleven aircraft aborted our formation for various malfunctions before we ever crossed the English coast. Three more aircraft aborted after we had departed the English coast. We were now down to a formation of eight operational aircraft.

Dingle's voice came over the intercom, although it was calm and controlled it conveyed a sense of urgency. "I need help in the cockpit. Chuck and Mac have both passed out." Dingle was making reference to our engineer and our copilot. We were at 29,000 feet. The temperature was between 48 to 52 degrees below zero. The intense cold had caused the bomb bay doors to malfunction. They had to be closed if we were to keep up with the formation. Chuck Allred, our engineer had used a portable oxygen bottle and proceeded to the bomb bay. He cranked the doors to the closed position and attempted to return to the cockpit. His oxygen supply exhausted, he collapsed as he crawled into the cockpit. Without a thought for his personal safety, copilot Ed Meginnies climbed out of his seat and gave his own oxygen supply to the stricken engineer. Chuck had not even had time to recover before Ed too collapse on the flight deck. Dingle had no choice. We were flying in formation and he could not leave the controls even for an instant. He could only watch in anguish as his flight engineer and copilot remained inert on the flight deck. Chuck, now with fresh oxygen, a gift of life from Ed Meginnies who had surrendered his own oxygen responded. He quickly reconnected the stricken copilot's oxygen and helped him back to his seat. The act was a typical demonstration of the personality of Ed Meginnies. He never gave thought to his own safety when he surrendered his life-giving source of oxygen to save the engineer.

Fortunately we were recalled while over Belgium. This was truly a milk run. There were no Luftwaffe fighters and no flak. We landed at Knettishall at about 1630 hours. Returning to base with us were many complaints about frostbite. The cold had been intense and had taken a heavy toll.

I caught my ride to Pine Tree and went to the WAAC day room where I was to meet Genevieve. Instead of Genevieve I was met by a bevy of older WAAC women. They asked me, "What are your intentions?" "Will you be nice to her?" "Genevieve is innocent and a good girl, she does not know about aircrew members." I weathered the interrogation by the self appointed guardians of Genevieve as they assured themselves her virtue was to remain intact. I convinced the ladies of the WAAC detachment of the absence of ulterior motives on my part. They were satisfied. I was in love. After stern warnings they allowed me to visit with Genevieve. We shared a wonderful evening by the huge fireplace. Later in the night when I departed it was Genevieve who led the way. She wrapped her arms around my neck and passionately kissed me goodnight. She whispered, "Please be careful when you fly."

October 20th the Duren, Germany mission was back on the board. Take-off was again set for around 1030 hours. This time we would form up and again fly over the target at 29,000. We were doing much better than we did on October 18th. We started out with nineteen aircraft and only three aborted. Our P38 escorts were with us to and from the target area. Flak was meager. There was no battle damage.

We returned and landed around 1600 hours. It was a mission to enjoy. Even an easy mission was fatiguing work. We were usually up early and then flew about seven hours at high altitude while on oxygen. Eyes ached from staring into the bright blue sky searching for the Lufwaffe. After landing I learned we were not to fly again until November 3rd. I quickly showered and caught my ride to Pine Tree. Genevieve was waiting. I spent the evening wrapped in her arms watching the embers of the huge fireplace. When it came time to catch the return courier ride to Knettishall, I told Genevieve I was not flying again until the first week in November and asked her to go to London with me. She agreed to go. Shameful as it may have been my thoughts were lustful.

13
LONDON

Genevieve met me in Thetford and we caught the train to London. I do not recall how long it took to make the trip. But I do recall the touch of her hand as we sat together in the compartment. Time passed quickly as it can easily do when you are with someone you love. Before either of us expected, we were in London. A taxi took us to the Barclay Hotel where we registered with the clerk. He gave us separate but adjoining rooms.

Once in my room I removed my jacket and necktie, brushed my teeth and gave a gentle tap on the door adjoining our rooms. Genevieve had already changed to a dress. It was the first time I had ever seen her in other than a uniform. She was breathtakingly beautiful. Passionate feelings surged through my body. I wanted to touch her and feel her close to me. I resisted the urge and hoped she was not too observant.

We were surprised by a knock on the door. It was the maid wanting to know if we would like to have tea. "It's tea time now," she said. I gave an inward sigh of relief. The change of pace was needed. Tea and some little cakes arrived quickly. I just as quickly tipped the maid and sent her on her way. We sat around a small table and shared. Tea never tasted better.

Typical of the English weather a mist blanketed the city giving the impression of evening arriving before its time. In a distance Big Ben added an eerie resonating deep bong to mark the hour. The moment was overwhelming. I was in a hotel with a beautiful woman in one of the world's most renowned cities. The tea and cakes had served only to whet our appetites. But for the moment our minds were not on food nor were they on Big Ben.

I held Genevieve close enjoying the sweet scent of her hair and the touch of her hands. One moment we were kissing passionately and the next we were on the bed. I felt her body cling to mine. I touched her and she gave a little shudder and asked, "Wing Ding, what have you done to me?" I looked at her and smiled. It was then I saw the tears in her eyes and asked her what was wrong. Her answer shocked me. "Wing Ding," she said, "I have never been alone with a man before. Until I met you I always thought I would go to a convent." She then added the final blow by saying, "I love you so much Wing Ding. I would do anything for you." She was trembling with emotion.

Genevieve Marie might as well have been wearing a chastity belt. What a terrible time I elected to become stricken by my conscience. Genevieve was there, in my grasp. I had only to make the move and she would have surrendered. But I could not. Nothing she had said or done had left me physically impotent. I suffered mightily with my desires. My love and respect for this beautiful woman was sufficient to cause me to desist. I could not take advantage of her. I knew she would still be a virgin when it came time for us to leave London. I held her in my arms and told her of my love. She quieted, then ceased trembling and fell asleep in my arms. I quietly crept back to my room, put on my pajamas and tried to sleep.

I fell asleep only to be awakened by the sounds of the air raid sirens. Not too far away there was the explosion of bursting bombs. A nearby antiaircraft battery was hammering away. I knocked on the door between our rooms. It opened immediately. Genevieve rushed to me saying, "I'm afraid, please stay with me." I noticed she had changed into a nightgown, one of those flimsy things girls wear. It was apparent she was not wearing anything underneath the flimsy thing. Bombs at the moment were not really on my mind. We foolishly went to the window and pulled the protective curtains aside and watched the search lights probe the sky in a crisscross fashion.

I took her back to her bed and she asked me to stay. I slept with Genevieve wrapped in my arms for the next two nights.

The remainder of our pass was spent doing all of the military tourist type things. We visited The Tower of London, Big Ben, The Wax Museum and a show the name of which is long forgotten. Our two nights in London ended quickly and we were soon on the train headed back to our units. Whether it was my respect for Genevieve or fear of the bevy of biddies in her outfit, I will never know the reason for my almost out of character conduct. In my heart I knew dear sweet Genevieve was not meant to be mine. I also knew from where she worked she would have knowledge of when I was flying and her prayers would be with me. Perhaps those prayers were reward enough.

14
BACK TO THE KITCHEN

My three days in London with Genevieve left me in a quandary. British beer was beginning to taste better. My thoughts turned to the local pub. I had not been there for nearly two weeks and felt a need to visit my British friends. Even though it was getting dark as I left the base I opted for the short cut across a farm field, down a narrow lane. When I came to the fence I lifted the bicycle over the steps of the stile and started across the field. It was getting darker now and the path was difficult to see. Several times I found myself off the path risking a collision with the rocks of a stone fence.

As I approached the pub I could hear the sounds of the accordion and voices raised in song. I parked my bicycle in front of the pub and entered. The music stopped. Everyone stared. The same old pensioner who had suggested we should fly at night broke the silence, "Yank, we thought Jerry had done you in for sure," he said. I saw Barbara sitting in the corner. "She's been waiting there every night, Yank," the bar keep told me and at the same time handed me a beer. I went over to where she was sitting and noticed she was crying. She said, "I thought I lost another one. Wing Ding, where the bloody hell have you been?" I could not bring myself to tell her I had been to London with another woman. "You know you should not ask such questions," I told her. She apologized and asked me, "Do you have to go back to the base tonight?" I told her I did. We sat and quietly enjoyed our beer. The accordion was again squeezed into life and once more happy voices echoed throughout the pub. I remained at the pub with Barbara for about one hour. She then leaned over and asked me to go home with her for a little while.

With Barbara I had no problems of conscience. I quickly agreed. Several hours later I headed back over the short cut to the base. It was too dark and too risky to ride so I walked and pushed the bicycle.

As I neared the mess hall area my stomach growled, telling me I had skipped the evening meal. I peered into a window of the mess hall and saw no one. It appeared no one was working. I found the door unlocked and entered the kitchen. It was the first time I had been in a kitchen since leaving Myrtle Beach, South Carolina. I boldly turned on a light. It did not take long to discover food. I helped myself to a few squares of peach cobbler and was busily eating when I heard voices.

I put the sheet pan down and grabbed an apron and a cook's hat. Five officers, all slightly inebriated, came through the unlocked back door. They asked for something to eat. At first I refused and told them I would get in serious trouble if I fed them when the mess was closed. One of them thrust a few pound notes in my hand. The others also chipped in. "What the hell," I thought, "I cannot let them go to their quarters hungry." I recovered the sheet pan of peach cobbler and told them it was all I had. They thanked me profusely and took off with their loot, the entire sheet pan of peach cobbler. I waited until I was sure of their departure. Then I removed the hat and apron and beat a hasty retreat.

Several days later as we were leaving a briefing Dingle said to me, "Wing Ding one of the navigators tells me there is a cook here who is a dead ringer for you. You don't have any relatives in the group, do you?" I shook my head indicating I did not. Our navigator, Renslar Pomery, suggested I check and see if I might have a relative in the group. Although I agreed Lt. Pomeroy's suggestion was a good idea and indicated I would check, my thoughts told me they already knew the answer.

My late night sale of peach cobbler netted me almost five pounds in English money. I considered a repeat performance. However, the risk of someone recognizing me was too great. My arduous escape from kitchen to the world of aviation was not yet a faded memory and I had no desire to return to duty as a cook.

15
BACK IN THE AIR

November 3, 1943, we were about to fly our eleventh mission. It was to be a late take-off of around 1000 hours. The target was Wilhelmshaven. When it was announced we would be fully escorted by P-47's a short cheer went up in the briefing room. However, we remembered their absence on our return from Schweinfurt and hoped for the best. Preflight preparations were the same as always. Flak was predicted as meager except for over the target.

The mission was exactly as predicted. Fighters never appeared and though our altitude was only 23,000 feet the flak was too low to bother us. Of course I whistled and of course Mac complained. The only thing different was Dingle laughed. We returned to Knettishall at 1615 hours. Everyone was happy to have enjoyed what we had to class as a milk run.

When the word was passed listing November 4th as a no mission day I decided to go to Pine Tree and see Genevieve. The sun had set by the time I located the courier. The driver, usually the same Sergeant each day, would always listen eagerly to my stories of the missions. There never was a need to embellish them. The truth was far more exciting than fiction. Upon arrival at Pine Tree I found Genevieve waiting. She embraced me with all the love and passion in her heart. She gave a little shudder, held me close and said, "Wing Ding you make me feel so good." We again sat in front of the fireplace in the lounge of the WAAC day room with arms wrapped around each other. She was strangely silent and finally asked me, "Wing Ding, can we go to London again?" Her question came as a surprise. Even more surprising was when she told me she wanted to return to the Barclay Hotel. Her words lingered lustfully in my mind during the long ride back to Knettishall.

The briefing officer's pointer traced the red line across parts of Holland and Belgium to the Ruhr Valley, a place called Gelsenkirchen, the site of an iron foundry on the Dortmund River. His voice droned without emotion, "You will be engaged in the destruction of a very important iron works and marshalling yards."

We were the lead group and started out with twenty-nine aircraft off the ground around 1000 hours. Six of our aircraft returned to base early for various mechanical problems. We were over the target at 28,000 feet with twenty-three aircraft. It was bombs away at 1333 hours. The mission was not exactly successful. We might as well have been hauling nickels (leaflets). We missed the primary targets, the iron works and the marshalling yards.

Flak over the target was intense and nearly every aircraft took a hit. Bohne flying My Devotion in composite lead with Major Chamberlain lost two engines to flak. By the time they reached England the other two engines were running rough and the left wing was severely vibrating. Flight Officer Bohne determined the situation out of control. He ordered his crew to bail out. They all landed safely. But the fire from their crashing bomber ignited a large stack of straw; it burned until the following morning.

2nd Lt. Bramwell, flying his seventh mission in Flak Suit was hit on the way in to the target. They pulled out of formation, dropped their bombs and headed down with their number one engine on fire. Bramwell determined Flak Suit would no longer survive. He gave the order to bail out. Three members of the crew, bombardier 2nd Lt. J. J. Maiorca, flight engineer T/Sgt. H.C. Johnson and right waist gunner S/Sgt. G. Watt evaded capture. The radio operator and the tail gunner were both killed. The others ended up as prisoners.

2nd Lt. R. M. Walker and his crew were on their third mission in Pistol Packin Mama. They fell behind soon after bombs away and started down with bomb bay doors still open. Engine number two was feathered and number three was smoking as they started down. Eight chutes opened. But it did not go well for the ball turret gunner. His parachute opened prematurely and became entangled with the tail. He rode Pistol Packin Mama to the ground. The right waist gunner apparently never left the airplane and was killed in the crash.

We faced almost ten days of crummy weather. Even our practice missions were curtailed. I made the most of it by managing a three-day pass to London. My first destination was Rainbow Corners USO at Piccadilly Circus. I had been in the club for only a few minutes when I heard a lilting voice ask, "What are you looking for sergeant?" I looked and saw a most attractive lady, petite in size and perhaps in her late thirties. She introduced herself as Adele Astare Cavendesh the sister of Fred Astaire. Rapport was immediate. Adele took me under her wing and clucked like a mother hen. She warned me about all the places where I could get into trouble and cautioned me to avoid them. Little did she know how her warnings would serve only as a guide; I checked out all the places on her forbidden list. I did however heed her warnings about the Piccadilly Commandos. I enjoyed seventy-two hours of luxury, great stage performances and the stories Adele told about Hollywood and the people she knew from the world of make believe. She also introduced me to a former ballerina named Flip who worked at Rainbow Corners and lived alone. Flip was a remarkable lady with an even more remarkable body and calluses on her feet from dancing.

When I left London the weather was the usual pea soup mist. It clung to the ground and was so dense even Big Ben sounded like a muffled gong. It was no different at our base. I had a choice; go to Pine Tree to see Genevieve or to the pub. I decided on the pub and Barbara. The ability of the courier to stay on the road in the miserable weather caused me concern. Taking my chances at 25,000 feet seemed to be less of a risk than sleeping in a Jeep zipping over a fog shrouded narrow road. I had finally located most of the big rocks on the short cut route to the pub. I had also learned to limit my intake of beer. This I found improved my ability at darts and anything else

I wanted to do. In addition it made the ride back to the base less of a challenge.

The patrons of the pub never seemed to change. My arrival was usually greeted with the announcement, "Cheers, our Yank is back." They made me feel welcome. The accordion player would squeeze out the same songs night after night. I never joined the singing until after several beers. It was some sort of a balance. I had to drink enough beer to stifle my inhibitions to a point where I would sing. I did not realize how close our relationship had become until one evening they presented me with a set of my own darts. It was then I knew they cared. I was deeply moved.

We were up and flying on November 13th, headed for Munster. The weather was some of the worst we had ever seen. By the time we reached mid-channel it was apparent the mission would be scrubbed. The groups were in disarray; formations were badly confused. Fortunately a recall was sounded. We returned to Knettishall happy to be able to get back on the ground in one piece. I often thought about the stories of the early airmail pilots and how they flew in marginal weather. Well, for certain the 8th Air Force pilots did them one better. Many of our take-off and landings were on the negative side of marginal.

We were up early on November 14th. I found myself hoping it would be better than October 14th; at least I would have my parachute with me. The charge of quarters rousted us out at about 0300 hours. When we arrived at briefing we learned our destination would be Bremen. The red line led across the English Channel then over the Zider Zee and to Bremen. Plans called for us to put up 22 aircraft. We were to fly as the high group of the 45th Combat Wing.

The group was off the ground by 0750 hours with the exception of Lt. Simon. He blew a tire on take-off. Quickly they switched to B-17 LiL one and were off the ground at 0831. It has oft been said, "If you are going to have a bad day there isn't much you can do about it." This was obviously a bad day for LiL one. They were searching for the group when at sixteen thousand feet the propeller on engine number four ran away. The engine was shut down. However the propeller failed to feather and continued to rotate like a windmill, causing severe vibrations. LiL one shuddered as if it would come apart. In fact it started to come apart. The cowling and engine cover on engine number four ripped off. The entire aircraft continued to shake dangerously. Lt. Simon determined the aircraft could no longer be controlled and was unsafe to land. The alarm bell sounded throughout the bomber. The crew needed very little encouragement to leave their vibrating aircraft. All ten men hit the silk. B-17F 42-30213 LiL one became history. One of those bailing out was the navigator, 2nd Lt. R. L. Gudgel from Spokane, Washington. Bob Gudgel was on his seventh mission when he learned how to operate a parachute. He landed with minor injuries.

Two more of the twenty-one aircraft taking off from Knettishall experienced propeller trouble and were forced to abort. Lt. Paul Swift, who had skillfully saved his crew when they crashed on takeoff with a full load of bombs on the Schweinfurt mission experienced a loss of oil pressure and was unable to feather the propeller on engine number two. He returned to base without further difficulty. Captain Chaffin, flying as deputy lead, aborted from 27,000 feet when the prop on engine number four ran away and would not feather. He had descended to 7,000 feet when the number four engine burst into flames. He prepared to ditch in the English Channel and sent out the emergency message. Then a relatively rare event took place. His aircraft was struck by lightning and further radio communication was not possible. Despite the problems he landed successfully. The remaining eighteen aircraft continued to Bremen where they found minimal flak. Approximately fifty Luftwaffe fighters made one pass at the group but disappeared with the appearance of our escort.

An explanation about the extensive mechanical problems is in order here. It would be a grievous error for anyone to get the idea our ground crews and maintenance crews were sloppy. This was not the case. The 8th Air Force was growing and critical equipment items such as spark plugs and generators were at times in short supply. Additional ground crews, the life-blood of an operating air force had been hastily trained. Then too, the airplanes themselves were in a constant state of modification, improvement and repair from battle damage. Not enough credit can be given to those on the ground; they kept us in the air. Their skill made the difference. Because of their dedication our aircraft were ready to fly.

Our fourteenth mission to Rjukan, Norway was classified as secret. We bombed the heavy water project where the Germans were working to develop a nuclear weapon. Take-off and departure were unusual. We were off the ground with minimal visibility at 0630 hours. The weather made it difficult to form up. One aircraft lost power in engine number two and aborted. Another lost the formation when we entered clouds and never did rejoin. As we flew over the North Sea we ran into icing conditions. The tail of one B-17 iced up causing severe control problems. They dropped out of formation, dumped their bombs at sea and turned back. The group was left with seventeen aircraft to complete the mission.

Although we were flying low, at only 12,500 feet, the combination of moisture and intense cold caused the lead bombardier's bombsight to become frosted and he could not line up on the target. The deputy lead took over and we made a wide turn to set up a new bomb run. Bombs were away at about 1150 hours. Two enemy fighters were seen. One ME109 came up behind the formation and fired two rockets. I bit down hard on my frozen Milky Way and fired at the rockets. Both rockets moved through the formation and exploded at a lower altitude. The fighter then made two passes. His 20mm guns hit one aircraft without wounding anyone and did not inflict major damage.

There was good news at our debriefing. Dingle told us we had one more mission to fly before we were to go to the Flak Home. We would spend about ten days in an English mansion with servants and breakfast, lunch and dinner served by staff. Clean sheets and real beds all promised a short but memorable life of luxury.

We would then have only ten more missions before our tour was completed. We were now a veteran crew. We also knew we were flying on borrowed time. Anything over ten missions put a crew into the borrowed time category. Using the estimated loss rate of four percent per mission and a tour of twenty-five missions it was not difficult to come to a "luck running out" conclusion. Skill in the use of algebraic equations was not essential for figuring the odds. We all had the experience of seeing crews go down near the end of their tour.

Upon hearing we would not fly the following day I decided it was time to head for the pub. I peddled my bike with care through the field. I had by now learned the location of almost every large rock and small stone along the route. On arrival the usual patrons greeted me with warmth. The accordion whipped out a version of "Roll Me over In the Clover" and Barbara raised her glass and called out, "Cheers." Someone handed me my darts, which they kept at the pub, and challenged me to a game. My ability compared to the regular dart players meant the Yank was buying the beer. I don't think many of those in the pub even knew my name. To them I was known either as Wing Ding or Barbara's Yank, the guy who brought candy for their children and cigarettes for the others. The pub keeper called time and Barbara and I left the pub. I pushed my bicycle as we walked together. I was looking forward to a soft warm bed and Barbara.

We were prepared to fly to Gelsenkirchen on November 19, 1943. However there was a change in plans. Dingle told us we would be going to the Flak Home earlier than scheduled. The officers would go to their rest home and the enlisted men to a different location. I am ashamed to say I do not recall where it was located other than it was in the southern part of England. We were flown to a location nearby and then transported by a truck. The mansion itself was huge. Each man had his own room. The rooms were heated and equipped with large soft beds. At night the bed was turned down and in the morning a butler came to announce breakfast and a schedule of the day's activities.

Much to my delight I discovered the young maid who was assigned to my room was more than a little friendly. I am sure she had gone through prior interludes with my predecessors and would continue with following replacements. But for a young tail gunner, nineteen years old she was a remarkable tonic to relieve my combat fatigue. I spent ten days in recovery.

On our return to Knettishall we were in for a shock. Our ground crew chief, M/Sgt Paul Irelan met us and told us Tiger Girl had gone down on November 26 while on a mission to Bremen. The pilot had been 1st Lt. G. E. Branham. He and most of his crew were on their nineteenth mission. The Command Pilot on the mission was Captain Jerome Davidson; for him it was his seventh and final mission. Just after bombs away, at approximately 1217 hours the formation had made a sharp turn to get out of the flak pattern. Two incendiaries dropped from the 96th Bomb Group flying as high group and struck Tiger Girl. One caught her on the left stabilizer and the other struck near the waist door. The tail came off. There were two parachutes. One was the radio operator, T/Sgt. F. P. Grande who was on his 14th mission. The other was the navigator, 2nd Lt. Bob Gudgel who was on his 8th mission and second parachute jump in the month of November 1943. Things did not go well for Lt. Gudgel. While descending he was struck by antiaircraft fire and subsequently had his leg amputated by the German doctors. Tiger Girl, B-17G number 42-3555 became history at 1220 hours, November 26, 1943.

16
ON BORROWED TIME

The loss of our airplane, especially the way it was lost and the loss of friends was disturbing. Almost everyone flying on Tiger Girl had been near completion of their tour of twenty-five missions. Again in our mind was the approximate four-percent per mission loss ratio. We were now flying on borrowed airplanes and on borrowed time.

From November 26 until December 11, 1943 it appeared as if we were never going to be able to complete our tour. Weather and some commitments to drop leaflets occupied the group's activities. However on November 29th the mission was to Bremen. Of the twenty-nine aircraft taking off four aborted the mission for mechanical reasons or a physical problem of someone on a crew. The realities of high altitude hazards were accentuated. S/Sgt. Raymond Wilbur, engineer on Lt. Ramsey's airplane died from anoxia. Another friend was lost when the pilot was forced to ditch on the return route. S/Sgt. J. P. Riley flying on his twentieth mission had filled in as ball turret gunner on a crew flying their first mission. He and seven others did not survive the ditching.

Our fifteenth mission did not come until December 11th. We flew as part of a task force to bomb the shipyards at Emden. From the onset the mission was plagued with bad weather conditions. Shortly before we reached the target the Luftwaffe hit us causing a loss of five aircraft. One of those was from our group. Six parachutes were observed before their airplane blew up. Of the thirty-two aircraft over the target seven had flak damage. To add to the problem our bombs fell short of the target area. We would have done as much good if we had never flown.

I cleaned my equipment and once I was assured there would be no mission the following day I caught a ride with the courier to Pine Tree and shared a few very happy hours with Genevieve. I spent the evening wrapped in her arms. She seemed more passionate than ever and again asked when we could go back to London. I promised her we would go as soon as possible. I said goodnight with Genevieve holding me tightly until the movement of the courier Jeep forced her to let go.

December 13th marked our sixteenth mission. We were steadily getting closer to the magic number of twenty-five. After take-off we formed as part of the low group and headed across the North Sea flying south of Heligoland Island and entered the continent flying over the Kiel Canal headed for the Kiel naval yards and ship building center. The Luftwaffe made a half-hearted attack. But it was deadly for Lt. Cwiklinski, navigator on Lt. DeJean's crew. A 20mm cannon round burst in the nose killing him. The intense flak over the target area was magnified when the lead aircraft could not get the bomb bay doors open. We made a second run on the target, giving the antiaircraft gunners on the ground a second bite of the apple; we were the apple. Out of the forty-three aircraft making the bomb run only six escaped battle damage. We were fortunate to get off without heavy losses.

I do not recall why we did not fly several missions during the last part of December. It could have been aircraft maintenance or some other operational reason. We seemed to be hanging around with nine missions to go. Counting to the end was definitely not good for crew moral. I managed to stir things up. I found a source where I could buy carbide stones. Some may recall the old acetylene lanterns once used by miners and others to light their way. Such lanterns or lights burned the acetylene gas generated when water was added to the stones. I took a bottle and combined a few stones and water. Next a condom was placed over the top of the bottle. In short order there would be a large balloon filled with explosive acetylene gas. The condom-balloon was then rolled under the bunk where another gunner was relaxing while reading the Star and Stripes or just dozing off. A smoldering cigarette rolled under the bunk to join the inflated condom would quickly result in a puff of black smoke and a whoosing sound. The recipient would invariably react as if his airplane had been blown up. Curses filled the air while those in on the joke would laugh uproariously.

During the next ten days I almost wore out the bicycle riding to and from the pub. I had developed good relations at the mess hall in exchange for showing one of the cooks how to bake really good cake. This enabled me to get a variety of hard-to-come-by items. These things and my own candy and cigarette rations gave me a good source of Christmas items for my friends at the pub.

Christmas Eve was special. I caught the courier and went to Pine Tree to see Genevieve. We spent a wonderful evening in front of a huge fireplace. The world could have come to a stop. Neither of us would have noticed. We were oblivious to all activities other than our cuddling and loving. Genevieve suddenly gave a little gasp,

"Oh," she asked, "What have you done to me to make me feel like this?" I did not reply. I only held her closer and thought about what I would like to do but should not do. A repeat trip to London was steadily becoming more appealing.

Our seventeenth mission was scheduled on December 30, 1943. The target was the I. G. Farbenindustrie Chemical Works at Ludwigshaven. The 388th would furnish aircraft for both the "A" and "B" flights. Aircraft were off the ground between 0815 hours and 0850 hours. Following a rendezvous with the 45th Combat Wing five of our airplanes aborted for mechanical reasons.

The group ran into severe prop wash over the target causing a near mid-air collision. The B-17 of Lt. A. W. Carlson went out of control, rolled over and broke in half at the radio room. There were only four parachutes seen going out and opening. Shortly after bombs away My Day piloted by Lt. Comelia had a fire in engine #3. He put his B-17 in a dive and was successful in extinguishing the fire. But the propeller on the #3 engine failed to feather and twisted off severely damaging the nose section. My Day, now alone and crippled became food for the Luftwaffe. They quickly attacked and knocked out engine #2. The crew fought on, steadily losing altitude. As they crossed the coast, well under a thousand feet, My Day was again struck by flak. There were no options remaining. They were forced to ditch in the English Channel. Air Sea Rescue responded to their call for help. Even so, a combination of the impact on ditching and hypothermia cost six of the ten-man crew their lives.

17
WE LOSE MIKE

On January 4, 1944 we flew our 18th mission. I celebrated my twentieth birthday by returning to Munster. When we arrived at our airplane our copilot, Ed Meginnies was conspicuous by his absence. Dingle was in his seat, warming up the engines and doing preflight check when a Jeep came to a screeching halt near the right wing tip. A grinning Ed Meginnies ran from the Jeep and climbed on board. We did not learn until later the reason for Mac's late arrival. On his first solo flight Ed Meginnies had worn a pair of polka dot shorts. Considering them a good luck charm he carried them with him and wore them on every combat mission. On this particular morning, upon arriving at the briefing, Ed Meginnies discovered he was not wearing his lucky shorts. He implored the operations officer to lend him a Jeep to rush back to his quarters to retrieve and don his good luck underwear. He had worn those shorts on every mission. They were never washed between missions; he feared washing his luck away. Perhaps not too fastidious, but a good luck charm for sure.

Take-off at around 0700 hours was completed in the usual poor visibility. We formed up and never saw the ground again until we returned around 1300 hours. Our fighter escort was excellent and the Luftwaffe wisely avoided paying us a visit. But the flak gunners were busy. They picked us up at our altitude and direction from Rhine on the Em River and tracked us on to Munster. Although the flak was not especially heavy it was accurate; 30 of our 36 aircraft suffered damage. Five were hard hit. Another friend, tail gunner,

Dennis Tobias received serious head and chest wounds from flak. I could feel the "borrowed time" noose drawing ever tighter.

Despite knowing we would have an early take-off the next day I caught the courier Jeep to Pine Tree. I had considered going to the pub but did not want to drink and did not want to take a chance on not being present for the mission. The courier Jeep rattled along, driving on the wrong side of the road by American standards. The sergeant driving paid little attention to the hazardous mist hanging over the road. When we arrived at Pine Tree I found Genevieve and some of her friends had planned a surprise party for me. Although I would have preferred to be alone with Genevieve I could only express my gratitude and hope for a chance to be alone with her. Such was not to be and I soon found myself shivering as the courier Jeep bumped along the narrow and winding return trip to Knettishall.

The heavy fog challenged the driver. He ran off the road twice and I began to think I would not make it in time to be ready for the 0630 hours or earlier scheduled take-off. I securely buckled the passenger side safety strap to keep from falling from the moving Jeep. I tried to sleep. Sleep did not come and I had visions of missing the mission. We arrived at Knettishall at 0400 hours. There was barely enough time for me to change clothes and make it to the mess hall and then to briefing.

When the briefing officer pulled back the curtain I was pleased to note our destination was to be Bordeaux, France. "An easy target," I thought, "and a good way to complete my nineteenth mission." Someone said it would be a milk run. A milk run it was not. Dingle, flying deputy lead, had us off the ground around 0730 hours. We were bombs away at approximately 1035 hours with moderate to intense very accurate flak. Our B-17 rolled and shuddered in reaction to a near burst of flak. A moment later our navigator, Pomeroy spoke on the intercom. "Mike has been hit," he said, making reference to our bombardier, Mike Chaklos. At the same time we were busy with a combination of FW 190's and ME 109's making persistent and deliberate attacks coming in at the front of the formation and diving down toward the rear. Their approach and departure was so quick there was little opportunity for a shot. They stayed with us for about fifteen minutes. The uninitiated may view fifteen minutes as a short time. It may well be a short time, but it is not a short time when you are under fighter attack.

As we approached the Brest Peninsula a new group of dedicated Luftwaffe pilots challenged us. They were mostly interested in crippled B-17's, but they also came at us from the tail. I was satisfied to see my tracers dance on the wings and fuselage of several of the attackers. However, there was no way I could make claim for a confirmed kill. It was a case of close but no cigar. Other gunners were also on the targets.

Our lead aircraft was hit during one of the head-on fighter attacks. There was a fire in the cockpit. Colonel David, Group Leader took over the controls from the wounded pilot, Captain Bailey. He dove out of formation and put the fire out. The bombardier, Captain Bartuska moved into the copilot seat to assist Colonel David. At 10,000 feet they again came under intense fighter attack. The gunners knocked down four fighters and the others gave up the chase. Nine of the ten men on the crew were treated for wounds.

Navigator Pomeroy again spoke on the intercom. "I think Mike is dead, there is no response," he said. His words ran through the crew like a bolt of electricity. Mike had been close to all of us and now the odds had taken their toll.

Sioux City Queen left the formation with one propeller feathered and was immediately jumped by fighters; they shot up the tail. Seven chutes were seen. We were to learn later the ball turret gunner and the copilot died of wounds. Both waist gunners were taken prisoners and six members of the crew evaded capture. Later reports told of the price of their evasion. Lieutenant LaForce lost one leg and Lieutenant Plytynski lost both legs while crossing the Pyrenees Mountains into Spain. The so-called "milk run" had been flown at a high cost. There were four dead men and sixteen wounded by flak or fighters. I had only six more to go. But for Mike the tour was over. He would go to the American Cemetary at Madingley.

Rocket Damage

18
BACK TO LONDON

For reasons long since forgotten we did not fly again until January 21st. I took advantage of the interlude and decided to go to London. I went to see Genevieve and learned she would not be able to get a pass. Rather than sit around the base I decided to go alone. The ride from Thetford to London promised to be somewhat long and lonely. I climbed in a compartment and was pleased to find it was already occupied by a chubby but attractive WREN, the British equivalent of our WAVES. She told me her name was Penny and she was stationed in London and had been home to visit her mum.

Never having before met an American she displayed some initial shyness. This soon departed as the train rolled through the countryside. By the time we arrived in London Penny had convinced me she should spend the final day of her leave showing me the sights of the city. The day was so enjoyable we extended it to the morning. I made it a point, partly out of sentimental reasons, not to go to the Barclay Hotel. Breakfast at Oxford Circus was my treat. I bid Penny a cheerful goodbye as she left to report for duty. Her parting comment was, "Cheers, love, remember a bad penny always shows up."

London in those days was filled with military personnel from all types of services and a horde of ladies known as Picadilly Commandos who haunted the streets at night in search of customers. Their special tactic was groping prospective clients in hopes of creating a business-like atmosphere. It was said the average was about twenty gropes per block.

Arguments and brawls were not uncommon. One such donnybrook took place near Picadilly Circus. Just off the street, down a flight of stairs were men's toilets. At times the facilities were crowded and one had to wait their turn. I was in the lavatory in the process of waiting my turn to use the urinal. Four of the dozen or so spaces were occupied by military personnel dressed in kilts. All was quiet and orderly until six Australians entered. One of the Australians seemed to be in a hurry. He pushed his way to the front of the line. He took his swagger stick and poked it up under the rear of the Scott's kilt and loudly said, "You ladies should go someplace where you can sit down and pee properly." The Scott who had been the recipient of the swagger stick turned about and proceeded to urinate on the Aussie. The battle was on; I hurried up to the street and stood outside in the cold with all thoughts of having to use the toilet facilities a distant memory. The sounds of the donnybrook subsided. Up the stairs and out of the lavatory came the four kilt-attired Scott's. They were adjusting their kilts. I cautiously returned to the lavatory. It was immediately obvious who had prevailed. The Australians did not look too good.

Having survived the battle of the lavatory I decided to go to Rainbow Corners and see if Adele was working. When I arrived she greeted me warmly and chastised me. She told me Flip, the ballerina to whom she had previously introduced me had been asking where I was. Adele lectured me for not being more considerate. "Flip has been wanting to see you again," she said. I told Adele I would be back in a couple of hours and took off to see the show at the Windmill Theatre. My next two days were spent with Flip at her apartment. She danced for me.

19
SIX TO GO

When I reported back to Knettishall on January 11th I found we were not scheduled to fly. Jimmy Jones told me I had lost two friends. S/Sgt. Zaskiewicz, a ball turret gunner and S/Sgt. Brinker, a tail gunner had gone down on a recalled mission. We compared notes and found we each had six missions left on our tours. I told Jimmy about my feelings of borrowed time and reminded him about Lt. Eccleston and his crew. On December 20, 1943 they had taken off to fly their 25th mission. They were last seen going down in flames shortly after bombs away. All were killed. Jimmy laughed and commented as to how he had long been on borrowed time. In one of his early missions while flying as tail gunner on Gremlin Gus he escaped death. Gremlin Gus, flying in bad weather, after dark, scraped a hill. When it crashed shortly thereafter on another hillside, Jimmy Jones was not on board. He was in the broken off tail section, dazed but relatively uninjured, in the dark and on foot.

Since we were not scheduled to fly for nearly ten days I spent my time either peddling my bicycle to and from the pub or taking the wild night ride from Knettishall to Pine Tree and return. Genevieve never failed to remind me she was praying for my safe return from each mission. Barbara on the other hand was much more matter of fact. Her view was she would lose me no matter what. Either I would be shot down or I would return to the United States. Fortunately neither lady knew about the other. This arrangement was within my control. The outcome of the final six missions was not.

The mission to Calais, France on January 21, 1944 marked our twentieth mission. It was also our first mission since the loss of Mike Chaklos. I could not help but remember how Mike appeared when he was removed from our airplane. He had only one mark on his body. He had been struck in an artery in his groin. The wound, although mortal, appeared to be no more than a small dot about the size of the end of a little finger.

The run to Calais gave me cause for apprehension. We flew the mission at only 12,000 feet. Broken clouds at the target made accurate bombing difficult. As a result there were several bomb runs while the lead bombardier did his aiming. Fortunately there was minimal flak and no fighters. It ended up as one of those missions you would not want to miss. Credit for a mission flown was obtained at a very low price.

The weather was absolutely crummy for the seven days following our trip to Calais. I didn't mind. I found myself balancing my desire to complete my tour and a return to CONUS against leaving England. Some of my ties had developed into rather pleasant emotional circumstances. I again set up my routine of riding the courier Jeep to Pine Tree and spending time with Genevieve. When it was not convenient to make the trip to Pine Tree there was the pub and Barbara. There was a difference. With Genevieve it was passion and desire; with Barbara it was more physical.

January 29th found us headed for an early morning briefing. The red line on the briefing officer's map indicated our route would be over parts of France and Belgium on our way to Frankfurt on the Rhine. We had an early morning take-off for our twenty-first mission, the kind Dingle liked so much, climbing blindly through the overcast until we broke out in the clear weather. Five of the group's aircraft aborted for mechanical reasons. The bomb run was made at 24,000 feet utilizing PFF (radar equipment). Fighters attacked some of the other formations, but left us alone. Flak was low and off to one side of the formation. However, Mary Ellen, B-17 #42-32856 was hit by flak while over the target. They left the formation and did not make it back to England. Two more friends were lost when the airplane went down. Ball turret gunner T/Sgt J. L. McCullough on his 13th mission and tail gunner, S/Sgt. M. O. Moore, on his 14th mission were killed. I was beginning to have my doubts. There were four missions left to fly.

My doubts were further reinforced on January 30th. We were not flying but as was my custom I went to the flight line to watch the group as they returned from Brunswick, Germany. According to reports the flak had been moderate to intense over the target area. F/O M. P. Bianchi had to leave the formation. One propeller was feathered and another had failed to feather. I learned I had lost another friend, tail gunner, S/Sgt. J. H. Marshall. Also killed was the right waist gunner, S/Sgt. E. S. Wolf. Both were on their 13th mission. My thinking was ridiculous; in my mind I had the thought they had gone down in my place while I beat the odds. As hard as I tried to dispel the thought it continued to nag me.

Our twenty-second mission to Frankfurt on February 4th clearly defined the cold weather and minimal visibility problems we faced. The winter weather was miserable. Most of our departures found the pilot's eyes locked onto the instrument panel. It was not uncommon for the visibility to be limited to the wing tips as we climbed to the clear skies at altitudes of 10,000 to 15,000 feet. Temperatures were cold beyond description and frostbite took a heavy toll. Intense cloud cover obscured the targets and most of the bombing had to be done using radar. At best the accuracy of our effort on each such mission was questionable.

Colonel David flew the lead on the Frankfurt mission in a Pathfinder equipped airplane. As we approached the target he lost power in the #1 engine. The problem was exasperated when the propeller would not feather and eventually froze. To add to their troubles, the bomb bay doors failed to open. Colonel David had no choice. He was forced to leave the group and return alone. The deputy lead, also flying a Pathfinder equipped B-17 assumed the lead and continued with the mission.

Flying over the Ruhr Valley was sometimes necessary. It was also an open invitation to the German antiaircraft gunners to have target practice. February 4th was their day. The flak over the Ruhr was intense and accurate. The German gunners demonstrated their skill. Almost every one of our aircraft suffered battle damage.

B-17 #42-31781, piloted by Lt. DeJean received a direct flak hit on the right wing slightly before bombs away. The damage was severe. They went out of control and flipped upside down; the right wing was in flames. They were last seen going down in flames. They were still out of control when they entered the heavy clouds at 16,000 feet. Depending on the circumstances, escape from an out-of-control airplane is virtually impossible. The centrifugal force keeps the hapless members of the crew firmly locked in position all the way to the ground.

For the majority of the DeJean crew it was their fifteenth mission. Only the bombardier and the radio operator were able to escape from their plunging airplane. They survived to become prisoners of war. Odds were hard to figure. About three weeks earlier, December 13, 1943 while on a mission to Kiel, a head-on fighter attack resulted in Lt. DeJean's aircraft taking a direct hit in the nose from a 20mm cannon round. It killed his navigator. He managed to bring his crippled bomber home. He too had entered the borrowed time era.

We were up and flying again on February 5th. Our mission was to maul various Luftwaffe airfields in France. Our primary target was cloud covered; therefore we moved to the secondary target. I personally liked missions of this type. As a rule there was minimal flak and we would be hitting the Luftwaffe on the ground. We made our bomb run from 22,500 feet. The target, a repair depot for Junkers aircraft located slightly south of Paris was well covered. Two FW 190's attacked the formation. One of these was shot down. All of our aircraft made it back to Knettishall.

The group was scheduled to again hit airfields in France on February 6th. I had hoped we would be able to fly our 24th mission. But we were not scheduled to fly until February 10th. I took turns and rode the courier Jeep to Pine Tree to share time with Genevieve or pedaled my nearly worn out bicycle to the pub to shoot darts, drink beer and spend time with Barbara.

Nose Job
(B-17 flown home by Lt Larry deLancey after mission to Colonge, Germany)

20
THE FINAL TWO

February 10th our 24th mission started out with one of those early morning wake-up calls. We fumbled around in the dark, damp, chilly early morning and headed to the mess hall. From breakfast we went to briefing and saw the long red ribbon mark our target as Brunswick

The take-off at 0740 hours was up through the usual wall of near invisibility. On our way in on the coast of Holland we received intense and accurate flak from the coastal antiaircraft guns. Heavy damage was inflicted on about half of our aircraft.

Soon after crossing the Zuider Zee the Luftwaffe made an appearance. One group came under attack by approximately thirty FW 190's. Shortly after 1100 hours we were hit again by FW 190's flying in small groups. On our approach to the target the familiar twin engine rocket launchers were back in business. They followed their usual pattern of hanging back, just out of range and firing the rockets into the formation. I could only see one possible defense. I tried to fire short bursts at the approaching rocket. I readily admit, I never saw one blow up because of my efforts. But I felt better. I disliked rockets.

Just prior to bombs away Bad Penny flown by Lt. Evans of the 561st Squadron left the formation with #3 engine feathered. Enemy fighters quickly hit them and they went down. As inappropriate as it may have been my thoughts reflected back to my recent trip to London. I kept saying to myself, "A bad penny always shows up." They did not. Only three of the crew survived. Hell's Bells, flown by

Lt. Feeney of the 501st Squadron took a heavy flak hit while over the target. Hell's Bells left formation out of control. Seven of the crew managed to bail out before it crashed. Both of these crews had made it into the borrowed time zone. Each had less than ten missions remaining until their tour was complete. The 561st Squadron lost one more crew. Lt. Tolles's B-17 with #4 engine feathered had fighters pressing home the attack. Somewhere after the coast of Holland they apparently went down in the English Channel. There were no survivors.

Our debriefing was a solemn affair. We all were keenly aware we had one mission left to fly and the potential of not making it was brought home by the day's loses. The weather gave us no choice. We had to wait until February 13th for our 25th and final mission. I made good use of the time. Bad weather or not I caught a ride on the courier Jeep to visit Genevieve. When I arrived she greeted me warmly and told me how much she loved me. We spent a torrid evening; coming as close to making love as possible. Fortunately the day room did not offer much privacy. She again told me she wanted to go to London before I left England. I promised her I would try.

I considered going to see Genevieve again on February 12th, but heard we would fly on the 13th and did not want to take a chance on the courier Jeep not making it back in time for the mission. Another consideration was a need to go to the pub and see Barbara and the others. The weather was cold and wet and the shortcut across the fields muddy and slippery. Riding the bicycle was far more work than it would have been had I trudged through the mud.

"Cheers Yank," greeted me as I entered the pub. My pint of beer showed up without a word out of my mouth. Someone handed me my darts and I knew I was going to buy the beer. I told Barbara I was flying in the morning and could not stay late. She immediately took my darts and put them away.

She said, "Yank, I am not going to have you much longer. Let's go home." I finished my beer and we left. I remained with her until 2100 hours and then returned to the base and cleaned the mud off my shoes before I crawled into my bed.

There was no early wake-up on February 13, 1944. Our twenty-fifth and final mission was scheduled to have a late take-off. We were going to hit military installations in the Calais area of France. Although everyone knew it was our twenty-fifth mission, no one wished us good luck at the briefing. We might as well have been a new crew flying our first mission. Dingle had us off the ground around 1330 hours and it was bombs away at 1519 hours at an altitude of only 19,000 feet.

The 388th flew as low group, one of three groups of the 45th Combat Wing. Two of our aircraft aborted for mechanical reasons and we went over the target with twenty-one aircraft. Flak was moderate but very accurate. Over half of our aircraft had minor damage. Two had major damage and just before bombs away the lead bombardier was hit by flak causing him to miss his aiming point. All of the group's aircraft landed at Knettishall before 1700 hours.

I remained in the tail for the landing. I was suddenly trapped by my emotions. Had it all really happened? Survival of the tour slowly became a reality. Dingle moved our B-17 to the hardstand and shut down the engines. Everyone remained in place. The entire crew was silent. Then almost as if on a signal a cheer went up as we scrambled to the ground. We had beaten the odds. Radioman Bill Pross mentioned how perfect it would be if Mike had made it to the end. But the memory of Mike was in our hearts and the touch of sadness failed to quell our exuberance. M/Sgt. Irelan, our crew chief had a photographer and Mike's dog standing by. He brought Mike's dog to the front of the B-17. Stan Gajewski held the dog and we had our crew picture taken.

We spent minimal time in the debriefing room and then had our own rather personal celebration. After the celebration settled down I return to the tail of our B-17 and removed my gun barrels. I took the barrels to the armament shack and gave them one final cleaning before I gratefully put them away. Suddenly we were finished flying combat. Everyone was excited and wanted to go someplace, anyplace. But they did not seem to know where. I knew where.

Although the water was cold I showered, put on clean clothes and caught the courier Jeep to Pine Tree. I wanted to share the evening with Genevieve. She cried with joy and told me how much she had worried each time I had flown. My return ride to Knettishall in mist and fog was more hazardous than my final mission. The courier driver, operating with only blackout lights drove as if he knew every turn in the road. Every now and then he demonstrated a lack of knowledge and we careened around curves with the Jeep barely clinging to the edge of the road. If he was trying to impress me with his driving ability he succeeded.

There was a big let down. I had no more missions to fly and found myself thrust into the position of instructing new gunners on identification and tracking procedures. I had no idea when I would be going home and there was no rush to get up and go to the flight line each morning. It was as if I had been forgotten and left to fend for myself. If I did not go to Pine Tree I went to the pub and shared the night with Barbara. She was most philosophical about the fact my time in England was drawing to a close. Her complaint was a compliment. She lamented about not being able to replace me. "I'm getting too old to train another one," she said. As I held her close in what was to be a final embrace she handed me my dart case. "Remember me when you use these," she said. There were no tears.

Weather kept the group on the ground until February 20th when they went to Poznan, Poland. Having no other duties I rode my bicycle to the flight line to see how some of my friends had fared. The mission had been a long one and the 388th had provided an "A" group and a "B" group. Two aircraft from the "B" group did not return. I learned they had come under fighter attack at the Danish Coast on the way in and way out.

21
GOING HOME

On the morning of February 24, 1944 I was called to the orderly room and told to have my gear packed and be ready to leave in thirty minutes. There was no time to say goodbye to my friends in the pub and no opportunity to contact Genevieve and tell her why we were not going to keep our planned date in London. Within the next two hours I was on board a train headed for Liverpool with orders to report to the transportation officer. I was going home. I was carrying one bit of memorabilia, my darts from the pub.

When I reported to the transportation office I found I was to return on a Liberty ship. Having heard reports about such ships being built at the rate of one a week, I had some apprehensions. Rumors had them breaking up when the ocean became rough.

Unfortunately I can no longer recall the name of the ship on which I returned to the United States. I do recall being met by the Captain when I boarded the ship. I was in a group of about ten others. The Captain greeted us warmly and welcomed us aboard his ship. I could not help noticing the cleanliness of the ship and how everything seemed to have a special place. We were shown our quarters and told we could not go ashore.

I had expected the trip home would be much like the trip overseas. Such was not the case. We were assigned hammocks but there were far more hammocks than there were passengers. In fact the crew outnumbered passengers. I located my hammock and decided to take a short nap. When I awakened I felt the motion of the ship. I went on deck and in the early morning light observed a line of vessels moving out to sea in Liverpool Bay. Our ship was part of the convoy line.

Breakfast consisted of real eggs and bacon. For some this was not much of a treat; their stomachs had trouble adjusting to the gentle pitch and roll of our Liberty ship. Three days into our voyage the weather turned foul. The winter skies opened up; the wind blew and the snow came down. Waves grew in proportion to the increasing wind. They reached gigantic proportions. The ship ceased its gentle pitch and roll. One moment we were on top of a wave and a second later our minuscule Liberty ship would dive headlong into a solid wall of water. The decks were awash and no one moved unless they had a firm grip on part of the ship. The storm lasted for the better part of five days. My stomach survived and I found there was an abundance of food with minimal diners.

On the morning of our eighth day out the weather cleared; the sun made an appearance. With the improving weather the seas settled somewhat. As if by some miracle appetites were restored and even those with queasy stomachs returned to the mess. The remainder of the crossing was relatively smooth

On the evening of day twelve of our voyage the Captain informed us we were dropping anchor in the outer harbor where we would wait our turn for a pilot to take us to the main harbor. I had trouble sleeping and was on deck to greet the rising sun. It was a beautiful day. A look down at the water told me we were underway. I saw the pilot boat come along side our ship and watched the pilot as he swung onto the ladder and climbed on board.

Then I saw it! In a distance the Statue of Liberty slowly became visible. My God, what a beautiful sight! There was a football-size lump in my throat. I stood by the rail and unashamed let tears of joy roll down my cheeks. I thought of my friends, those who didn't make it. I recalled the mid-air collisions; crashes; fighter attacks; bursts of flak and B-17's spinning with the crew locked in position, unable to escape. Somehow it all seemed like a dream. But here I was, coming to America. The sounds and words of the Star Spangled Banner and God Bless America echoed in my mind. A lieutenant was standing next to me; he turned, grabbed me and sobbed. Until then I had been in reasonable control of myself. But then I lost it. We clung to each other, looking for some sort of magical relief from our emotions. The relief came in the form of a blast of the ship's horn. We stepped back and our sobs turned to laughter and shouts of joy. "This is my home town," the Lieutenant said and started to point out the sights. It was then I noticed; he was pointing with the stub of his right wrist. There was no hand, only a cap of white over a stub.

It seemed as if time stood still. We were docked; the band was playing and everyone was wondering when we would debark. Someone must have said something because our debarkation was almost immediate. From there it was to customs. My head was spinning with excitement. Before I had time to regain my composure I had joined a group of officers and non-commissioned officers who were being ushered on board a bus. A captain welcomed us home and told us we were headed for Mitchell Field on Long Island for processing. It seemed we were always being processed for something or other.

What a change two weeks had wrought! We were assigned our quarters, issued new uniforms and even had a tailor available to make necessary adjustments without charges. We were told we could go to the city and had only to report to the orderly room at 0800 in the morning for further assignment.

The exact date, like so many things of the era escapes me. About ten of us, were told to be in uniform with ribbons, for transportation to New York City. We were told we were to be guests of honor at a "Wings Club" dinner at the Waldorf Astoria Hotel. Somewhat of an overwhelming experience for a young staff sergeant barely twenty years old.

During the evening I was offered a free telephone call home. What I learned came as a shock. Mother told me John had been shot down and killed. She had very little in the way of details. But from past experience I knew in my heart the probable accuracy of the report. Nevertheless I assured Mother such reports were not necessarily correct and promised her I would find my brother. I kept the news to myself during the evening. The next morning I was in the orderly room looking for orders to return me to the 8th Air Force.

22
THE CAMPAIGN TO RETURN

The thought of returning to the 8th Air Force was foremost in my mind. The probability of becoming a casualty was not considered. My immediate goal turned into a campaign to get orders back overseas. It did not take long to learn Mitchell Field did not have the authority to issue overseas orders. Every person I talked with looked at me as if I was a lunatic. When it became apparent Mitchell Field could not issue overseas orders I decided on orders out of Mitchell Field to any place. I got those orders in record time. Within the week I was saying an emotional goodbye to an attractive and very sympathetic civilian clerk in the personnel office who tried her best to have me change my mind. When she failed to convince me she added my name to orders sending me to Lincoln, Nebraska. I was sure I could hook up with a crew headed for the European Theater of Operations.

My new orders authorized a thirty-day delay en route. I caught a Greyhound bus and started my journey. I planned to stop in Hershey, Pennsylvania, but we paused in Lebanon, Pennsylvania for a rest stop. While at the bus station the military police checked my orders. This time there was no apprehension or concern on my part. I could not help but notice how polite they were. I was headed for the refreshment counter to get a Coke when I heard someone call my name. I turned and saw a corporal named Robert crossing the room. He had his hand extended in friendship. My first reaction was joy in seeing him. My second reaction was a flashing memory of a copy of the World Book crashing into my face while I sat in study hall nearly five years prior.

I didn't shake Robert's hand. I hit him as hard as I could. He went down on the floor; his nose was bloody. He had a confused look on his face. The look quickly faded when I said, "Now you bastard, you know your place." Robert was experiencing total recall. The disturbance in the rather small terminal did not go unnoticed. Two military policemen grabbed me and took me into custody. I offered no resistance as they moved me away from the gawking bystanders and led me away from Robert to the office of the area Provost Marshal. "Oh crap," I thought as I observed a young lieutenant who was about to sit in judgment of my conduct. "Sergeant, you are in serious trouble. What do you have to say for yourself?" he asked. I told him the story of the World Book incident. He looked at me over a pair of horn-rimmed glasses and asked in an amazed tone, "Do you mean to tell me your were getting even for something he did over five years ago?" I nodded my head in agreement and mumbled, "Yes sir." He had one of his men bring in Robert. I noticed Robert's nose had stopped bleeding and thought, "I should have hit him harder." The lieutenant then asked Robert if he recalled the incident with the World Book. Robert said he did and had long been ashamed of his act. The lieutenant then told me I would have to remain in his custody until the next bus left. I spent the next half an hour in his office drinking coffee and telling him stories of combat and London. He personally saw me on the bus, shook my hand and asked me not to come back. I promised him he had seen the last of me.

I could smell the chocolate long before the bus reached Hershey. The aroma alone stirred old memories of my high school days. As we rolled past familiar territory and the large farms I reflected on how much my life had changed in such a short time.

My week in Hershey was spent renewing a few prior high school friendships and accepting an invitation to speak to the local Rotary club. I made sure to visit Mr. Hunchberger at the bakery. He looked at my wings and stripes. He quickly figured out I was no longer a baker. I was sorely tempted to hang around Hershey for a few additional days. However; I was anxious to be on my way back to the 8th Air Force and hanging around Hershey would not help. It was time to be on my way.

I boarded the train at Hershey and after a change of trains found myself on the Delaware Lackawanna & Western Railroad. I sat in the Pullman car, looking out of the window as the train rolled on next to the Delaware River. We went through Delaware Water Gap into the mountains and finally through East Stroudsburg. From there the train followed the Broadhead River from Henrysville to the curve of the old tunnel several miles short of the village of Mount Pocono. I heard the whistle blow and thought of our father who had once fired the boiler of DL&W engines, perhaps this very same engine. The train wheezed to a stop at the station of the village of Mount Pocono, Pennsylvania.

Although it had been my intention to get off the train and go home, I did not get off. I continued to sit and stare out of the window. I was three miles from home. I spoke to no one. When the train pulled out of the station I continued to sit and stare out of the window at the passing countryside. I could not bring myself to go home without my brother.

Two days later I got off the train in Chicago. The city had not changed. Girls without guys were everywhere and I was there. Pauline was the first to be called and whenever she was busy there was Beverly. However there was a difference. This time I was truly a veteran; a Staff Sergeant, wearing wings and ribbons. I also had no need of partial pay. Part of my time overseas had been spent sharing the proceeds of a crap game set up and run by another gunner and myself. I found Chicago to be as great the second time around as when I first visited. If anything it was better. Unfortunately I could not linger long to enjoy myself. Much like a migrating bird I felt a need to get to Lincoln Air Base. I had a mission to accomplish.

Someone had a bad idea. I arrived at Lincoln Army Air Base to find I was about to be assigned to a make-up crew of veterans who would fly around the country to promote the sale of war bonds. My first thought was some public relations type must have had one drink too many when the war bond sale idea was sold. I had my name removed from the operation before the ink on the mimeograph had time to dry.

From then on I ended up becoming a perpetual visitor to every unit with a commanding officer who in my mind might have authority to issue overseas orders. Time and time again I was politely tossed out on my ear and told not to come back. But I went back and sometimes was clever enough to get in to see the commanding officer. Unfortunately all I was getting was a lot of empathy minus action.

Dates with young ladies, mostly one night to one week stands were the common event. I was wobbling back to Lincoln Field one night during inclement weather. The night was graced by drizzle. I was wearing my raincoat; in the right pocket was a pint bottle of some sort of alcoholic beverage, perhaps whiskey. When I dismounted from the bus, at the main gate I noticed the presence of the Officer of the Day, a 2nd Lieutenant. My first thought was to conceal my bottle. Without thinking I eased my right arm out of the sleeve of my raincoat. The empty sleeve remained tucked into the pocket. I then held the bottle close to my body with my right hand. The bottle was well concealed by the folds of the raincoat. I realized my error when I approached the Lieutenant. I had to salute him. I did so with my left hand. I was only a couple of steps past him when he called to me and asked, "Why did you salute with your left hand?" I replied, "I am sorry sir. I am with the returned veteran's group and haven't been issued my artificial arm." He was obviously embarrassed and said, "Oh, I am sorry." I brazenly responded, "It's OK sir, it is only off at the elbow," and vigorously waggled my right arm so only the elbow appeared to be moving. I hastened through the gate without further conversation.

I had been at Lincoln Army Air Base for about a month. I had no assigned duties and spent my days on the flight line working with a couple of the crew chiefs putting to use the knowledge I had gleaned from M/Sgt Irelan. The rest of the time it was eat, drink and sleep. I did plenty of each. There was a problem. I was drinking too much and I could not remember with whom or where I last slept.

The orderly room sent word for me to report to Headquarters. When I arrived there the clerk told me he had orders sending me to Miami Beach, Florida as cadre. I went to see the Adjutant, hoping to have the orders changed. I recognized the Adjutant as the Officer of the Day who had challenged my left handed salute. He informed me in positive terms as to the permanence of the orders. He then smiled and said, "Sergeant I see you have had your arm fixed." We both laughed. He stood up, turned serious, shook my hand and said, "I hope you find your brother." For a fleeting moment I thought about ignoring the orders to Miami Beach and going to an airfield, any airfield where I might catch a ride back to the ETO. After some cogitating I discarded the idea and decided to go to Miami Beach.

I enjoyed the three-day train ride and reported for duty at Miami Beach. While there I spent my time either at Buck Grundy's Sand Bar or on one of the recreational fishing boats. I spent so much time on the boat they thought I was crew. I recall two things about the several months I spent in Miami. Jewish girls were the same as Gentile girls except they did not want their parents to know they were dating anyone other than a Jewish boy.

23

DYERSBURG

Sometime during the later part of May 1944 I managed to have myself transferred to Dyersburg, Tennessee as an instructor. It took me two days to make the trip from Miami Beach to Dyersburg. The trip was by Pullman all the way. By now I was becoming accustomed to the luxury of the first class train accommodations. But it was without the many interesting embellishments I had enjoyed on a previous train ride. In fact I thought the train would never get there. When it did get to Dyersburg I was thrilled. The place was jammed with B-17's. They were taking off and landing and flying around the countryside. I began to feel as if I had returned to where I belonged.

I reported for duty during the first week of June. "D" Day was big news. My main concern was the war might end before I could get back overseas. When I reported for duty I learned I was going to assist in training new crews during their transition phase. It soon became apparent why Dyersburg was known as the Bloody Battle of Dyersburg. I quickly learned all pilots were not equal in their ability to fly a four engine aircraft and all pilots were not cut out to become efficient and effective leaders of men.

When I reported to the flight line for my first day of duty I was pleased to find myself in the cockpit as the flight engineer. Somehow a new designation had managed to show up in my records jacket. I had no doubt as to my ability. I had spent hours reviewing the G Manual M/Sgt Irelan had given me. My familiarity with the airplane gave me all the confidence I needed. Besides at twenty years of age and with a tour of combat behind me I was ready for the world. Little did I know how frightening my part of the world was about to become.

Pilots reporting to Dyersburg for training were not novices. Many of them had close to sixty hours in the cockpit of a B-17. But it was not long before I began to think some of them should not be hanging on to the yoke. There were those who obviously viewed themselves as having mastered the airplane; they tended to ignore the formal procedure of the checklist and did it all from memory. I silently marked those in my mind as pilots headed for disaster. And there were those who would haul the B-17 into the air. More than once I stood between pilot and copilot and gritted my teeth while we experienced the pre-stall shudders as the props chewed into the air seeking airspeed. Oh yes, the battlers; they fought the controls, on every landing. But worst of all were the "hot shots"; the ones who wanted to demonstrate their ability to fly only slightly over the tops of trees. Then there was another group. Pilots who seemed to have been born to fly. They followed procedures as if procedures were a religion. Their movements were sure and skillful. It was almost as if they were a part of the airplane.

I cannot say I enjoyed my assignment at Dyersburg. I was there for less than two months. I never left the base. Weather permitting I flew constantly. Evening entertainment was at the WAAC club were there was dancing, cold beer and friendly smiles. Being ungifted in the art of expressing myself on the dance floor I limited my relationship to conversation, cold beer and a friendly smile. I enjoyed the walk up to the top of the hill where one could find seclusion and moments of non-enduring romance.

24

THE RETURN

Summer was coming to an end and I was not any closer to returning to England than when I first arrived at Mitchell Field. Crews reporting to Dyersburg were already filled with their full compliment of personnel. This offered minimal opportunities to join a crew. Then my luck changed. I heard of a tail gunner who had been grounded. The pilot was desperately in search of a replacement so they could be on their way overseas. I quickly tracked down Lieutenant Martin Hertz, the pilot of the crew and told him I would like to be his replacement tail gunner. He looked at me and asked, "Have you finished your transition training?" I replied, "No sir." He then told me they could not use me. I told him, "Lieutenant, I have already flown one tour of combat as a tail gunner. I think I have sufficient qualifications." Lt. Hertz looked as if he had discovered gold. He changed his mind and personally initiated a request to have me assigned to his crew. I was on my way back to the European Theater of Operations.

This time there was no Liberty ship plowing its way through wild seas. I was flying! My goal was to return to the 8th Air Force and now my goal was within my grasp. I was not overly concerned with our route of travel. Our first stop was Bangor, Maine. Our stay was short and after one night of rest our nose was pointing toward Goose Bay, Labrador, a comparatively short flight over rather barren and uninviting terrain. The weather was in our favor for the flight to Goose Bay. But it changed for the worse soon after our arrival and threatened to delay our departure for the next leg of our flight, to Meeks Field, Iceland.

Contrary to what had been predicted the bad weather failed to develop. We were on our way, from Goose Bay to Iceland. Words barely do justice to the beauty of our night flight. Moonlight-enhanced large cumulus clouds watched us race past as we moved ever closer to our destiny. But the vastness of the sky and a dark foreboding ocean far below revealed our insignificance. The navigator, like the rest of us had no desire to test the Air Sea Rescue Service and as we neared Iceland he displayed his proficiency. He had us on target and Lt. Hertz set us down in a perfect three-point landing. We were shown to our quarters and informed there would be no passes.

We languished on Iceland for two days before receiving clearance to depart. Of all the temporary destinations during our trip to the ETO Iceland was least impressive. The standard joke had a pretty girl behind every tree. But, there were very few trees. Iceland was definitely not my kind of territory.

We left Iceland and headed for the British Isles. Strangely I no longer recall exactly where we made landfall. I do recall boarding a train and going to The Wash for gunnery school. When I arrived at The Wash, a training area on the eastern coast of England I learned what was in store for me. I was to be pulled from the crew and would remain at The Wash as a gunnery instructor. I found this unacceptable. However, a S/Sergeant has little choice when it comes to assignments.

Again good fortune was with me. On my third day at The Wash one of the officers invited me to go pub-crawling with him. I agreed without giving the matter a second thought. I accepted the bicycle he loaned me and we were off to see the village. All went well until the evening ended. After we returned to his office the reason for his friendship became known. He was seeking a lover. I had been selected. I avoided his advances on the pretense of being ill from drinking too much beer. Shortly after breakfast I was in the orderly room. I offered a deal. Send me to the 92nd Bomb Group immediately. I also requested leave time so I could visit the 388th Bomb

Group at Knettishall. There were no questions asked. Orders were cut including fifteen days of leave to allow me to visit the 388th Bomb Group. It was my intention to go to the 388th and have my assignment changed.

I wasted no time in getting out of The Wash. I was a passenger on the next train to London. On arriving it was as if I had never left. Adele was still at Rainbow Corners. The Windmill Theater had not closed and the Picadilly Commandos were still working the street. After making the necessary rounds I caught the train to Thetford and a bus to Knettishall, the home of the 388th Bomb Group. I arrived early on a Sunday morning and located the officers' quarters. When I entered I found Dingle, now a captain assigned to train new pilots.

Needless to say he was surprised to see me. I told him I wanted to be transferred to the 388th so I could fly my second tour with my old unit. Dingle told me it was not possible but took me to see the group adjutant. Again the answer was no. Nothing worked. I remained assigned to the 327th Squadron of the 92nd Bomb Group.

Having determined I could not get my orders changed I borrowed a bicycle and went to see Barbara at the pub. Again, I was disappointed. Barbara was no longer there. She had moved to London and no one knew her address. I returned the bicycle and bummed a ride with the courier to Pine Tree. I wanted to see Genevieve.

It would not be possible to adequately describe how Genevieve greeted me when I paid my unannounced call. She cried and then she told me she had met someone who did not fly and had been going out with him. From what I learned I decided dear sweet Genevieve was probably not going to be entering a convent. I bowed out gracefully and without too much reluctance headed for London. There were still ten days remaining on my leave. I planned to stay in London and enjoy the sounds and sights of the big city.

25
THE COMMANDO

It was well after dark when I arrived in London. I made my way to the Oxford Circus area and went into Lyons Corner House. I sat there drinking my beer and feeling somewhat left out of the magic circle. Genevieve had a new love, Flip the ballet dancer from Rainbow Corners was on holiday in Wales and I was alone. An attractive lady came over to my table. I spotted her as a Commando, but in my loneliness thought, "What the hell," and invited her to sit down.

She came right to the point. "Yank, would you like a bit of fun?" she asked.

"No thank you," I replied. She came back immediately and asked me if I only liked men. I laughed and said, "Not at all, I like girls. But I left the seminary to come and serve my country. When this war is over I will go back to the seminary and become a priest." A look of shock came over her face and she quickly crossed herself and said, "I'm sorry."

"Don't be sorry," I said with a smile and asked her name. She told me her name was Molly and she came from Dublin, Ireland. I offered to buy her dinner and she declined.

Our conversation continued. "Yank, don't you ever go out with girls?" she asked. I put on my most pious look and told Molly I had taken vows of chastity and therefore was intent on keeping myself pure. Molly told me about her life in Dublin and how she had come to London to help out in the war effort. She claimed she was not a real Piccadilly Commando but admitted she did date men sometimes if she liked them.

"Yank, I'm lonely. Why don't you come to my flat? We can talk and eat something," Molly said.

"Oh, I couldn't do such a thing," I told her. However, she asked again and I finally agreed to go with her. We caught a taxi and rolled slowly through the fog to somewhere in London, stopping only long enough for Molly to purchase something for dinner.

The bong of Big Ben, muffled by the dense fog reverberated with a dull and ominous sound. Molly complained about the chill of the night and snuggled closer as the taxi chugged along. She put one hand inside my jacket and cautiously crossed her knee over my leg. Her embrace was more than a friendly hug. I gently pushed her away and reminded her of my vows.

After winding around the fog-shrouded streets we finally arrived at Molly's apartment building hidden away among a hundred identical other buildings. Molly guided the way with her tiny flashlight and I followed. Once inside she turned on the gaslight and the small wall mounted gas heater to take the chill off the room. I looked around. It only took a glance to see everything. The room consisted of a small two-plate gas burner and a tiny sink next to a table barely large enough for two. At the far end of the room was a small bed. A makeshift closet contained her limited wardrobe. I sensed immediately I was seeing the kitchen, dining room, lounge and bedroom all contained in a space of less than four hundred square feet. "The toilet and bath is down the hall," she said.

Molly took a bottle from the shelf and offered me a drink. She poured about three fingers into each of two glasses. "Cheers," she said and tossed her drink with one quick motion. I did the same and by the time it was halfway down my throat recognized it as gin of a questionable quality. "Make yourself comfortable," she said as she helped me remove my jacket and motioned for me to sit on the bed in the corner.

"I bought fish and chips," she said. "I hope you like them."
"One of my favorites," I replied. Molly then poured another two

glasses of the 'not so good gin' and brought the fish and chips to where I was sitting. Again it was "Cheers". We sat there, eating and drinking. After the third hit from Molly's bottle of gin I noticed there was an improvement in quality and flavor.

By the time we finished the fish and chips I heard the distant bong of Big Ben announce the hour of eleven or twelve. When I told Molly I had to be leaving she insisted, "It is too late to get a taxi. Stay here tonight. In the morning we will go to Hyde Park." She promised she would not do anything to cause me to break my vows. It was either the gin or circumstances or perhaps a combination of both. I was feeling good.

I removed my clothes and placed them along side the bed. In the dim light I could see Molly dropped out of her costume faster than I would have bailed out of a burning bomber. "I just want to sleep with you," she mumbled and pulled me down along side of her, on a bed barely large enough for one person. I thought Molly had stripped down to her slip, but when she wrapped her arms around my neck and snuggled I found the slip had disappeared. If Molly had gotten any closer she would have been on the other side of me.

My physical reaction was normal; however I insisted on being true to my vows. I fell asleep only to be awakened by the air raid sirens and the sound of antiaircraft fire. I asked Molly if she wanted to go to a shelter. She indicated she did not want to go to a shelter, she only wanted to be loved. I surrendered.

When dawn arrived Molly was filled with remorse for causing me to break my vows. I decided I had to stick to my story. We never did get to go to Hyde Park. Molly decided once the vow was broken I was free of my obligation.

The next day we went on a train ride to Cambridge. As we rode along Molly continually commented about how much greener it was in Ireland. When we returned to London after sun down; Molly was in a depressed mood. The next morning she told me she was going back to Dublin. I helped her pack her meager possessions; two small suitcases held it all. We went to the station. When it came time to say goodbye she held me close and cried. "Yank, you have made me look at myself. I am going home to Dublin. I will pray for you every day." With her final goodbye she gave me a small envelope which she said contained an Irish blessing. I put the envelope in my pocket and helped her get on the train; there was one final embrace before it was time for me to get off. I watched Molly through the window as the train departed. I was glad I had never told her of my deception. Her words, "I will pray for you everyday," remained with me as I turned my focus to joining the 327th Squadron of the 92nd Bomb Group at a place called Podington. I could not help but wonder what it would be like in a different unit.

26
BACK TO WORK

I wanted to see Genevieve one more time even though I was sure she had a new love. I took a detour via Pine Tree before going to my new unit. I spent the evening with her in the lounge of the day room. She asked me why I was treating her so coldly. I told her I thought she was romantically involved with someone else and I did not want to interfere. Genevieve was visibly upset and denied being romantically involved with anyone.

She berated me for leaving England without ever saying goodbye. I told her the reason for my sudden departure and how it had not been possible for me to contact her before I returned to CONUS. In a moment, too short to describe, everything returned to the way it was before my departure. She reminded me of my promise to again return to London with her. We snuggled in the day room until long after the legal hour for visitors. I finally went to the transient barracks and found a bed for the night. Early the next day I caught a bus to the hospital to see Haley Thompson, a member of Genevieve's unit who had recently undergone surgery.

I knew the Glen Miller orchestra was located near the hospital and decided to go there and see if I could see any of the orchestra members. I arrived at the orchestra's compound shortly before lunch. I did not expect the reception I received. I was a combat veteran; the members of the orchestra were musicians who had not been exposed to combat. To them I was the important person. When I told them about visiting the orchestra during their rehearsals when they played at the Hershey Bandstand one of them called Major

Miller to come over. I told him I still had his autograph from Hershey. I was amazed when he recalled I was the kid who was learning to play the trumpet. We talked for a few minutes and he asked me to stay and have lunch and to sign their guest book.

I left the orchestra's location and headed for the 92nd Bomb Group fully stoked from the excitement of the day's events. I arrived at the 92nd late on the afternoon of August 10, 1944, and found my way to the orderly room where I presented Special Orders 218, Headquarters Station 112 dated August 5, 1944 assigning me to the 327th Squadron. I had expected to be questioned about the extra leave I had taken. To the contrary, I learned I was a gunner without a crew. I located Lieutenant Hertz and found the crew had been disbanded. He told me the enlisted men had been reassigned to other units. I was chagrined. I had returned to fly not sit on the bench as a substitute.

It took me a few weeks to become adjusted to my new surroundings. The only flying I did from the day I reported until nearly the 10th of September was practice missions. But on September 11th the group was headed for Merseburg. I had never been to Merseburg and wanted to make the mission. It took only a short search to find a tail gunner who was suffering with a severe head cold. I checked in as his replacement. No one questioned me. No one asked who I was or how many missions I had flown. To the crew I was a spare gunner. To me the pilot and crew were people I did not know and I was not interested in making friends. All I wanted to do was fly and they were my ticket to the show.

I found there had been changes. The oxygen mask had a simple but effective safety catch which greatly reduced the chance of an accidental disconnection. Oxygen supply failure at high altitude was serious and had cost a few gunners their lives. The waist windows were now closed. No longer did the vicious freezing winds howl through the waist. My next discovery did not come until we were assembled. I looked to my rear and gasped in amazement. My first thought was of a gigantic flock of crows coming off the roost. Everywhere I looked I saw bombers, miles of bombers. This then was the bomber stream.

I could not help but reflect back to the days in 1943 when we thought a hundred aircraft over the target was a big mission. I was still musing over the changes and thinking how great it was to have fighter escort to and from the target when I heard someone on the intercom report fighters in the area. I searched the sky and observed only a few. The fighter attack was coming in from the front of the formation. Not so the flak; it was coming up and was in such a quantity I decided there had been another big change. The flak was more intense and seemed to be more accurate than it had been in 1943.

Flak at target

No one had to tell me we had been on a rough mission. I had seen at least half a dozen aircraft go down. On landing I learned we had lost eight aircraft, one of which went down in friendly territory. I marked Merseburg in my mind as a place best avoided.

The next day was dedicated to shopping for a bicycle. This time, more aware of what I was doing I hunted around and found one in excellent condition. It even had a small generator and a tiny light. The light was a joke. It was too feeble to be of any use other than to have some Bobby or Air Raid Warden shout the usual, "Turn off your light Yank." I suppose having been bombed mercilessly they had good reason to be light sensitive.

Determined to test my new transportation, I peddled my way off base in search of a pub and a pint of British beer. I had my darts in a carrying case and thought I would like to try my hand. I had practiced religiously ever since I left England and now had in mind an opportunity to win back some of the beers I had earlier bought when at Knettishall.. The bartender greeted me with cordiality and poured my drink. I eased over to the side where a game was in progress and asked a few questions about scoring and rules. I was soon invited to participate in a game. I used house darts for the first round and lost. I agreed to another game, raised the ante and broke out my own darts; the same ones my friends near Knettishall had given to me. I won the next three games. By the time the third game was finished most of those in the pub were observing. I collected my winnings and then spent it all buying drinks for the house. It was still early when I left the pub amid echoes of, "Hurry back Yank" and returned to Podington. I decided to check out the NCO club.

Because I had been off base I was wearing a class A uniform with ribbons. When I entered the club a gunner challenged me because of my Distinguish Flying Cross. "Hey, aren't you the new guy who just checked in?" he asked. I told him I was and asked him what it was he wanted. He made some comment about my wearing a decoration I had not earned. Not being a person short of words when sufficiently annoyed and plied with a few drinks I told him he was full of shit and would do well to mind his own business. He loudly proclaimed his opinion regarding my wearing of unauthorized decorations. When I walked out of the club he was sitting on the floor with a dazed look on his face. I was off to a great start in a new outfit.

There was another mission scheduled for September 13th. I checked and found the tail gunner was still suffering and again took his place. I laughed as I left the barracks, telling him, "You will have two more missions on your tour after today." When I arrived at the mess hall I found myself sitting across from my acquaintance from the NCO club. He had a fat lip. "Who the hell are you?" he asked. I told him, "They call me Wing Ding. This is my second tour. I came back to find my twin brother, John who was reported killed over Athens, Greece." He offered his hand and said, "My name is John too. I am sorry about my remarks last night." We talked all through breakfast. I learned he was a waist gunner flying his seventh mission. We shook hands and I promised to buy him a beer after the mission.

We finished chow and went to briefing room. A hush fell over the room as the briefing officer made his appearance. Someone called, "attention," followed by an immediate, "be seated." John sat next to me in the briefing room. He said, "Lord, I hope we don't have to go back to Merseburg again." The briefing officer droned on and I thought, "All briefing officers sound the same." He finally pulled the curtain aside and a strong murmur ran through the room. Merseburg again. The briefing officer assured us of a strong escort and commented briefly on the anticipated flak. "It will be heavy," he promised.

John and I rode the same truck out to the aircraft. As he dismounted the last words he said to me were, "You owe me a beer." I never had a chance to buy the beer. The route to the target and the promised flak was as briefed. The flak was not the heaviest I had ever seen but it was deadly and accurate. We lost four aircraft in the vicinity of the target. I observed what I thought was John's B-17 in flames. It blew up. I did not see parachutes. There were several large holes in our tail and waist section and number three engine was running rough. We returned to base without further incident. The ground crew chief counted sixty holes. I was convinced my second tour was not going to be a milk run. The flak was making up for the missing Luftwaffe.

13

SHOT DOWN

The weather was miserable and I expected to end September without being able to fly another mission. I kept myself busy by going to the flight line and helping various crew chiefs when they were short handed. Most of them were surprised to find a tail gunner who would volunteer to work on the line. When I was not working I would peddle my bike off base and throw darts with my friends at the pub.

On September 22nd while at breakfast I met a Texan, S/Sgt. Guy Weddel, a waist gunner on the crew of Lt. Conrad Thorall. Guy had completed three missions and was about to fly his fourth as a fill-in on the crew of 1st Lt. Edmund Dornburgh to temporarily replace a wounded waist gunner.

Guy told a story of having been forced down in friendly French territory on his third mission. He expressed anger when he related how their tail gunner had claimed his guns were jammed and deserted the tail while under fighter attack. Pounded by 20mm hits they ended up with only one good engine, one dead engine with a prop they could not feather and two sick engines. Crippled and without radio their B-17 continued to lose altitude until they were skimming over the rooftops of Frankfurt. They remained airborne long enough to make it to friendly territory where a P-47 led them to fighter strip A-64, at St. Diezer, France.

According to Weddel they were stranded at A-64 for three days. The field had no shower facilities and they had to scrounge for rations. Although the shortages were not much of a hardship it was sufficient motivation for them to hunt for a quick way back to England. During a search of the area they located an abandoned twin engine Cessna AT-17 trainer parked at one end of the strip. Also at the field was an A-20 pilot who had been forced down by enemy fire. He was now without an airplane. The A-20 pilot looked over the AT-17 and said, "I think I can fly this thing." There was no hesitation. Guy Weddel and Mel Engle, navigator squeezed into the rear seat. The A-20 pilot and John Willet copilot of the Thorall crew were in the front seat. They were unable to get fuel from the grounded B-17 and had only enough fuel in the trainer to allow them to get airborne and quickly search for another airfield where they might find fuel. After a minimal warm up they were airborne. Just as the engines were near to sucking on air they found an abandoned airstrip near Paris. There was not enough fuel to make more than one pass. The A-20 pilot skillfully landed on a runway littered with wrecked trucks and trash. Moving from truck to truck they were able to siphon an estimated thirty gallons of fuel which they transferred to the AT-17. Realizing their fuel situation was marginal they talked the situation over before deciding to take off for England. Weddel continued his story. "We were flying not over 500 to 1,000 feet over the water when about half way across the English Channel one engine ran out of fuel and died. The propellers of the AT-17 cannot be feathered and the dead engine's propeller began to windmill. The windmilling action of the propeller created a drag causing us to rapidly loose altitude. From my seat in the rear I could see Willet and the A-20 pilot scrambling to get the engine restarted. They hit the tank switch and vigorously operated the primer pump. We were almost in the water when the engine came to life. Ahead the White Cliffs of Dover came into view. I wondered if we could clear the cliffs and if we had enough fuel to make land fall. We crossed over the cliffs with little altitude to spare and set down at the first bit of smooth terrain we could find." After he finished his story Guy asked me if I might be interested in joining their crew as tail gunner. I did not answer, only shook my head and laughed. It was later in the day

I began to think Guy Weddel was cursed. I went to the control tower to watch the group return. The B-17 of Lt. Dornburgh and his crew on which Guy Weddel was flying as a replacement waist gunner had not returned.

The notice on the Aero club bulletin board announced the Glen Miller orchestra would appear at the Sports Arena on the afternoon of September 23rd. I knew I would not be flying and planned to be at the Arena early to get a good seat. I was there at least an hour or more before the scheduled performance and managed to say hello to a couple of the musicians I had met at the hospital. When the performance started it was Major Glen Miller who said hello. He stepped up to the microphone and said, "Before we get started I want to say hello to a tail gunner friend from Hershey, Pennsylvania. He then called my name and asked me to stand up. I darn near drowned in my moment of temporary prestige.

L/R Colonel Reid and Major Glen Miller

27
THE INVITATION

On September 27th there was mission to the cathedral city of Cologne. I was fortunate and found a tail gunner who did not mind being replaced. I went to breakfast and was surprised to see Guy Weddel. I asked him what happened on the mission he flew with the Dornburgh crew. He told me they had been hit bad by flak and had to put down on the continent. He again broached the subject of my replacing their tail gunner. I made no comment.

We sat together through the briefing and heard the promise of escort and a prediction of light flak. I remembered Mike our bombardier on my first tour. Mike was killed when a small piece of flak penetrated the artery in his groin. Ironic as it was this took place on a day when there had been hardly any flak at all. My thought was, light flak, heavy flak, it makes no difference. I considered the flak to be light. However, at the debriefing I ran into a highly irritated Guy Weddel. I asked him what was wrong and he said, "The son-of-a-bitch did it again. When the flak started he left the tail and came to the waist and tried to hide." He then asked me, "Would you consider being our tail gunner?" I laughed and said, "Shit, man you have flown five missions and been shot down on two of them. Why in the hell would anyone want to fly with you?"

However, I needed a crew as badly as the Conrad Thorall crew needed a tail gunner. On October 7th, I again filled in for a tail gunner, this time on the Conrad Thorall crew. It was rapport from the beginning. My first mission with the crew was to Ruhland. Flak was light as we approached the target. The leader of the low squadron, Lt. Kerr left the formation after being hit in engines #3 and #4. We were bounced around by the flak but did not suffer damage. After we landed Guy Weddel commented, "Wing Ding, I know we don't have to worry about the tail with you back there."

While we were at the debriefing someone told me the chaplain wanted to see me. I went over to where he was and asked him what he wanted. He asked, "Do you have a twin brother by the name of John Carson?" I told him I did and he had been reported killed December 20, 1943 over Athens, Greece. The chaplain's words echoed in my ears. He said, "Your brother is alive. He is a prisoner." I thanked him and tried to control my emotions. But the news was too much. I did not trust myself to speak. In my heart there was nothing but joy and thankfulness. I had found my brother and he was safe. My excitement did not allow me to sleep. I tossed and turned until nearly dawn. I wanted to share the news with someone and thought of Adele Astaire. I asked for and received a pass to London. Thus, Adele became the first person I told about John's survival. She suggested I stop flying and take a ground crew assignment. I never gave the matter a second thought. Instead I bought a ticket for the show at the Windmill Theatre and enjoyed the scenes while thinking how much John would enjoy the show. I sat through two runs of the same show before I left the Windmill and went to one of the Corner Houses to get something to eat.

Who can recall what it was they ate in London half a hundred years ago? I suspect the answer would almost always be no one. But I have good reason to remember the girl. She was seated with a friend at the table next to me. I could not help but notice her frequent glance in my direction. I managed to strike up a conversation and introductions revealed her name to be Sue. I soon found out her friend was from Liverpool and about to catch a train home. With this bit of information Sue became a person of importance. We went to the station and saw Sue's friend depart. Sue said she would like to see a show. We went and from the show to a pub for a few drinks. The few drinks led to an invitation to go to Sue's place. She lived in a typical working girl's single apartment, not unlike the one Molly had occupied.

Before we went to bed Sue turned off the gas pilot lights. This she explained was necessary in case the pressure should be disrupted during an air raid and then come back on. The gas entering through the pilot light vents could asphyxiate people in their sleep. Sounded like a good idea to me.

I think it was about two o'clock in the morning when I awakened. I felt something moving across my chest. At first I thought it was Sue's arm. I reached for my flashlight and right then and there damn near died. The bed had a third occupant! A large rock python of at least six or more feet in length was waving his tongue in the air and eyeballing me as if I might be his next meal. I bumped Sue and said, "Wake up, there's a snake in the bed!" Sue excitedly warned me, "Don't hurt him Yank, it's mine."

Her explanation was simple. She was a dancer and used the snake in her act. She kept the snake in a box under her bed. But on chilly nights the snake would wiggle out of the box and come to the bed for warmth. I had Sue put her dance partner back in the box and tried to go back to sleep. This was my second experience with reptiles. I was hoping there would not be a third.

Standing L/R Conrad Thorall (p) Allen White (b) John Willet (cp) Melvin Engle (n) Front Kneeling Joseph Moses (e) Andrew Vehmire (bt) Gene Carson (tg) Frank Cummings (r) Guy Weddel (w) 327th Sqd., 92nd BG

28
MY BROTHER'S STORY

It was with considerable excitement I made my way to the Customs House at 2nd and Chestnut streets in Philadelphia. I never had a second thought. I signed my name, John W. Carson and enlisted in the Army Air Corps. My heart beat as if it would come out of my chest as I was sworn in with a group of others. When the oath was concluded I turned to a guy about my age and shook his hand. With wide grins and much emotion we both exclaimed, "We made it!" Although he is but a distant memory of the past, I still recall his name, Francis J. Slocum. I never saw him again. Little did I know in those days there would be many whom I would never see again.

The Army Air Corps wasted no time. The group I was with promptly left Philadelphia and went to Ft. George G. Meade in Maryland for a brief initial indoctrination, inoculations, receiving of uniforms and quick lessons on the intricacies of military life. In about a week many of us were on a slow train on our way to Keesler Field, Biloxi, Mississippi for basic training. Keesler was splitting at the seams with trainees and we ended up in a tent city as members of the Army Air Corps Unassigned. It seemed every drill sergeant at Keesler spoke with a Southern accent, dipped snuff and delighted in teaching us "Yankees" the rigors of the military. I endured basic training believing at the end things would improve. Things did improve. We were all assigned duties commensurate with our experience. My experience being limited resulted in my doing thirty days of KP, peeling potatoes, and washing pans while waiting to ship out to somewhere.

During this waiting period I attended class and heard an inspiring recruitment speech by Captain Ralph DePalma of Indianapolis racing fame. He was touting the benefits and privileges of being an aerial gunner. Captain DePalma stressed the thrill of flying, quick promotions, flight pay and freedom from the more mundane chores of military life. His speech fell on ripe ears. As a basic trainee fully involved in the more mundane chores of military life, I needed little convincing. I think all I heard was the part about a quick promotion, flight pay and the silver wings. When I compared the glory and glamour of the picture he painted to the day in and day out drudgery I was currently experiencing the grass on the other side of the fence looked much greener.

Sufficiently inspired by the prospect of a glorious future I quickly signed up for the program and requested radio operator training. My first training on my new venture was at the Stevens Hotel on Michigan Boulevard, Chicago, Illinois. What a change of life style this presented. We were the first radio operator's class at the Stevens Hotel. We lived in the hotel, ate in the hotel and went to class in the hotel. I began to really appreciate the value of my decision. When radio operator's school ended I shipped out to Tyndall Field, Florida for training as an aerial gunner. Despite a few bouts of airsickness training went well. At the completion of gunnery school I received my promised promotion to S/Sgt and the silver wings of an aerial gunner. My next stop was the replacement depot, at Salt Lake City Fairgrounds, Utah. I was at the Fairgrounds for a week or so and then off on another train ride. This time to a rather desolate area, Blythe, California where I was assigned as first radio operator for a senior officer on a B-24.

At this time my twin brother, Gene was cook at Hamilton Field, California. He managed to fly to Blythe and spent a day with me. He arrived looking like the real thing. He was fully equipped, had his own parachute, leather jacket, flight suit and helmet. No one would have suspected he was a cook engaged in unauthorized barnstorming around the country. We spent a wonderful day and night together. The next day he was down at the flight line where he caught a flight back to Hamilton Field. I smiled as I reflected on his ingenuity which always seemed to take him to wherever it was he wanted to go. Little did I know at the time how soon I would again see him.

Knowing well my brother's desire to fly, I tried to help. In my naiveté and unfamiliarity with military protocol I wrote a letter to General Hap Arnold asking to have Gene assigned to my unit. My letter received immediate attention. It was returned via channels with disastrous results. I received a stern lecture on military procedures and was removed from my position of first radio operator on the B-24 crew. The next day all of the other B-24 first radio operators were promoted to the grade of T/Sgt; I remained a S/Sgt and became the assistant radio operator on a B-17 flown by Flight Officer George A. Levchek. Assistant radio operators normally flew in the ball turret. However, claustrophobia and airsickness made it impossible for me to fly in the ball. I traded my position with the tail gunner and he took over the ball turret.

We were now a part of Lt. Col. Plummer's Provisional Group and training in earnest to deploy as replacement crews. We received our new B-17F; our pilot promptly named it "Julie-A", no doubt in honor of our pilot's girl friend. With our new B-17 we moved to Rapid City, South Dakota for further training. It was now summer and much of our flying was low level over the Black Hills and Bad Lands. The summer air was turbulent and airsickness was a regular visitor to many members of the crew.

I was in for a surprise. Without warning or prior announcement a new aerial gunner made his appearance at Rapid City. It was my twin brother, Corporal Eugene T. Carson. He had managed to do the impossible. Somehow he had moved out of the kitchen and was here as a replacement gunner. He was on temporary duty as a clerk in the orderly room while waiting further assignment. I thought of one of our grandfather's expressions, "The fox is watching the hen house." We walked outside; when I asked him how he did it he grinned. Then I told him of my concern. He knew nothing about the guns and other procedures. We went to the armament shack and I watched him strip and reassemble a fifty-caliber machine gun with speed most gunners could not match. I shook my head in amazement; knowing my brother I knew for him almost anything was possible. Our phase training completed we moved to Grand Island, Nebraska which was to be our jumping off place. I wondered what my brother was doing. I soon found out. His next appearance was at Grand Island where he was assigned to a replacement pool. We had time for one quick goodbye before I departed with my crew.

Our trip from the United States to North Africa was uneventful but exciting. We detoured slightly to buzz Milwaukee, Wisconsin the home of our navigator, Jack Drummond. From there it was on to Bangor, Maine, then Newfoundland where we waited for favorable weather before flying to Scotland. From Scotland we made it to Casablanca and then to Tunis our final duty station where we again lived in a tent city. Showers became an infrequent luxury, enjoyed whenever the water wagon came around.

29
THE GLITTER FADES

It did not take long for the glitter and glamour to fade from my new silver wings. My first mission found fighters lined up on our tail. The shock of first combat caused me to either go blind with fear or else I was too damned busy praying and shooting to recall what took place. I was suddenly faced with the stark realization this was real; I was at war and training was over.

But there was much more to come. On nearly all of our missions we had some form of engagement, flak or fighters. It did not matter whether it was the ME 109 or the FW 190, both were deadly adversaries. The Germans were great pilots. I found myself busiest on the bomb runs. It was there I was either warding off fighters or praying. I suspect they may well have been simultaneous acts. My thought was to keep the fighters outside of 800 yards from our airplane. If they could get inside of 800 yards you could count on being hit.

I vividly recall the day our waist gunner, S/Sgt. Clayton Kahler made a kill. The ME 109 came through on a frontal attack. He was high, off our right wing when Kahler opened up on him. The tail of the ME 109 came off and the pilot bailed out. His chute opened in my field of fire. I had my guns trained on him and for a fleeting moment nearly pressed the butterfly triggers. Fortunately I could not bring myself to shoot. I have forever been thankful for my moment of self-control at such a critical time.

The initial mission of the 15th Air Force to Wiener Neustadt, Austria proved to be a difficult day. Fighter attacks were heavy and when not firing I found myself counting blossoming parachutes and out of control aircraft as they fell from the sky. We were hit! A cannon shell damaged a propeller and forced a reduction in power for the engine. A supercharger on another engine failed. Soon after bombs away we were confronted by all sorts of German fighters. Directly to our rear a B-24 crew was bailing out. Their parachutes were floating between us and approximately twenty-seven or more German fighters. There was no way I could fire without endangering the lives of the B-24 crew. I had to wait until they dropped to a lower level. Of course the German pilots obviously felt no restriction and continued to work us over. We took another hit from behind and my new gun covers were reduced to rags.

Our running gun battle continued. In addition to our propeller and supercharger there was other flak and fighter damage. Fortunately the fighters left us, either to refuel or to look for other quarry. But being crippled we were unable to keep up with the formation. Our pilot, Philip Devine knew he could not fly our seriously crippled B-17 back to our base in Tunis and opted to put us down in Sicily. We waited there over night while a maintenance crew gave us a replacement propeller and a new engine. The next day we returned to Tunis.

As the war progressed our unit moved from Tunis to Foggia, Italy. I was still seeking the evasive fifth stripe of T/Sgt. and learned of a first radio operator vacancy on the crew of Lt. Dave Rohrig. During the later part of December 1943 I had my first indication of having made a bad decision. It was my twenty-seventh mission; we were flying on a B-17 named "What a Tomato". Fighters jumped us and severely wounded our tail gunner, S/Sgt Corley. I will always believe Corley was a contributor to our trouble. He had two previous kills and wanted another. He had a habit of waiting for fighters to get in close before he fired. However this time he waited too long; a fighter moved in and Corley was severely wounded during the attack. Cannon shells from the fighter took off our right wing tip and crippled our hydraulic system. Jagged foot-long holes appeared all along the fuselage. "What a Tomato" took on the appearance of a sieve and began to vibrate like an overloaded washing machine.

We had dropped out of formation and were continuing our battle with the Luftwaffe fighters when our own fighters arrived and pulled our ass out of the fire. One of the B-17's from our group dropped back and joined us, flying along side. They kept looking us over and the radio conversation was not at all encouraging. The pilot of the other B-17 kept saying, "I don't think your going to make it Dave." Admittedly, "What a Tomato" was one hell of a sick bird. But the skill of Dave Rohrig nursed it back to our base.

Damage to ball turret

30

SHOT DOWN

Our next mission was to strike the Airdrome at Athens Greece. "What a Tomato" was in no condition to fly and we were assigned to fly the B-17 "Eager Beaver". We did not expect fighters but were told the antiaircraft fire would be accurate. It was accurate. We were flying lead and had already taken a few minor hits from flak. As we turned on the IP (indicated point) all hell seemed to break loose. I was about to reach for the front door of the radio room door so I could look into the bomb bay and report when the bombs had cleared when I heard pilot Dave Rohrig, on the intercom. He asked the bombardier, Lloyd Haefs, "How are you doing Lloyd?" Haefs replied, "I am going to drop them any second Dave." The response was no sooner out of Lloyd's mouth when we took a hit under the aircraft. At the time of the hit I had my hand on the handle of the radio room door to the bomb bay. But I never had a chance to open it. I looked up and out of the radio room toward the tail of the "Eager Beaver" where I observed two bursts of flak tracking to the rear of the vertical stabilizer. I never saw the third burst. It probably struck in the area of our waist door or it could have been slightly aft of the waist door. The rear radio room door splintered from the explosion and struck me in the face. For a moment I was stunned.

"Eager Beaver", now minus its tail, rolled over and started down. I looked to the rear and saw figures struggling in the dust and smoke in the waist area. I tried to assess my own situation and found myself straddling the radio room gun. We were at 21,500 feet upside down, out of control and headed down. I was tangled in the debris looking at the ground. Centrifugal force and tangled metal had me locked in place. I could not extricate myself. I heard the engines screaming in a high pitched moan and realized I was trapped. I tried to cover my fear by fainting. It did not work. Then I thought, "This is going to cut my legs off; no it is going to kill me." My next thought was, "Please God, I don't want to go to Hell when I die." Somehow, I cannot explain how, I extricated myself from the tangled wreckage. I fought my way back through jagged metal of what was once the waist. I bailed out and pulled the ripcord of my backpack.

I do not remember the opening shock of my parachute. But I found myself floating in air. Below bombs were going off; above me the antiaircraft shells were exploding. I was convinced I was someone's target and decided to get out of the battle area. I pulled down on the shroud lines of my parachute to slip out of the area. This was a bad decision. I found I had started an oscillation. I began to swing like a pendulum. The motion coupled with the stress of the moment made me sick. I looked down and saw I was going to land in a field. Off in a distance I observed two soldiers with rifles and fixed bayonets running to where I was going to land. They did not approach my projected landing site nearly as fast as I did. My landing was not easy. The ground was hard and I hit with a thud. I was immediately taken into custody, but not before I had time to stay on my knees and say a prayer of thanks for having been spared. I quickly took account of my physical condition and noted I had no serious wounds other than surface wounds from the splinters of the rear radio room door.

On my second day of captivity along with waist gunner Walter Chesser and ball turret gunner Louis Crawford, I was loaded on a JU54 Trimotor and flown from Athens, Greece to Solonika, Greece. Chesser having suffered a broken leg was in pain, but Crawford was in relatively good condition. We were held at Solonika until late in January when we were all loaded on a German troop train and headed for Germany. The trip was uneventful until somewhere in Yugoslavia. Partisans attacked the train killing and wounding some of the German soldiers on board.

On our arrival in Frankfurt Main we were marched through the streets. The attitude of the population was hostile and frightening. Credit must be given to our guards for the protection they gave us. We remained at the Frankfurt Main interrogation center for several weeks and then boarded another train for Hydekrug, East Prussia the site of Stalag Luft VI. Shortly after departure I became ill and it was determined I had acute appendicitis. In an act of human kindness I was taken off the train at Thorn, Poland and put in a German military hospital. The hospital also had a number of British soldiers as patients. My operation was successful and I was to eventually recover. However, six days after surgery my sutures became infected. The doctors reopened the incision. This procedure was done without the benefit of anesthesia and was, to say the least, painful.

31
LIFE AS A POW

Still recovering and only two weeks after my appendectomy I was transferred to a Stalag XXA. This was a British prison holding mostly prisoners captured at Dunkirk. After three months at Stalag XXA I was shipped with one guard to Stalag Luft VI, another frightening journey. My guard enjoyed showing me off to every Hitler Youth Group congregated at various stations on the way. You can bet they were not friendly.

At Hydekrug I met many old friends as well as Chesser and Crawford. But the unusual thing was the Eighth Air Force men from the 388th Bomb Group flying from England. They would come up to me and ask, "Wing Ding, we thought you finished your tour." One of them, a gunner named Lew, had used my brother's old parachute harness with "Wing Ding" stenciled on it. The question was always the same, "How did they get you?" I would explain to them they had me mixed up with my twin brother Eugene Carson

Around mid July 1944 the Russian advance made it necessary to evacuate Stalag Luft VI in Hydekrug. About 2,500 of us were crowded into the holds of two dilapidated coastal coal tramp steamers. The trip to the German port of Swinemunde took five days. As I think back I am reminded of fishworms in a can. Men were ill or suffering from wounds, nevertheless they were stacked in the hold without thought of their comfort or survival. The trip was a horror of horrors; there was no water to speak of and there was no way to relieve the body. There were no sanitary facilities at all. The stink was incredible; I could not bring myself to go down into the hold. I went only half way down, seated myself on the drive shaft and clung to a ladder for the entire five days.

On debarking we loaded into box cards for an overnight trip to a rail station near Stalag Luft IV. To prevent escape our shoes were taken from us and we were handcuffed in pairs. Many of the men were ill or wounded. As for myself the incision of my surgery was still draining. On arrival we were permitted to retrieve our shoes but remained cuffed to a partner. Now we were double-timed through a cordon of young German guards who used bayonets, rifle butts and dogs to keep us moving. To fall meant dog bites and to lag behind also meant a jab from a bayonet or a blow from a rifle butt. I was handcuffed to a Jewish gunner; as I recall his last name was Adler. In order to give us maximum protection I instructed him to dump his personal belongings (our homemade knapsacks) and get in the center of the column. It worked and saved us from any major injury as the column ran a distance of one or two miles to Stalag Luft IV.

Like everyone else I settled into the routine of obedience and slow starvation. We had a daily ration of bread, the content was 50% bruised rye grain, 20% sliced sugar beets, 20% saw dust and 10% minced leaves or straw. When fortunate we enjoyed a little margarine, boiled potatoes and soup. The soup was a mixture of potato, turnip, carrot, dehydrated sauerkraut, rutabaga, kohirabi and a small amount of what was probably horse meat. About twice a week we were given cooked barley and millet. Our Red Cross parcels, when received were share with other prisoners. The Red Cross parcels were regularly pilfered and choice parts eaten by the guards. Like everyone else, I found myself suffering from serious malnutrition and steadily lost weight.

The meager rations were matched by meager bathing and sanitary facilities. Each lager had open-air latrines. They consisted of two back to back twenty holers and urinals. These were for day use only. At night each barracks had a two-hole latrine which was shared by 240 men. There were no facilities for bathing and the fleas, lice and bedbugs had a field day.

Late in October 1944, I was approached by a couple of new prisoners. They were from the 92nd Bomb Group located in England. It was the same story as before. They wanted to know when I had been shot down. It was then I learned about a second tour gunner. They were not sure of his name. They only knew him as Wing Ding. However, from their description and stories about the second tour gunner's activities I had no trouble in knowing the identity of the gunner. They were talking about my twin brother. I knew in my heart, he had come back looking for me. I was determined to survive.

Midair collision

32

WAITING FOR JOHN

I flew with Conrad Thorall as his tail gunner again on October 15th to Cologne. My attitude had changed. I believed my brother was safe in a prison camp and no longer in danger. Now my motivation was to end the war and see his release. I thought him safe, sitting out the war in a prison camp. I had no idea of the hardships and deprivation the prisoners had to endure.

My thoughts went back to another October week in 1943. I remembered four days: Bremen on October 8th; Gydnia on October 9th; Munster on October 10th and Schweinfurt on October 14th. Our losses of men and aircraft nearly put us out of business. During those October days of 1943 we were at times outnumbered by Luftwaffe fighters. This was no longer the case. Now the long-range P-51 escorts to and from the target insured us there would be minimal enemy fighters. But the flak was accurate and constantly bounced us around.

We returned without damage and I found the late in the day landing with rapidly closing weather more of a challenge than the mission itself. After the mission we had the usual debriefing and learned we would not be flying for approximately five days. I decided to spend my free time by visiting Cambridge.

Compared to London Cambridge was somewhat on the dull side. The patrons of the pubs were friendly and more than willing to allow a Yank to join their dart games. I won some, but in the long run the pub veterans ate a hole in my wallet. The ladies were much different from those found in London. They were perhaps more reserved and not so brash and bold. Needless to say, Cambridge had its fair share of attractive young ladies and they were friendly.

While in Cambridge I visited a small medical supply store where they sold manufactured human skeletons for use by anatomy students. I was going to buy a full sized skeleton to take back to Podington. Because the price was a bit too high and it was too cumbersome to carry, I settled for a very fine looking replica of a skull. The skull was dubbed Yorick; I carried Yorick to Podington in my gas mask case. The mask it once contained had long ago been discarded.

With much ceremony Yorick was mounted over the inside of the barracks door. A small red light was installed. If a mission was scheduled the light would glow. Alas, poor Yorick; he was in place less than a week. What a stir he caused. Someone without a sense of humor objected to his presence.

I was ordered to attend a discussion on the subject of Yorick. I reported to the squadron commander's office as ordered. When I entered I found myself in front of the squadron commander, the flight surgeon and the chaplain. They gave me no choice. Remove Yorick or else. The flight surgeon said he thought I might need a rest. The chaplain suggested I consider the impact Yorick might have on the morale of others. The squadron commander, bless him, struggled to keep from laughing. In the end he said, "Wing Ding, take the damn skull down."

On October 21st there was a dance at the Aeroclub. I decided to go and have a look. I entered the club and was surprised at the number of ladies. I was even more surprised to see members of the WAAC. I wondered if it could be possible for Genevieve to be there. I did not wonder long. A member of the WAAC group collared me. "Genevieve is here," she said. We soon located her and my evening became a success. We slipped away from the crowd and went to where we could communicate in private. The evening passed far too quickly. As we said goodnight she reminded me of my yet unfulfilled promise of another trip to London.

I was back in the tail of Conrad Thorall's B-17 on October

22nd, destination Hanover. Yorick went with me, carefully wrapped and in a sack. I quietly tied the sack to the tail fin of a bomb and returned to my tail guns. When I heard the call, "bombs away" I could not help but grin and say, "Alas, poor Yorick; his era of fame was short. I knew him but not well."

Winter weather flying in England left much to be desired. Many of our departures and our return trips were hazardous. Taking off more often than not meant climbing to altitude in the most adverse weather conditions imaginable. The danger was increased by an overloaded sky containing hundreds of others all seeking a clear sky and their rendezvous destination. Unfortunately for many the rendezvous destination came as a mid-air collision. Return trips, often near dusk with a low ceiling also required skill and a bit of good luck. More than one crew was lost when they flew into the ground or attempted to share the another bomber's air space. It was a dangerous business we were in. Marginal visibility became as big a hazard as the fighters and the flak.

Still in the tail, I flew again with the Thorall crew on October 26th, this time to Bielefeld. Guy Weddel after his prior experiences had come to the conclusion I carried a rabbit's foot in my pocket. I continued to marvel at the sight of the bomber stream and wondered what our bombs were hitting when we dropped them through the clouds.

The month of October ended with a trip to Munster on the 30th. Someone asked me how many missions I had flown since my return. I was not sure because I had flown without being on the crew list and the credit went to someone else. My goal was not to complete a required number of missions and go home. All I wanted to do was fly. I flew four missions during the first nine days of November as Conrad Thorall's tail gunner. Then had a break until November 25th. I am not sure, but I think the crew went to the flak home.

During mid November I had a pass and planned to meet Genevieve in London at the Barclay Hotel. When I arrived at the hotel she was waiting for me and told me she had already registered for a room. I started to register and she told me it was not necessary. "We can share the same room," she said. I almost jumped out of my skin with excitement and anticipation. We went to the room and barely had time for the door to close before we were involved in a fit of passion. There was a knock on the door. "I ordered tea," Genevieve said and added, "I want this to be like the first time." We enjoyed our tea and after a torrid and amorous half-hour I was the one who suggested we go and see a show. We caught a taxi to Rainbow Corner and picked up tickets.

I am not sure either one of us paid much attention to the actors on stage. Our dedication was more directed to a script of our own making. We went to one of the Corner Houses after the show and then returned to the hotel and our room. Genevieve said she wanted to take a bath. I sat impatiently for about thirty minutes until she came out wearing a beautiful negligée. I gathered my toilet article kit and headed for the bath.

I came out of the bathroom clad in my pajamas hoping my emotions were not too obvious. If Genevieve objected she did not say so. She was under the covers waiting for me. Our three days of bliss ended all too soon. On the last evening Genevieve asked me, "Wing Ding, why did you make me wait so long?" I had no answer, I too wondered the same thing.

On November 25th we were back in the air. The flak was moderate to intense, but for us there was no significant damage. Being a tail gunner had taken on a different image. On most missions the Luftwaffe was conspicuously absent from the sky. The intense excitement once experienced during a mission was a thing of the past. There was little to do other than sit in the tail and watch. However, there was no let up in the antiaircraft fire. The density and the accuracy of the German antiaircraft defense had turned the sky into a gigantic shooting gallery; we were the clay pigeons.

I was tired of riding in the tail and had been spending more and more time on the flight line working with several of the ground crew chiefs. I had a goal. I wanted to move to the flight engineer position. I wanted to see where we were going and I wanted to be promoted to T/Sgt.

Conrad Thorall did not fly on November 26th so I filled in for another tail gunner. Fighters were reported to be in the area and flak was intense. The B-17 of Lt. Kirkbridge was hit by flak and forced to land behind friendly lines. S/Sgt Arthur Wilson, the ball turret gunner was killed and a waist gunner wounded. The lead aircraft of the Group was also hit and was forced to land on the continent with two fatalities.

November 30th was a rare day. Visibility was good and we bombed Merseburg from 28,000 feet. The flak was of the usual Merseburg quality and took out the B-17 of Lt. Arthur M. Smith. Although they went down in a flat spin seven of the nine man crew managed to bail out. Lt. Smith was not one of the survivors.

33
A PURPLE HEART

It was a rainy day, early in the month of December 1944. Actually it was not a heavy rain, but a drizzle combined with a mist so heavy you could cut it with a knife. I thought about going to the flight line and decided against it. Then I remembered a newly acquired flare pistol and flares I had liberated from a no longer serviceable B-17.

I stood in the barracks doorway fiddling around with the flare gun. I don't think I intended to fire it, but after I loaded it the urge to shoot seemed to take over. I pointed it out of the doorway and pulled the trigger. As one might logically expect, it fired. The bright red flare arched through the shroud-like mist into the direction of the approaching figure of the deputy squadron commander riding his bicycle. The flare moved in his direction as if guided by a spirit. The deputy, no fool, had enough sense to bite the dust. I think it might be more appropriate to say he bit the mud.

I made no attempt to run or hide. I stood there and laughed at the sight of the major going in one direction and his bicycle going in another. He climbed to his feet. Mud covered his entire uniform. His face was contorted in anger. In a flash he zeroed in on the smoking flare pistol. He demonstrated no sense of humor as he ordered me to report to the orderly room. He stated his intention to have me reduced to private and put on permanent guard duty. I figured I had pushed my luck one notch too far. He seemed to be really pissed. He picked up his bicycle, shook his fist in my face and rode off, headed to his quarters to clean up.

I went to the orderly room as ordered and reported to the first sergeant. He instinctively knew I was in trouble. He asked, "Wing Ding, what in the hell have you gotten yourself into this time?" I told him the story in detail. I did not notice the squadron commander standing in his office partially concealed by the door. The squadron commander stepped out and asked, "Wing Ding, what the hell am I going to do with you? You are supposed to shoot Germans not people on our side." He confiscated my flare pistol and booted me out of his office.

December 1944 was one of the most miserable and coldest Decembers in over fifty years. Flying time was limited because of the weather. On December 4th we went to Kassel. If ever there was a milk run this was it. The flak was light and there were no fighters thanks to our escort. We were off to Merseburg on the 6th. The Merseburg mission was also easy. Again, light flak and heavy fighter escort.

Along about the 10th of December I flew as a flight engineer on a practice mission. I have no desire to embarrass anyone or cast a cloud on a pilot who may well have relatives or friends read this story; therefore the date and the name of the pilot are not essential.

It was late in the afternoon, evening was not far away. Flying conditions were marginal and we had been instructed to land at an alternate field. The pilot's comment as clearly as I can recall was, "The hell with it, I have a hot date. There is no way I am going to divert." He turned and flew away from our base for a while. He then turned again, lined up on a signal and headed towards what he thought would be Podington despite the navigator's strong advice to divert. We were slowly letting down as we approached what he thought should have been the runway. The altimeter was creeping lower and lower and the fog became thicker and thicker. We were below 500 feet and there were no runways in sight or signal flares to indicate a runway. Suddenly the fog thinned. On our right there appeared a tall brick chimney; on our left there was another structure. Rooftops were reaching up toward our ball turret. I looked at our airspeed and saw it was 140. Although I did not have a lot of time to think about it my thoughts were, "This is not too good."

Everything took place in a matter of seconds, but it seemed to take forever. The navigator came out of the nose and popped into the cockpit area. He was busy making the sign of the cross. The pilot panicked; he let go of the controls, covered his face with his hands and screamed, "Jesus Christ we are all going to die." Our copilot was not ready to die. He took over the controls, eased the throttles forward, raised our right wing to clear an obstruction and continued to climb out of what seemed to be a forest of tall chimneys.

Off to our left we spotted two yellow flares. Someone knew we were there and they knew we were in trouble. The copilot turned the B-17 like a liaison aircraft. In a flash we were over a runway, down on a runway and stopped. I knew I had been given another chance to live.

On December 15th Thorall was not flying and I went to Kassel as the tail gunner on the crew of William Lambert, an easy going Texan. I had become very comfortable flying on the Thorall crew and was not pleased with the change. However, on reaching the airplane I was made to feel welcome by a friendly crew.

I flew again with the Lambert crew on December 18th. We took off in the fog and bombed marshalling yards at Ehrang. Our return was under equally difficult weather conditions. But the flak was light and there were no fighters. The most exciting part of the mission was the take-off and the landing. I thought the weather was the worst I had ever seen.

December 23, 1944 the weather demonstrated it could become worse. I was having my last ride as a tail gunner and was back with the Thorall crew. The fog was so bad we had trouble finding our aircraft. I was sure we would not fly. Then out of the dense fog came the green flares. The mission was on! We were going to Ehrang to hit the marshalling yards.

Flak on the mission to Ehrang was light, but it was there and a burst came near our tail. There was a sharp crack. My head snapped backwards. I knew I had been hit, but did not know the extent of my wound. A jagged piece of flak cut the left cheek of my face and another caught me just above my left eye. There was more of a burning sensation than there was of pain. My oxygen mask was still operable and the bleeding not too severe. I decided to wait until we landed to report being hit.

34
OUT OF THE TAIL

December 28th was a big day. The sutures of my relatively minor wound had been removed. I was well on the way to healing. A goal had been achieved; I was in the cockpit as flight engineer for the William Lambert crew. For me this was a new combat experience. I could now see the flak long before we entered the field of fire. My first impression was awesome. Before I had always watched the flak while we were in it or while other groups were flying through it. Now I had the opportunity to contemplate our potential fate well in advance. I immediately developed new respect for pilots.

New Year's day I went to Magdeburg, with Lt. Peters as the pilot. My notes do not indicate his first name. Probably because I was not on first name basis with the average officer. I had been to the same target area before but this time was different. I was up front where I could see the full show. Somehow we missed our timing and were either too late or too early for our escort and we ran into a dozen or so of the Luftwaffe. For the first time I had an opportunity to fire the top turret guns in combat. One thing was apparent; the fighters did not demonstrate the same degree of aggressiveness as those I had seen during 1943 era. Again, as usual the flak was of more concern than were the Luftwaffe fighters.

January 2nd we were headed for a place called Bitburg. It was one of those rare days when we had visual bombing. The pilot was Lt. John Bosko. I had never flown with Lt. Bosko before but he was some sort of a legend. During an August 1945 mission to Merseburg while on the bomb run his aircraft was struck in the open bomb bay by flak. The damage was incredible. The radio room was destroyed and the ball turret gunner killed. Aileron and elevator cables were cut. Fully armed bombs, not yet dropped failed to explode. A fire in the bomb bay increased the probability of armed bombs still on board exploding. Working in an open bomb bay in a faltering aircraft the crew managed to extinguish the fire and drop the bombs. As if by some miracle Lt. Bosko and his copilot kept the crippled B-17 in the air. They nursed it along, steadily loosing altitude until they were over England. When the second engine died Lt. Bosko order the crew to bail out. He and his copilot then landed the battered B-17. I felt privileged to fly with him as his engineer.

January 4, 1945 marked my 21st birthday. I knew we were to fly the next day so my celebrating was limited to going to Aero Club but I did not drink. It was in fact a very dull birthday. I left the club and rode my bike out to the flight line and drank coffee with the ground crew. I owed them much for all the lessons they had so willingly taught me. Among the things I tried to learn was code. This was a failure. My radio skills were limited to turning the equipment on and searching for music. I never did learn to tell the difference between a dot and a dash.

On the morning of January 5, 1945 prior to our trip to Niederbresig, Lt. Peters assembled the crew. He announced I had been promoted to T/Sgt and would continue to fly as engineer for his crew. My promotion was celebrated by a genuine milk run. Flak was scarce and we had an escort of over a hundred fighters. I wondered how my brother was doing and thought it was good and was safe in the prison camp.

I was not scheduled to fly on January 6th but I filled in to cover for a hung over tail gunner. He had suffered all night with the dry heaves and was in no condition to fly. Our trip to Cologne was uneventful. I thought about the Luftwaffe's rare and intermittent appearance and wondered when and where we would see them again. I also noticed I was having trouble staying awake. Although the long hours spent searching for nonexistent fighters in the sky was boredom, it was not sufficiently boring enough to make me wish for the intense fighter activity we had experienced in 1943.

On January 10th I was again in the cockpit with Lt. Peters. We were headed for Gymnich to bomb the airfield. The flak was heavy and on the way in our lead aircraft with Captain O'Halloran and Major Bideganeta took a severe hit on the right wing and lost the number #3 engine. They continued on; a second hit cost them engine #4. They left the formation and quickly lost their final two engines. The B-17 was now, for all practical purposes, a glider. They opened the bomb bay doors and dumped the bombs. Captain O'Halloran then maneuver his "glider" to an open field in friendly territory where he skillfully made a wheels-up landing in a field covered with snow.

One other B-17 took hits and lost three engines and was forced to land near Liege. Tragically the waist gunner bailed out at about three hundred feet and was killed when his parachute failed to open. The remainder of the crew escaped injury.

Shortly after bombs away a burst of flak knocked a hole into our airplane behind the copilot's seat. Miraculously no one was hit. But an oxygen line and a hydraulic line ruptured. The fire was immediate and intense. Nothing, absolutely nothing short of having your wings fall off is more attention grabbing than fire in the cockpit. The pilot cannot divert his attention from his formation flying and there is insufficient room for the copilot to help. I grabbed the fire extinguished from the bulkhead and sprayed the area. A box of flares was starting to burn. I threw the burning box out of the still open bomb bay. The fire died as the oxygen at the location diminished. The B-17 is provided with four oxygen systems operating at a pressure of 400 pounds per square inch. Each system is separate to minimize the impact of failure of a system in combat situations.

It was not to be my day. As we prepared to land the ball turret gunner announced the landing gear was not down. The pilot told me to crank it down. I moved to the bomb bay and prepared to crank the gear down. I inserted the crank and started to crank the gear down. I was on the third turn when the copilot decided to try the landing gear switch one more time. The drive motor to the landing gear turned on causing the crank to turn. The crank struck my right elbow knocking me partially onto the bomb bay doors. I had no parachute on and hung on to the walkway with my left hand as I stared at the ground from the partly opened doors. My right arm was useless; I was sure it had been broken. When I managed to get back into the cockpit I proceeded to tell the copilot he was a dumb shit. It did not relieve my pain. But it made me feel better. Later, at the debriefing his apology was profuse. So was mine. I knew there was no excuse for my insubordination. Fortunately, the damage to the arm amounted to no more than a severe bruise.

Despite my arm still throbbing on January 13th I decided to fly. My choice was a good one. There was good visibility and a minimal amount of flak. We bombed a railroad bridge at Karlsruhe with good results. The mission was, for us, a genuine milk run.

Contrails

35

THE SECOND PURPLE HEART

January 15th should have been one of the easiest missions of the war. We were going to bomb marshalling yards at Freiburg. The cloud cover forced us to use PFF (pathfinder) and there was no way to tell how successful we had been. The flak was sporadic and it seemed as if we would escape without damage.

Shortly after bombs away a near burst of flak appeared to the front of our airplane. I recall seeing the red flash in the center. Several quick companion bursts followed. They had our range. I heard the sharp crack and at the same time felt the pain. No one had to tell me I had been hit. Unlike the first time I had been wounded, this one really hurt. I came down out of the turret and doubled over. A dark stain was appearing on the front of my flight suit at the crotch. I remembered Mike, our first tour bombardier and how he had died when his femoral artery had been cut with flak. He had not bled. I was bleeding. I was sure my penis had been blown away. Because of the pain I had trouble breathing. I pulled myself back into the turret and turned my oxygen on full. I cautiously looked down; the bleeding did not seem to be severe, but I could feel it running down my right leg.

I reached inside of my suit and tried to assess the damage. The slightest touch caused excruciating pain. I was sure I had been totally emasculated. I had determined I was not going to die. But my thinking was I would have to sit down to pee for the rest of my life. For some reason the thought struck me as funny and I laughed. The flight back to our base took forever and I went directly to the base hospital and from there to the Seventh General Hospital. I was overjoyed to learn my injuries were actually slight. I still had one of the family jewels intact and to my way of thinking one was a lot better than not having any.

I spent the remainder of March and almost all of February at the hospital. The food was great and regular passes were available. I took full advantage of everything they had to offer. Numerous times during February I had asked to return to duty. The hospital adjutant kept telling me to wait. One day while in the mess hall one of the hospital corpsmen told me I would be going home soon.

The prospect of leaving without finding my brother pushed my button at the wrong time. Within minutes I was in the office of the Commanding Officer. I told him I was not going to fly any more but had to wait for my brother. My persuasiveness prevailed and I was on my way back to Podington. My return route was rather circuitous. It took me through London and three days at the Barclay Hotel with Genevieve. She was pleased to learn I had fully recovered.

I came back to Podington and flew a mission with Robert E. Williams on March 1st. I was quite comfortable being back in the air, although I was still very sensitive in the area of my groin. We went to the marshalling yards at Reutlingen. The weather permitted a visual bomb run. The destruction to the yards and buildings rendered them useless. Captain Williams was back in the air on March 2nd, this time headed for Sachsische where we helped to put the finishing touches on a coal drying plant storage facility. Bombardiers were again provided with an opportunity to bomb visually. The results were impressive.

On March 4th a visitor came to my barracks. Flight Officer Anthony L. Marozas from Chicago asked me to fill in as his engineer. I thought back to a practice mission and recalled a near crash when a pilot had used bad judgment and nearly cost me my life. The copilot of the practice mission had been Flight Officer Anthony L. Marozas. I did not have to think long. He had my answer without hesitation or reservation. Although I had only flown with him one time, he had left me with no doubt as to his ability and skill as a pilot.

A 1st Lieutenant from Texas was assigned as our copilot. I thought it unusual for us to have a pilot who was a Flight Officer and a copilot who was a 1st Lieutenant, but said nothing. We flew a couple of practice missions as a crew and our copilot was impressive. He knew how to fly in a tight formation and his landings were smooth without a lot of cockpit movement. He was a really good pilot. We learned he already had flown five missions and were happy to have an experienced man in the right hand seat.

On March 9th we were on a mission to bomb Kassel. As we approached the IP and prepared to bomb under visual conditions the flak to the front of the formation was moderate and accurate. There were no fighters in the area and I was out of my turret, standing between the pilot and copilot. I noticed the copilot had covered his face with his hands. He removed one hand for a moment, turned toward me and gestured wildly as he pointed to the flak bursting to our front. He continued to keep his face covered, but soon after bombs away he caught a glimpse of a/c 44-8326 flown by Lt. Fred Stewart take a burst of flak. It exploded; only two parachutes were seen. At the sight of the loss our copilot became extremely distressed and was barely able to function during our return to base and during the landing.

I had a serious discussion with Flight Officer Marozas and he wanted to give the Lieutenant one more chance. However when we flew pathfinder missions to Dortmund on the 10th and to Molbis on the 17th of March our reluctant copilot was suffering from blocked sinus and did not fly with us. I thought it was unfortunate he missed the two missions because both were in the milk run class.

Our sick copilot had recovered enough to fly with us on March 18, 1945. The briefing officer pulled back the curtain to reveal a long red line all the way to Berlin. He predicted intense and accurate flak. I wondered how our copilot would hold up?

We turned on the IP. Far ahead the flak appeared like a dark cloud. As we continued on course the dark cloud began to demonstrate the familiar individual octopus shaped black bursts of flak. Moving still closer we now could see the ball of orange explosion in the center of each burst. I turned my attention to the copilot. He was again covering his face. A burst slightly above and to the front of us knocked a hole in the windshield on the pilot's side. I quickly checked and determined Mr. Marozas had not been hit. But we had serious problems. I saw Mr. Marozas pull down his goggles to protect his eyes from the subzero blast of air coming through the windshield. In the meantime our copilot decided he had seen enough. Without warning he seized the controls and tried to turn us out of the flak pattern. How we missed being involved in a midair collision will forever remain a mystery in my mind. With two men struggling for control we moved through the formation without direction. Mr. Marozas continued to struggle for control of the airplane without success. The copilot had lost his steel helmet. Flak continued to pummel us. I took the fire extinguisher and hit him hard enough to knock him out. I was temporarily without oxygen and nearly passed out. I reconnected my oxygen as Mr. Marozas slowly moved us back into position in the formation. The copilot remained slumped in his seat until well after we left the target area. In retrospect I know the entire incident took place in less than a minute, but it seemed like a long slow bad dream while it was happening.

Later I was called to testify before a board of officers as to the copilot's conduct during the two combat missions he flew with us. Despite his actions I felt genuine sorrow for him and testified with reluctance. I never learned what happened to him and I never saw him again.

On March 20th I again filled in for a tail gunner on a mission to Hamburg. Flak was minimal and fighters continued to be nonexistent. It was obvious the war had to be coming to an end. Even the anti aircraft fire for most targets had become sporadic. On March 28th I flew my final mission. We went back to Berlin, a place where we could still count on having moderately intense flak. However, this time I flew with a copilot who was capable of conducting himself with the courage required of a man in the right hand seat.

I reported to sick call around the end of March and found myself grounded because of a severe ear infection. Pending the flight surgeon's determination I decided to go to on leave to London. I returned from London on April 5th and was told Flight Officer Marozas had been shot down on April 4th. On further inquiry I learned he and the crew had been taken prisoner but had been held for only a short time before being retaken by British troops. When they finally returned about two weeks later Flight Officer Marozas had a vivid scar at least six inches long on his left cheek where the surgeons had operated to repair a badly broken jaw.

Somewhere during the period of the second tour I had lost count of the number of missions I had flown. The mission count was not important, I was not flying with a goal of going home. I was waiting for my brother who unbeknown to me was marching across Germany in one of Europe's worst winters in nearly one hundred years. I had no idea he was slowly starving and getting weaker with each passing day. In my ignorance I continued to be thankful he was no longer flying and safe in a prisoner of war facility.

Two out

36

JOHN'S WINTER WALK

On February 6, 1945 in one of the toughest winters Europe had experienced in a long time we set out on a forced march. The guards told us our march would last only three days. Seventy-five days later we were still marching. Our three day forced march did not end until April 26, 1945. The march led us from Stalag Luft IV near Gross, Tychon, Poland to Halle, Germany. I was but one of nearly 9,500 others who endured the march.

The march was, as some have said, "savage". Most of us were malnourished and for the most part in need of medical care. It would have been a test for a healthy well-trained paratrooper. For us it was a test of pure guts and a determination to survive. The winter weather was bitter cold and we were nearly starving. There was no way to take a bath. Fleas and lice feasted on our bodies adding discomfort to our problems of hunger, exhaustion, frozen feet and dysentery. In many cases the survival of a prisoner was the result of another prisoner sacrificing his own comfort and well being to care for the less fortunate.

We marched on in misery. Each day was a new ordeal. My feet were giving me trouble. I sort of lost track of time as I plodded on day by day. The winter weather eased and seemed to be warming. But, food remained a rarity, body lice and fleas continued their feast. They did not seem to mind our malnourished bodies.

It was near the end of April when we marched through the front lines at Bitterfeld, Germany. A pair of P-51 fighters flew over us at a low altitude. Their canopies were open and their wings waggling.

I am sure I was not the only man who choked back sobs of joy over the end of our incredible journey. There was no longer anyone in control of the prisoners so another guy and I bummed a Jeep ride to Halle and holed up for a couple of days at the German airfield where we found beds and showers. We convinced the local Military Government to give us rations and located a BMW motorcycle with which we toured the area. The next day a C-47 landed at the airfield. We satisfied the pilot, a colonel, as to our identity and talked him into giving us a ride to Rhemes, France where we were deloused, issued clean clothing and fed. From there I went to Camp Lucky Strike where all former POWs were congregating. I managed to persuade authorities of the need for me to go to London because my twin brother was waiting for me.

I crossed the English Channel in some sort of a British ship and managed to make my way to London. When I arrived at the Rainbow Corner Red Cross Club at Piccadilly Circus I made inquiries. A kind lady, Adele Astaire told me she knew my brother, Gene, and would contact him. She arranged for us to meet in the Red Cross Club on VE night.

The night in London was one of the greatest in our lives. I can still see my brother coming down the left side of the hall to greet me. He was taller and a T/Sgt. We hugged each other for the first time since I had last seen him in Rapid City, South Dakota. He showed me around London, taught me how to drink English beer and took me to the Windmill Theater a burlesque house open twenty-four hours a day. The Windmill Theater was a great place. You paid your money to go in and when the curtain fell on the show for intermission everyone scrambled over seats to work their way to the front row. Here I met a very nice young member of the cast, Valerie Ware. She was about eighteen, blond and attractive. I still remember her address, 39 Marlow Dr. N. Cheams, London, England.

It was a reunion to remember, and the lights were on in my heart as they were all over London.

Victory

37
NORTH AFRICA AND HOME

John left England and I returned to Podington. Combat was over and now I spent time flying on several sight seeing trips to the Rhur Valley for the benefit of ground personnel. I had to decide what I wanted to do. The 327th was being reassigned to Port Lyautey, French Morocco in support of the Green Project which was intended to provide support service for the relocation of prisoners of war and other high point personnel to the United States. The squadron commander, Lieutenant Colonel James A. Smyrl asked me to be his engineer. Despite having more than double the number of points required for rotation to the United States I wasted no time thinking about an answer. I am no longer sure of the date of our departure from England. But I vividly recall the flight. The moon was bright; scattered cumulus clouds were sprinkled across the sky. Our B-17 had been stripped of all war time equipment and we flew at an altitude of 5,000 feet. I had never seen the sky or the ocean appear with more elegance.

We flew back to England around the middle of July for a conference and I managed to reach Genevieve. She told me she was soon to return home but wanted to see me. We managed to spend three days at the Barclay hotel in London. We left the hotel to eat and see a few shows, but most of our time was spent in our room. In the end we parted with love. Genevieve was returning home and I was to return to North Africa. I think we both knew our romance had come to an end. She looked at me and told me, "Wing Ding, I have no regrets." I returned to French Morocco with a clear conscience and a happy heart.

My time at Port Lyautey was coming to an end. Colonel Smyrl was about to return to the United States and I decided to go with him. We flew to England and then home on a B-17. Before leaving England I made a heartbreaking trip to Cambridge and visited the American cemetery and said goodbye to Mike and others. As I walked among the markers I silently cried my heart out. The following poem, written by and unknown author says it all.

Michael J. Chaklos
January 5, 1944

THEY CAME TO MADINGLEY

If chanced I wandered Hardwick way
From Cambridge on a sunny day.
By pleasant lanes in early May
And here I parked, an hour to stay.
Then o'er the trees against the sky
I saw Old Glory flying high
And remembered nearby lay
War Dead of the U.S.A.

'T was Madingley I'd choose to stay
Where often aged couples stray
From several thousand miles away
And at a grave to stand and pray.
Maybe o'er their only son
And clasp the medal that he won
As he was on his fateful way
To come to Madingley to stay.

He may have come from Santa Fe.
He may have known the Great White Way.
Some came who knew Pacific spray
Blowing in from 'Frisco Bay
They came from North, East, South and West
Certain their own state was best;
Reckless too with love or pay
Then came to Madingley to stay.

By various paths they made their way
To come to Madingley to stay,
Some bombed Schweinfurt in the day
And, in air-combat's lethal fray
A bullet does not ask what race,
Not even colour of a face

And some could fall to "friendly" stray
Then come to Madingley to stay.

And these at Madingley do stay
Are very much the same as they
Our Brits; in France or in Maylay.
And "Senseless slaughter" some may say
But such are easy words to speak
For Belsen's chimney ceased to reek
Due to young men such as they
Who came to Madingley to stay.

Oh do not let the Dead March play
O'er these at Madingley do stay
For they were young and old-style gay,
Play their music of the day;
Tunes of Dorsey, songs of Bing.
Let them hear Glenn Miller's swing
Then too the crosses well may sway
With those at Madingley do stay.

Although, in truth, those boys don't stay
I've 'Knowledge" and I hereby say
The empty bodies are not 'They'
Below in that cold Cambridge clay;
Such happy souls don't stick around
In that well-tailored burial ground
But you be sure they see you pray
And pray for you, as you for they.

Author Unknown –

Wee Willie 91st Bomb Group

On arrival in the United States I found my next duty assignment was the National Airport, Washington D.C with duty on one of the "Brass Hat Squadron's B-17's". While there I met a WAAC M/Sgt. Margaret Hayes. Maggie worked at the Pentagon for General Eisenhower. We soon became close friends and shared many evenings talking about our past and hopes for the future. Maggie was promoted to Warrant Office and convinced me I should go to Officer Candidate School. At the time the Air Force did not have an OCS program so I opted to go to Infantry OCS and then jump school.

It was then I decided on the demise of Wing Ding. Somehow it did not seem appropriate to aspire to troop leadership while being known as Wing Ding. I queried a plastic surgeon and quickly found I could not afford the surgery required to remove my tattoo. However I had made up my mind. I learned there was a "do-it-yourself" method. The method consisted of rubbing the tattoo with gauze and salt until the skin began to seep. It was then permitted to heal until a scab formed. When the scab peeled it had tinges of color. The process was then repeated, each repetition resulted in a lightening of the tattoo. It took more than six months, but the identity of the tattoo slowly disappeared and became an unidentifiable faint scar. And as the scar faded so faded Wing Ding to become a historic memory of a life once lived and a war now over.

For a long time in my possession was an Irish Blessing given to me by Molly. It read:
"May the road rise up to meet you.
May the wind be always at your back.
May the sun shine warm upon your face.
Let the rain fall soft upon your fields
And until we meet again,
May God hold you in the palm of His hand."

As I reflect on the words of Molly's Irish Blessing I am forced to conclude:

The road did rise up to meet me and I found the wind always at my back. The sun did shine warm upon my face and the rains fell soft on my fields. For what reason I will never know, God chose to hold me in the palm of His hand. He let me look deep into the shadows from where there was no return. But then He gave me strength and led me back into the light.

I could write forever, but I could never express it with more truth and dignity than did Col. Bud Peasley in this beautiful passage:

"The tumult and the shouting have died away. The B-17's and B-24's will never again assemble into strike formation in the bitter cold of embattled skies.

Never again will the musical thunder of their passage cause the very earth to tremble, the source of sound lost in infinity and seeming to emanate from all things, visible and invisible.

The great deep-throated engines are forever silent, replaced by the flat, toneless roar of the jets and the rockets.

But, on bleak and lonely winter nights in the English Midlands, ghost squadrons take off silently in the swirling mist of the North Sea from ancient weed-choked runways, and wing away toward the east, never to return.

On other nights the deserted woodlands ring with unheard laughter and gay voices of young men and young women who once passed that way.

Recollections of all these fade a little with each passing year until at last there will finally remain only the indelible records of the all-seeing Master of the Universe to recall the deeds of valor excelled by no other nation, arm, or service. These sacred scrolls will forever remain the heritage of the free and untrampled people of this earth."

Colonel Budd Peasley,
C.O. 384th Bomb
Group (H), 8th Air Force

Gene Carson 82nd Airborne 1956

ACKNOWEDGMENTS

This story has been under construction for almost two years. It was written at the behest of my daughter, Esther H. Price. She often urged me to put down on paper my war time experience with the 8th Air Force. It was not easy. There were things I did not care to remember. Ever so slowly I made the transition and finally started the story. I could not devote full time to writing because I had a business to run; therefore my writing has been done in the early morning and late evening

On June 18, 1999 I asked R. J. Rake-Herrmann from Sierra Vista, Arizona to assist me with proof reading and editing. Her initial reaction was to decline. Fortunately she read part of my original draft and changed her mind.

Her attention to detail and the long hours she spent proof reading and editing have undoubtedly served to improve the story you have read. I am grateful. Her work was a labor of love and has added much to the content of this story.

There are still living from our original crew pilot, Otis C. Ingebritsen and copilot, Edward J. Meginnies. We have become good friends and they contributed essential information. We flew our twenty-five missions with the 560th Squadron, 388th Bomb Group, Eighth Air Force, mostly in 1943 and without fighter escort.

My second tour from August 1944 to the end of the war was with the 327th Squadron, 92nd Bomb Group, Eighth Air Force. Navigator Mel Engle and waist gunner Guy Weddel have helped me fill in details of a tour when the Luftwaffe no longer ruled the sky. However, the fighters had been replaced in part by extremely accurate antiaircraft fire.

I am indebted to two friends, no longer with us, Edward J. Huntzinger for use of his excellent reference, "The 388th At War" and John S. Sloan for his "The Route As Briefed". There are two other great reference works, "B-17 Nose Art Name Directory" by Wallace R. Forman and "The B-17 Flying Fortress Story" by Roger A. Freeman. In addition there is a Combat Recon Marine, Wayne Sirois, known to his friends as Crunch, a superb graphic artist who did the art for the cover of the book.

I must note with appreciation the time spent on The Heavy Bombers web site created by Scott Burris. The site enabled me to communicate with others who shared and cared. Many were pilots, navigators, bombardiers and crewmen who contributed to revitalizing a fading memory. Also were the widows, sons, daughters and grandchildren who told the same story over and over. It, was, "I wish I had talked to him about it while he was still living." To name one is at risk of slighting others.

There one final person, my twin brother, John W. Carson, who when he was reported killed motivated me to return to search for him. I am grateful to him for telling the story dealing with his time as a prisoner of war. It represents the first time we have ever talked about it.

Bomb Drop

EPILOGUE

Fifty-seven years ago is a long time to remember. Some of what I have written has brought back memories and once again a dreams of days spent in another life. A life of excitement, and moments wondering whether or not there would be a tomorrow.

Let the reader be aware, in writing this story I have altered a few names and dates. This has been necessary to protect the image and details when I was of the opinion it might embarrass an individual or his family.

Today, as I look back to 1942 until mid 1945 there are times. I find it difficult to accept the fact, I was there and I did it.

Printed in the United States
24409LVS00001B/247

BORN TO BE A DOCTOR

BORN TO BE A DOCTOR

A Memoir

PAUL BURNS, MD
WITH BARBARA A. LANGHAM

Based on oral interviews conducted by
Thomas M. Hatfield

Dedicated to those who made my dream possible
My family, teachers, colleagues, nurses, and staff at Seton and the office
Most of all to the patients who trusted me with their health and life
Especially to my wife, Toni

Copyright © 2018 by the Dolph Briscoe Center for American History, University of Texas at Austin
All rights reserved
Printed in the United States of America
First edition, 2018

Requests for permission to reproduce material from this work should be sent to Office of the Director, Dolph Briscoe Center for American History, University of Texas at Austin, 2300 Red River Stop D1100, Austin, TX 78712-1426

∞ The paper used in this book meets the minimum requirements of ANSI/NISO z39.48-1992 (r1997) (Permanence of Paper).

Library of Congress Control Number: 2018945107

All photos courtesy of the Burns family, unless otherwise noted.

Special thanks to my wife, Toni, for her work restoring many of the old family photographs.

Contents

Foreword Ernest Butler	vii
Preface Don Carleton	ix
Introduction	xi
Chapter 1. The Calling	1
Chapter 2. Schooling for a Career	30
Chapter 3. The Army and Internship	44
Chapter 4. Vietnam	61
Chapter 5. Residency	93
Chapter 6. The Practice	110
Chapter 7. My Enriched Life	148
Chapter 8. Restoring the Ranch	178
Acknowledgments	211
Appendix	213
Sources and Methodology	221
Index	223

Foreword

It was chance that Paul Burns and I would meet for the first time in a summer job in medical school. We had each attended different undergraduate schools and had grown up on opposite sides of the state—he in Brownwood in West Texas and I in Mabank in East Texas. Paul went to Vietnam before his residency, and I was sent to a regional base in central Illinois where I reexamined where I wanted to live and the type of practice I wanted to have.

I chose Austin despite not knowing anyone there and audaciously started out by myself in a space large enough for two physicians, which proved to be very fortunate. After several months of being on call 24/7 with no vacation days, I welcomed a call from Paul, whom I knew and who also wanted to live and practice in Austin. Because we had been in the same training program for otolaryngology, we worked together efficiently from the beginning. We had similar small-town values for work and patient care. We cofounded the Austin Ear, Nose, and Throat Clinic, one of the earliest incorporated medical practices in Austin, at the beginning of our association.

From the outset, Paul demonstrated his ability to work hard, start out early, and be exceptionally well prepared for all his challenges in medicine and our practice. He was candid, honest, and always unselfishly interested in a successful practice. He never refused to see a patient, regardless of whether they could pay or not, and was particularly dedicated to unfortunate patients with head and neck cancer. These patients always required more attention and care, which meant less financial compensation. In addition, he documented almost everything he did because he knew where he had been and definitely knew where he was going in the future.

By the time he retired, our clinic had ten physicians with several branch offices serving the needs of Austin and the surrounding area. The clinic would develop into a great success and continues today with fifteen physicians. The same basic principles still apply. This may be the biggest success of both our lifetimes.

Paul always enjoyed listening to piano, as his mother had taught him to do, and still does. It's not surprising that he became involved in the arts early in his career. He served on the boards of the Austin Symphony and later the Austin Lyric Opera. He created the position of the opera company's physician and was recognized for his expertise on vocal disorders in singers. After a series of challenges, the opera company paid off its debts and became a significant regional company in the United States.

Throughout our practice and long friendship, we knew we could depend on each other completely. One Sunday in August, for example, I was driving my family—my wife, Sarah, and our children, Robert and Linda—to Lake Travis for an afternoon of sailing. On the way out Ranch Road 2222, our car overheated as we climbed up the long hill close to Ranch Road 620. I stopped the car and walked to the nearest pay phone. I called Paul and asked if he would pick us up and bring us back home and said I would have my car towed back to Austin.

As it turned out, Paul had just finished a night class at the University of Texas on automobile repair so he could work on his new V12 XKE Jaguar convertible. (What most people don't know is that Paul once had a penchant for flashy sports cars.) "It sounds to me like the thermostat has frozen shut," he said. A little while later, he showed up with a new thermostat, gasket, sealant, and tools. He replaced the thermostat by the side of the road, and we were on our way.

It made no difference if either of us needed help, whether it was operating on a critically ill patient on Christmas Day or replacing a stuck thermostat by the side of the road on a hot afternoon. I could count on Paul, and he could count on me.

Ernest Butler, MD
October 2017

Preface

I first met Paul Burns more than thirty-five years ago because of his extensive map collection. At the time, he was one of the most active map collectors in Texas, and he had assembled a fabulous collection of scarce, unusual, and rare examples of historically valuable cartography. Dr. Lewis Gould, who was a friend and colleague of mine on the faculty of the university's Department of History, is the person who told me about Paul and his map collecting. Lew was a patient of Paul's ear, nose, and throat clinic, and Paul enjoyed discussing maps with him during office visits. Lew asked if we could give Paul a special behind-the-scenes tour of the center's massive collection of maps, and I was delighted to do so. That tour began a friendship with Paul and his lovely and charming wife, Toni, that has now lasted nearly four decades. During these past years, I've enjoyed discussions with Paul during many meals and sessions at his office (I too became a patient!) that covered a wide variety of intellectually stimulating topics. I also learned about Paul's fascinating personal history: his youth in rural west central Texas; his experiences in medical school and his insights into the medical training of the era; his tour of duty as a physician in Vietnam during that ill-fated war; his involvement in helping to found a pioneering ENT clinic in Austin, just at the time of the city's takeoff as a major metropolis; his imaginative collecting activities; and the innovative work he has done and continues to do in restoring his family ranch.

I'm pleased that Paul has decided, with the editorial aid of Barbara Langham, to share his recollections of these experiences with a wider audience, and that he has allowed the Briscoe Center to publish them as *Born to Be a Doctor*. I want to thank my friend and colleague Dr. Thomas Hatfield for skillfully conducting an oral history with Paul that served as the basis for this memoir. Those interviews are now part of the Briscoe Center's Oral History Collection. I also want to thank Dr. Holly Taylor, the Briscoe Center's chief editor, for her expert work on the text and her guidance of the project.

Born to Be a Doctor is published as one of a series of books the Briscoe Center has produced that preserve the historically important memoirs of individuals whose papers or oral histories are at the center, or whose lives are closely connected to the center's collections. Through stewardship, scholarship, and outreach, the Dolph Briscoe Center for American History increases knowledge and fosters exploration of our nation's past. As a leading history research center, the center collects, preserves, and makes available documentary and material-culture evidence encompassing key themes in Texas and US history. Researchers, students, and the public use the center's collections for a wide range of academic, professional, and personal purposes. These collections also inspire our own projects, including books, exhibits, programs, documentary films, and other educational materials. The Dolph Briscoe Center for American History is an organized research unit and a public service component of the University of Texas at Austin.

> Don Carleton
> Executive Director and J. R. Parten Chair
> in the Archives of American History
> The University of Texas at Austin

Introduction

I have always felt fortunate that I was born in the state of Texas, in America, and in 1938. As I look back over almost eighty years, I am still astonished at what a wonderful and happy life I have lived. Although I have never taken the time to examine how the pieces of my life came together, I *have* questioned why I was able to live a life that was fulfilling and interesting every day.

Knowing that memory is tricky and often fails, this book is my attempt to record a way of life and *living* life that is disappearing. Perhaps I am writing this because I am almost eighty years old. Perhaps it is because I have long regretted not asking my grandmother, my mother and father, aunts and uncles, friends, and teachers more questions about their lives. Perhaps it is the long ago admonition from Mr. Leroy Preston, the finest teacher I ever had, still echoing in my memory all these years to "learn from the lives of other people."

Practicing medicine has defined my life. Everything I have accomplished has radiated from my core desire to become a doctor. This book takes my life from its beginning during the Great Depression in a family with just enough money to live on—but no more—repeated illnesses as a child, and staying with my grandmother, to the University of Texas and Baylor College of Medicine. The book shows how my life was influenced by listening to my mother play Chopin and quote Shakespeare, building fences with my father on the ranch, going to war in Vietnam, treating patients, and finally devoting time and effort to the ecological restoration of our family ranch. Any full life has both tragedy and joy, and I have had my share. Still, I look back in awe and wonder and think, What a life.

Mr. Preston was an exceptional teacher. He taught civics during my junior year in Brownwood High School. Several of us decided to take his class together, and many of the best students at the high school were in this class. For the first few minutes of class, we discussed national and world events. Then he would lecture the rest of the hour. It was thrilling to hear him bring history and civics alive. He was not married—teaching was his life. He was early middle-aged, did not own a car, and rode a bicycle to school every day. Today I can still see him sitting on his bicycle, bolt upright wearing a suit and tie, dignified and professional. He required us to go to the library every day and read the *Fort Worth Star-Telegram* that the librarian carefully placed on a long pole to keep it together. He taught us how cities and governments function and why all citizens have responsibilities. He encouraged us to read widely and to always include biographies. He wanted us to read biographies of people from all walks of life to study their achievements, learn from their missteps, understand what made them flourish or languish, emulate their successes, and avoid their failures.

Mr. Preston also taught my father's Sunday school class at the Coggin Avenue Baptist Church in Brownwood, and many years later, I visited the class with my father. After thirty years, Mr. Preston remembered our class well, even our exact seating arrangement. He said it was the most enjoyable class he ever taught. I think it interesting and telling that both teacher and students thought it was the best class of their lives. In life, you never know when the most ordinary comment or action will affect another person.

Every summer our small Baptist church in Blanket, Texas, held a revival meeting with a church service every night for a week. The Methodist church across the street had a similar meeting, and to support their church, we dismissed our regular Sunday night service to visit their church. One particular night has resonated through my memory all these years. It was an exceptionally hot August night, the church was full, the ladies were fanning nonstop, and some of us had to stand outside and look through the window. The old pastor said one line over and over, his voice at a fever pitch, and seventy years later I still hear him: "I would not give a dime for your use-ters [what you used to do]. It's your now-sters that count." It was such a simple statement, but the nine-year-old boy inside me has repeated it throughout my life.

When I was a senior at Brownwood High School, my wonderful physics teacher, Mr. Tracy Hayes, was discussing an answer to a test question that I have long forgotten. A heated discussion erupted among students about some principle of physics. After a few minutes with no sign of compromise in sight, a classmate held up his hand and said, "Let's take a vote and see who is right." Mr. Hayes, who had sat back throughout the discussion and let us all talk, silently stood up. The class hushed and he quietly said, "Scientific principles are never settled by a popular vote." In a few quiet words, he said a lot about how to live and not let the crowd control you in science or in life.

This book began over a decade ago when various family members asked me about Vietnam; they were curious and I seldom talked about it. Many people also asked about my medical practice. It made me uncomfortable because I believed it was *the patient's story*—not mine—and I never wanted to violate a patient's confidence. Generally, I talked about Vietnam only with other soldiers who had also experienced it, and medicine only with other doctors. Frankly, through the years, I was simply too busy to dwell on it. I have always wondered, however, if my reticence is the reason my children did not go into medicine. Because I never talked about the satisfaction and joys of medicine, they saw only the long hours and fatigue. I tried writing down my experiences, but I was not successful.

Once when Tom Hatfield and I were talking over dinner, I told him my dilemma. I asked what advice he could give me on how to tell my life's story without violating the sacred trust to family, patients, and soldiers. He thought for a minute and said, "Let me conduct a series of extensive interviews of your life. You have done so many different things while practicing medicine in a time of historic change." I was elated because I knew Tom could do it with understanding and sensitivity.

Being a physician was a calling: it is who I am. Intelligence and talent are not enough for a happy and satisfying life. It takes hard work, perseverance, and curiosity as well as charity and gratitude. My family nurtured me through every part of my life, from rearing me on a ranch, to sacrificing for my education, to giving support when I was in Vietnam, to standing by when patients needed me.

I hope this book will show the reader how a few off-the-cuff words, as surely as monumental events, can lead to a life filled with wondering, adventuring, helping people, and supporting the environment, and all the while learning something every day.

I have had a wonderful life, and this book is my attempt to honor and show my gratitude to all those who guided and educated me and made my life possible.

PAUL BURNS, MD
OCTOBER 2017

BORN TO BE A DOCTOR

CHAPTER 1

The Calling

The call came in midafternoon, when my Austin office was full of patients, as it usually was in my practice in the early 1980s.

"Dr. Burns, we need you here right away," said the voice on the line. Dr. Dick Shoberg was the anesthesiologist on a child's throat surgery, and the surgeon had asked him to call me. "We can't stop the bleeding," he said. I left immediately, pausing only to ask my office staff to make sure my surgical team—Debbie Lane and Jerry Baker—would meet me in the operating room.

Hurrying from my office in Medical Park Tower across the parking lot to Seton Hospital, it occurred to me that the surgeon had probably nipped a tiny vessel of the carotid artery and was trying to stop the bleeding with coagulation, the standard procedure. Another riskier procedure came to mind, and even though it allowed only a thirty-second window, I felt confident I could do it.

One look into the child's throat and I knew I was exactly right. First, I applied suction to the point of bleeding—which in itself could mean more blood loss and death. Then, using a hemostat (surgical clamp), I grasped the tiny blood vessel, sewed it closed with a single stitch, and tied the knot. Silence ensued, except for the monitoring machines. The stitch held, and the bleeding stopped.

"OK, you can finish up," I said. As I was changing out of scrubs, the surgeon asked me to accompany him in speaking to the child's parents. "No, I need to get back to the office—lots of patients waiting," I said. But he insisted. "The patient is my best friend's daughter," he said. I couldn't refuse.

"This is Dr. Burns," he said to the parents. "Your daughter's fine, but at one point, we couldn't stop the bleeding. Dr. Burns did it and saved her life." The parents didn't know what to say, and I felt embarrassed. It was an awkward moment. We nodded to each other, and I returned to my office to continue seeing patients.

The next week I encountered the surgeon in a hall of the hospital. He stopped me, looked me square in the eyes, and said, "I'm retiring." He was an excellent surgeon, one of Austin's finest, and had been an outstanding ear, nose, and throat (ENT) physician for many years, but the bleeding episode gave him pause. He realized it was time to go.

Why am I relating this incident? I certainly did longer, more complicated surgeries in my twenty-three-year career as a surgeon. Why does this particular one stand out in my memory?

When I look back over my life, I can see that the decision to become a doctor seemed to have been made for me. No one ever told me I should become a doctor, and nobody pressured me. I never got doctor books or kits to play with. I just knew that's what I would do. You might say I was born to be a doctor.

My medical practice gave me a way to earn a comfortable living. But money was never the main goal. I treated everyone who sought my help, regardless of ability to pay. I treated patients because it was the right thing to do. Patients thank me decades later for the way I told their father he had cancer, or for talking to an ill child before I did an examination, or for coming to the hospital in the middle of the night because I was worried. I now count these words of gratitude among my greatest accomplishments.

I believe that work is not just what you do for a living, but what you really do with your life. When I wasn't treating patients, I was spending time with my family or working at the family ranch. It was my family that nurtured me in every phase of my life. It was my family that supported me in all endeavors I chose to pursue, whether studying history, collecting rare books and maps, traveling to the world's great art museums, or serving on the board of the Austin Lyric Opera. I always consider myself fortunate because I loved what I did every day. Even now, in retirement, every day is exciting and challenging.

Excelling in a career and gaining the respect of colleagues is often attributed to intelligence, talent, and luck. But I believe it's the care and compassion you bring with you day in and day out, regardless of the type of job or field. When you reach a certain level of your profession, your colleagues are generally just as smart and talented as you are. Success is more likely due to hard work, attention to detail, discipline, sacrifice, judgment, and character. Those who accomplish more and do their job better are generally those who work harder.

As we age, we see time differently—we just do. The young will have to take my word for it. Maybe we see ahead and behind and realize that there is more behind us than in front of us. I have realized that now is my time to be an example, to consider how I may influence others, and to hope that what I have done will be a part of what shapes and enriches other lives, for good.

This book is a way to begin.

Why Did I Decide to Become a Doctor?

One Christmas when I was about four years old, I lay wheezing and coughing in bed, while my maternal grandmother, Mommie Winn, prayed fervently at my side. My parents had brought me from our ranch fifteen miles away to my grandmother's house in Brownwood because it was the nearest town with a doctor. The doctor had come and gone, but nothing could be done. In those days, the early 1940s, there was no treatment for asthma.

At one point, I couldn't breathe and was turning blue from lack of oxygen. In near desperation, Mommie went to the living room, took a small gift from under the Christmas tree, and brought it to me. "Santa stopped by early and wanted you to have this," she said. As I grasped the gift, my wheezing slowed ever so slightly. In a few minutes, my breathing improved and the coughing became less frequent. I raised myself in bed and began unwrapping the gift. It was a toy! I hardly noticed the tightness easing in my neck and chest. In an hour or so, I was able to go to sleep holding that toy. It was my only gift that Christmas. But it was a treasure.

My maternal grandmother, Mary Etta "Mommie" Winn, had a tremendous influence on my life, beginning in childhood.

Anyone looking at my early life might surmise that my asthma—as well as other family medical events in childhood—influenced my becoming a doctor. The desire to alleviate suffering and heal sickness may indeed have taken root in my subconscious.

More important, I think, was how my grandmother and my parents responded to the ill, the disabled, and the dying. For example, my parents as a young couple experienced the death of their first child shortly after birth. Like many other families who buried children in those days, they shared the grief and steadfastly went on with their lives.

Mommie showered her kindness on everyone, including my mother (*right*) and Uncle Paul Winn (*left*), for whom I am named.

Naturally, when I was born healthy and strong in 1938, my parents hoped that I would remain so. But I started having asthma attacks when I was about nine months old. The attacks were so severe sometimes that my father would stay up all night holding me upright so I could breathe better, and he would carry me in his arms, walking in the yard as I struggled for every breath. My parents once took me to Fort Worth to see an allergist, and I took allergy shots for a while, but they did no good because allergy was not the problem. The attacks became less frequent and less severe beginning when I was eight or ten. Treatment did not become available until the 1960s.

When I stayed with my grandmother, I witnessed firsthand the care and compassion one human being can give another. In her case, it was the care she gave her brother, Estel Rowland. He had left home shortly after the United States entered the First World War in 1917, along with thousands of other young men determined to crush the German kaiser. Joining the army also provided a way to escape his stepfather's beatings. Estel survived a mustard gas attack, only to suffer recurring cancers of the head and neck. When the tumors grew too large, he would go to the VA hospital, have them removed, and get skin grafts. Most of the skin of his face and neck had been replaced, and his nose and ears had been removed as the cancer destroyed them. Mommie understood his distress and took care of him, allowing him to live in one room of her house. She brought his meals there so he could eat alone. He did not want anyone to look at him while he ate because he was so horribly disfigured. I always liked Estel, but he rarely talked to me and never mentioned the war. Mommie would take care of him for the rest of his life.

Mommie's compassion resided deep in her psyche, no doubt strengthened by her religious faith. A devout Baptist, she quoted frequently from the Bible, but not obtrusively. Once, when she was ironing, she said, "I'm ironing love into this shirt." Everyone adored her. I'm sure that her care and tenderness was one reason my parents sent me to stay with her during bad asthma flare-ups.

I saw my parents commit to a lifetime of care and compassion for my little brother, Billy. I was five years old when he was born in 1943. My older brother, Pierce, was nine, and our younger sister, Mary Margaret, was three, and both enjoyed good health. Even though I was only five, the memory of my parents bringing Billy home from the hospital is one of the most vivid of my life.

As Mother told me many years later, she could feel that this pregnancy with Billy was somehow different. After delivery, when she saw Billy for the first time, she knew he was not like other children. When Dr. Scott came to see my parents the next morning in the hospital, he explained that the baby was "not right"—the exact words he used—and that he would never be right. Billy had Down syndrome, as it would be called three decades later. Dr. Scott spoke about cognitive disability and the physical health problems they could expect and recommended that the baby be immediately put into a home, which was the accepted thing to do. There was a long pause. No one knew what to say. My dad told me later that the news was like "being kicked by a horse." Finally, Mother quietly said, "No, he's family. He will always be with his family. He stays with us."

Mother stayed in the hospital about a week, while Mommie stayed with us at the ranch. It was one of the few times she kept us there, so we sensed that something serious was going on. Then one morning, my father left to bring Mother home. All day we watched the long dirt road that led to the house. Sure enough, about the middle of the afternoon, we spotted his black 1940 Ford two-door sedan and all ran out to the porch. When Daddy drove up to the house, I started to run to greet them. But my grandmother reached out and grabbed my hand and held it tightly. I thought it was strange that I could not run down and say hello to Mother. She was leaning back in the seat, looking straight ahead, not looking at us, and not saying a word. Daddy got out, went around and opened the door, reached down and picked her up, and carried her into the house. She was holding the baby in her lap. No one said anything. Daddy put Mother in bed and laid Billy in a small bed beside her. I thought this was strange because none of us got to sleep in the same room as Mother and Daddy. I think everybody there knew the family would never be the same.

Billy lived at home with us, which was unusual in those days. I do not know of another child with Down syndrome who was kept in the home

My mother, Ona Louise Winn, was a cultured young lady in Brownwood, excelling at piano and the arts.

while I was growing up. Generally, children with intellectual disabilities were sent to live at a state institution in Austin. But Mother was adamant that Billy would always be a part of the family and would always live a normal life. When she began teaching school in the nearby town of Blanket, he went with her every day and eventually learned to read and write. He changed our lives. He changed my life.

The final event that could have influenced my decision to become a doctor happened to my mother. When I was entering my senior year in high school, I went to Austin to represent Brownwood High School at a student council workshop. Pierce was away on a naval cruise as part of the University of Texas Reserve Officer Training Corps program, and only Mary Margaret was at home. As she described it to me later, she woke up in the middle of the night when she heard Mother crying uncontrollably. Daddy took her outside and walked her back and forth between the house and the barn trying to comfort her. At daylight he took her to the hospital in Brownwood. I think the doctor could not make a diagnosis and had her transferred to a psychiatric hospital in Fort Worth, 150 miles to the east. Daddy called me in Austin and told me what had happened. I caught a ride with a friend who was going to Fort Worth. I first saw Mother after she had had an electric shock treatment. She was unconscious. Over a couple of hours she became minimally responsive, but obviously she was very sick.

Mother had many electroshock treatments, and Daddy was with her for each one. At that time the doctors didn't give a general anesthetic beforehand. They just brought the patient into a dark room, put the electrodes on the head, and pushed the lever. The patient went into convulsions and grand mal seizure that lasted at least a minute and sometimes longer, then remained unconscious for hours afterward. My mother told me many times that it was the most horrible time of her life. Looking back, I think it was unbelievably cruel.

After spending six weeks in the hospital, Daddy brought her to Mommie Winn's house in Brownwood to recuperate. Soon after that, he bought a house in Brownwood and we moved to town permanently. From then on, Mother lived in fear that she might have to undergo electroshock treatments again. What had caused the illness? Was it the stress of teaching school, caring for Billy, and managing a thousand tasks at the ranch, mostly in isolation? After years of medical practice, I decided that she must have had severe pathological depression.

My family's responses to these events—my asthma, Estel's disfiguring cancer, Billy's Down syndrome, and Mother's depression—certainly influenced me. But the influence would be on how I treated patients in my medical practice, and not on my decision to become a doctor.

My Role Models in Hard Work

My parents, especially my father, served as excellent role models in the life lesson of hard work. Daddy was well educated, deceptively so. In college, he had majored in English and studied astronomy, but he never talked about that. After graduating in 1927, he got a coaching job at Comanche High School but stayed only a year. He loved athletics but didn't see a future in coaching. "I didn't think I could get ahead in coaching," he told me later.

In addition, he loved the outdoors, he loved animals, and he loved what he did as much as anyone I ever knew. Unfortunately, ranching, like everything else in the early 1930s, took a turn for the worse in the Great Depression. Daddy worked from sunup to sundown just to make a living so that we could eat and pay the bills and make payments on the land. He worked so incredibly hard. He never took us hunting or fishing and never played games with us. I don't remember him ever sitting down and talking to me. Our survival demanded constant work. The same was true of my friends' fathers.

My mother, who had met my father while both were attending Howard Payne College, was not prepared for ranch life. She had grown up in Brownwood, where her family owned a grocery store and a restaurant. As a "town girl," she had lived a comfortable life, became an accomplished pianist, and studied the arts and literature. At that time she and Daddy were the only ones in either family who finished college. Her education might have made her feel less accepted by some of her in-laws, which could have been a factor in her depression later.

Unlike other ranch wives, Mother never chopped wood, mended fences, or rounded up cattle. Daddy was very protective of her. She worked primarily in the house—cooking meals, baking bread, canning, churning butter, cleaning, and mending. Monday was laundry day, for example, and it took all day—heating water in the old iron pot, scrubbing clothes on the washboard, rinsing out soap, squeezing out water in the wringer, and hanging the laundry on the line outside to dry. And through it all, she fed and bathed us, nursed us through illnesses, and guided our education.

My father, George Pierce Burns, a handsome and athletic graduate of Howard Payne College in Brownwood, quit coaching after a year in favor of ranching.

My father worked harder than almost any man I knew. Here he stopped long enough in 1939 to hold me in his arms. The building on the right was our first home.

Both my parents lived by the maxim that anything worth doing is worth doing well. Daddy, for example, insisted that fence posts be put into the ground exactly right. The posts had to stand at the same height, even if it meant digging the hole deeper in solid rock. It wasn't for show; it was just the way it should be. Likewise, Mother practiced playing the piano almost every day. In her mind, a sixteenth note was not an eighth note. Plus, she played for the sheer joy of it. Fortunately, I absorbed their desire to do everything as well as I possibly could.

When the United States entered the Second World War in 1941, Daddy realized that he could no longer support the family on ranch income. He took two jobs, one with the Coleman Production Credit Association and another with the Federal Land Bank in Brownwood. He was responsible for making loans to farmers and ranchers to buy livestock or land. It was a perfect fit because he knew everyone in the county. I asked him years later if he ever had to foreclose on anyone. He thought for a minute and said, "Yes, once a man just could not pay and I had to take his cattle." Though he felt bad for the farmer, my dad could take solace in the fact that he had made only one bad loan in twenty years of making loans every day.

As young children, we helped with a few small chores. When we came home from school, we gathered the eggs, fed the chickens, and made sure the cattle had enough water. Then we played until dark. After supper, we read and did homework. Because I was small and sickly, Mother protected me more than Pierce, so my chores were minimal. As we grew older and my asthma became less severe, Pierce and I helped Daddy tend the livestock and work in the fields. Mary Margaret helped Mother around the house.

In the summer, after breakfast, Daddy would give Pierce and me a job to do during the day. Much later I found out the reason was to keep Pierce and me busy and out of Mother's way. We usually dug postholes or hoed weeds in the cornfields. It was hot, backbreaking work. Pierce helped Daddy with the hardest tasks, like driving the Farmall tractor to plow or bale hay and riding the combine to sack the oats that poured out from its spout. Daddy gave me the easier and less dusty jobs, like driving the Ford pickup.

In the spring, we had to find every calf and lamb the day it was born and treat it for screwworms. We would hold the newly born animal down and place a black daub on the umbilical cord to kill any screwworms before they hatched. We also had to watch for any animal that got a nick or scratch where the screwworm fly could lay its eggs. It was a daily race against death. If you lost only a few animals, all the profit for the year was gone.

Treating sheep for stomach worms was even harder. We would catch a sheep, hold its head upright, put a metal tube down the side of the mouth, and force the medicine down the throat. Daddy was so coordinated that he could jump off his horse, catch a specific animal out of the hundred or so in the bunch, and instantly dispatch the medicine. To this day I have never eaten lamb, and neither Pierce nor I enjoy riding horses.

Ranching proved doubly difficult during the 1950s when Texas suffered one of its worst droughts. With no rain, the crops did not grow, and there was no grass for the livestock. We had to supplement the cattle's feed, and that sapped the profits. Many times, we ran out of water in the ranch ponds and had to water the livestock at the house from the windmill. The cattle would get so thirsty that they would stand around the water trough all day.

The low rainfall forced many farmers and ranchers to sell their land and move to Brownwood and other urban areas, but Daddy held on to the ranch. Even though he and Mother lived in town, he worked at his town job all day and then drove to the ranch and worked there until after dark. It was a grueling schedule.

The only day he and Mother took off was Sunday. Mommie and Mother were members of the Baptist church. Daddy went to church with Mother, but he never joined, which was always a bit of an issue. During my early years, we worshipped at the Baptist church in Blanket, and after moving to Brownwood, we went to Mommie's church, Coggin Avenue Baptist. It was a big part of our lives.

During the 1950s, we followed a routine on Sundays. Mother got up early and put a roast in the oven before we left for church. When we got home, it was cooked. Mother insisted we eat Sunday dinner in the dining room with our best china and a freshly ironed tablecloth. For the rest of the day, we read or talked or listened to Mother play the piano. (Most Americans would not have television until a decade or two later.) No one did any work on the ranch. Sunday truly was a day of rest.

Christmas was a special time. About two weeks beforehand, the whole family went into a pasture or wooded area and chose the best cedar tree. Daddy chopped it down, and we decorated it with a small collection of ornaments. On Christmas Eve, Mother played Christmas songs on the piano. We opened a few gifts on Christmas morning and then went to Mommie's house for Christmas dinner with all the Winn family.

At the Blanket Baptist Church, the traditional service took place the Sunday before Christmas Day. One year Christmas fell on Sunday. We woke up early and left for church as usual. We drove the nine long miles on a bad dirt road to Blanket. As we got close to the church, we saw other members of the congregation standing around a blackened patch of ground. The church had caught fire that morning and burned down. We joined the congregation in stunned silence. Some of the women were quietly crying. In those days, fire was a constant hazard, and its destruction a calamity.

In addition to working hard, our parents taught us the value of money. When I was eight or nine years old, they opened an account at the Blanket State Bank for each of us. Every year, Daddy gave each of us a calf and made us responsible for its care. When the calves were grown, we could sell them and deposit the money in our bank accounts. We were free to spend our money on things we wanted, but I saved most of mine. That practice began a lifelong pattern of saving money and spending it wisely.

Growing Up on the Ranch

I believe Mother divined early, while I was still a baby, that I would go to medical school, an idea that must have seemed implausible for anyone living in Brown County at the time. Both she and Daddy had graduated from college, and they were determined that their children would finish college as well. But why medical school, and why me? Perhaps it was because doctors were among the most highly educated and respected people in our community and she saw something special in me.

For the first four years of my life, we lived in a little house built originally for the hired hands and intended as temporary housing. It was so primitive that you could see light through the cracks in the walls. It had one main room with a cookstove in the middle where Mother cooked. The children slept in that room, and Mother and Daddy had a small separate bedroom.

Like most Texans in rural areas, we had no electricity and used kerosene lamps for light. The only heat came from the wood-burning cookstove. In the winter before we went to bed, Mother would hold a quilt in front of the stove and get it nice and warm. We would jump in bed, and Mother would lay the warmed quilt on us and pile more quilts on top. She would heat water on the stove, pour the water into a hot water bottle, wrap a towel around it, and put it under the covers close to our feet.

Water came from a well pumped by a windmill between our house and my dad's parents' house, which was about two hundred yards away. Water was piped to the kitchen faucet—the only running water in the house. In winter when the fire went out in the stove, the water froze in the faucet and pipes. We also relied on the windmill to provide water for the garden where we children grew the vegetables the family depended on. When the water got low in the storage tank, we would dig little trenches for the water to go to each plant. We stood and watched to make sure no water was wasted.

When I was about three years old, my mother woke up early one cold winter morning and saw flames coming through the roof of my grandparents' house. She screamed to Daddy, "Your parents' house is on fire!" Clapping his hat on his head, he ran up the hill to their house. My grandparents got out unharmed, but the house burned to the ground. Nothing was left but the foundation, a bathtub, and a couch and chair sitting in the front yard. Everyone felt the tragedy and devastation. Grandfather Burns had a stroke soon afterward that left him partially paralyzed. Mother said he was never the same after that. It seemed to

My grandfather, Simon Pierce Burns II, and his wife, Mollie, lived near us on the ranch. Their home (behind them) burned to the ground when I was about three years old.

break his spirit. He and Grandmother Burns moved to Brownwood to live out their remaining years.

We had no refrigeration. Daddy built a cooler that evaporated water to keep the milk a few degrees cooler than the room. Even though we raised cattle, we did not eat beef because we had no way to keep it from spoiling. Soon after the first "Norther," or cold front, the men would kill hogs and smoke the meat or bury it in salt to preserve it. We ate the cured pork as well as potatoes, canned green beans, and canned peaches during the winter and early spring. In the late spring and summer we ate fresh vegetables from the garden. Occasionally, we ate a chicken that Mother killed and cooked the same day. She would kill the chicken by grabbing it by the neck and wringing it until the neck broke. Then she would pull out all the feathers, cut it up, and fry the pieces.

Daddy milked our two cows every morning and evening. During the day, often with the help of one or two hired hands, he tended the cattle and sheep, planted or harvested crops as the season demanded, and did maintenance, such as mending fences. That meant that Mother was alone all day, with only the children. Sometimes the wind would blow with a moaning sound that frightened her.

When Daddy would come back to the house after dark, he would start whistling about three hundred yards away so she would know he was close. It was a little routine he had to keep from surprising her at the door. They had an extremely close, loving relationship.

One hot day in the summer of 1938, she was sitting barefoot outside on the small porch. She was seven or eight months pregnant with me and needed to get off her feet. Suddenly she saw my dad galloping on his horse toward the house. He had no shirt on. He had been working in the pasture all day, and she thought, *Oh, no, something must be wrong. Please, God, what more can we take?* He clambered off the horse, holding something in his shirt. He beckoned for her to come inside. He had been working close to the dirt road, he told her, and an ice truck from Brownwood that was making deliveries in the area had gotten lost. The driver asked Daddy for directions. After Daddy complied, the driver asked if he could pay for the information. "No," Daddy said, "but I would like a small piece of ice." The driver chipped off a chunk, Daddy took off his shirt, wrapped the ice in it, and raced the mile or so to the house. It was the only ice Mother ever had on the ranch. She and Daddy made some iced tea and sat at a table on the porch drinking tea and holding hands. She said that she never drank iced tea again that she did not think of that incident. Forty years later when she told me the story, tears came into her eyes.

Early in World War II, about 1942, the army built Camp Bowie at Brownwood. All the houses on the land for the army post had to be removed. Daddy bought one of those houses and had it moved to our ranch. He and Mother picked a beautiful hilltop with old mesquite trees and a view of Brownwood fifteen miles in the distance. He hired carpenters to add two bedrooms, one for Mary Margaret and one for Pierce and me. (After Billy was born, he slept in our parents' room.) Later Daddy added a garage.

To us, it was a tremendous luxury. At first the house didn't have electricity, but it did have an indoor toilet. (I remember one of the men who worked at the ranch saying, "Having a toilet in the house ain't sanitary.") The windmill pumped the water into a storage tank to give us running water and that great luxury, hot water. Shortly afterward, we began using butane to heat the house.

Before the house was wired for electricity, we used a wind charger to power our radio. This simple device, situated outside a window, used a three-feet-wide propeller that charged a car battery under Pierce's desk. The battery, connected by a wire to the radio, allowed us to listen to President Roosevelt's fireside chats and *Your Hit Parade*, both favorites of my mother. My personal favorites were *The Shadow* and *Tom Mix*, the crime-fighting cowboy. I listened to the radio every day—KBWD 1380 Brownwood on the dial. There was a call-in show at night and you could call and request a song dedicated to your girlfriend, so all the school kids listened.

Daddy had the house wired for electricity about 1947, but the actual delivery of electricity from the power line to the house was delayed for a short time. The electricity came from an electric cooperative in Comanche that had been created in the late 1930s by the federal Rural Electrification Act.

One night when we were eating supper, Mother glanced around the table where a kerosene lamp was providing light and got up from her chair. She went to the wall, flipped the switch, and the whole room lit up. It was a miracle! Never again in my life did I ever see such a dramatic change.

Electricity changed our daily lives in remarkable ways. Daddy bought a refrigerator and later a freezer that enabled us to keep perishable food from spoiling. He would slaughter a cow or calf to provide fresh beef and freeze parts we could eat later. We no longer had to clean and fill kerosene lamps, and electric lights in every room allowed us to read and study long into the night.

Mother had always wanted a telephone so she could call her mother in Brownwood. Daddy put up a telephone line strung between mesquite poles that he installed along nine miles of roadside fences to the nearest telephone connection. Whenever our phone stopped working, he had to drive the nine miles looking for a break in the wire. The telephone enabled us to communicate more readily with family and friends.

Aiming for Medical School

Growing up in such humble circumstances, I know that my parents spent most of their life sacrificing to give us a good education. Their single-mindedness toward our education manifested in several ways.

First of all, my parents started me in school at age five. With my September 25 birth date, I would ordinarily have started a year later. Additionally, although we lived in the Owens School District, my parents realized we would get a better education in the nearby town of Blanket. Owens had probably thirty people in the town and a one-room school, whereas Blanket had about 350 people and a larger school.

Getting us into Blanket proved to be a hassle because of the rules against transferring to other districts, but my parents persisted. With that battle won, they faced the daunting task of getting us to school every day. Daddy would drive us to a bridge where the Blanket school bus would pull over and stop to pick us up in the morning. If it was cold, Pierce would build a fire to keep Mary Margaret and me warm while we

I'm standing outside our new house in September 1944, ready for the first day of school at Blanket Elementary.

I won second prize in the Brown County Livestock Show for my Hereford steer, "Charlie," which I raised as a 4-H project. I'm barefooted because I wore my one pair of shoes only to church and school.

waited. The bus ride itself took about an hour, but it was great fun. In the afternoon, we walked home from the bus stop, about three-quarters of a mile.

We attended grades one through eight at the Blanket school. Generally, every grade had its own room. When there were two grades to a room, the teacher would teach one grade in the morning and one grade in the afternoon; the idle side would do homework or just sit the rest of the time. I had wonderful teachers. Ms. Isla Reid, who taught fourth or fifth grade, was one of the greatest teachers I ever had.

All the students in grades one through four at Blanket Elementary gathered for a photo in 1944. I'm second from right on the bottom row, and my brother Pierce is second from left on the top row.

I became close friends with all twelve boys and girls in my class. None of our families had any money. Some of the kids didn't have shoes; they would come to school barefooted. One of my best friends lived in a house with a dirt floor. When I visited him, I didn't think anything about it—that was just the way it was. Only later did it dawn on me that his house had such a primitive floor.

Despite having so little money, my parents made sure to provide educational opportunities at home. They made sure each of us had a separate desk for reading and doing homework. Mother often played the piano, which she had brought from her childhood home in town. Besides exposing us to music, her piano playing profoundly influenced us in all the arts. She also read to us from the classics in literature—works by Shakespeare, Dickens, Hardy, among others. She recited Portia's mercy speech from Shakespeare's *The Merchant of Venice* so often that I could still quote parts of it years later.

My family had just arrived home from church when we posed with our white 1948 Ford pickup. *Left to right:* Daddy, Billy, me, Mary Margaret, Mother, and Mommie Winn. My brother Pierce probably snapped this picture.

After we moved into the new house, Mother established a rule. During the summer after lunch, she would first read to us or play the piano. Then we all had to lie down for an hour in a different room, be quiet, and take a nap or read. I usually read *Compton's Encyclopedia*. I was fascinated with all you could learn from the multivolume set. I read it so often and so carefully that eventually I could turn to any page at random and tell you what it was about.

Mommie Winn also emphasized learning. When we stayed with her, she would read Bible stories as well as other books. Every Bible story had a moral that I incorporated into my being without realizing it. Sometimes when she read, she would get so drowsy that she fell asleep. I would shake her awake and say, "Read, Mommie, read."

I excelled in school from the first grade on and graduated from the eighth grade as valedictorian. Nobody ever told me to make good grades. Maybe everyone just assumed I would. For my part, I enjoyed studying and learning. I loved being alone to read and think, due in part to Mother's rule about resting after lunch. Both she and Daddy supported me quietly and unobtrusively. Those years were some of the most pleasant in my life. I think it was an ideal childhood.

Blanket had a high school but did not offer chemistry, physics, advanced math, foreign language, and government. It had no chemistry and physics labs. Mother and Daddy must have realized we would never be able to compete with students from big cities unless we went to the larger high school in Brownwood. Again, they shouldered the daily burden of getting us better schooling, but now it meant driving us the fifteen miles into town, a long way in those days of bad roads.

When it was time for me to transfer in 1952, I worried about keeping up with my new classmates. Coming from a class of twelve at Blanket, suddenly I had to compete with a class of 165 at Brownwood, and most

Our eighth grade class celebrates graduating from Blanket Elementary in 1952. I was valedictorian (*standing, third from right*).

of them had grown up together since the first grade. I felt the Brownwood students were much better off than we were and much better educated and had all the advantages of living in a big town. I told Mommie how I felt. Fortunately, she had taught a girls' Sunday school class at Coggin Avenue Baptist Church her entire life. She asked one of her students, Peggy Parks, who would be in my class, if she would loan me her yearbook from the year before. I memorized every student's picture and name. The first day that I went to ninth grade, I knew all 165 students in my class by sight and could call them by name. I was accepted right away and quickly made friends. It showed the preparation I put into the new adventure. Later in life I thought there was no excuse for not being better prepared than everyone else.

Another reason I was accepted was that I made good grades. At our ninth grade graduation, I was the highest ranking boy in my class. I did academically well for the rest of high school. My grades earned me membership in the National Honor Society, and my classmates elected me to the student council and president of our junior class.

I enjoyed all my classes and had great teachers—as good as any I've ever had in my life. My Spanish teacher, Ms. Ruth Cole, had been a classmate of my mother's at Howard Payne College. Mr. Tracy Hayes, my chemistry and physics teacher, and Mr. Leroy Preston, who taught civics and history, were superb. I give them credit for my love of those disciplines ever since.

One of the things at which I did not excel was sports, which was disheartening. My dad was extremely athletic, and Pierce was good at football. I was always small and weak, plus I had poor eyesight and didn't want to wear glasses. At Blanket when they did the annual eye exams, I would slip down to the front of the class and memorize the eye chart so that I could call out the numbers and letters perfectly. I didn't wear glasses until I was in about the fifth grade. My eyesight was so bad that I could never see a baseball being thrown or hit. I could never see a football until it was right on top of me. I tried out for football but was not big enough, and I ran track but was never fast enough. I played tennis my last year and was okay but not great.

When the US Supreme Court ruled against segregation in May 1954,

The Calling 27

At Brownwood High School, my grades earned me membership in the National Honor Society, and my classmates elected me to the student council and president of our junior class.

the Brownwood School Board decided to integrate grades nine through twelve the next school year. Up until that time, black students had attended R. F. Hardin High School (named for a former buffalo soldier who started a "colored" school in Brownwood in the 1890s). Thus, in September 1955 black students attended classes with us. There were no incidents because frankly no one thought much about it.

When Mother got sick and quit teaching at Blanket, I realized that it would be good if I could bring in some money. No one told me to get a job; it was something I wanted to do. I got hired as a soda jerk at Doc Barkley's Palace Drug my senior year. In addition to serving sodas, I made ice cream in a hand-cranked freezer, waited on customers, wrapped gifts, and delivered prescriptions. I started about four o'clock after school and worked until ten at night when we cleaned up, mopped the floors, and closed the store.

Having a job after school meant that I could not study as much as I had before. I would get home about ten thirty, eat a bite, and go straight to bed. The only time I had to study was one hour of study hall at school. My grades did not deteriorate that much, but it was enough to knock me out of the possibility of being valedictorian of my high school class. That honor went to my best friend, Johnny Minear.

I had many good friends, and we would often hang out together. We would drive out to the ranch, go dove hunting, take long hikes, and fool around. I bought an old car, a 1947 Chevy coupe, for three hundred dollars with my wages (fifty cents an hour) at Palace Drug. My friends and I would drive around on a summer afternoon without any purpose in mind. We would drive through Brownwood, go around the circle, stop at the Dairy Queen, talk and laugh and tell stories, and look for girls. It was an ideal time to grow up. Everyone felt safe. Unlike today, we could be gone all day with no contact with parents, and they never worried about us.

When I got my driver's license at age fourteen, I took a trip with my younger cousin Rowland Winn to Big Bend National Park, which is about 350 miles west of Brownwood. Daddy let us use the pickup, and he gave us maybe five or ten dollars for gas. We didn't have enough money to eat in a restaurant or stay in a motel. Mother made us enough sandwiches for several days and we put a bedroll in the back of the pickup. We drove to Big Bend and spent two or three days out there. We camped by the side of the road and slept in the truck bed. No one else was around for probably a hundred miles in every direction.

One morning the pickup would not start. No cars had come by for hours, and there was no pay phone anywhere. We had parked on an incline close to a stream but just far enough that I thought if Rowland and I would push the truck and get it rolling, I could jump in, slam it in second gear, and pop the clutch to get it started. It worked. We jumped in and headed down into the park. On another day, as we were driving up into the Chisos Basin, the truck overheated. We let it cool down and then poured water into the radiator. After that, we didn't have any more trouble and made it home just fine. It was a huge adventure. Although I was only fourteen and Rowland only ten, my parents had confidence that we could handle any problem that came along.

Although Brownwood had a small Baptist college, Howard Payne, my parents wanted to send us to the University of Texas at Austin. My brother Pierce had gone to the university and become an engineer. All my life I had assumed I would go there; I never really considered going anywhere else. Mother and Daddy thought it was the best university in

Texas and would give me the best chance of getting into medical school. Mary Margaret went to the university for her second year of college, after a first year at Howard Payne. She returned to Howard Payne, completed her degree in three years, and became a teacher.

I remember the first time I walked across the campus at the university. I stared up at the Tower, marveled at all those stately buildings, and got caught up in the jumble of thousands of students. I'd never seen anything like it in my life. It was awe inspiring. I knew the university was the ultimate in science and literature and the arts. I envisioned the professors as almost godlike. I realized that it was a grand time and a grand opportunity. Maybe the real beauty of it was that my parents and grandmother didn't push me. It was something I wanted to do. I remember thinking that this was going to be tough. It was going to be a different world. This was not Blanket, and it wasn't Brownwood; I would have to compete with students from big cities, like Houston, Dallas, and San Antonio. I knew that this was the big leagues. But there was no question in my mind that I was going to excel.

CHAPTER 2

Schooling for a Career

On the last day of freshman physics at the University of Texas, I took my seat for the final lecture of the semester. Surrounding me in the four-hundred-seat lecture hall were premed, science, and engineering students, surely some of the most brilliant freshmen at the university in that spring of 1957. When the professor came in, he took his place at the lectern and said, "Something has happened in this class that has never happened to me before." He paused for a moment, then continued: "During this entire year, one student has made 100 on everything—every exam, every pop quiz, every laboratory assignment, and every lab exam." Everyone glanced around, wondering who that might be. "I'm going to reward that student by not making him take the final exam," the professor said. "He's free to miss the exam because he already has an A." Then he called my name.

It was one of those rare times in a life when a single event reveals a special insight. I realized that a boy from a small rural school could compete academically with anyone at the highest level. From that time on, I was no longer intimidated by the students who had grown up in the big cities, who had gone to prominent high schools, and who had enjoyed all the privileges that wealth and social status could provide. I realized that I was as smart as any of them and that hard work and perseverance would make the difference if you wanted to rise to the top academically.

Our parents' hard work and thrift enabled us to get a good education. It was not until they both died and we had access to their records that we realized how much they had sacrificed. Their standard of living, recreation, and any luxuries were all secondary. They never once mentioned it to us, but they obviously had a lifelong commitment to each of us to make sure we got a good education.

The University of Texas

Leaving home for the University of Texas in the fall of 1956 was a huge event. I had traveled out of Brown County and even out of Texas several times but always with family members. This time I went alone and I knew it was not just an overnight stay.

I lived in Roberts Hall, located just south of Gregory Gym. The dorm was not air-conditioned, but it was what we could afford. Starting with the second semester, I roomed with Johnny Minear, my best friend from high school who had gone to Texas Tech University but then transferred to the University of Texas. He was an excellent student and studied as hard as I did. (He eventually earned a master's degree from MIT and a doctorate from Rice and enjoyed a career in the geosciences.)

Because dorms were noisy all the time, I studied between classes and in the evenings in the Main Library in the Tower. I went straight to the back and sat in a corner where I could be alone. I felt regal just walking in the door. I sensed that I was carrying on the tradition of generations of people who had studied there before. It was my kind of heaven.

To be sure I got into medical school, I knew I had to be at the top of every class. Many classes, especially the sciences, were graded on the curve. That meant that if everyone made, say, 92 or higher on a test, only the top five or ten percent would make an A. So I had to do better than ninety-five percent of all the other students in class, which meant making a grade close to 100 on every test.

In those days, our classes were huge. My chemistry and physics classes, for example, would have four or five hundred students. I loved those big classes for two reasons: First, I could look at the grades when they were posted to know where I stood in relation to everybody else. In a class of five hundred students, for example, I had to be in the top five percent, or the first twenty-five students. Second, the very best professors taught those classes. If classes had only twenty-five students, then you had many possible teachers, and you might not get the truly eminent ones.

I was privileged to have such world-class professors as Dr. T. S. Painter, the father of modern genetics who had served as president of the university; the master history professor Dr. Otis Singletary; and the famed ichthyologist Dr. Clark Hubbs in biology. I never got to know any of my professors personally. Maybe I was a little intimidated by them because I was from a small school. I had them on pedestals.

One of the hardest courses I ever took in my life was French. I had taken Spanish in high school and had done well. But I wanted to take something different, and I chose French because it was so beautiful. Once I got into the class, I could have kicked myself. I found I was not particularly good at French and it didn't come naturally to me, so I just had to learn it by brute force. But at the end of my second year in the language, the French teacher called me in for a conference. I had never talked to her outside class. "You're the best student I have," she said. "Would you consider majoring in French?" I was flabbergasted. I took that as one of the greatest compliments of my whole college career.

Another class I struggled with was sophomore English, where we studied great American writers like Faulkner and Hemingway. The professor was excellent (I don't remember his name), and it was a wonderful class, but I didn't do well on the exams. At the end of the second semester, I came out with a B. It was the only B I ever made at the university. That meant I would not have a perfect 4.0 grade point average, and I really worried about that. I was selected for Phi Beta Kappa my junior year, which indicated I was in the top five percent of my class.

Mother and Daddy didn't want me to get a job in college because they realized that it would compromise my education. They insisted that I not work, even though it was very hard on them. That was one reason I never went to a movie, never ate in a restaurant (only the university cafeterias), never had a beer, and never went to a party the entire time I was at the university. I knew that those things, even though they cost a few pennies more, would make my parents' sacrifice even greater.

I loved football, but I went to only a few games. While studying on Saturdays during home games, I could hear the roar of the crowd in the stadium. At that time, the Longhorns had just acquired a young head coach who would go on to become one of the greatest coaches in the university's history—Darrell Royal. He coached the team from 1957 to 1976 and would still be coaching when I returned to Austin to start my medical practice.

During the school year, I would go back to Brownwood maybe every three weeks, mainly to see my girlfriend, Leta Lu Huff. I didn't talk to her by telephone because long-distance calls were too expensive. Most of the time that I was at the university, I didn't have a car, so I would hitchhike. I would ask a friend to drive me to the edge of Austin (where Lamar Boulevard now connects to Highway 183), where I could catch a ride. After getting stuck a couple of times in Lometa, I learned to ask the driver first if he was going to Brownwood or at least to Lampasas or Goldthwaite, where I could get a ride. Sometimes it took two or three rides to get home.

Summers were different. I went home and worked my old job at the Palace Drug. I alternated shifts with Dabney Kennedy. We both opened the store at eight in the morning, and then one of us would get off at six, and the other at ten. So I was off at six every other night. It was a great job because my friends would come by and have a fountain soda. If we were not busy, I could visit with my friends while I cleaned up.

I finished my studies at the university in three years, lacking only a government course to get a degree. (I never got it.) In my third year, I applied to all three medical schools in the state—University of Texas Medical Branch at Galveston, Southwestern Medical School in Dallas, and Baylor Medical School in Houston. I knew I wanted to practice in Texas, so there was no point in applying out of state. I felt fairly confident that I would get in, but I still had some lingering doubt. Much to my delight, I heard from all three immediately asking me to interview.

My first interview was with the head of the anatomy department at the University of Texas at Galveston. He asked me all the usual questions, and we talked for an hour. At the end, he said, "Well, I hope you choose us because you're the kind of person we want in this medical school." It was like a heavy weight had been lifted from me. At that moment, I knew I would get accepted by all three, and I was. I chose Baylor

My entire family—including my sister, Mary Margaret, shown here with her husband, Fred Byrom, and their children, Marietta and Paul—assumed that I would finish medical school. There was no plan B.

because I thought it was the best. It was also the choice of many of my friends, including Tommy Coopwood, and I was excited about continuing my studies with them.

Baylor College of Medicine

In the fall of 1959, when I started medical school, the Baylor College of Medicine occupied a prominent place in the Texas Medical Center. Methodist Hospital, Baylor's principal teaching hospital, and the Texas Medical Center Library, where I studied when I wasn't studying at home, were short walks away.

Hermann Hospital was the first hospital established on the site that would become the Texas Medical Center. It opened in 1925, more than three decades before I arrived. Three hospitals—MD Anderson Cancer Center, St. Luke's Episcopal Hospital, and Texas Children's Hospital—opened in the medical center in 1954. Ben Taub Hospital would open about the time I graduated from medical school in 1963. I would spend much of my residency from 1966 to 1970 practicing in Ben Taub.

The VA hospital, the other teaching hospital, had been built in 1946 after World War II. It was about two miles away from Baylor at the intersection of Almeda and Old Spanish Trail, which meant we had to drive there for clinical work.

While I was in school and residency, much of the Texas Medical Center consisted of large expanses of open land and trees. Today it's the largest medical complex in the world. It has two medical schools, seven nursing schools, a dental school, two pharmacy schools, and twenty-one hospitals, among other medicine-related institutions.

The first two years of medical school consisted of lectures in the basic subjects, such as anatomy, physiology, histology (cell structure), biochemistry, embryology, genetics, and neuroanatomy. I found them all

At Baylor Medical School, my friends and classmates stand with Dr. Denton Cooley in our senior year in 1963. *Left to right:* Jim Cecil, Jerry Marcontell, Dr. Denton Cooley, Tommy Coopwood, me, and Dwight Odom.

fascinating. All were important in becoming a doctor, but we considered anatomy absolutely essential. In anatomy lab in the afternoons, we would dissect parts of a cadaver (four of us to one cadaver). Because we knew the cadaver had once been a living human being, we treated it with respect. Unfortunately, the cadavers were submerged in formaldehyde, which emitted a strong odor. When I got home after lab, I would change clothes in the garage so I wouldn't stink up the whole house.

Our professors knew us by name, and we greeted each other when we passed in the halls. But we didn't really know our professors personally. We understood that we were held to high standards, and if we made a mistake, we would have to leave school. Dr. Michael DeBakey, the famous heart surgeon on the Baylor faculty, was especially terrifying. He tolerated absolutely no errors.

As medical students, we worked with doctors on the Methodist Hospital staff to care for patients. We would be on duty for thirty-six hours, then off for twelve. It was exhausting. But we had to be there. No one called in sick, because it was too hard to find another student to cover your shift. Fortunately, while we were on duty, the hospital cafeteria provided us three free meals a day, plus a fourth at 2:00 a.m. Some grumbled about the hours, the fatigue, and the time spent away from our families. But we accepted the schedule as "just the way it is."

Financial and Family Issues

As thrilled as I was to begin medical school, the lack of finances continued to plague me. For some reason I still do not understand, I could not get help with a scholarship from Baylor. My grades were good, and the need was surely there. Other students got scholarships, but none came my way. Mother and Daddy had helped as much as they could but really couldn't spare any more money. I couldn't work because medical school was a full-time job.

I felt the lack of money more acutely because I had a family to support. I had married my girlfriend during my last semester at the University of Texas, and she was pregnant with our first child. Most of my friends were also married, but only one had children. When our daughter Margaret Ann was born (October 28, 1959), I was only about three weeks away from final exams. I felt enormous pressure because I didn't know how I was doing in comparison with other students.

When we brought Margaret Ann home, she cried around the clock. I found it almost impossible to study. When she was about a week old, Mother came down to help. "Well, she's just hungry," Mother observed. "If you'd give her an extra bottle every time she cries, then she won't cry anymore." Sure enough, we did that, and I could study a lot better from then on. I remember taking my good friend Jerry Marcontell over to see our baby girl, and he said, "That is the most beautiful baby I have ever seen."

When we went to Brownwood that first Christmas, we got a call from Paul Winn, the uncle for whom I'm named. Daddy and I went down to his drugstore, Winn Pharmacy, to talk to him. To my surprise, he offered to loan me $150 a month for the rest of medical school, the equivalent of $1,000 a month, or $12,000 a year, in today's money. It was a godsend. We paid $70 a month for rent and utilities, which left $80 for groceries and everything else. That was barely enough to get by, but that's what we lived on. I wouldn't be able to pay it back until years later, after I had been in practice five or six years.

When we went to Brownwood for visits, Mother and Daddy would give us beef from the ranch that I would pack into the freezer of our refrigerator at home. Meals were simple. We had some kind of beef almost every day and fish maybe a couple of times a year. The only groceries we could afford to buy were vegetables, bread, and eggs and bacon for breakfast. We ate at a restaurant maybe twice a year, unless family came and took us out, which was rare. Occasionally I could eat free at the hospital. Even so, I do not remember ever wishing for more variety. I simply accepted that we had to live within a tight budget.

The first semester, we lived in a small house on the east side of Houston in a rough neighborhood. It was the only house we could afford. Leaving my wife and baby alone all day proved too unsettling, so we moved to a better neighborhood only a block away from my friend Jerry Marcontell. He and I took turns carpooling to school every day, which meant my wife could have the car every other day if she needed it.

Because my brother Pierce lived near Houston when I was in medical school, our families visited each other on occasion, allowing our children, Fierce Jr., Margaret Ann, and Laura, to play together.

By this time Pierce and his wife, Reba, were living in Pasadena, southwest of Houston, where he was working as a chemical engineer for Lubrizol Corporation. Their son Pierce Jr. and our daughter Margaret Ann were only a month apart in age and enjoyed playing together. Going to visit them was a big treat.

When I started my third year of medical school, my wife and I were expecting our second child. The due date was around Christmas or New Year's Day. But the doctor planned to go hunting over New Year's and didn't want a delivery to interfere with his schedule. When the baby didn't come by Christmas, he decided he would induce labor on the twenty-seventh. And that's when our daughter Laura was born, December 27, 1961. I was off for Christmas break, and Mother stayed with us a few days to help take care of her. "She's a perfect baby," Mother said.

Learning Medicine with Friends

In medical school, I was doing exactly what I had dreamed about doing since age four. Although I was concerned about my rank in class, I felt confident I would graduate, because I knew I was as smart as everyone else. I had known several of my classmates at the University of Texas. Everybody had been Phi Beta Kappa, everybody had been at the top of their class, and nobody was a slacker. Many had come from other universities all over the nation. Being surrounded by people like that was a wonderful, pleasant way to learn.

Five of us became close friends—Jerry Marcontell, Jerry Litel, Tommy Coopwood, Richard Spangler, and I. My friends were all brilliant people, as smart as I've ever known in my life. All had the highest character and integrity; we trusted each other implicitly. We went through almost every rotation together for the four years of medical school. Even though I rarely see them today, I still feel close to them in memory. Sadly, Jerry Litel and Dick Spangler have died.

We went to class at eight in the morning and had an hour off for lunch. We all brought a sandwich from home because none of us could afford to eat in a restaurant. The five of us would sit in a car, eat lunch, talk, and then go back to class. We had either lab or more lectures all afternoon and finished about five. We would eat supper, study, and go to bed. The routine continued the next day.

At home when I was not studying, I played with Margaret Ann and Laura. I was one of a few medical students who had children, and I always thought I was fortunate to have them while I was young. I would get home around five, play with the girls, and eat supper. The girls would go to bed early and I would study until I went to bed. Both children were an absolute delight.

The first two years I would get up by 6:00 a.m., but the last two years I had to get up by five because we had to draw blood and do lab work before the staff doctors got there. Frequently, we were on call and had to spend the night at the hospital, which limited my time with my daughters. I had many weekends off that allowed us to do things together as a family. It was a furious schedule, but I do not remember thinking it was hard or that I was tired.

Medical school was intense because we all realized that the knowledge we acquired would make the difference in how good we would become as physicians. The more we learned, the better we could be. If we missed something, we could do harm. Medicine was no longer theoretical. Although my close friends and I would do anything to help each other, we were also competitive. It may sound paradoxical, but competition was vital. We spurred each other on to study harder and move forward at the same high level. Each of us delighted in finding some obscure fact or condition that we could drop into the conversation at an appropriate time to intimidate each other.

Between our first and second years, we were encouraged to participate in basic research. Six of us hooked up with Dr. Carlos Valbonna of the Texas Institute for Rehabilitation and Research (now part of the Hermann Hospital system), which cared for paralyzed and severely ill patients, especially those with polio and cystic fibrosis. He came up with an astounding project for us. We would isolate a dog's beating heart with the lungs attached, remove it from the animal still beating, isolate it, and monitor the chemical changes in the blood and their effect on the heart and lungs. As far as we could tell, we would be the first to do this exact experiment. It was a huge project for medical students to pull off.

We would arrive at the dog kennel at about five in the morning and get our dogs out of their special pen. We put the dogs on leashes and walked them across the medical center to the institute for surgery. Jerry Marcontell and I prepared the dogs, set up the heart-lung apparatus, and ran all the lab tests. Tommy Coopwood, acting as the surgeon, began at about seven or eight to isolate the heart and lungs, and ran the experiment until the heart quit beating. It took several days to run the lab and analyze the data.

One morning when we went to our dog pen, we found the dogs unusually well groomed and well fed. As we walked them across the medical center in the darkness of morning, we noticed they were extremely friendly but we did not think much about it. We removed the heart and lungs and began the experiment. At about nine the school's head of research called, yelling into the phone: "Where in the hell are Dr. DeBakey's dogs?" We had no idea what he was talking about. He said that Dr. DeBakey had implanted a new heart valve in the dogs and was watching to see how it worked before implanting it into the first human. We explained that the dogs had been in our pen. "I don't care what pen they were in," he thundered. "You bring the dogs back immediately!" We told him the dogs were already sacrificed. Everyone went berserk. Surely Dr. DeBakey would kick us out of medical school. The powers quickly huddled and decided that we should "get out of the medical center immediately and stay hidden at home until this blows over." They agreed never to tell our names, and we agreed to hide out until it was forgotten. We did that and never mentioned the incident while we were in medical school. Later we were told that Dr. DeBakey's staff was able to do an autopsy on all the dogs and got the information needed.

At the beginning of our fourth year, we elected class officers. My close friend Richard Spangler was elected president. I and another student were nominated for secretary/treasurer. The vote ended in a tie. A second and third vote ended the same way. So we decided that one of us would be secretary and the other treasurer, but we never decided who would do which. It didn't matter anyway because we weren't expected to do anything. The election was merely a convention.

Feeling the Pressure

From what I understand, the atmosphere and the attitude at Baylor was different from that at the medical schools at Dallas and Galveston. At Baylor we did not have any exams except the final exam. I never knew where I was in relation to the class, but I had a good idea because I was with my fellow students all day, every day. By contrast, at Galveston students would have an exam every Saturday morning, and then they had the weekend off. The students could get together and have some fun. At Baylor we weren't able to do that. It was supposed to take the pressure off us so that we did not worry about an exam every week. But on the other hand, it put more pressure on us because we never knew how we were performing until the end.

The pressure intensified the last two years, when we did our clinical rotations. We had a year of surgery, internal medicine, and pediatrics and a final year devoted to subspecialties, such as psychiatry, orthopedics, otolaryngology (ear, nose, and throat), gastroenterology, and obstetrics. In every rotation, we began learning to read X-rays and studying the diseases and conditions that affected each subspecialty.

Periodically, we presented a case to assembled staff doctors. A professor would grill you with questions and expect you to answer promptly and correctly. As you approached the limit of your knowledge of a particular condition, you realized you were on shaky ground. When the professor would ask another obscure question and you weren't sure of the answer, you would make an educated guess. Then suddenly, from somewhere in the room, a strident voice would call out: "Wrong!" It was Tommy Coopwood. He gleefully jolted us whenever he could.

Mistakes were made of course, and the professors were quick to correct them. One day in a large assembly of staff and students, Dr. DeBakey got fed up with what he was hearing and remarked: "You fellows make the same mistake day after day and call it experience." That statement stuck with me all my life, especially when I served in Vietnam.

At the end of the fourth year, the school ranked how we finished in class: top third, middle third, or bottom third. I finished in the top third. Even though I felt good about that, I was always acutely aware that I was surrounded by people who were as smart as I was.

When we started medical school, our class consisted of eighty-four students, all men except for three women. One classmate was Karen Teel, who would practice as a pediatrician in Austin for many years. Of our class, everyone graduated (except one who left voluntarily the first day). At the end, none of us would say that medical school was fun, but most of us would say it had been extremely rewarding. Baylor could take comfort in the fact that it had accepted only those students who were capable of finishing.

I recently asked my sister, Mary Margaret, if she had ever heard my parents talking about what would happen if I didn't get into medical school. Not once in her entire life, she said, did she ever hear our parents or our grandmother discuss or even hint that I wouldn't get into medical school. There was no plan B. I was going to medical school and they just assumed I would get in and make it.

Selecting an Internship

When I graduated from medical school in 1963, it was time to arrange an internship. I wanted to intern in the army for two reasons. One, it would provide excellent training and give me a lot of responsibility. Two, the internship would pay a living wage, something I desperately needed. I would make $256 a month, which would have been about $2,000 a month, or $24,000 a year, in today's money. All the interns would earn the same salary, and we would all live in government housing.

I was fortunate to get my first choice—Madigan General Hospital at Fort Lewis, Washington, in the US Army. Traveling to Madigan turned out to be a huge adventure because we drove halfway across the nation with everything in the trunk of our old Chevrolet. I looked forward to spending more time with our daughters and learning to ski.

CHAPTER 3

The Army and Internship

As a medical doctor on active duty at Fort Lewis, Washington, I was immediately commissioned a captain in the Medical Corps. I walked in with absolutely no military training, not even an orientation. We arrived at the hospital, put on a uniform, and went to work the same day.

On the first day, I looked up and saw a lieutenant colonel coming toward me. I had my captain's bars on, which usually meant one had been in the army for several years. I had never saluted anyone and didn't know whether I was supposed to salute first or wait. I remember breaking out in a cold sweat and thinking, *I have no idea what I'm supposed to do here.*

I was in the army, but I was green.

THE ARMY IN MY BACKGROUND

Despite my bewilderment, the idea of military service had been interwoven in my life. Like many young men in the 1960s, I had grown up hearing about the Second World War and seeing photographs of fathers and uncles in uniform in Europe, Africa, and the Pacific. I thought them heroic. I was only three when Japan bombed Pearl Harbor, prompting the United States to enter the war. But I remember the huge impact the war had on my family and our community at the time.

In 1940 the War Department relocated Camp Bowie from Fort Worth to Brownwood as a training center for the Texas Army National Guard.

The Army and Internship

Once the US Congress declared war in December 1941, Brownwood changed from an isolated rural village to a bustling town. The population exploded from 13,964 in 1940 to 23,479 in 1941.

Among the eight divisions trained was the guard's Thirty-Sixth Infantry Division. The camp couldn't house all the soldiers' families, so Mommie rented out rooms in her house. Five families lived with her, each in a separate room and all sharing one bathroom. The soldiers would come home about six in the evening in a jeep. If I was staying with Mommie, I ran out to greet each one. They would pick me up and carry me into the house. It was exciting.

A year or two later when the division pulled out, the soldiers with all their trucks and tanks marched in a huge parade through downtown Brownwood. Mother, Mommie, several of the soldiers' wives, and I stood in front of the Lyric Theatre on Center Avenue. "All the soldiers look alike," Mother said, "but you can tell what kind of man he is by the woman on his arm." Those words stuck with me for the rest of my life.

In the evenings, the world news came on the local radio station. At six everyone gathered around to hear Gabriel Heatter, a commentator who began every broadcast with the same phrase: "There is good news tonight." Everyone was absolutely quiet as we listened for any news of the Thirty-Sixth Infantry.

My father was too old to serve in that war. Many years later, he told me he got his draft notice near the end of the war for the invasion of Japan. In August 1945 the United States dropped atomic bombs on Hiroshima and Nagasaki, and he didn't have to go.

Japan surrendered in September 1945, and the division came home as a unit in December. Several of the wives lived with Mommie until the war's end.

Young men continued to be drafted until 1973, the year the US military changed to an all-volunteer force. Thus, when I finished medical school in 1963, I was obliged to serve two years to satisfy a military obligation plus a year of internship and four years of residency to become a physician specializing in otolaryngology. I could have stayed at Baylor for the internship, but I would have earned only $135 a month, and I needed more than that. I applied for an internship in the army, which paid nearly twice as much. I reasoned that I could move from the internship into my military obligation and then do the residency.

I anticipated that I would get excellent training in the army, and I had a favorable attitude toward it because of my family's World War II experiences. Then, too, I wanted the adventure of it. From the day we arrived, I liked Fort Lewis. Seeing all those snow-capped mountains and verdant green forests gave me the first inkling that I had made the right choice.

The Internship at Fort Lewis

Although young doctors at Madigan Hospital came from all over the nation, I soon discovered that I was the only intern from Texas. We all had different backgrounds but were eager to learn. We were all good doctors who worried about our patients. Most important, I began to do what I had dreamed about since childhood: practice medicine.

My first rotation was ear, nose, and throat (ENT). I enjoyed it so much that I'm sure it's why I decided to specialize in it. Two excellent doctors, Dr. Carl Lineback (who actually came to Austin and practiced at the same time I did) and Dr. Ray Rosedale, supervised me. As interns, we were on call every other night, or every third night depending on the rotation, for the entire year. Being on call meant working most of the night, but I expected it and it was what I was trained to do.

I enjoyed all my rotations except one: obstetrics/gynecology. It was one of the few times in my life that I believe I was treated badly. The colonel (whose name I've surely repressed) ran a rotation that was almost inhumane—for both the interns and the patients. We interns worked thirty-six hours straight evaluating pregnant patients and delivering babies. Then we had twelve hours off. We went home, ate supper, and immediately went to sleep. But the clincher was that on our night off, we had to come back in at seven and make rounds for an hour. It was exhausting. I went for weeks without seeing daylight.

As for the patients, they had to suffer through labor without adequate anesthesia. This colonel did not believe in spinals or epidurals,

The Army and Internship

I did my internship at Madigan Hospital at Fort Lewis, Washington. The army internship paid a living wage, something I desperately needed to support my family. (Credit: Madigan Army Medical Center.)

which can relieve much or all of the pain of labor. He made us deliver every one of those women with a pudendal block, a local anesthetic injected in the vaginal area. Those women suffered for hours. It was horrible. We stayed with them the whole time and it was something we all wanted to forget. He was a full colonel, and other than the general who was the head of the hospital, he was the second-highest-ranking officer, so no one could touch him. We delivered a lot of babies and got pretty good at it, but I never wanted to go into another delivery room the rest of my life.

It was during this rotation that I first thought seriously about Vietnam. Young pregnant women would come to the obstetrics clinic in the afternoon and wait in their hospital gowns in a long hall lined with chairs. I will never forget the sight—an endless hall as far as you could see lined on both sides with young female faces, all pregnant and eager to see the doctor. I was always dead tired but I knew that I and a couple of other interns had to see every woman, often forty a day. We had to carefully examine them, talk to each one, and see how the pregnancy was going. It was one of those times in medicine that I learned that no matter how tired I was and no matter how many patients I had to see, the patient in front of me wanted one thing: my total concentration.

In taking the medical history, I asked about their husbands. I felt surprised and almost overwhelmed that every one of their husbands was a soldier who was either in Vietnam or soon would be. These women, like us, were young, innocent, and trusting. Even if they had to wait all afternoon to see me, none of them ever complained. They just wanted to be sure their children were all right and they were doing the right thing. Hanging over it all was Vietnam. I surely did not know what it would mean for these women and what it would mean for me, but I had a vague feeling of foreboding.

One afternoon, feeling dead tired as usual, I picked the next chart off the door rack and read the name and age of the patient. I had never seen this woman before, but that was not unusual because we just saw who came to the clinic that day and rarely saw the same person twice. I quickly scanned the chart and made mental notes: first baby, no complications, lab OK, young healthy woman, close to term, regular visits to the clinic with no problems.

I opened the door and introduced myself as Dr. Burns. We were all captains, but in a tiny defiance to the army we referred to ourselves as "Doctor" rather than "Captain." She and I talked a few minutes about the pregnancy and lab results. The routine was for me to see the next patient while the nurse put the current patient in the stirrups for the exam. When I came back into the room, I examined the abdomen first and then listened for the baby's heartbeat. As a pattern that I followed throughout my entire career in medicine, I was absolutely careful and thorough with the exam. In those days, the diagnosis was made by physical exam—no CT (computerized tomography) or ultrasound, just a stethoscope and eyes, ears, and hands. For the life of me, I could not tell which way the baby was facing. I just could not palpate the baby's head completely. I looked at the chart and saw nothing noted in the previous exams. I felt again and again and I just could not feel the head.

Interns were not allowed to order X-rays on pregnant women without the resident's approval, but no resident was in the clinic that day.

The nurses and clerks all liked me because I rarely got behind, but today I was getting behind. The nurse, a major, narrowed her eyes as if to say, "What is going on? Let's move it." Finally, I said, "I just cannot feel the baby's head. We need to send her to get an X-ray."

After seeing a few patients, the nurse came with the "wet" film, meaning it had not been read. I placed it on the viewing glass and looked for the head, to see which way it was positioned. I gulped. There was no head. The baby was anencephalic.

When I got the resident on the phone, I could tell he was irritated. He knew he might get into trouble because he had not ordered the X-ray and the clinic had missed the diagnosis for months. "Look," I said, "I'll put your name on the X-ray, and you'll get credit for making the diagnosis. Now, what do I do with the patient?" "Tell her," he said and hung up.

I agonized: How does one deliver devastating news? I was an intern just out of medical school. Summoning all the courage and compassion I could muster, I went in and spoke quietly, kindly, unhurried, but absolutely honestly. It would be the way I told patients bad news a thousand times, later in my practice. I was never upbeat when it was not warranted. We talked alone for a few minutes. She did not say much and did not cry. I told her that in unusual circumstances an intern could request to deliver a patient and I would be called when she came in, if she would like. She said, "I'd like that."

By chance I was on call and in the hospital when she arrived in labor in early evening. She labored long and hard for hours. At almost daylight she delivered the baby. The baby had no head, the lungs heaved a couple of agonal breaths, I did nothing, and the baby died. I told the mother the baby was dead. "Was it a boy or girl?" she asked. "A boy," I said. I did not show her the baby and she did not ask. She quietly cried. I could not help from crying myself but quickly stifled it. "I'm sorry," I said. She thanked me for being kind and helping her. I saw her once in the hospital after that but never heard from her again. I wondered many times if her husband went to Vietnam and made it back, and I wondered if today she was thinking about her first baby.

When I finished the internship, I came away with a hundred such episodes seared into my mind, never to be forgotten, and never to be told because they were too personal to me and might be misunderstood if taken out of context. So when someone asks, "How was internship?" I think, *Well, which patient? Which day? Which time that I had been up for thirty hours without sleep?* It's not something you can put on a bumper sticker. Dickens probably got it closer than anyone: "It was the best of times, it was the worst of times." But this much is certain: you never can say you do not remember internship.

Two historical events occurred that year—one that shocked the world and another that gradually seeped into the nation's conscience. In November, while on pediatrics rotation, another intern and I were hurrying across a parking lot to the neonatal intensive care unit. We were about halfway there when someone came to meet us: "President Kennedy has just been shot." I was stunned. "The president? Shot?" It was hard to believe. As the day wore on, we heard news snippets about an assassin who had fired at the president's motorcade in Dallas. The president had died, and Vice President Lyndon Johnson was sworn in. It was a grim moment for the entire country and the world.

The second event happened the following January when the US surgeon general, Dr. Luther Terry, released the first federal government report linking smoking to cancer, heart disease, and other serious conditions. It received little attention at the time. I had never smoked, because of my asthma, but many doctors, old and young, had a habit of lighting up several times a day. Years later in my medical practice, as smoking declined, I saw a corresponding drop in head and neck cancers.

I left my internship feeling that I was extremely well trained. I had performed or assisted with many surgeries and had given general anesthesia under supervision. I had full confidence in my ability to handle medical emergencies because I had done that all year.

Basic Training in San Antonio

As soon as the internship was over, we headed to Fort Sam Houston in San Antonio for basic training. All my friends from medical school were there, along with hundreds of other doctors. We went to class to learn army rules and regulations, had rigorous physical workouts, shot rifles, used gas masks in a gas-filled room, and so forth. But we didn't see patients, and we didn't take medical calls. I had enough money for my family to live on—a huge relief. It was almost the only time in my life I had no responsibility. Mainly I remember just fooling around with friends.

Vietnam was something in the distance, and none of us thought much about it. At some point, we were told that if we did get sent to Vietnam, our biggest risk would be ambush and capture. The ambush training, at Camp Bullis northwest of San Antonio, was led by a young second lieutenant, a big man who must have weighed 250 pounds. As he talked, he twisted his face into a stern frown. Obviously he had never been to Vietnam. At the end, he said, "Captains, if you are in an ambush in Vietnam, the way you survive it is to charge immediately into the teeth of the ambush." He repeated the phrase several times for emphasis: "Charge into the teeth of the ambush." We all looked at each other and thought, *Really?* After the lecture we all agreed it was stupid. In Vietnam, every time we roared down a road in Vietcong-held territory, we would say, "Grab your .45 and run into the teeth of the ambush." That joke never failed to make us laugh.

After basic training at Fort Sam Houston, we were each assigned to a regular army unit. If you interned in the army, you had preference in your next duty assignment over those who were inducted. I chose Fort Carson, Colorado, the primo duty station in the world. I wanted to be in a line infantry unit, so I volunteered for the Fifth Mechanized Infantry Division. It was all armor, with tanks and armored personnel carriers designed for warfare in Europe. The division was called a STRIKE unit and stayed on constant alert. If war broke out, this unit would be the first to go. We were constantly training in the field and ready to go anywhere in the world. The location in Colorado was perfect because I wanted to ski as much as possible.

Ralph Levin, who had interned at Letterman Army Hospital in San Francisco, and I became good friends, probably because we both planned to go into ENT after the army. We volunteered to be battalion surgeons. I don't remember his assignment, but I was assigned to the Second Battalion, Sixty-First Infantry, Fifth Mechanized Infantry Division, which consisted of a thousand men. My medical unit had four armored personnel carriers—three to evacuate wounded and one as my command vehicle. I learned to drive it battened down with just a small slit to see out. It was a grand adventure, and I knew at the time I would never get to do anything like it again. I also had a jeep and driver, but most important, I had two sergeants who had been in the army nearly thirty years. I quickly learned that I would take care of the medicine, and they would take care of everything else.

On my first field training exercise at Fort Carson, we went out for about a week in simulated war games. We drove in fits and starts for about an hour and stopped. In my open jeep, it was bitterly cold, with the temperature hovering about ten degrees above zero. It began to snow, and the north wind was blowing. A sergeant came to my jeep and with a twinkle in his eye said, "Doc, you might be needed in the cracker box [slang for ambulance]. You know, it has a heater." I was quick to say I was OK. I didn't want the men to think I couldn't take anything they took. We started up again, and I said nothing about how freezing cold I was.

A message came on the radio that we should proceed to a certain area and wait. Colonel Snell, the battalion commander, came by in a few minutes and pulled up beside my jeep. "Doc," he said, "set up in this area." I quickly told my men to begin unloading the trucks and set up an aid station. Because I had grown up on a ranch and had probably worked harder than ninety percent of the men, I was eager to show that I was no wimp and could work just as hard as they could. I began helping to unload all the equipment. Although it was chaotic, we were making progress.

After a few minutes of furious activity, I looked up to see my sergeant standing just beside me. He was the movie picture of a drill sergeant—tall, muscular, almost regal—and close to the end of a thirty-year career and to retirement. "Sir," he said, "could I have a few words with the captain in private?" "Sure," I said, somewhat taken aback. We walked about fifty yards to the extreme edge of the clearing, well away from the men.

"Sir," he began in a calm, low voice, "will the captain permit me to say a few words?" He used the third person—captain, not doc—and was formal and polite. "Yes," I answered.

"Sir, the captain should never pitch in and help the men unload a truck and direct them when I am present. The colonel will tell you what to do, you should then turn to me and give me simple orders, and I will have everything done just like you and the colonel like it. The captain is here to treat the wounded and save men's lives."

Neither of us said anything for a long time. I let what he said sink in. In a few words, he had covered leadership, command, respect for each man doing his job better than you can, and respect for each other. I learned that good intentions can be a disaster. Finally, I said, "Thank you, Sergeant."

We walked back to the area, I stood back, and he took over. He barked a few orders, and with military precision, the aid station took shape.

I learned a lifelong lesson that day that made me a much better surgeon in the operating room and a better doctor in office practice. I needed to surround myself with the best people and concentrate on surgery and medicine and let my surgical and office staff do their jobs. I learned that everyone I meet can do something better than I can.

By intuition I knew that in addition to caring for the health of the troops, my job was to always make the colonel look good. Colonel Snell turned out to be one of the greatest men I've ever met. He had been with the Tenth Mountain Division in the Second World War, and this was his last command before retirement. He was one of the grand old commanders, a perfect gentleman, fair, tough, and the kind of person you wanted to lead you into battle. He was especially kind to me. He knew, for example, that I was trying to save money for my residency, so he allowed me to take a part-time job. I worked on call overnight in a mental hospital in Pueblo, about forty miles south of Fort Carson. I would drive there in the evening, spend the night, and drive back in time for seven o'clock roll call the next morning.

Battalion Surgeon

Our battalion was the last in the entire US Army to be mountain ski–trained in case NATO needed a division in the mountains of northern Europe or Russia. We spent the winter of 1964–1965 at Camp Hale, Colorado, where we practiced cross-country attacks on skis or snowshoes with armored vehicles. I held sick call every morning, treating mostly broken arms or dislocated shoulders. It was the coldest I have ever experienced in my life—below zero every day. One night it dropped to thirty-five degrees below zero without the chill factor. The snow was also great for recreational skiing. If we finished training early, Colonel Snell would let me go to Vail about fifteen miles away and ski by myself. It was exciting and fun.

I never will forget the first time I saw the power of a US mechanized infantry division on an attack. We were at Fort Carson on a simulated warfare game, and a member of our battalion went out in front on a scouting mission. It was at night but just before daylight. The next thing I knew the colonel radioed me that the scout had turned his jeep over in a ravine, crushing one man to death and injuring three others. "Captain, we've got some actual casualties out in no-man's-land in front of the battalion. You need to get out there and see what you can do for them, but we are not going to call off the attack."

My sergeant and I jumped into a jeep and raced for the ravine. I got out and started trying to resuscitate one of the men. I could see maybe two or three hundred yards up a slight incline before it disappeared over the horizon. After about fifteen minutes, the entire Fifth Mechanized Division came over that hill in a simulated attack. Hundreds of giant tanks and armored personnel carriers were coming straight toward us. The noise was deafening. In that second, I understood what it would be like to face an American mechanized infantry unit in combat. I thought there isn't anybody in the world that can match the US Army when it's all geared up.

During that year, I volunteered for a month of amphibious training with the marines at Camp Pendleton, California. We learned how to load and unload a medical unit with all its vehicles on a ship and bring it ashore. The training ended with a landing exercise off the coast of Pendleton. Ships were everywhere, along with helicopters, tanks, and armored personnel carriers. At 2:00 a.m., dressed in full battle gear, I looked to my sergeant, who nodded that we were ready. The ship's speaker blared, "Away all boats," and landing craft swung over the side, followed by a net. A strong wind was blowing, causing the landing craft to rise and fall on ten-to-fifteen-foot waves. The men had to crawl down the net, which was about five stories high, with a sixty-five-pound pack strapped to the back and jump onto a landing craft. The trick was to time the jump at the exact moment so you would not be slammed to the steel deck or, worse, get crushed between the vessels.

Because the battalion surgeon always goes last, I was still on the ship when the commander called a halt to the boarding because of the storm. The landing craft circled the ship for an hour and a half. As far as I could tell, almost every soldier in the landing craft was vomiting. When the wind died down slightly, the boarding resumed. I climbed onto the net, which was slick and wet, and made my way down. Just when I was about three feet from the landing craft, I reached out my foot just as a wave caught the craft and propelled it upward. Everyone on the net got thrown to the steel deck. We stood up and shook ourselves out, just glad we made it. We circled in the landing craft for half an hour and then headed for the beach. I thought of it then, as now, as a grand adventure—dangerous even without anyone shooting at you.

In summer 1965, we started hearing more on the news about Vietnam. In July President Johnson ordered a buildup of sixty-five thousand troops as a way of showing the world America's commitment to halting the spread of communism in Southeast Asia. My division was supposed to be called up first, but evidently the army decided to keep it in reserve in case it was needed in Europe. Many of the division's battalion surgeons, however, were ordered to Vietnam. I had gotten to know them when we all met at the officers' club for coffee.

Getting Orders

"Doctor, you're going to Vietnam." The words cracked like a rifle shot. *What?* I thought. *Vietnam?* During the previous two years—internship and basic training—I had heard of Vietnam but mostly as rumors. I was aware of US military advisors there, but it seemed so far away.

"You have fourteen days to report to Fort Gordon," the colonel was saying. I came out of my semistupor, thoughts racing wildly in my head. *I go where? What about my family?* In the back of my mind, another thought arose: *Wait. I don't have to go. I have asthma. That's a one hundred percent way of getting out of this.*

But I chose to go. I'm proud to this day that I did. I realized that I had a great life. Everything that I'd wanted to do in life I had done up to that point. It was a free country, and I loved it. It had given me opportunities that I couldn't have imagined. I believed that if I accepted the benefits of living in this country, then I had the obligation to go if my number came up. I surely wasn't going to volunteer for Vietnam, but, if my number came up, I had a moral obligation to go. At that time, many young American men accepted the calling just as their grandfathers and fathers had done in the two previous world wars and Korea.

All my friends were called up. We all got the same orders the same day. It was unexpected because it removed all the battalion surgeons from the highest priority unit in the army.

The fourteen days I had to get to Fort Gordon went by in a blur. I remember driving across West Texas and thinking how desolate it looked. I remember wishing that I had not gotten orders for Vietnam and thinking that I wanted to go into my residency at Baylor, where I had been accepted. I rented a small house in Brownwood for my family and helped unpack our belongings. One afternoon I drove out to the ranch with Daddy and my daughters, who were five and three at the time. We didn't do anything but feed the cows.

Just before I left for Fort Gordon, Mother took me aside. "Daddy is real worried about you and afraid you may get sick," she said. They had heard on the news that the Vietcong had put a price on the head of

American doctors, and they worried I would be out in the jungle alone without protection. "I'll be careful," I said.

I flew out of Brownwood on Trans-Texas Airways, changed planes in Dallas, and then continued to Atlanta. I missed the connection in Atlanta and had to sleep on the floor in the airport to catch a flight to Augusta at 4:00 a.m. You could fly half fare if you were in the military and in uniform. It was so early in the buildup that no one paid any attention to the military.

It took a few days for everyone to arrive and be processed. Several friends from Fort Carson and the Fifth Mechanized joined me. There were seventeen doctors in all, many of whom I got to know well. We were assigned to old World War II army barracks, which they called the BOQ, with six of us in one room. When we complained that we couldn't sleep at night because the bare windows let in too much light, we were told, "Close your eyes."

At Fort Gordon, we were assigned to the Forty-First Civil Affairs Company. At that time, "civil affairs" was a new concept the army was developing. In our first meeting, we were told that we would be organized into sixteen teams, each with a doctor, an engineer, a lawyer, a combat infantry officer, an intelligence officer, and five enlisted men. The doctor would treat the Vietnamese. The engineer would evaluate such things as water supply, dams, irrigation, and any building project that might help the Vietnamese. The infantry officer, a lieutenant, would arrange security and command the team. The intelligence officer, always a second lieutenant just drafted into the army, would gather intelligence. The lawyer's function was vague from the start. Although medical doctors were captains, we were outside the chain of command.

I was assigned to a team that would ultimately serve with the First Air Cavalry in Pleiku. We were told we would be working with the Vietnamese—"winning their hearts and minds"—but were given no information on culture, language, or mission. We were as elite and educated a unit as could be assembled, facing a month's trip across the Pacific with nothing to do. We pleaded for something to study on our own, but nothing was available. Our biggest risk would be capture, they said, and they "didn't want a bunch of POWs with dental problems." So we got our dental care done. We asked if we could volunteer at the post hospital at Fort Gordon. "No," they said, "just stay around the company area." To break the monotony, six of us rented a car so we could go out to eat lunch every day.

During our time there, we had two mysterious visitors. One, a professor of surgery at Georgia Medical School in Augusta, would occasionally come out but never really had anything to do with the doctors. He was sophisticated, well educated, and well respected. After a month or so, three of us, including Ralph Levin and I, decided we would try to talk to him to see if he might know what we would be doing in Vietnam. He invited us to his home a week later. When we arrived, we nearly went into shock. The home was palatial. A butler ushered us in, took us to a glass-enclosed garden, and gave us coffee and sweet rolls. After a half hour or more, the butler told us the doctor was tied up but would be with us shortly. So we waited, feeling out of place in our fatigues.

Finally, the professor came in. (I don't remember his name.) He was in his late fifties and articulate, tall, and impeccably dressed, like a Southern gentleman. We explained the little we knew and asked him to tell us more. He said he went to Vietnam regularly and that we would be treating Vietnamese civilians but he couldn't tell us anything other than that. After a pleasant but inconsequential conversation, he excused himself and left. Then his wife came and talked to us for a few minutes, told us we could leave, and graciously took us to the door. We saw the professor once more in the company area talking to the commander. Months later, the commander confided to me that the professor was just as much a mystery to him as to us. One of the doctors saw him at Saigon during our tour and found him distant and unwilling to talk, possibly because he was with a young Vietnamese woman.

The other mystery person came to see us the night we were getting ready to pull out for Vietnam. We had been told someone from Washington would be visiting, but we were too busy to pay attention to him. This quiet, extremely dignified man walked around the company area, somewhat aloof. He had come down on the train and went back by train as soon as we left. (He said he never flew in airplanes.) Our commander

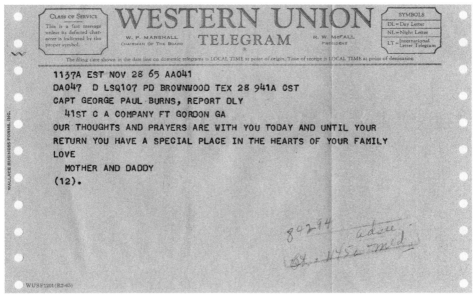

I received this telegram from my parents about two hours before we left Fort Gordon on our way to Vietnam.

told me later that the man knew all about us in great detail but would say nothing about his role. Our commander thought he was from the CIA and was probably the one who had thought up the concept of our company.

Originally we were told that we would leave in the middle of the day and fly from the Augusta airport to San Diego. A day or so before we left, our orders changed. President Johnson had decided that he did not want any troop movements during the daytime because he thought the American people would get nervous if they realized how many troops were going to Vietnam.

The night we pulled out, a gentle rain began falling at about 10:00 p.m. We were all quiet and introspective, without much talking and no joking. If we'd had any doubts, we all knew now that we were headed for war. Throughout my time in the army, I received letters and packages from home—from my wife, relatives, and friends. About two hours before we left Fort Gordon, a Western Union runner handed me a telegram. "Our thoughts and prayers are with you today and until your return. Love, Mother and Daddy." I tucked it in my fatigue pocket, kept it with me while I was there, and have it among my most treasured possessions.

We boarded buses at about 2:00 a.m. and rode to the airport in a long convoy. The movie *We Were Soldiers Once . . . and Young* about the Ia Drang Valley depicted our pullout exactly. Sitting by a window, I saw the rain gently streaking along the glass, with freeway lights reflecting off the pavement. No cars were on the freeway, and the only sound was the hum of the bus engine. No one said a word. The whole trip to the airport was eerie and ghostlike. Ever since then, when I have driven on a freeway at night in rain and no traffic, I think about that trip to the airport. It's not an unpleasant flashback, just a lonely, quiet, and sad feeling.

CHAPTER 4

Vietnam

When we landed in San Diego, we didn't talk much. There was really nothing to say. We knew we were part of an elite unit of physicians and other professionals. While other doctors were assigned to a Vietnamese provincial hospital or a US military unit, we were going to Vietnam to treat the Vietnamese and help win the war. We were going because it was our duty and we had a job to do. We knew we would encounter danger, but we were willing to risk it.

As we soon discovered, however, our mission was no clearer in the combat zone than it had been in the States. Even worse, those at the highest levels of command didn't seem to understand or care. Most troubling was that we had no medical equipment—no X-ray, no surgical instruments, no laboratory, not even a stethoscope.

My high ideals gradually turned into disillusionment. I learned, as the Prussian military theorist Carl von Clausewitz had written 130 years earlier, that war is complex.

But I'm glad I went. My experiences would inform my practice of medicine and remain with me for the rest of my life.

On the Way to War

Our transport ship, the USS *General LeRoy Eltinge*, was first launched in September 1944. It had been used to ferry troops to both the Asian-Pacific and the European-African theaters in World War II. It had been deactivated and then reactivated for the Korean War in 1950, and then deactivated and reactivated again for Vietnam.

Our voyage was the ship's second to transport troops to Vietnam. At 523 feet in length, it carried 5,000 troops in a space designed for 3,823. Only about 150 were in our unit, and most of the rest were replacements for the First Air Cavalry, which had fought a major battle at Ia Drang Valley a few weeks earlier (mid-November 1965).

The ship had few modern conveniences. Because of an inadequate heating system, we steered toward the equator. There the tropics and overcrowding made us wish for air-conditioning, which was limited. The enlisted men slept in the hull in beds made from webbing and hung from metal hooks. Officers slept in a tiny metal room with four rows of bunks, five feet high with about a foot and a half between bunks. Between the rows of bunks were aisles perhaps twelve inches wide. Thus, a room about six feet by thirteen feet held sixteen men. Lights-out was at 10:00 p.m., and the trick was to fall asleep before somebody started snoring.

We were awakened at about six every morning and not allowed back in the bunk room until bedtime. A man was permitted to stay in a bunk if he had a medical slip for seasickness. One poor lieutenant got seasick when we left and never recovered until we landed. He was the happiest man I have ever seen to get to Vietnam.

With so many troops on the ship, each person had to be assigned a place to stay during the day. My place was on one of the upper decks, a steel plate about two feet square. It had a vent from the bakery, so I smelled fresh bread all the way to Vietnam. It reminded me of the times I stayed with Mommie Winn when she pulled freshly baked bread from the oven.

We asked for books to read but got nothing. The trip could have given us the chance to learn some of the Vietnamese language and read about the country's history and culture, but the opportunity was missed. When we were together with other troops, we spent the time talking to friends.

We ate in the officers' dining room. The doctors mostly sat together, so we all got to know each other during the twenty-six-day trip. We had three good meals a day, although we ran out of fresh vegetables in a couple of weeks and had to eat canned food the rest of the time. One day we hit a typhoon, with waves coming over the main deck. That day only three of us showed up for lunch, which showed that I have a great appetite and the ability to withstand an upset stomach at sea.

We wore fatigues, but near the equator we could take off the shirt and wear only the undershirt. We all looked the same. The navy crew, however, wore starched white uniforms and never mixed with us.

About the third or fourth day out to sea, a navy officer came walking down the deck toward me. To my surprise, it was Larry Smith, a medical school classmate from Baylor. After his internship, he went into the navy and was assigned to this vessel as the ship's doctor. We were both glad to see each other, and we visited occasionally but not often. He had one of the few air-conditioned rooms on the ship, and I always thought he was afraid that if we got too friendly I would want to hang out in his room. He told me the voyage was top secret and thus no communications could leave the ship for any reason.

About two weeks into the voyage, he asked me to see a patient with him. "I think he has appendicitis," he said. Larry had started an IV with antibiotics dripping but hoped he would not have to operate. In examining the patient, I found an elevated CBC (complete blood count), pain in the right lower quadrant, slight fever, and rebound (pain after pressing on the stomach). "Yes, I agree that it's appendicitis," I said, "but how are we going to operate?"

As a navy doctor, he outranked me, so he would be the primary surgeon and I would assist him. But who would give the anesthesia? The ship commander made a request over the loudspeaker that anyone with experience or training in anesthesia should report to the sick bay. No one came. Larry had had a surgery rotation but no anesthesia. That left me, who had had a month's rotation in anesthesia.

Larry thought we should put the patient completely under with a general anesthesia, but I disagreed. In addition to having an old anesthesia machine, we had encountered a frightful storm. I realized a lot can go wrong in high winds and crashing waves in the middle of the Pacific. I argued for a spinal and was confident I could do it, having done several as an intern. Finally, I convinced him to do it my way. Larry informed the ship commander about the procedure, and the commander turned the ship to go with the waves to steady the ship as much as possible.

The anesthetic procedure requires elevating the upper body so that the level of anesthesia is exactly right. The anesthesia, which is heavier than the spinal fluid, goes down through the spinal canal and anesthetizes the nerves in the lower part of the body. To begin, I sat the patient up, put a needle in the spinal canal, drew back spinal fluid to be sure I was in, and injected the anesthesia. Then I laid him down on the operating table, and just as I did, the ship took a huge roll so that his head plummeted straight down. It was almost a deadly complication because the anesthesia could paralyze the chest muscles, making the patient unable to breathe. I grabbed the crank on the operating table and cranked it up to force the anesthesia away from the head and chest muscles. Just as I had his head up, the ship rolled the other way, so I cranked the table down. Every time the ship rolled, I'd crank the other way. I kept him from being totally paralyzed, but the anesthesia level was lower than what we needed to make the incision. So we injected a local anesthesia into the incision site where we needed to cut. We told the young soldier it would hurt but it was the safest way to go. He was awake, so we could talk to him the whole time. He never once moved or said anything. The appendix was badly inflamed and retrocecal (tucked behind the colon), but we got it out.

I saw Larry only one more time after the war. Several years later we encountered each other at a medical meeting. We greeted each other warmly and swapped a few stories. "You know, Paul," he said, "I've been hoping we would see each other again." On his next voyage to Vietnam after ours, he said, exactly the same thing happened: He had a soldier with appendicitis and no anesthesiologist, but he had a doctor with some training. "We put the patient to sleep with the old machine, and his blood pressure started falling. He got worse and worse no matter what we did. We couldn't do the surgery, so he died on the table." An investigation later showed that the canister that absorbs carbon dioxide on the machine was defective. The patient died of asphyxia. "The more we would pump him with what we thought was oxygen, it was really building up CO_2 that was not absorbed by the machine, and so we killed him," Larry said. "I just wanted to tell you that you made the right decision by not using that machine, because we would have killed that patient, too."

Except for the appendicitis operation, the trip was uneventful. Because we had nothing to read and no radio, Ralph Levin suggested we try to solve math problems. He proposed we figure how far we could see a flag flying twenty feet above the water when we were standing on deck. For days, we calculated the curvature of the earth and the angles of the triangle from our perch to the top of the flag. Having no trigonometry tables made it much harder, but we finally remembered enough college math to solve the problem.

In one of the bull sessions among doctors, we were telling how far we each had to travel to reach the first duty assignment. I learned that the date one began traveling determined one's commissioning date. That is, if you were promoted to captain before someone else by even a single day, you outranked him. Because I had traveled from Houston to Fort Lewis, I had started traveling earlier than any of the other sixteen doctors in our unit and thus outranked them. Not knowing what the implications might be, I approached our company commander, Major Wiggins. He was career army, and rank was everything. When I told him I outranked the other doctors, he frowned and squinted his eyes. "I'll get back to you," he said. Two or three days later, he found me and said, "You're exactly right. I'm making you in charge of all sixteen doctors in the country."

My new rank turned out to be a double-edged sword. On the one hand, the higher rank had perks. On the ship, for example, I was allowed to move down to the field grade quarters, which meant I slept in a small comfortable bunk on the floor with no one above or below, and I could take a regular shower. The high-ranking officers had never hinted to us that they had better quarters, and I never told my friends of the improvement.

Once we deployed, however, I had to go into the field more than the other doctors, which increased my risk. It also gave me the opportunity to see the big picture. While other US doctors were assigned to a Vietnamese provincial hospital or to a village, I saw the medical care system for the whole country. I spent time with most American units and could see what effect we were having on the population. I saw on the ground the relationship between the US forces and the Vietnamese civilians. I saw the medical care of the Vietnamese people in the cities, villages, and hamlets. I was probably the only person in a position to see the country's entire health care delivery system. My vantage point gave me unique insight into the effectiveness of our doctors in the civil affairs unit.

Trolling the Saigon River

Our transport ship was supposed to land in Nha Trang on the eastern coast of Vietnam, but we were diverted to Vung Tau downriver from Saigon. At Vung Tau, the ship commander came on the speaker and said that our landing orders had changed. As a show of force, our ship would go up the Saigon River with no security and no escort to show the world that the Saigon River delta was safe.

A small group of infantry with M16 rifles boarded the ship and were stationed behind the steel plates as cover. If any boat came close, a Vietnamese with a loudspeaker would tell the boat to turn around. The riflemen had orders to fire across the bow of every boat and, if it did not stop and turn around, to kill the occupants. All troops were ordered below deck, but because I now had some rank, I went topside to see what was going on.

For a few miles, we steamed slowly up the wide, beautiful, flowing river. At first we saw no small boats because the Saigon River was almost a mile wide at the mouth. When the river narrowed to about three-quarters of a mile, we began to see sampans with two or three persons on board casting nets and fishing. The infantry grew a little more alert as boats were now about three hundred or four hundred yards away. I inched forward to the top of a stairwell, then crawled to the edge of the stairwell's steel plate, getting a view of the whole river. An infantryman was sitting beside me about a foot away with his rifle resting on another

Vietnam

On December 22, 1965, we got our first view of Vietnam from the troopship. It was a solemn moment.

steel plate. All was quiet except for the ship's engine as we cruised up the river. Several sampans were now within one hundred yards.

I never heard the rifle, just the bullet hitting the steel plate and ricocheting off the steel deck and the ship. Who knows where it came from, but it seemed as if each soldier opened fire on the sampan in his sights at the same time, the bullets hitting about a foot or two in front of the sampans.

For almost an entire day we repeated the same dance. Most of the sampans seemed to be carrying a single man or woman, probably just crossing the river as they always had. As we neared the harbor, the crew began throwing depth charges off the side every thirty seconds to kill anyone who tried to swim out and attach an explosive to the hull. Every sampan that came close or did not seem to stop quickly enough got a few quick shots across the bow.

I got my first sight of Saigon two days before Christmas. We moored in Saigon harbor in midafternoon on December 23. Except for a few hours in Guam, we had not seen land for twenty-six days.

From the ship's rail, we looked out over the harbor and Saigon beyond. Here finally was Vietnam. How terribly foreign and unknown and foreboding it all seemed! Vietnamese with heavy loads on their backs and heads scurried around on the crowded dock. Exotic sounds and smells filled the air. I vividly remember three men taking a break on the dock in the shadow of our ship sitting strangely on their legs, smoking an opium pipe, and passing it back and forth. They rested a few minutes and then went back to work.

We talked but mostly were quiet with our own thoughts. We realized that in a few days we would be on the ground with a combat unit and would be expected to provide some type of medical care. We were not really afraid but we had no idea what lay ahead, except that it was something we had never before encountered and it could all turn out very badly. It was a sobering sight.

No one was allowed off the ship except for a half dozen men sent out to resupply vegetables and find out about our landing. One man in the advance party was a big disagreeable lieutenant that no one liked because he was always picking fights and causing trouble. The party left in a borrowed jeep and was expected to return in two or three hours. We all watched from the deck. After three hours, we became concerned. Finally, after about five hours, the jeep came wheeling around the corner of the dock, driving much too fast on the crowded waterfront. The party jumped out with fresh food, which meant we would have a good Christmas dinner. About two days later, the lieutenant came down with one of the most resistant cases of gonorrhea I have ever seen.

That night, the crew continued to throw depth charges off the side, making it impossible to sleep. The next morning, Christmas Eve, we headed back down the Saigon River to the South China Sea. All the way, the riflemen fired at sampans that came too close. Even so, I was able to see the incredible beauty of Vietnam—the wide, calm river, sampans everywhere, tall trees lining the shore in the distance, and blue skies with fluffy white clouds. It had been an absurd trip, risking the lives of five thousand men just to make a point.

The Landing

After returning to Vung Tau, we turned and steamed north up the coast to Nha Trang but out of sight of land. The ship, which had a speed of seventeen knots, was going as fast as it seemed capable of moving. The sea was calm, and the sky was blue with an occasional cumulus cloud. It was oppressively hot, but the breeze and the ship's speed helped. When I lay on my back in my assigned area of the deck, I looked straight up at the blue sky and clouds. *It's just like the sky at the ranch*, I thought. In the weeks that followed, I would lie on my back and look at the sky several times, believing for a few seconds that I was in Brownwood. It would bring me feelings of comfort and safety during some of the worst times in Vietnam.

In midafternoon on Christmas Day, in response to the ship commander's order, all five thousand troops crowded shoulder to shoulder on deck. The ship seemed to slow and a deathly quiet settled over the men. When we were all in place, the commander walked to the top of a catwalk and stood on a small platform with a rail around it.

"Tomorrow at daylight we will make an amphibious landing," he said. "We expect it to be unopposed but we cannot be sure. Everyone has been issued his full amount of ammunition. You will be up at 0300 and dressed in full battle gear. The landing craft will begin circling at 0500, and the first troops will board as soon as there is enough light. We will get you as close as we can, but the beach slopes down and the landing craft will drop you a fairly long distance from shore."

Then he turned to a tall, slender, blond soldier standing close by,

My army medical unit, the Forty-First Civil Affairs Company, landed amphibiously on the Vietnam shore from the troopship that had carried us across the Pacific.

tipped his head, and said, "Lieutenant." The lieutenant sang "Danny Boy," the Irish ballad about war, death, and returning home. He sang a cappella in a beautiful, clear tenor voice with no embellishment, slowly and almost mournfully.

When he finished, a hushed silence fell upon us. The song transformed five thousand men like nothing I have ever seen. Until that moment, we were on a grand adventure. We were part of the mightiest army on earth and going to war. That experienced commander, who looked like he was surely of retirement age, was telling us that after tomorrow nothing would ever be the same, and that many would die. If you went home, home would be different, the country would be different, and we would be different.

When the lieutenant finished singing, the commander stood quietly for several seconds. Then he said slowly and straight from the heart, "Good luck, men." As it turned out, most of the troops were going to the First Air Cav, and many did not survive.

Finding it hard to sleep that night, we had no trouble getting up at 2:00 a.m. At daylight on December 26, 1965, we loaded onto the landing craft, just as we had done with the marines at Camp Pendleton. The landing craft circled and then took us to shore in one wave. About a hundred yards from shore as we waded to the beach, I looked to my right and saw the tall, lanky soldier we had operated on. He raised his rifle over his head and shouted, "Thanks, Doctor, I feel good!"

Nothing happened as we landed. On shore, we loaded onto a deuce-and-a-half (two-and-a-half-ton cargo truck) that took us to our base camp, where lush green jungle stood against a backdrop of high mountains. We soon learned that the previous night Vietcong sappers (demolition commandos) had attacked the area. They had breached the security and swept into the area throwing satchel charges into the tents. Now we knew we were in a war.

Life in the Jungle

The company headquarters in Nha Trang was set up in tents. We affectionately called it "tent city." The temperature in the tents in the afternoon got up to 135 degrees. You never got away from it. Day and night our clothes were soaked with sweat, and gradually we learned not to think much about it. Several of my doctor friends were at the US hospitals, which had air-conditioning. I was never in air-conditioning in Vietnam. I knew that if I ever went into air-conditioning, it would last only a few minutes and I would have to go back into the oppressive, unrelenting heat.

Then there was the constant rain. When you got wet, you could not dry out for days. Your clothes just stayed wet because the humidity hovered around one hundred percent night and day. So we tried to stay dry as long as possible. At times, I went for days without a shower. I promised myself that if I got out of Vietnam I would take a shower anytime I felt like it. To this day, and it has been fifty years, if I'm at the ranch and get hot, I take two or three showers a day.

I always carried a pistol, probably the same kind the army had used in the Second World War, a .45-caliber Model 1911 Automatic Colt Pistol. I was never without it, except when back at base camp, which wasn't that often. I didn't carry a rifle, and most of my doctor friends didn't either. Carrying a rifle would have contradicted our role as doctors. Our job was not to fight but to help the sick and wounded. A handheld pistol would allow us to defend ourselves if necessary.

As part of our medical civil affairs program, our job was to treat the Vietnamese sick and wounded. By contrast, doctors in US military field hospitals treated wounded American soldiers. We were not a MASH (Mobile Army Surgical Hospital) unit, like the ones that had been used in the Korean War and were depicted in the movie and the long-running TV series.

Treating the Vietnamese would prove difficult because we had no equipment, no X-ray, no laboratory, not even a stethoscope or a flashlight. Furthermore, all medication had to come through Vietnamese supply channels, which would prove extremely inefficient.

At first not much happened, and unrest grew. The doctors looked at me, wondering, *What's going on? When are we going to see some patients?* We were all idealistic, eager to help the Vietnamese, do some good, and help win the war. Although I went along to planning meetings at MACV (Military Assistance Command, Vietnam) headquarters, I was never allowed to sit inside. I had no information to pass on to the other doctors.

Eventually our sixteen teams deployed all over the country, each to a different provincial capital and attached to a different military unit, such as the marines, the First Air Cav, the 101st Airborne Division, the 173rd Airborne Brigade, or the First Infantry Division. Once attached to a military unit, the leadership of each team shifted to the unit commander.

Sick Call

In most teams, the unit commander typically would decide to hold sick call in a village or hamlet. An army unit would sweep through the area first, and the next day a medical team would go in to treat the sick and wounded. We always had an interpreter and someone to show us the way. Usually my jeep would follow a truck or deuce-and-a-half mounted with a .50-caliber machine gun. Eight or ten infantrymen would sit in the back of the truck with weapons. They were as afraid as I was because we had no way to tell where an ambush or sniper fire might come through. Our routine was to go down the road as fast as possible, get in and out quickly, and come back a different way before dark.

We never knew how many would show up for sick call. Sometimes it was a few Vietnamese, but many times hundreds came. Often the whole village turned out, pushing and shoving in a festive mood, to see what goodies the Americans were giving out that day. In addition to war wounds, they had every disease imaginable, from malaria, parasites, and plague to anemia and cancer.

One of the most common serious diseases was tuberculosis. But we could not diagnose it exactly without X-ray or laboratory. Nor could we follow up to ensure the patient took the antituberculosis drug for the prescribed one year of treatment. Often the drug was not available through the Vietnamese supply channel, and it was not practical to give a patient a year's supply, because the drug might be sold to the Vietcong, traded for other drugs, or forgotten.

Most of the sick were children and elderly. Children were always tough because we didn't speak the language. Many of the children had skin infections like impetigo, which turned out to be something we could treat. Someone came up with the idea of bringing potable water in a small trailer that was towed behind the deuce-and-a-half. All the trailer holes had been welded shut so water wouldn't leak out, and a board was floated on top so it wouldn't splash out. We showed the mothers how to wash their children's skin infections. We gave them a small bar of soap (furnished by major US hotels, the same size used in guest rooms today) and antibiotic ointment. It was often our best cure.

The Vietnamese were almost frantic to see an American doctor because they realized we were the best in the world. We heightened their expectations and then did not deliver. It turned out to be so simple and obvious. People know if they get well after seeing the doctor: you're cured or you're not. We were not curing anybody, other than those with skin infections and a few wounds. We were seeing rare, devastating illnesses and doing little to change lives long term.

I am examining a patient with a skin infection, a common malady in Vietnam and one of the few conditions we had the resources to treat.

Mothers of sick children were especially unnerving. It almost made me cry to see the look in the mothers' eyes when they handed over their sick children with the fervent hope and expectation we could help. The thing that tore my heart out was that I knew I could help them but did not have the simple equipment and medicines to do my job. It makes me feel bad to this day that the Vietnamese put so much faith in the American doctor.

To hold sick call, we would go out into the jungles during the day and come back into a base camp at night. There was no alternative: you couldn't put a secure perimeter around a village at night. When we'd come out of the village in the afternoon, the Vietcong would go back into it at night.

One day I drove my jeep by myself to the Special Forces camp outside Nha Trang to get a haircut. As I approached the camp, I saw people scurrying around and heard shots and shouts. I had no idea what was happening. Fortunately, the commotion ended as I arrived. Within a few minutes, I realized that I had driven my jeep into an ambush. I was not injured, but others were. It turned out to be the only ambush I was ever in. But it showed me that you could never know where or when you might get killed.

Vietnamese Doctors and Hospitals

We knew at that time that Vietnamese doctors were paralleling us on the other side. They would come into a hamlet after we left and spend the night with the Vietnamese. A diary kept by a North Vietnamese doctor was found by an American soldier after our forces killed her. She had been in the same area that I was in, but a year later. The diary was translated and published in 2008 under the title *Last Night I Dreamed of Peace*. It's one of the most emotional books I have ever read. It showed, as we suspected, that the North Vietnamese were winning the psychological war.

The Vietnamese had their own provincial hospitals, often primitive by American standards. At that time, a Vietnamese patient's family stayed with the patient, the whole family slept in the patient's bed, and they cooked their meals in little kettles in the courtyard and gave medication to the patient.

Many Vietnamese hospitals dealt with diseases rarely seen in industrialized nations. In one hospital, for example, I saw a ward of nothing but rabies cases. The ward was kept totally dark to prevent any stimulation from light that might cause patients to have seizures.

I saw a cholera ward that I would later have doubted existed were it not for the pictures I took. The ward had long rows of patients, each lying on a cot. Each cot had a hole with a bucket underneath. Cholera patients have diarrhea so severe they die from dehydration. The staff would put the patient over this hole so that the diarrhea would go straight into the bucket. Then they would toss the excrement out a window and put the bucket back in place. Each patient could have only one or two IVs a day, and those who needed more died. The vast majority died of dehydration. There was not much we could do.

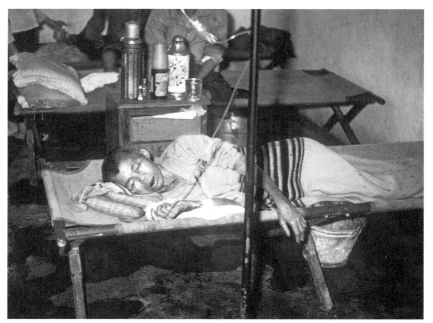

In the cholera wards of Vietnamese hospitals, a patient would lie on a cot with a hole in it where the diarrhea effluent dropped into a bucket underneath. The bucket was emptied in the yard.

A village in the central highlands of Vietnam provided the backdrop for one of the many sick calls we held during my tour of duty.

I visited most of the provinces and spent some time in many of them. The Vietnamese doctors that I observed in those hospitals were excellent surgeons but poorly trained in internal medicine. The nurses, too, had little training in modern medical practices. A few nurses were sent to the United States for training, and most did not return. The head nurse in a US I Corps province hospital came back from training in Denver and introduced the practice of recording each medication a patient received and the time. It was revolutionary in Vietnam. Even the best hospitals in the country had not done this before.

Rather than going out into the villages and hamlets, some of our teams hooked up with a provincial hospital. Several teams worked in Catholic and Mennonite hospitals and ended up doing a lot of good. I talked to some Catholic nuns and Mennonite doctors and saw their almost unbelievable courage and dedication. They were willing to risk death every day to do what they thought was right. They served for years at a time, which was the ideal way to help.

When I heard the Southern Baptists had a mission at Nha Trang, I thought that as a Southern Baptist I could find some way to put the vast resources of our company to good use. I found the small room the mission used for Bible study and asked to see the missionary. The Vietnamese woman at the desk said he was not there and would not be back for several days. She gave me directions to his home and suggested I try there.

Two or three days later, Ralph Levin and I took our jeep and after much trouble found the home. We were astounded. It was a palatial compound maybe five acres large with a security fence around it. The guards, who were expecting us, checked us through the entry. We drove up a long, winding driveway with immaculately landscaped lawns on either side, nodding to gardeners as we passed. We were met at the portico by a butler and a maid, who cordially invited us in. The butler told us the lady of the house would be with us shortly.

After thirty minutes or an hour, the missionary's wife came out. I believe she was an American. We explained that we had seventeen doctors with really not much to do. But we had the power of the US Army behind us so we could do anything that she wanted in helping the Vietnamese, such as taking care of sick people. To our astonishment, she told us in no uncertain terms that she didn't want anything to do with us. "Just leave our mission alone," she said. As I reflected on the situation, I decided they had set themselves up as a king and a queen in a poor country. All they did was hold Sunday school with a dozen or so Vietnamese and maybe Bible study once or twice a week. That was it.

I learned a lot from that experience. I learned that many people were profiting from the war. They might have written reports about the number of Vietnamese they served, but the reports might not have accurately reflected their work. A report could assert the good being done for people, which sounds great in the United States, but actually nothing was being done, or the work was counterproductive. I wrote to the Southern Baptist Convention, urging the leaders to look into the missionary's abuse of the Church's goodwill. I never heard anything back. As a result, I chose not to contribute to foreign missions and became suspicious of nonprofits.

Turning Points

It became obvious to me, after we had been in the country for a few months, that some things needed to change. There were several turning points for me.

One was a cholera epidemic. I was in Nha Trang, back at our base camp. A South Vietnamese commander told us about a severe cholera epidemic about fifty miles south, down toward Cam Ranh Bay, in a remote village that was mostly controlled by the Vietcong. The area was not secure, but we were out there all the time anyway and we wanted to help save lives. Several of us frantically scrounged cholera vaccine and IVs. It was Friday after five in the afternoon when we finally had everything ready. We knew it was dangerous, but we all had volunteered to go and were confident we could make it. I went to the South Vietnamese commander who had brought word of the epidemic and told him what we had arranged, and all he needed to do was take us down there. He looked at me and said, "Captain, it's five thirty on Friday afternoon, and we don't work on the weekends. Bring your equipment back on Monday

I rode to sick call in a jeep, often following a deuce-and-a-half truck mounted with a machine gun.

morning and we'll take you down there." I said, "By then they're going to be dead." I argued with him strenuously at the top of my voice. He said calmly, "No, it's a weekend, and we're not going." We didn't go Friday, and we didn't go Monday either. I thought, *Something's wrong with this whole war.*

Another time, I was called at around nine or ten at night to go to a little house in a remote village. A Vietnamese civilian told us a woman was in childbirth and the Vietnamese midwives couldn't deliver the baby. In their eyes, if the American doctor would come, he could save the mother and baby. I eagerly went down. I thought I was pretty good at delivering babies because I had delivered many in internship. When

I got to the patient, she was bleeding heavily. I looked around. They had absolutely no equipment, no IV, no forceps. There was no way to put the patient to sleep to do a C-section. The midwives were pretty darned good, they had done everything, and they were probably better at it than I was. All we could do was sit and watch. Both the mother and the baby died.

I had always known we were not effective without any equipment, but that night was different. It was no longer a theoretical concept but a reality right in front of my eyes. I thought maybe some of the bureaucrats who had sent us over without any planning or equipment would feel differently if they had been there that night. I never went out again. When they called me to help with a delivery, I didn't go anymore because there was nothing I could do.

Being in charge of all the other doctors in our teams, I had a unique opportunity to evaluate civil affairs. No one else had that perspective. It occurred to me that talking to the big brass might help, if I could only get to them.

Early in 1966, I heard that Major General Byron Steger was coming to Nha Trang. I had gone to the ceremony at Madigan where he had received his first star. He had received his second star while I was at Fort Gordon. Now he was the top general for all medical aspects in the Pacific. Here was my chance. Ralph Levin and I arranged an invitation to a cocktail party for General Steger at the MACV headquarters. Because we knew we would have only a minute with him, we practiced exactly what I was going to say. I knew he would recognize me because he had a quirky way of remembering people's names.

We arrived at the cocktail party early and immediately felt out of place. When General Steger came in with his entourage, we had to wait for about thirty minutes until we felt we could approach him. When we did, I said, "General Steger, I'm Paul Burns. I was one of your interns at Madigan." He said, "Oh, yes, Captain Burns, one of our finest interns." I'm sure he barely knew me at Madigan, and I doubt he knew how I did there. He asked how I was doing and what my job was. "I'm in charge of all the medical affairs of our civil affairs company," I said. I explained how I had been all over the country and that I was convinced that civil

Arriving for sick call, this time at a Catholic school in the jungle near Bien Hoa, we were overwhelmed with patients. Tragically, we never had the necessary medical equipment and had only an hour to see patients.

affairs in Vietnam was counterproductive. I told him that the doctors were eager to do a good job but they were not effective and never would be the way it was organized. He looked at me, put his hand on my shoulder, and said, "Captain, I know you and all of you young men out here are doing a fine job. Keep up the good work." He turned around and walked off. Ralph and I stood speechless. We had never expected that response. The general's mind was closed, and the visit was just for show. I knew at that moment that the civil affairs concept would never be successful in Vietnam. I also realized that this war was not worth being killed over.

I learned much later that General Steger's whole purpose in coming to Nha Trang was to evaluate civil affairs in Vietnam. He was to decide just what I asked him about: how to organize medical care to the Vietnamese civilians, whose command it should be under, and how the doctors should interact with our chain of command and with the Vietnamese. But our commanders seemed more interested in their careers than in Vietnamese civilians. As far as I could tell, no one was particularly interested in whether civil affairs was effective or not. It was much like Defense Secretary Robert McNamara's later emphasis on numbers—the body count of the Vietcong after an engagement. American officers were more concerned about their efficiency reports, or ERs. If we saw fifty patients one day, they wanted us to see seventy-five the next day. No one asked how many patients were cured.

I have always felt conflicted about Vietnam. I served in an elite unit with physicians and other professionals. We did our best. I was proud of our work there and still am. At the same time, I feel extreme remorse because we accomplished little or nothing. We never had a clear mission. We were never told in specifics what we were to accomplish. Our company commanders were never able to articulate a mission because they never had the clout to tell the people up the chain what we could or should be doing. I didn't know it at the time, but our leaders in Washington didn't have a clue either. Early on, President Johnson was focused on getting his Great Society program passed by Congress, and military leaders disagreed on how to win the war. Many books have since been written about our failure in Vietnam, but I believe the army scholar H. R. McMaster came closest with his meticulous analysis of the shortcomings of both the administration and the military in *Dereliction of Duty: Lyndon Johnson, Robert McNamara, the Joint Chiefs of Staff, and the Lies That Led to Vietnam* (1997).

From my vantage point on the ground, I could see that our policy in Vietnam was fatally flawed. I wasn't sitting in some office in the Pentagon or at the CIA dreaming up something that might have sounded good on paper. I could see that medicine as a tool of psychological warfare is incredibly complex. I saw the physical toll that the war took on civilians and their dismay and distress when we could do nothing. I got a firsthand look at the medical delivery over the whole country. I saw on the local level what the Vietnamese needed and what we could and could not accomplish. I think I understood the medical aspects of civil affairs as well as anyone because, as far as I know, no one had as much experience and insight as I did. I saw what we were doing on a daily basis and desperately wanted to tell someone that it was not working. But no one seemed to understand or really care. In my entire life, I have never seen such arrogance and misplaced self-confidence at the planning level.

The Best and the Worst

I saw the best and the worst in the Vietnamese. Most civilians were uneducated and desperately poor. But inside they were just like us. They wanted to be safe, raise their families, earn a living, have enough to eat, and enjoy what comfort and pleasure they could muster. They clung to their children just as I clung to my daughters and wanted them to be safe and happy.

I also saw the best and the worst in American soldiers. One night at base camp I saw a couple of lieutenants trying to make out with two teenage Vietnamese girls. Their mother worked in the base camp picking up trash and doing other menial tasks. I had never paid any attention to the girls; I didn't know anything about them, not even their names. At the time, I didn't think much about it. But when I saw the men hassling the girls another time, I realized they were not trying to make out with the girls—it was rape. As a captain in the Medical Corps, I didn't have any authority over them because I was out of their chain of command. I wasn't much older than they were either. But I decided I couldn't pass it by. "Look," I said to the lieutenants, "if you ever bother those girls again, I will see to it that your careers are ruined. And if the army doesn't do it, I'll do it myself." They let the girls go.

Two incidents still trouble me today. The first happened one day when I was getting ready to leave base camp to go on sick call in a village. The Vietcong generally knew where we were going, and it was obvious which roads we would take. Right before we were to leave, someone came in and said sick call was canceled. I asked him why. "Last night some Vietcong soldiers were captured and interrogated. They had an ambush set for where you were going today." Interrogations were always conducted by Vietnamese, and I don't know whether torture was used in this particular instance. But those Vietcong were tough guys, and I'm sure they didn't give up that little bit of information freely.

That incident taught me that I cannot sit here and say philosophically, "Well, I'm totally against torture. Torture is wrong." It's not all black and white. I'm sitting here today because a harsh interrogation yielded information about a planned ambush.

Another time, a person (I don't remember his name) told me about free-fire zones. These were areas completely controlled by the Vietcong, and anyone in those areas was the enemy and could be killed. This person told me that on a day when he wasn't busy, he would occasionally go up in a spotter plane, fly over a free-fire zone, and shoot people. B-52s would bomb these areas, but this man would go there in a small plane and shoot people out in the open with his .45. Then the pilot would circle back so he could empty another clip into his victim. When he told me that story, he asked if I wanted to do it. "It's exhilarating," he said. I declined and didn't think much about it at the time. But it troubles me today that I didn't criticize him for doing it.

These incidents show how war can affect you. When you're there at the moment and you see those bodies coming in, you see wounded Vietnamese in hospitals, and you see terrible destruction all around, you wonder, *Who am I to judge?* It's easy to feel morally superior when you're back in America surrounded by luxury and comfort, but it's more complicated than that. We should be careful about criticizing what a soldier does in the heat of battle or over enemy territory.

The war was hard on the doctors in our company. At least one doctor was injured in a mortar attack and received a Purple Heart. Another doctor refused to go out on a dangerous assignment, and I volunteered to go in his place. (I could have sent another doctor, but I decided that if I were not willing to go, I could not ask anyone else.) The doctor was sent back to the States with a medical discharge for shell shock (what we would call post-traumatic stress disorder today)—the only person I knew in my company who left early. Fortunately, we did not have a single doctor who was killed while I was there. That's because we were very careful. And we were lucky that the Vietnamese soldiers who got us in and out of villages were not spies or Vietcong.

Despite the tension and strain of war, I think the doctors, to the person, found their service rewarding. We thought we did some good and you could always help a few. After the army, I never saw or heard from any of those doctors again, except for Ralph Levin. We ran into each other at a medical meeting in Chicago about five years after we left Vietnam. He did his residency at the University of Chicago. I learned later that he died young of a brain tumor.

Leaving Vietnam

With the end of my two-year army commitment approaching, I asked my commander for permission to write an after-action report. I wrote it in pencil in the field, and a sergeant typed it on a manual typewriter in a tent at the edge of the jungle. He attached a second carbon so I could keep a copy. In that five-page report, which is printed in the back of this book, I condemned the lack of an explicit mission for our civil affairs company and the lack of medical equipment. I described the primitive medical care in Vietnamese hospitals and the impossibility of improving it among an uneducated populace: "Healing the sick is not something that can be passed out like rice." I suggested that those in policy-making positions were not interested in a true program so long as it looked good on paper. There was no way to scientifically determine the psychological impact of our medical care, I explained, and holding sick call from village to village "possibly does more long-lasting harm than good." I suggested training the Vietnamese so that they could assume responsibility for their own health care, a process that would take a minimum of six or seven years. After I turned in the report, no one ever called me or asked me to explain my findings. I wondered whether anyone paid attention to it. At least I gave the army my honest appraisal and recommendations.

Before my departure in late June 1966, I didn't tell anybody I was leaving, except a few close friends. It was kept secret because killing someone during his last few days in Vietnam was an insidious way to demoralize us. It got everybody's attention. The morning I left, I put my belongings in my duffel bag, and another doctor and I got in my jeep and headed to the airfield, which was several miles away. We left Nha Trang, a secure area, and went through an insecure area to get to the airfield, which was secure. We stopped at a checkpoint, got out of the jeep, and carried our duffel bags through the gate to the helicopter. Just as we were getting ready to leave the insecure area, out of the corner of my eye I saw someone running full speed right toward me. *Someone's got a grenade*, I thought, *and they're going to toss that grenade on me, and I'm going to die right here on my way out of Vietnam.* I jerked to my right to see who it was and saw a Vietnamese woman only ten steps away. I vaguely recognized her, and I could tell by the look on her face that she was not going to kill me. She thrust a folded piece of paper at me and never said a word. I put it in my pocket without looking at it, and in a few steps reached the secure area. I threw my duffel bag into the waiting helicopter, jumped in, and felt the helicopter lift off. The person beside me said, "What in the world was that?" I said, "I have no idea but I thought I was going to get killed."

Some time later, I opened the paper. It was a handwritten note. At first I was confused. Then I realized it was from the mother of those two teenage girls. She thanked me for chasing off those lieutenants. I'd never suspected she knew about it. The note was written in very poor English, so she obviously had someone translate her message. It was fairly short, but she said she knew I was leaving, she would never see me again, she would always think of me, she wished that sometime she could see me again, and she wished me well. The note was signed, but the name didn't mean anything to me. I never knew anything about that Vietnamese family. I just saw that something was not right and did something about it. Someone could have shot her as she ran out to us, but she was determined to thank me. I think that incident made me a better doctor. A small bit of kindness or concern or help may have a profound effect on someone sick, or worried, or in trouble. You just never know.

Our helicopter flew to Tan Son Nhut Air Base in Saigon. We were supposed to go out the next morning but were delayed. Lots of men, mostly from the First Infantry Division and the First Air Cav, were stuck there too, probably because of some scheduling problem. We slept on the floor for a couple of nights, waiting for a departing plane. We saw

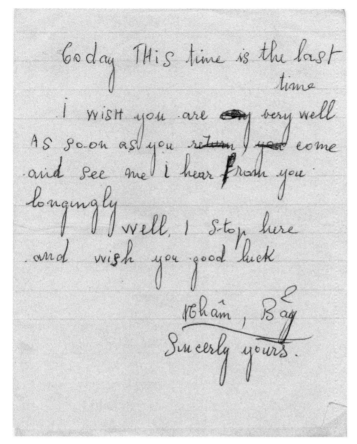

A Vietnamese woman rushed to get me this handwritten note as I was leaving the country in order to thank me for preventing other soldiers from accosting her daughters. It has served as a reminder that a small bit of kindness can make a big difference.

planes leaving with civilians in newly tailored, soldier-of-fortune jackets and carrying Australian bush hats to show the folks back home they had been to Vietnam. They were probably from the State Department and the press corps. Having to wait while they were treated royally was one last indignity.

I was desperate to leave Vietnam because I had been accepted for residency at Baylor, which would begin July 1, and I had no way to tell Baylor—or my family—that I would be late. The army allowed us only one phone call a year, and I had already made mine a month earlier. Letters were completely out of the question because they took two weeks to get to the States and two weeks to get back. I had no way to notify my family, and I knew they would worry when I didn't show up as expected.

One afternoon while waiting, we learned that a Vietnamese band would entertain us that night. The band arrived at about dark and set up in a temporary building that had a tin roof, sides of cheap plywood, and screen netting to keep out the mosquitoes. After dining on C rations, about two hundred of us went to hear the band. We were surprised to see a small stage with huge speakers and a few lightbulbs. We were even more surprised to hear them sing American pop songs, all from memory with no accent. After playing for a couple of hours, they started singing "Detroit City," the classic Bobby Bare song.

When they got to the chorus, the soldiers all joined in. They cranked up the volume and sang the chorus three or four times: "I want to go home, I want to go home." The men got louder and louder. It was wonderful. Everybody was singing at the top of his lungs. A sergeant who had fought with the First Infantry Division for a year went to the front door, tore it off its hinges, and slammed it down. The Vietnamese band kept singing. When they realized what had happened, they sang louder. We all sang louder. Other men started ripping down the screens and pulling down the plywood sides. When the building was about half gone, I yelled to a friend of mine, "Man, I don't want to get in trouble, so I'm getting the hell out of here." We left. When we went by there the next day, nothing was left but a pile of tin and plywood.

The next day I checked in as if nothing had happened. "Captain, can't get you out of Saigon, but I think I can get you out of Pleiku," the corporal said. "I'm gonna fly you up to Pleiku today and maybe you can get out of there within a day or two." I flew to Pleiku and the next day I and a couple of hundred men from the First Air Cav waited by the runway for a big jet cargo plane to land. The major in charge took a group of us aside. "Men, we don't like these planes getting mortared on the runway," he said. "We're gonna bring this thing in, get those men off that plane as fast as we can, and when the last man comes by you, I want you running to that airplane. They're gonna keep the jets running as high as they can, and as soon as the last boot lifts off the ground, the plane's gonna start down the runway while the back cargo door comes up. So get on that plane if you want to go home."

The plane touched down and came to a hard stop. The back door was already down and the new men were streaming off. The departing men welcomed them to Vietnam with all the obscenities they could think of with a few suggestions of what they could expect. We ran to that plane, scrambled up the cargo door, and strapped ourselves into the webbing on the sides of the plane. As the cargo door slowly came up, the plane headed down the runway with every jet screaming and the plane shaking. The pilot circled that big jet just as hard as that thing could possibly climb, straight up and circling until we got up. And when we finally leveled off, there was a huge shout. We knew we were out, we were away from the antiaircraft fire, and we were going home. In that moment, I experienced enormous relief. It surprised me. My mind had been operating at a peak of intensity the whole time I was in Vietnam, and suddenly it was over.

I got word that the pilot of the plane wanted to talk to me. "Captain, you're the ranking officer on the plane so you're in charge," he said. "We're gonna land and get fuel in Taiwan and in Japan. It's your responsibility to get every one of these men back on the plane. We're not waiting for anybody, and it's your ass, you're getting everybody back." I protested: "Look, I'm a medical officer and can't be in command of infantrymen." He said, "Captain, I'm not gonna argue with you. You're in charge." That was my last order in Vietnam.

I didn't have any trouble getting the men back on the plane in Taiwan and Japan. We flew across to Alaska and then to San Francisco. I don't remember much about the flight. We all slept.

Getting Out of the Army

I don't remember exactly where we landed in San Francisco, but it was probably Travis Air Force Base. I was tired and wanted one thing: to get out of the army. The clerk asked if I was having any trouble with an illness or anything else. "Man, I don't have any trouble at all," I said. Did

I want to apply for any kind of disability, such as hearing loss? "I am perfect," I said. "Okay, Captain, [stamp], you're out."

I headed for the San Francisco International Airport, still in the same US Army uniform I was wearing when I left Pleiku a few days before. I caught the first Braniff Airways flight I could get on that was going to Dallas. To get half-price fare, we had to fly in uniform and on standby. I didn't have enough money to fly any other way.

When I boarded the plane, I found a seat by a window. A young woman sat down in the aisle seat next to me. We said nothing. Well into the flight, she observed my uniform and asked where I had been and where I was going. "Vietnam," I said. "I'm going home." She asked what it was like and what I did there. I naively answered her question, completely unaware of the growing opposition to the war at home. When I finished explaining how we treated wounded and sick Vietnamese, she looked at me with mocking eyes: "Did you kill any Vietnamese babies?" Her sarcastic voice slashed me like a knife. I was speechless. I had done my best, braved horrific conditions in the jungle, and risked my life trying to help people, and this is what I got.

I landed too late in Dallas to catch the evening Trans-Texas flight that flew over our ranch every afternoon at five thirty. That night I slept on the floor at Love Field (DFW would not open until 1974) so I would be sure to catch the early morning flight to Brownwood. I called my family and told them I would be home the next morning.

When I disembarked in Brownwood, I was surprised to see a small group of people standing by the runway. They were holding a handmade sign: "Welcome home, Paul." A motel on the outskirts of town had a much larger sign on its marquee: "Welcome home, Dr. Burns." I was the first from my town to go to Vietnam. Before the war ended, eleven Brownwood men would be killed in Vietnam.

I was thrilled to see my family. I hugged my six-year-old daughter, Margaret Ann, and reached out to my four-year-old, Laura. To my chagrin, she turned away, not knowing who I was. It took weeks for her to get comfortable with me. Later as I reflected on it, I realized Vietnam had a profound effect not only on the soldiers but also on their marriages and children. Some marriages did not survive.

Vietnam

When I returned home from Vietnam in June 1966, the Holiday Inn in Brownwood greeted me with this marquee.

I was eager to go to Houston to start my residency, but my father persuaded me to delay by one day to speak to the Rotary Club, in which he was an officer, at the Hotel Brownwood. The next day I walked into a packed, standing-room-only crowd. They welcomed me with a long standing ovation. I told them that the doctors in our company were the cream of the crop, smart, dedicated, willing to do whatever our country asked of them. We could win the war in Vietnam, I said, but I doubted we would.

What I didn't know at the time was that I would have a recurrent nightmare. In the nightmare, I'm standing beside a man in Vietnam who gets shot in the chest and the blood squirts on me. I would wake up sweating and terrified. In another version, I get orders to go to Vietnam and I think, *Oh, no, I've already been there.* But I can't get out of it and

I get shipped out. I'm issued weapons and then arrive in Vietnam. At that point, I would wake up. I would feel helpless and couldn't go back to sleep for hours. Sometimes I would have the nightmare frequently and then go weeks without it. Reading a book or talking about Vietnam would trigger the nightmare to come back, just as vividly as if I were still there. So I tried to avoid the subject altogether.

In addition, I would sometimes have a frightening flashback. When driving down a remote highway, like between Goldthwaite and Brownwood, all of a sudden I would think, *My God, this could be an ambush.* It would happen in a millisecond and then I would realize where I was.

I understand that today returning soldiers have access to therapy and counseling. I guess it helps. But I didn't want therapy and I didn't have any. I used to think I worked through it pretty well on my own, but recently, after reading Sebastian Junger's *Tribe: On Homecoming and Belonging*, I came to think I had the advantage of belonging to a "tribe," my fellow students at Baylor, where I felt needed and supported.

Another reason I don't talk about Vietnam is that no one would understand. Like the passenger on my flight home, people who haven't been in it don't understand what war is like. They don't understand why you do things in war that you would never do otherwise. War is surprisingly like the medical profession: you're admitted to an exclusive club. Soldiers and surgeons don't talk about their finest or lowest hour except to other soldiers and surgeons. We don't need accolades from the public. The highest praise is a simple nod from a fellow soldier or surgeon that he admires what you did.

CHAPTER 5

Residency

My first choice for a residency program was Baylor, where I had finished medical school. I thought it would be as good a residency as any in the world, and I believed I would be as well trained as it was possible to be trained in the ear, nose, and throat (ENT, or otolaryngology) specialty.

I started the program a few days late because of the delay in leaving Vietnam and the need to move my family from Brownwood to Houston. Not only did my fellow residents have a bit of a head start, but they also assumed that my service in Vietnam made me experienced in medicine, particularly trauma medicine.

Actually, the opposite was true and I knew it. I had spent two years without taking care of any patients and I was a little rusty. I had not been in an operating room during that time. I had been in Vietnamese hospitals, but I never once set foot in a US hospital, not even a hospital anteroom. When I first began caring for patients at Baylor, I realized I had forgotten small technical details, such as how to put the tube in the IV. Fortunately, I remembered the basics of surgery because they had been deeply ingrained in my brain during previous training.

What made things worse was that occasionally I would wake up while on call with horrible dreams about Vietnam. If I sat up for an hour or two in the middle of the night, the nightmares would go away and I would be able to go back to sleep. Over the years, the dreams seemed to come in waves. I had a lot at first and then there were periods when I didn't have quite so many, but they would always come back.

Practicing Medicine as a Resident

Residents practice medicine under the close supervision of well-established professionals. The training lasts for three to seven years depending on the program and the specialty. My residency was one year of general surgery and three years of ear, nose, and throat. As residents, we took on increased responsibility each year, gaining more independence with each step up the ladder.

At Baylor, residents were given full responsibility for a patient's care, even if we were in our first year. It was our job to call for help if we needed it. A first-year resident would call a second-year resident, and if the latter needed help, he or she would call a third-year, and so on. Experienced staff physicians were always available, particularly for seriously ill patients or complicated cases. If you didn't need help, it was your responsibility to go ahead and treat the patient and then answer to the staff physician either in the clinic or on rounds at the hospital. One of my fellow residents who erred in not calling for help was promptly dismissed. (Fortunately for him, he completed his residency in another program and was able to practice medicine.)

We had grand rounds once a week. Each resident chose his or her most difficult case and presented it to a group of staff physicians. Each presentation began with a complete history and physical, then the results of lab, X-ray, and any special tests, and finally the diagnosis and proposed treatment. Staff would question every decision and expect us to defend the care and quote the pertinent studies from the literature. It was always candid and straightforward.

Grand rounds took place in front of all our fellow residents, which meant huge peer pressure to do well. I always spent a few extra minutes memorizing all the lab and X-ray data in the hope that I could answer every question. It was no time to screw up. It was the traditional training of a physician, with a lot of give-and-take.

At the time, first-year residents were physically in the hospital for 100 to 110 hours in a typical week, which made it a grueling, sleep-deprived time. Often we would work 36 hours at a stretch without rest. Accreditation standards have since limited work hours to no more than 80 hours

Residency

At Baylor Medical School, the faculty physicians in the Department of Otolaryngology—Head and Neck Surgery were (*front row, left to right*) Ben Nail, Bobby Alford, Roy Sessions, and Ray Dickie. Residents were (*from left*) Sam Weber, me, Johan Yaneke, Allen Weaver, Gail Neely, Dick Grayson, Buddy Horwitz, Jack Rosenberg, Cary Stratton, and Doug Lamppin.

a week. The issue is how to balance physician training with patient needs. Fewer hours are believed to reduce mistakes by sleep-deprived doctors, but limited hours can also hamper doctors in following their patients and transitioning to incoming staff. Fewer hours also deprive residents of seeing the vast panorama of medical cases that you have to see in order to be well trained. If you're there only 40 to 60 hours a week, you're not going to see all those complicated, interesting cases that you need to know. In the middle of the night, you have more responsibility because your senior resident or the staff physician is asleep and you see the patient. You have to evaluate the case and then decide what to do and whether to call for help. Your judgment is on the line. If you're not in the hospital night after night, seeing patients and dealing with emergencies, then how are you to make good medical care decisions? In my mind, there's no other way to develop that judgment unless you actually do it.

The training programs have changed a lot, some for the better. I can honestly say that in my own experience and that of my fellow residents, errors were not made in the middle of the night because of fatigue. We got ourselves geared up for it and took care of patients no matter how tired we were. I think that we left with the advantage of having had vastly greater experience and responsibilities.

Some observers would argue that today's residents, with their use of electronic data systems, have faster, more accurate, and more efficient ways of storing and transferring patient records. But a disadvantage I have seen is the lack of doctor-to-doctor information exchange. At Baylor and later in my practice, I would personally hand off a patient's chart to the next doctor seeing the patient. Our vocal tone and facial expression conveyed subtle and not-so-subtle concerns that a computer screen cannot. And with the change to hospitalists (physicians who practice only in the hospital and have no office practice), the information gap has grown even wider. I understand that change is necessary and constant, and we take the bad with the good. The issue here is how the bad may affect the patient.

Truly caring about our patients was a theme that permeated residency at Baylor. It characterized several of my fellow ENT residents, notably Richard Grayson, Jack Rosenberg, Allen Weaver, Sam Weber, Melton "Buddy" Horwitz, and Gail Neely. All went on to brilliant careers and were some of the greatest people I've known in my life. Buddy and Gail were a year behind me, and both became internationally renowned. Buddy's career included teaching ENT at Baylor, and Gail chaired the University of Oklahoma's ENT department for a number of years. Sam is clinical professor of ENT at Baylor and the University of Texas Medical Branch at Galveston, and was chief of otolaryngology at St. Luke's Hospital for many years. Richard is still practicing ear, nose, and throat in Pensacola, Florida. Three have passed away: Allen died from a tumor in his spine, Jack from Lou Gehrig's disease, and Gail from pulmonary fibrosis. They all made the four years of residency some of the best of my life.

First Year: General Surgery

I began my residency under Dr. Bobby Alford, the chairman of the otolaryngology department. I spent three months on his service and was with him much of every day. My group was the first group of residents that he fully trained. He was a superb ear surgeon, the person that I would use as a model of impeccable clinical judgment in my practice. He always made the right diagnosis. He also had ultimate power over a resident's career prospects. He determined whether you finished your residency and whether you were eligible for national ENT board certification. He was uncompromising with us. He tolerated nothing but the best. He expected us to be the best residents in the whole Baylor program and did not tolerate anything less than that. He was such an exceptional physician and educator that the ENT department at Baylor now bears his name.

For my year of general surgery, I had three months of facial plastic surgery and neurosurgery, three months in charge of the emergency room at Ben Taub Hospital, and six months of general surgery. This first year prepares you in a broad sense to be a more complete surgeon. You develop skills that are common to all surgery, you learn to handle any emergency, you see many surgeons operate, and, most important, you get a concept of the entire field that can come only from firsthand experience. You cannot learn this from a simulator or out of a book or by an explanation from someone. That is why the training is so long. You have to be there to worry about the patient and to learn from the best in the world.

My first rotation was facial plastic surgery and neurosurgery, a combined rotation for three months. It gave me a real love of plastic reconstructive facial surgery that I carried over to the rest of my career. I enjoyed doing rhinoplasties (nose) and otoplasties (external ear) and did a lot of them later in my Austin practice. The neurosurgery rotation was excellent. I would see a head trauma case first in the emergency room and call the senior resident if the patient needed to go to surgery.

My second rotation, being in charge of the emergency room at Ben Taub, was the plum rotation for general surgery residents. Ben Taub, which was named after a Houston philanthropist, had opened just three years earlier (1963) as the city's public hospital in the Texas Medical Center. At that time it was the largest emergency room in the world. It was, and still is, one of the finest teaching hospitals anywhere in the world and is unsurpassed for its emergency room care.

I had the good fortune to have the Ben Taub rotation in October, November, and December of 1966. My routine was to arrive at the ER at 6:00 a.m. and make rounds with the doctor in charge from the previous twenty-four-hour shift. We would see every patient in the ER and go over what the problem was, what had been done, and what needed to be done. I would check the physical findings on each patient, go over the lab work, and look at each X-ray. I read every X-ray myself because I was responsible.

Usually there would be some lulls, but on payday Saturday before Christmas in December the stream of emergencies never stopped. On payday Saturday, many workers spend their paychecks on drinking sprees, get into fights, and come in with knife and gunshot wounds. Two cases from that night, December 17, 1966, stand out in my memory.

The first occurred at about 9:00 p.m. Although it was fairly routine for payday Saturday, it signaled that we had a bad night coming. The EMS technicians brought in a man who had been shot in the face and abdomen. He was drunk, fighting everything we tried to do, vomiting Chinese food, and bleeding from his nose and mouth. We started two IVs with large catheters, began fluids, and ordered blood. We immediately took him to X-ray and got skull, chest, and abdomen films with contrast injected to outline the kidneys. Looking at the films, I was relieved to see the brain had not been hit. But a catheter in the abdomen was showing blood, and we were barely keeping up with the bleeding. We quickly sent him to the operating room, and the crew immediately cleaned the ER for the next case.

In a second gunshot case, a man arrived in the emergency room barely conscious and obviously bleeding to death. "Multiple gunshot wounds," the EMS technician said. We moved the man immediately to the operating bed of the shock room and swung into action. A nurse cut off his clothes, revealing several gunshot wounds in his chest. Simultaneously, two interns inserted IV catheters and began fluids and blood in his veins, a nurse attached EKG leads, and I inserted a tube in his trachea and began breathing for him. He was losing blood faster than we could replace it.

I reached for the knife that was always on the wall, cut open his chest, and inserted rib spreaders. I was astonished to see five tiny holes in his heart, each squirting out blood with every beat. One shot to the heart should have killed him, but this man had five! I closed each hole with a well-practiced suture and put in chest tubes to inflate the collapsed lungs. We waited. The bleeding stopped, and the lungs began feebly filling and expelling air. When he was stabilized, we sent him to intensive care. He went home a few days later.

During my twenty-four-hour shift that payday Saturday, we had twenty-four shock-room cases (that is, gunshot or stabbed patients in shock when they came in), plus a hundred or so lesser injuries from auto accidents and drunken brawls. It was thought to be an all-time record up to that time, a fact the staff fully appreciated.

The next Monday at rounds, I presented my most complicated case, knowing I had handled the ER extremely well. The senior staff physician gave the slightest nod of his head and said quietly, "Good job." I was profoundly moved. Superior performance was the norm, and almost no one was acknowledged for it.

Being in charge of the emergency room was a bit like going to Vietnam in that it establishes one's reputation with peers. If you can handle the emergency room in the busiest time—some would say chaos—and if you do it well, then you have a little status among the other residents. It was a rite of passage.

By far the most unusual case at Ben Taub—not on payday Saturday but another night—happened when two EMS technicians came in, one pushing an end of the stretcher and another running alongside holding a metal chair whose steel leg was implanted in the patient's skull. The man had been drunk, got into a barroom fight, and was knocked down. One of the combatants had picked up the chair and hit him in the head, driving the chair leg into his brain. The technicians had wisely not tried to pull it out. The patient somehow made it to the hospital still alive. We recognized this was no job for the ER. We stabilized him as best we could and sent him to the operating room. There a neurosurgeon extricated the chair leg, and the man died.

At Ben Taub I worked every other day, twenty-four hours on and twenty-four hours off, for three months. I was on for twenty-four hours seeing emergencies straight through, never stopping, and rarely getting any sleep. I went home dead tired from being up all night and went straight to bed. I slept until the middle of the afternoon, got up about three or four, ate supper, and went right back to bed. I knew I had to get as many hours of sleep as I could because for the next twenty-four hours I would be up all day and all night again. For three months I didn't do anything but work and sleep. Fortunately, I had no worries about my family. I knew my wife was taking good care of our girls.

A few residents broke under the physical, mental, and emotional strain. If you broke, you were dismissed from residency and you had to find another one or do something else. It was ruthless and we all knew that. There was no real dishonor in being dismissed from a good residency program like Baylor's. Some very good doctors just could not do it and were dismissed. But we all realized that if you could handle the emergency room, then you could probably handle everything else. I was thrilled to get the ER rotation but more thrilled to finish it. It was as hard as anything I have ever done.

My next rotation was also at Ben Taub, not the emergency room but general surgery. It was another plum assignment. I got to do a fair amount of surgery, such as repairing a hernia or removing an appendix, and dealt with constant trauma, such as a stab wound to the bowel, for example. Much of this surgery occurred at night.

The last rotation of my first year of general surgery residency was at the adjoined private hospitals, St. Luke's Episcopal and Texas Children's, in the Texas Medical Center. The disadvantage of this rotation was that I didn't get to do much myself. On a private hospital rotation, I would work up the patients for the private doctors, assist the doctor in the surgery, but mostly just watch how a doctor handled a case.

Among St. Luke's legendary staff were Dr. William Seybold, chief of surgery, and Dr. Denton Cooley, renowned heart surgeon. With Dr. Seybold, I observed that many doctors would ask his opinion, and he always told them exactly what he thought even if it was critical of them. I decided to do the same. Often when a fellow doctor asks for a second opinion, the doctor expects to hear a confirmation of his or her care. Something like, "Well, yeah, that sounds like a complicated case and it sounds like you're handling it well. I'm sure you've got a lot of experience and I'm sure you're doing just fine on it." I always felt that was a cop-out. Later, in my practice, when doctors asked me what I thought about their cases, I always said exactly whether I thought they were doing the right thing or the wrong thing. Then I went on about my business, and they went on about theirs. We stayed mutually respectful colleagues and good friends.

Dr. Cooley did not have me in his service, but if I wasn't doing anything, I could drop in and watch him operate. I learned a lot just watching him. I once found myself alone with Dr. Cooley in the surgical doctors' lounge. He was between cases and getting a cup of coffee. He was arguably one of the greatest surgeons alive and I felt awestruck to have the privilege of exchanging a few words with him. I asked him what I could do to be a great surgeon. He took the question seriously. "Go see the great surgeons of the world," he said after a moment. "Do not look at what spectacular surgery they are doing, but study each detail intensely and closely. How do they hold their scissors, how do they fit their fingers into the hemostat, how do they tie a knot? Study every minute detail because they have spent their lives getting each one exactly right. Practice it the rest of your life, and if you do that, you can be better than any of the great surgeons."

What he said was true. If you observe the tiny technical details of what made them good, then you could be as good as you possibly could be. Being a great surgeon is the sum of a thousand things put together perfectly. I did what he recommended. I went to see great surgeons operate, and there were many in Houston. I observed such details as which hand they used in different situations, how they positioned the hand to receive an instrument from the surgical nurse, how they held forceps in their fingers, how they handled tissue with forceps, which tissue they cut with a knife and which with scissors, and where on the shaft of the scissors they placed the index finger. Then I practiced those details. I would tie sutures to the back of a chair every night and practice tying knots. I would tie with the right hand, then the left, tie with one finger and then three fingers, tie a square knot, then a slipknot, slip a knot down and then secure it with a square knot or two, and tie it with a hemostat. I did it ten thousand times and never stopped practicing for my entire career. It's not the ten thousand times you do it. What makes the difference is that you are pushing yourself to do it better, smoother, and faster each time. I did the same thing with a hundred other motions in surgery until I could do them just right.

Gaining access to observe a surgeon in the operating room was easy in those days. All you had to do was ask the surgeon. There were no restrictions from the hospital, for example, nor any forms that you had to fill out. You just asked the surgeon if you could watch his surgery that day. If he said yes, then you scrubbed in, stood behind him, didn't get in the way, kept quiet, didn't disrupt anything, and just observed him. All the surgeons were glad to help, and I never had anyone say no. When I was practicing, if anyone asked me about observing in the operating room, I never said no. I even had reporters come into the operating room. I think there are restrictions on observing surgery nowadays, and I don't think there should be. I don't think any harm ever came from it and nothing but good comes of it.

Dr. Michael DeBakey at Methodist Hospital was different. He did surgery in an amphitheater setting. Observers would watch him from up above in a glass-enclosed ceiling where they could look down upon him. But all the other great surgeons let you look over their shoulder.

Three Years: Ear, Nose, and Throat

In the three years of ENT training, I rotated through all the subspecialty fields of larynx, voice, esophageal, ear, sinus, nasal, cancer, allergy, infections, trauma of the head and neck, and plastic surgery of the face. It is actually a broad specialty, a lot like family practice. That's the main reason I liked it. You can do mainly surgery or have only an office practice.

During the rotation, we would usually do surgery in the mornings, three or four times a week. In the afternoons we ran the charity clinics either at the VA hospital or at Ben Taub. If we were on call at night, we made rounds to see all the patients and then checked on them off and on all night, depending on how critical they were. If we were on call, we were ultimately responsible for their care all night. We were also on call for the emergency room, which would often keep us up the whole night. Sometimes we could slip in a few hours of sleep, eat breakfast in the morning, and then start the fourth eight-hour shift. In the morning, the nurses, the next set of residents, and the staff came in all fresh and rested. Meanwhile, you had been working for three eight-hour shifts and were starting your fourth just as it was getting light outside. It was hard, but we did it.

In addition to training under Dr. Alford, I learned ear surgery under Dr. Fred Guilford, one of the most famous ear surgeons who ever lived. He was the only professor in my residency that I didn't get along with. I suspect he did not particularly like me either. He was outrageously demanding, yet I learned a lot from him. What I didn't like was that he would constantly belittle the residents. I had been back from Vietnam only two years, and I was in no mood to let him belittle me. The day after Richard Nixon was elected president, on November 6, 1968, another resident and I were talking about the election while we were waiting for a patient to be brought in for surgery. Eight months before, in March, President Johnson had startled the nation by announcing that he would not seek reelection, which many observers attributed to abysmal public support for the Vietnam War. Dr. Guilford never liked anyone talking about anything at any time; we were supposed to sit around quietly waiting for him to say or do something. On this day, nothing else was going on, and Dr. Guilford lit into us with a storm of disparaging comments. I didn't apologize or back down: "We were just talking," I said. That innocuous response set him off again. "You're talking back to me," he ranted, spewing a fiery rebuke. Everybody stiffened, alarmed at what might happen next. As soon as I got out of Dr. Guilford's operating room, I went to Dr. Alford's office and told him what had happened, afraid that I'd get kicked out of residency. "Don't worry about it," he said. "I'll take care of it." Nothing did happen.

Another time when we were getting ready for surgery, Dr. Guilford asked one of the other residents, Wayne Buckley, how he was doing in residency. Wayne said, "Well, Dr. Guilford, I'm doing OK." Dr. Guilford was obviously eager for a fight. "Wayne, what do you mean you're getting along OK?" he said. "What kind of an answer is that from a resident? Getting along OK—is that the standard you have set for yourself, just doing OK?" "Well I'm doing as well as the other residents are, Dr. Guilford," Wayne said. "So that's your criterion, Wayne. If you're doing as well as the rest of them, then you're doing fine. Man, that's never been my standard." He just wouldn't let it slide. He seemed to relish railing against his subordinates. I deplored that. On the other hand, he made a good point: You don't compare yourself to those around you. You compare yourself to yourself. Are you doing the best that you possibly can? And even though I never really liked Dr. Guilford and I didn't like his hassling Wayne Buckley that day, I've never forgotten his point. Doing as well as everybody else is not a standard for evaluating your performance.

During the second and third year, a resident would have to be on call in the hospital every night. But the fourth year, a resident could be on call from home. On some rotations, we would be on call every third night. That was a real luxury, two nights at home and then one night in the hospital. We went in to the hospital only to do surgery that a junior resident could not do. If he had questions and you couldn't answer them on the phone, you would go in and help. In the final year, we also had the ultimate responsibility for the ward, answering only to the staff physician.

In those days we did not have cell phones but had a beeper or pager, a pocket-size electronic device that signaled important messages. When the beeper sounded, it would indicate whether a call was an emergency or routine and give a phone number to call. An emergency beep meant I had to call the number immediately. That was no problem if I was at home. But if I took the risk of going somewhere, like church, I could be out of touch for an hour. So I would keep the beeper on and run to the church office to make the phone call. Even though I could be on call from home my last year, I had to stay by a phone twenty-four hours a day, seven days a week, without any lapses. If the beep was routine, I could catch it as soon as I got to the hospital. If I was going to church with the family, they would drop me off at the hospital and come back for me later, because we had only one car. When the residents were presenting the case to staff in the calm of grand rounds, being unable to find a pay phone wouldn't fly with Dr. Alford or Dr. Sessions.

SUPERB BAYLOR STAFF

I did most of my head and neck cancer training under Dr. Roy Sessions. He was only a few years older than I was, but he had trained under Dr. Joseph Ogura, a world leader in ENT, in St. Louis. Dr. Sessions brought to Baylor the latest techniques in the head and neck cancer field, notably conservation laryngeal surgery (taking the cancer out but leaving half the larynx intact and preserving the voice, which is called a hemilaryngectomy, or supraglottic laryngectomy). It was a revolutionary concept but had the same cure rate as the traditional method. Because of its difficulty, it required extensive training—one could not just pick it up.

Because of Dr. Sessions's teaching, I became proficient in this advanced surgery and was able to bring it to Austin. No one else in Austin knew how to do it. It established me as the premier head and neck surgeon in the Austin area, and I immediately began doing all the head and neck surgery in this part of the state. Dr. Sessions was a wonderful teacher and came to be a great friend.

We learned facial plastic and reconstructive surgery from Dr. Bill Wright, who seemed to know instinctively how to fashion aesthetically pleasing facial features, especially the nose. He was a founding physician of the American Academy of Facial Plastic and Reconstructive Surgery.

Dr. Ronald Johnson supervised us in ENT clinics and was especially good in teaching sinus surgery.

In addition to learning procedural skills, we were expected to do clinical research. We would choose a specific topic, such as cancer of the parotid (salivary) glands, for example, and review cases in the literature, glean cure rates, and report complications. I had the honor of presenting one of my papers at an international ENT conference in Mexico City. My travel expenses were paid, and it gave me a break from the routine.

All staff at Baylor were superb. What we learned from their judgment, approach to patients, and skill at making the right diagnosis actually made the rest of our careers easier. We had seen everything in the ENT field, which bolstered our confidence. Doctors with limited experience at some residency programs are apt to feel uncertain about particular cases, which creates enormous stress for them. But when we finished the Baylor program, we felt that there was no ENT case that we could not take care of.

Hard Times

I don't think I realized at the time how hard residency would be. I am sure I did not think about it, because it was just something I had to do. It turned out to be extremely intense.

I don't remember what I was paid, but it was around $200 or $220 a month, or $2,400 a year. It wasn't enough to live on. Because I no longer received loans from my uncle, I took a few part-time jobs. One was holding sick call for an hour at the Rice University student health center. Also at Rice, I was hired to be in the stands during home football games to take care of any emergencies in the stadium. I also managed to scrounge up small loans to get me through.

There was a long three-year period when I rarely saw my daughters, Margaret Ann and Laura, except for supper every other night. Margaret Ann was often sick with asthma, which made it harder on me emotionally. Residency took its toll, psychologically and physically, but throughout it all, my family was very supportive. Fortunately, after the first year,

I could spend more time with the girls. In the last year of residency, I was home almost every night for supper and could play with them and read to them. It was the joy of my life.

Apart from the hard times, I remember residency with fondness because I worked alongside great residents. We were all in the same boat, all struggling and helping each other. We were all compatible and thought the world of each other. We respected each other, took care of each other, and covered for each other. There was no competition any more. We were all in it together, trying to be as good doctors as we possibly could. I think the support I felt in this tightly knit group helped me avoid some of the more debilitating effects of post-traumatic stress disorder that many of our military veterans experience now when they return from a war zone and are thrown into society.

At the same time, we were under the supervision of tremendous staff doctors, most of whom had no ulterior motives. They just wanted us to be good doctors—skilled in medical procedures, sincere in concern for patients, and competent in clinical research. Academically and intellectually, it was a pleasant time and I realized that I was getting better at practicing medicine. When I finished Baylor's residency program I was confident and knew I was well trained.

Takeaways

One thing I began to do in residency stayed with me throughout my career. Before a surgery, I would go over every step of it in my mind. Even if I'd done the surgery a thousand times, I would visualize the procedure in detail before I went to the operating room. Complicated surgeries like a radical neck dissection, removing a voice box, or removing a jaw have hundreds and hundreds of steps. If I went over those steps in my mind the night before—every step of it and everything I would do the next day—I never had any delays during surgery. Everything would be smooth and simple. The surgery would look easy. I think that was one of the secrets of my being an extremely quick surgeon. Visualizing the entire process beforehand applies to many fields other than surgery. It's another example of how intelligence and talent can take you only so far—you need hard work and perseverance to succeed. It's a simple little thing, and I don't remember how I hit upon it.

Another thing that stood me in good stead later on was knowing when to retire. We had a general surgeon at St. Luke's who was highly respected but he was getting older and operating longer than he should have. I noticed that behind his back the other doctors would make little snide remarks, such as, "Somebody had better stay close in case he gets into trouble again." Right then I decided that I would quit surgery when I was at the peak of my career, and I did. I operated until my fifty-fifth birthday. I thought I was at the top of my career and was the best at surgery as I had ever been. I quit on that day and never went back to the operating room. I decided it was important for me as a surgeon to stop when I was at my best so I would never harm any patients.

Dr. Alford had as much influence on me as anyone, other than family. I observed everything he did, not just the medical procedures but also how he interacted with patients, other residents, and professors. I watched how he handled medical school politics, from standing up for principles to nurturing egos to making compromises. We had the highest respect for him but never became friends with him. He drove himself to perfection and expected us to do the same. Many times in practice with a difficult patient I would ask myself, "What would Dr. Alford do?" and the answer would be clearer. Even to the end of my practice when I would get a call in the middle of the night and was stewing about whether I needed to meet someone at the hospital, I would ask myself that question. Then I would haul myself out of bed and head to the hospital. It is good to have a reference point in life.

At the end of my residency, I asked Dr. Alford what advice he might have for me. He simply said, "Concentrate your efforts, then you can have influence." I took his advice seriously. It helped me in many ways. I concentrated my surgery in one hospital so I could always work with the same people whom I knew to be the best. I concentrated my practice in what I was interested in and never strayed outside my area of expertise. I even followed that advice outside medicine.

Finishing my residency in 1970 marked eleven years of career prepa-

My brother Pierce, his wife, Reba, and their sons, Pierce Jr. and Todd, came to help me celebrate the completion of my residency in the summer of 1970.

ration—four years of medical school, a year of internship, two years in the army, and four years of residency. Finally, I was ready to hold myself out to the world as a fully trained and professional physician.

A few months before leaving Baylor, Dr. Alford asked me to stay on as full-time faculty. I was honored, and I thought seriously about it. I thought about how much I enjoyed the relationship with him and with the department. I thought about my frustration with the army's medical care in Vietnam. I thought about my parents' hard work and sacrifice to provide me with an excellent education. I thought about how a faculty position might impact my family. In the end, I decided that I belonged not in academia but in professional practice. Having the choice was an affirmation of my calling.

Looking back, I think residency training determined how good a doctor I would be and, to some extent, how successful I would be in life.

CHAPTER 6

The Practice

In declining the offer to join the Baylor Medical School faculty, I planned to go into practice in Houston with another resident and a Baylor faculty member. We were in the process of setting up a practice, and I was excited about the prospect.

One day shortly after making that decision, I was driving on a freeway in Houston, going between hospitals. The traffic was bad, with cars and trucks zigzagging between lanes and eighteen-wheelers thundering by. Out of the blue, I said to myself, "I'm not spending the rest of my life in this traffic." That day I told my colleagues I had changed my mind.

I began thinking about Austin, a university town with a thriving medical community of first-rate specialists who welcomed new, well-trained doctors. Austin was also appealing because my brother Pierce and his family lived there, and it would be closer to Brownwood for visiting parents and grandparents.

I heard that Ernest "Ernie" Butler, a Baylor grad, had started a solo practice in Austin a year earlier. I had met him by chance in the hall at medical school when he was a second-year student and I was a first-year student. The first time I saw him perform surgery, I was in charge of the emergency room at Ben Taub Hospital and he was a senior resident in ear, nose, and throat (ENT). A patient came in with a gunshot wound to the face and was struggling for every breath. Ernie calmly took a knife, opened the patient's neck, dissected the trachea, and inserted a tube, all in seconds. He made it look effortless. I thought we might make a good team.

As it turned out, his office had space for another physician, and he

Ernie Butler (*far right*) and I (*second from left*) founded the Austin Ear, Nose, and Throat Clinic in 1970. It gradually expanded to include (*left to right*) John McFarlane, Chris Dehan, Patrick Connolly, and Brad Winegar as partners.

was looking for relief from a round-the-clock practice. We agreed that I would join him and shook hands on the deal. It was one of the best decisions I ever made.

Setting Up the Practice

In 1970 we formed the Austin Ear, Nose, and Throat Clinic in Ernie's office in Medical Park Tower on Thirty-Eighth Street. The office building was the newest medical building in town and next door to the proposed site of the new Seton Medical Center hospital.

Ernie and I were ideal medical partners. Having both been trained at Baylor, we shared the same philosophy of practice. Although we both wanted to do general ENT, he was more interested in the ear portion of the practice, and I was more interested in head and neck work, so we complemented each other. He was also a superb office administrator; he was decisive and really enjoyed the business side. For all the years we practiced, we never had any real disagreements.

We started with the philosophical decisions that would guide our practice:

We would take everybody that called and asked for an appointment, whether they had money or not, and whether they had insurance or not. If you called our practice for an appointment, you got one.

We would try our best to see every patient the day he or she called. If a patient was sick and wanted to come in that day, we saw the patient that day. We didn't schedule way in advance unless the matter was elective and the patient wanted to schedule it in advance. Basically we saw everybody the day they called.

We would charge less than others in town so that it was easier for patients to see us without financial strain. When we started, we charged ten dollars for an initial visit and eight dollars for a follow-up. In terms of purchasing power, that was a modest sum that almost anyone could afford.

We would have a large volume and diversity of patients. We believed this was the only way we could stay up-to-date on ENT conditions and treatment.

We would always have the latest medical and office equipment available.

Our philosophy grew out of our beliefs. We believed we were practicing medicine in one of the best cities in the best country in the world, and therefore we had an obligation to every patient. Today that statement sounds odd and even corny, but we really believed it. At the same time we believed that our philosophy was the best for the patient. One of my strongest influences in this regard was my grandmother, Mommie Winn, the epitome of caring.

In the beginning, we met personally with every doctor in Austin and within about fifty miles. We met with specialists as well as general practitioners. It was a considerable undertaking because there were more than a thousand doctors in the Austin area at the time. We did not intend this as a marketing strategy. Rather, we wanted to know every one of our referring physicians personally so that when they called us or sent us a patient, we knew exactly who they were, and we could get back in touch with them and let them know what happened. In addition, we wanted to know doctors when we went to staff meetings at the hospitals. Of course, some doctors didn't refer patients to us, and if they didn't, we didn't know them well.

I don't think that's done anymore for several reasons. Principally, few doctors are solo or small-group practitioners today. Instead, many doctors are hired by corporations or groups that contract with hospitals for delivering medical care. They don't feel the need to know anyone outside their group. Plus, medical records are transmitted electronically, and doctors communicate by cell phone and e-mail. By contrast, when a doctor sent us a patient in the 1970s, we called the doctor or wrote him a letter that day. I knew the patients. I knew which drugs they were on and their history. It was an efficient way to practice medicine, and it worked well for us the entire time we were in practice.

My good friend and anesthesiologist Dick Shoberg recently reminded me that in those early years it was still a professional taboo for physicians to advertise. The Yellow Pages in Southwestern Bell's printed telephone directory (made obsolete in recent years by the internet) provided an office address, an office phone number, a notation of specialty training or area of interest, and the names of associates or partners in practice. Our practice, like that of others, grew organically—mostly through referrals from patients.

The Early Years

After training in one of the best medical schools in the world, witnessing horrific medical conditions in Vietnam, and completing a rigorous residency, I was ready to see my first patient in the practice. I was nervous: Would it be a difficult case? Would there be complications? Would I make the proper diagnosis? How would the patient respond? Would the patient come back?

I carefully reviewed the patient's chart, opened the door, exchanged pleasantries, and asked, "What seems to be the problem?" "My ear hurts," the patient said. I examined the ear in question, cleaned the ear canal, and observed inflammation. It was swimmer's ear, as simple as that. It was a humbling moment. I prescribed antibiotic drops and explained how to mix a solution of boric acid and alcohol to put in the ear after swimming. It was easy, almost disappointingly so. But the patient left happy, and I relaxed.

Ernie and I started with a staff of two: a receptionist and a nurse. The receptionist greeted patients as they came in, answered the phone, and took messages. The nurse did allergy testing, called the patients, and seated them in an exam room. Ernie and I each had two exam rooms.

We took medical histories on a paper form and recorded our notes on a simple chart. One quick glance at the chart gave us the exact information needed about the patient. We stored patient records in a filing cabinet. This system was inexpensive and worked well.

When ready to leave our office, the patient paid in cash or by check. The receptionist would give the patient a receipt and an insurance form to take home and fill out. The patient would file the claim with the insurance company and get reimbursed. The same with Medicare. We did not "accept assignment," which meant that money would be sent to the patient, not to us. If a patient could not pay at the office, we would send a bill at the end of the month. If the patient indicated an inability to pay, we did not charge. Our collections were good because our fees were so low.

We began with manual typewriters, an adding machine, and a bookkeeping ledger. Ernie did all the billing and accounting by hand. As office technology advanced, we adopted portable telephones, fax machines, and electric typewriters. We were the first medical office in Austin to use computerized billing and bookkeeping. We had a Wang computer and hired a computer expert to design the software because none was commercially available. When the software designer moved to Alaska, we were almost left in the lurch. But we soon hired another and were back up and running. We ran our spreadsheets on the first VisiCalc that was available. In 1979 when Apple came out with the Apple II Plus with an upgrade to 64 KB of memory, Ernie and I each bought one. We had the first personal computers of anyone I knew at the time.

I also used the Wang computer for recording survival and complication rates on my head and neck cancer patients. I wanted my cure rates and survival rates to equal or exceed those of MD Anderson. They did.

To keep our fees low, we had to run an efficient office with the bare minimum of personnel. We sent patients out to expert technicians for X-rays and lab tests. In the 1980s, we began accessing the latest imaging technology, including PET and CT scanning, and later MRI. Fiber-optic scopes replaced the metal bronchoscopes (and earlier hand-held mirrors and lights), which allowed us to more clearly see the larynx and trachea, making diagnosis easier and more accurate. These scopes and CT scans would revolutionize our practice.

When we started our practice, the standard local anesthetic for certain procedures was cocaine. It had been used by physicians since the 1880s because it was quick and helped reduce bleeding by shrinking blood vessels. One day when I had to remove a small tumor from a patient's nose, I reached for the bottle of liquid cocaine we kept on the shelf, dabbed a cotton swab with it, and inserted the swab into the patient's nostril. I waited a couple of minutes and then tried to snip out the tumor. The patient nearly bolted out of the chair in pain! I tried applying more, and the same thing happened. It occurred to me that someone had substituted another clear liquid in the bottle. This was in the 1970s when cocaine was gaining popularity as a recreational drug. (It had been illegal for the general population since 1914.) We had to switch to Xylocaine, which was less effective but worked well enough. We never found out who had stolen the cocaine.

One challenge we faced in the early days was that no hospital emergency room in town had a full-time doctor. When we got a call in the middle of the night about an ENT patient at Brackenridge, for example, there was no one to screen the patient. We had to get out of bed and go down and see them. It was one of the main reasons I chose to live in the central part of Austin. I never had to ask, "Do I really need to see this patient?" I could get dressed, drive a short distance, and take care of the problem.

For several years, we shared calls with John Youngblood, another ENT doctor who had his own practice. One of us—John, Ernie, or I—was on call every third night at Brackenridge. John later became a clinical ENT professor in the medical school at the University of Texas Health Science Center in San Antonio.

Following Dr. Alford's advice at Baylor, I concentrated my practice at Seton Hospital, which at the time was on West Twenty-Sixth Street in the University of Texas area. The hospital had been founded in 1902 by Catholic nuns, the Daughters of Charity of St. Vincent de Paul. The hospital moved to a larger campus on West Thirty-Eighth Street, practically next door to our office, in 1975.

When we started operating at Seton, we had to use whatever surgical crew they provided, and often they were not trained in the latest ENT surgical procedures. That meant that we had to hire a surgical nurse to assist us. As Seton's admissions increased, they agreed to train an ENT operating room crew and allowed us to have the same personnel for every surgery. This made a tremendous difference.

Although concentrated at Seton, we practiced in every hospital in town. When needed, we went to St. David's on East Thirty-Second Street, Holy Cross on East Eleventh Street, and Brackenridge on East Fifteenth, the oldest public hospital in Texas (founded 1884). Indicative of the era, Holy Cross was built in 1940 to serve all ethnicities; it was the first integrated hospital in the South. The other hospitals had opened to all patients after the passage of the Civil Rights Act of 1964. (Holy Cross later became a regional cancer care center, and then Seton bought the facility in 1984 but closed it in 1989.)

When I came to Austin, I made a decision that I kept during my entire practice: I would never drink alcohol—no beer, no wine, no liquor. I didn't want to be compromised in any way when I answered calls on my days off from the ER or from doctors in the operating room who wanted some help. I wanted to be in full possession of my physical and mental faculties for the benefit of patients and my own reputation. I realized that I was going to be busy, and that giving up alcohol was a small sacrifice. People would shake their heads when I declined a drink, but I never felt the need to explain it.

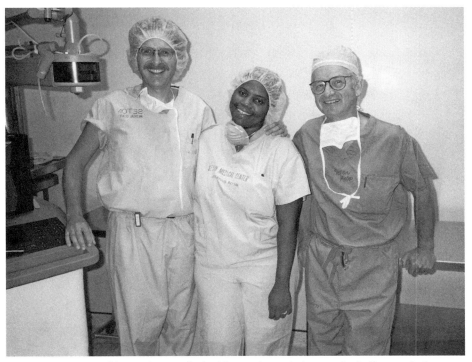

At Seton Hospital in Austin, I worked with superb surgical teams, including surgical technician Jerry Baker (*left*) and head nurse Debbie Lane, RN (*center*).

Throughout my practice, I took extra care of my hands and eyes because they had to be steady and accurate in surgery. I never used a chain saw at the ranch, for example. Later in my practice, I realized that working in the yard on weekends left my hands sore and tired, so I quit doing any yard work on Sundays.

As our practice grew, we saw that our decisions about our philosophy were doing exactly what we wanted. We developed an extremely diverse practice and a mirror of the general population. We saw the rich and poor, the educated and uneducated, and the famous and unknown. We saw the prisoners in handcuffs from the federal penitentiary and the president's wife all in the same day, and they sat together in the waiting room. It gave us an experience in medicine that kept us adept in making correct diagnoses in the office as well as in performing surgery.

Audiology and Hearing Aids

When Ernie and I started our practice, we contracted with an audiologist, Fred Martin, PhD, as a consultant to set up our soundproof booth and hearing test equipment. At the time, Fred was a young member of the audiology faculty at the University of Texas. He would go on to spend thirty-eight years in teaching and research at the university, write several books, including *Introduction to Audiology*, and receive many honors and awards.

While we were proud to have him as a consultant, we had so many patients in need of hearing and vestibular (balance) tests that we hired our first full-time audiologist, Carmen Tyler. In addition, we were one of the first medical offices in the state to acquire the newly developed electroacoustic impedance bridge to measure pressure in the ear (ear drum resistance) and screen for ear disease.

At first we sent hearing loss patients to commercial dealers for hearing aids but grew dissatisfied with the arrangement. If the patient had trouble with the aid and the dealer could not solve the problem, the patient would have to get another appointment with us. Often it was ear wax blockage deep inside the ear canal, which we would remove. To better control quality, we decided to have our audiologist dispense hearing aids. If there was a problem, the audiologist would just move the patient into an exam room and we would take a look. In addition, we could be sure every patient got the proper aid and fit.

As the clinic continued to grow, we added a full-service audiology department under the direction of Scott Haug, who worked with us for several years. Over the years, four audiologists worked with us—all smart, dedicated, superbly trained, and wonderful with patients, the young as well as the old—-Angela Wooten, Elaine Leatherwood, Gay Wucher, and Sharon Richardson.

Clinic Expansion

By the mid-1970s, our practice had grown substantially, requiring that we bring in a third partner. We wanted someone from the same resi-

The Practice

dency program at Baylor where we had trained. We knew that if he came through Baylor, he would be well trained and compatible with us and our practice. The first doctor to join our clinic was John McFarlane, a superb doctor and surgeon who happened to be from Brownwood. He was a few years younger than I, and I knew his family well. His father was a physician and his older brother, Joe, was an ophthalmologist in San Antonio. John was a wonderful man, one of the kindest, gentlest people I've ever known in my life, and one who absolutely cared about his patients.

A few years later we needed to bring in another doctor. This time, we violated our Baylor-only rule because we heard of a doctor who had trained at Duke University, one of the best residency programs in the world, and who wanted to come to Austin. Brad Winegar turned out to be the exact person we needed. He had trained in head and neck cancer surgery and was a superb surgeon, conscientious, hardworking, and smart. He integrated well into our practice.

In 1990 we brought in our fifth partner, Chris Dehan, a Baylor-trained doctor. He had planned to be a priest at first but later decided to become a physician. He was a superb doctor and conscientious, took loving care of his patients, and was a pleasure to be around. He was in the military reserves and was called to active duty for the first Iraq war in 1990–1991. He left us for six months or almost a year. I was always proud that we continued to pay him full salary the whole time he was gone. It was not required by law, but we thought it was the morally right thing to do.

Shortly thereafter, we were presented with a tremendous opportunity—a merger with three solo practitioners in Austin: David Tobey, Boyd Morgan, and Jim Eskew. Each was a perfect fit. David had trained at the University of Washington in Seattle, had worked for NASA, and taught ENT at the University of Texas Medical Branch in Galveston. He was especially interested in medical issues affecting singers and was involved with the Austin Lyric Opera, as I was. Boyd, who had trained at Baylor, grew up in a science family. His parents were chemists who had worked on the Manhattan Project, and his father codiscovered the element americium and established a program in nuclear radiochemistry at the

University of Texas. Jim, who trained at the University of Texas Medical Branch in Galveston, practiced in South Austin and smoothly blended his independent streak with compassion for his patients. All had successful but different practices and all practiced impeccable medicine. All were gifted with great intelligence and judgment, but most important, they had that hard-to-define quality of character.

Our first subspecialty partner was Patrick Connolly, in pediatrics. He was wonderful with children—and their parents—and one of the smartest people I've ever known. He expanded our practice in complicated neonatal cases, such as newborns with airway emergencies and congenital abnormalities.

We received many inquiries from doctors who wanted to join our clinic so they could practice in Austin. We turned down most of them, probably ten doctors a year. When we considered adding partners, we looked not only at their training but also at their wives. Recalling what my mother had said so many years ago about discerning a soldier's character by "the girl on his arm," I insisted that we meet the wives to ensure both doctor and wife were really good people.

During the entire time I was practicing, not a single doctor that we brought into the practice left our clinic. I don't know of any practice anywhere that had a record like that. One reason was that Ernie and I were extremely fair, financially and otherwise, with everybody that came in. They became full partners after just one year and paid almost nothing to join the practice. We never believed in their being subservient. We believed that the day they came they should be able to have the type of practice they wanted and be fully compensated for it, exactly the way we were compensated. Ernie and I never made any money off any of the new doctors we brought in. Our fairness contributed to our success.

In addition, Ernie set up the first profit-sharing plan in a medical practice in Austin, so every employee of our clinic could retire comfortably.

Running an Efficient Practice

We had superb office nurses throughout the duration of our practice. They had to be good if they were to assist with patients and keep us organized. Once, after our practice was well established, I had the receptionist keep track of the number of calls I received in one day. It turned out to be 150 people who wanted to talk to me personally that day. By screening calls and tending to matters that didn't need our immediate attention, our staff contributed to the efficiency of our office.

My most memorable office nurse was Mary Lou Stewart, who was always efficient and pleasant. After a number of years, I began to notice some subtle erratic behavior and vague medical symptoms. She had seen doctors about the symptoms but no one could make a diagnosis. I couldn't help worrying about her, even after I went home after work. One night I woke up at about two or three in the morning, and it suddenly dawned on me—she had a brain tumor. As soon as she got to the office the next day, I insisted she see a neurologist. Sadly, my suspicion proved correct. In spite of the best of care, surgery, and radiation, she lived for only six more months.

Early in our practice, we had a nurse whose mood was unpredictable from one day to the next. Some days she would be pleasant, and some days unpleasant. I always had to walk on eggshells around her. One day when she was in a bad mood, I went into Ernie's office. "We need to get rid of her," I said. "She should be wondering what kind of mood you and I are in rather than our worrying about what kind of mood she's in." Ernie said, "You're exactly right." So he fired her. That changed the tone of the office. From then on, we maintained a gracious, courteous staff. As I had learned from a sergeant in the army, it's important to have the right people around you.

When we opened our doors every morning, we started seeing patients on time. Occasionally we'd get behind in the office, generally because of emergencies. If we ran behind, patients rarely complained. Most understood when I explained that I had an emergency and there was nothing I could do about it. If they still were unhappy, I would suggest they might be happier seeing some other doctor.

Typically, I started the day by making early morning rounds in the hospital. I usually got up at five forty-five, went to the hospital at six thirty before everyone got busy, made rounds, saw all my patients, and discharged those ready to go home. I got to the office at seven thirty and

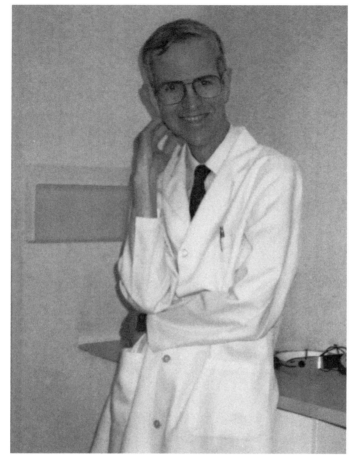

My partner Ernie Butler relaxes in a rare moment between patients—rare because we had a very busy office practice.

started seeing patients at about seven forty-five. I saw patients until a little before noon and then stopped for lunch. When I returned, I took a fifteen-minute nap from twelve forty-five until one o'clock. I could fall asleep instantly and would wake up totally refreshed. I saw patients until about six and then made rounds at the hospital or went home. I went for years without taking an afternoon off.

Like many busy professionals, I always had a lot on my mind. Maybe I had to prepare for a hospital staff meeting, return phone calls, or finish paperwork. But before I saw each patient, I cleared my mind of those distractions. When I pulled a patient's chart off the rack, I would flip

The Practice

When I was elected president of the medical staff at Seton, the administration presented me with a giant pack of Rolaids in a comedic warning of challenges ahead.

through and refresh my memory on who they were and what I'd done before—their personal history, marriage and family, and what they did for a living, for example. It took only a few seconds because I knew what to look for and where to look in the chart. Before I opened the door, I was focused on the patient. In the exam room, I never once let my mind wander. I got pretty good at blocking everything out. I think it was one of the reasons that I was successful in the office.

Through all my long office hours and visits to the hospital in the middle of the night, I was fortunate to have the support of my family—first my wife and teenage daughters and later, after a divorce, my second wife, Toni (whom I married in 1979), and her daughter, Robin. They protected me from household problems like plumbing and car repair (something I didn't fully realize until after I retired). They knew that I had accepted responsibility for taking care of patients and that sometimes it was a matter of life or death. There were lots of times when we were sitting down to supper or going to church or heading for a school function, and I would have to leave. They never complained. Without such support, it's hard to be a successful doctor.

Surgery

I usually operated three half days a week. If I operated in the morning I would be at the hospital at six thirty so that I could be available to talk to the patient's family and answer their questions. I was always the first surgeon to show up at the operating room. I learned early that if you arrived there first, you usually got to start first.

I performed many different kinds of surgery—removing cancerous tumors and repairing sinuses, for example. Actually, I probably performed as many complicated procedures as anyone in the state. I was the first in Austin to do frontal sinus surgery as well as conservation laryngeal surgery, which I had learned from Dr. Sessions at Baylor. Conservation means to preserve function while removing the cancer. Before that, the entire voice box was removed. With this new surgery came the need for restoration of the vocal function. I arranged for Anne Lueck, a superb speech therapist, to come from Scott and White Clinic in Temple once a week as needed to see all the voice patients before and after surgery. The combination of surgery and therapy allowed us to offer complete care, just like that at MD Anderson, Baylor, and major medical centers.

I also did cosmetic surgery, such as rhinoplasties (reshaping a bulbous or humped nose, for example) and otoplasties (repositioning overly extended outer ears, usually in children), but no face-lifts. I never did thyroid surgery even though the thyroid gland is in the head and neck area. I realized that Austin had excellent general surgeons—namely, Bob Askew, Tommy Coopwood, and Lamar Jones—who did that surgery, and that I didn't have anything to add to their fine work.

I did a lot of ear surgery, although not as much as Ernie. Actually, Ernie was one of the first ENT surgeons in the country to perform ear surgery exclusively on an outpatient basis. (Now it is the norm.) He could have become a part owner in Bailey Square Surgical Center, which

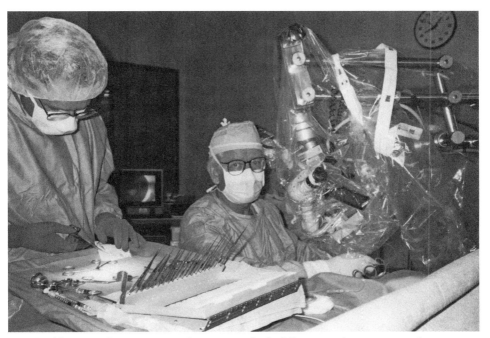

In this surgery I am reconstructing an ear and rebuilding an eardrum to restore hearing, assisted by surgical technician Jerry Baker. This delicate operation required the use of a surgical microscope, which is enclosed in plastic to keep the operating field sterile.

would have been very lucrative, but he refused because he thought it was a conflict.

As I explained earlier, before I went into a surgery, I mentally rehearsed the steps in a procedure. If I was going to do a complex procedure, I would go over it the night before, because it would take some time. I would always visualize the steps and review pictures in books. (This was before the internet and Google, of course.) If I encountered something unexpected—and I often did—on the operating table, I could quickly adapt. I think this mental rehearsal helped me enormously. It made the operation go quickly—no hesitation about what to do next, which instrument to use. That meant less time under anesthesia and fewer complications for the patient.

To be a good surgeon, one must have an impeccable knowledge of anatomy. This seems so elementary—knowing the body's structure and how all the parts fit and work together. At Baylor we learned anatomy primarily through hands-on dissection of cadavers. But today in some medical schools, students watch a demonstration of dissection, a process called prosection. I don't think that's enough. How can these fledgling surgeons be expected to instantly differentiate between structures, do exactly what's needed, and feel confident that they've done it right?

In talking with patients about their ailments, I always tried to be honest and straightforward. I never minimized risk. I never used the word "minor" in talking about surgery because I really believe there is no such thing when you put someone to sleep. It's major. I never told surgical patients they were going to do well. I told them exactly what I was going to do and what the complications could be. I always recommended a treatment. Certainly the patient has to agree to any procedure, but I think it's up to the doctor to give the patient an honest opinion of the best treatment. I always said, "This is what I recommend, and it's up to you to say yes or no." I would not give them two or three options and have them decide. I felt that they came to me asking my opinion, so I gave it to them. I did the same thing when a doctor called asking my opinion on a case. It was a lesson I learned watching Dr. Seybold at St Luke's Hospital during my residency.

In talking about surgery with head and neck cancer patients, I recommended strongly that they get a second opinion. I recommended that they to go to one of four hospitals: MD Anderson, the Mayo Clinic, Memorial Sloan Kettering, or Baylor. I knew what those doctors would tell the patient, and I knew they could call me to discuss the case. "They're not going to tell you to get some hokey treatment, and I won't have you coming back here for me to take care of all the complications," I said to patients. "If you want to go to some friend of your brother-in-law's to give you a second opinion, or you're going off to Mexico to get laetrile or something, find yourself another doctor." Some did. But those who got second opinions felt more comfortable that my proposed treatment was best. Talking frankly about second opinions cleared the air and never gave me any trouble.

Patients generally think of the surgeon as "the doctor," but no sur-

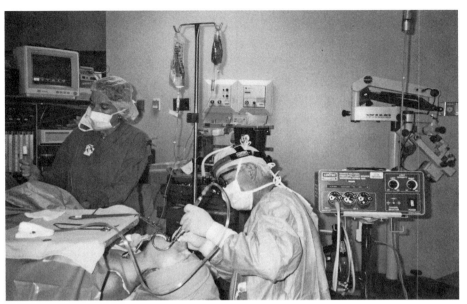

My head nurse Debbie Lane took this photograph of me during a tonsillectomy, one of several thousand I performed during my career. Behind me are pieces of standard surgical equipment: monitors, IV stand, fiber-optic light source, and surgical microscope.

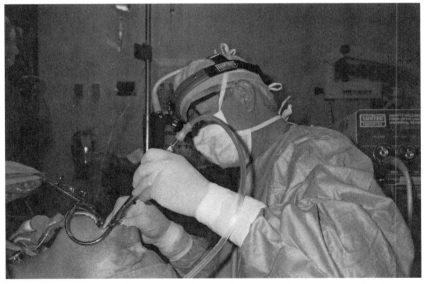

In this close-up of a tonsillectomy, my left hand uses a suction tube while the right hand removes the tonsil. This surgery also required the insertion of an anesthesia tube, tongue retractor, and a brace for holding the mouth open.

gery is successful—or even possible—without the anesthesiologist. This doctor not only puts the patient to sleep but also monitors the patient every second for changes in blood pressure, heartbeat, oxygen in the blood, and temperature. We worked in tandem. I could not have been successful without their keen judgment. Darrell Fabion and Milner Thorne provided anesthesia at Seton—just the two of them night and day—for many years. It's fair to say that the arrival of Dick Shoberg, Dennis Boyer, and then shortly later David Eden, David Hopkins, and Wayne Porter transformed the practice of medicine in Austin. Dick and Dennis initially practiced at Brackenridge before expanding to Seton. In time they added dozens of truly great physicians to their group, and I operated with many of them. I never had to worry about anesthesia when they were managing the patient, no matter how sick the patient was. Their medical judgment was always sound, and they were meticulous in the workup and care of every patient. We never had a death and never really any major complications in over thousands of cases and in many years of surgery. That is not an accident but skilled care day in and day out.

Critical to successful surgery are the nurses and technicians who work in the operating room. Julia Allen, a native of Lockhart and a graduate of Seton's nursing school, ran the operating room Seton at peak efficiency. "I never saw her sit down," said John Hilsabeck, a Seton administrator. "She was up and moving all the time handling the endless details of the operating room." (Julia died in 2009 at age ninety-six.)

The ENT team assigned to me was tremendous. Early on, Gail Downing served as head nurse, and later Debbie Lane took over. Both were registered nurses, extremely smart and professional. They made sure there was never any loose talk, joking around, or people coming through just to visit. Everything revolved around the patient's care. Neither Debbie nor Gail made any exceptions to that.

I always had an excellent surgical technician at my side, helping me with a procedure. Peggy Silvas, Janet Gunthrie, and Jerry Baker filled that role at one time or other. They assisted in complicated procedures that required hundreds of separate steps. Jerry and I, for example, could operate for six to eight hours at a stretch without saying anything. He would know exactly which instrument I needed next and when I would need it. He would know exactly how I needed the hemostat turned and which size hemostat I needed. He would know the exact curve of scissors I needed and the kind of suture I would need. Everything was there when I needed it. On rare occasions when the instrument wasn't exactly what I needed—I could tell by the feel if it wasn't—I just left my hand there a second and Jerry would remove that instrument and give me the one I needed. It was like a symphony: we communicated so well that we never had to say anything.

Coming out of a successful operation, even one lasting six to eight hours, I experienced a feeling of absolute peace and serenity. I would walk down the quiet hall, change out of scrubs, and cross the dark parking lot, feeling an intense sense of well-being. I knew the surgery had gone well, the patient had made it, and I had done a good job. A perfectly executed surgery is like a perfectly performed symphony. It's extremely difficult work, but every person rises to the challenge with a confidence acquired from years of painstaking practice and hard work. Everyone performs with precision and exact timing, coming together in splendid harmony. The feeling is a state of utter calm and quiet joy I have not felt anywhere else or any time since, but I'm sure other surgeons would recognize it.

Everyone on the surgical team was incredibly good, always pleasant, and never stressed, which made me a lot better. All of us felt that there was absolutely nothing that we couldn't do in the operating room. No case was too complicated or too hard or too dangerous. There was no life that we couldn't save. I was probably as busy as any ENT doctor in the state with such a diverse practice. I never had a death in the operating room, even though I took care of extremely sick cancer patients whose cases were complex. Nor did I have any major complications in the operating room. Furthermore, I never had to deal with a malpractice suit—never went to court, never had to settle, never even had a suit filed against me. The surgeon often gets most of the credit for successful operations, but we couldn't do it without a competent team.

Doctors versus Hospital Authority

In those days, the doctors were independent of the hospitals. Doctors applied for privileges to care for patients and do surgery in a hospital but were not its employees. Doctors with practice privileges made up the medical staff, who were primarily responsible for medical care. By contrast, the hospital provided the physical facility and the employees, such as nurses, lab technicians, and administrators, who served as support to the doctors.

Seton's medical staff consisted of 1,200 doctors with practice privileges. They governed themselves through committees. One committee, for example, determined whether a doctor was qualified to be on the staff, and which procedures he or she was qualified to perform. The ethics committee monitored doctors' decisions and, if necessary, set disciplinary measures (a rare event at Seton because all staff were superb). All committees reported to the executive committee and the president (medical chief of staff).

I served on Seton's executive committee for twenty years, perhaps longer than anyone else. I also chaired the ethics committee for many years. Late in my practice, I was elected president. (The position was a two-year term, but one also served two years as president-elect, as well as two years as past president—six years altogether.) Certainly I felt honored by my colleagues, but mainly I felt the enormous responsibility of guiding committees and maintaining high standards of medical care. The position also offered a tremendous learning experience. At one point, I went to a long-range planning session conducted by Ascension Health, the not-for-profit organization with which Seton is affiliated, in St. Louis. I learned a lot about their planning process and incorporated elements of it into my own life.

An anesthesia colleague, Dick Shoberg, followed me as president of the medical staff at Seton Medical Center.

For many years, I worked with Sister Mary Rose, the last nun who was the hospital's chief executive officer. While tension can exist between medical staff and hospital administrators, we collaborated well. I sensed that she was following a higher mission. Like the Catholic nuns I worked with in Vietnam, she was the epitome of charity and commitment.

Back then, unlike today, Seton had one vice president, John Hilsabeck. He ran the day-to-day affairs of the hospital, and he did it efficiently and with great concern for the patients.

All in all, because of its administration and medical staff, Seton was one of the best-run hospitals in the country at the time.

Patients

Many of our patients were ordinary middle-class people who worked in state government and university jobs, while others worked as auto mechanics and waitresses in small businesses. Some had jobs in the emerging high-tech industry (IBM, Texas Instruments, and Motorola had set up shop in Austin by the early 1970s), while others were prominent bankers and lawyers. A large portion of our patients lived from paycheck to paycheck or got by on food stamps.

One interesting group of patients were inmates from the federal penitentiary in Bastrop. The prison would attend to minor ENT problems but sent more serious cases (such as cancer and severe sinus infections) to us. The prison was very secretive about an appointment. They would call us the same day they were bringing the patients and never gave us their names in advance to avoid tipping off friends and family, thereby preventing an escape attempt. The guards, who always carried automatic weapons in cases, brought the inmates in, their chains clanking around their cuffed hands and feet, and had them sit down. The sight of them really cleared out the waiting room!

One of the dearest groups of patients to me were children with Down syndrome. As far as I know, I took care of almost all the children with Down syndrome in Austin. Having grown up with my younger brother, Billy, who had Down syndrome, I—and my sister, Mary Margaret— had experienced the disdainful stares and cruel remarks of strangers and grown very protective of him. It profoundly affected me in my practice, more than I realized at the time. Children with this type of disability are hard to treat. They have special needs and unusual conditions that require a lot of time. Many are hyperactive and unable to cooperate in a medical setting. But because of Billy, I understood the condition and enjoyed treating these patients. As a result, the kids loved me, their parents loved me, and they sent all their friends to me. Families with children with Down syndrome were a close-knit group, and they communicated with each other.

I ended up treating not only the children with Down syndrome but also many children with disabilities—including congenital deformities with grotesque facial features. Occasionally, we treated students attending the Texas School for the Deaf, the state-operated primary and secondary school on South Congress Avenue. Our audiologist communicated with these patients in sign language and translated for our staff.

Most of my head and neck cancer patients had little or no money. Generally, the vast majority of these patients were alcoholics and smokers, or at least had smoked and drunk heavily at some time during their lives. Many alcoholics would go into delirium tremens in the intensive care unit. Many were destitute. They didn't have insurance or money, but all were real characters. I enjoyed taking care of them—I just didn't get paid for it.

When I made the diagnosis on these cancer patients, I made a pact with them. "The treatment might be hard," I'd say, "but if you will stick with me, I will always stick with you. I will take care of you for the rest of your life no matter what happens." They understood that they could call me any time and I would always be there. I think that promise gave them a different attitude toward me than they might have had. It had no effect on changing their smoking and drinking—it didn't reform them one bit. They just liked me, and they would do anything that I told them to do except quit smoking and drinking. But with almost anything else, they would follow my instructions.

Sometimes they took my offer too literally. Once when I was in the office, for example, I got a call in the middle of the afternoon. "You have a call from the jail. Will you take it?" my nurse said. "If it's the jail, sure," I said. When I took the phone, the voice on the other end said, "Mr. [forgot his name] is ready for you to pick him up." "What do you mean pick him up?" I asked. "It's one of your cancer patients," the voice said. "He says you would always take care of him. He's ready to leave the jail and he wants you to come down and pick him up." I said, "Tell him there's no way I can get down there right now because I've got an office full of patients. He's going to have to get his own ride home."

A few days later when this patient came in, I asked him, "What in the world was this business about my picking you up in jail?" "Well, Doc, I didn't have a ride home and I thought, I'll just give Doc a call and see if he can get down here and pick me up," he said. "What did you do to land in jail?" I asked. "Doc, I didn't do anything," he said, which was so typical of my head and neck cancer patients. "I was at this bar and I got into a little trouble. It wasn't anything serious, and I had just left the bar on my own," he said. "I was walking down the street, minding my own business, and police cars came from every direction and picked me up. Sure enough, the first thing they did was find my gun in my pocket. Being as I'd been picked up before, they made a big deal out of it." He thought about it for a minute, and he said, "You know, Doc, the police are always doing that to me. I'll just be walking down the street and here they come and just pick me up and take me off." I paused for a minute and said, "You know, they've never done that to me." He missed my point: "Well," he said ruefully, "it sure happens to me a lot."

I treated many famous people, including state and national politicians. I won't mention all of them or go into detail, because of doctor-client privilege. But I will relate a couple of stories because they contain nothing medical or personal.

President Lyndon Johnson retired to his ranch about fifty miles west of Austin after leaving the White House in 1969. He was never my patient; he went to the Mayo Clinic for his medical needs. But I treated members of his family when they had ENT problems. They were referred to me by the obstetrician-gynecologist who cared for his daughter, Luci. She had a hearing loss, and Ernie and I operated on her shortly after Johnson came back to Texas.

Every time President Johnson wanted to talk to me about his family, his assistant, Tom Johnson (no relation to the president), would call me. He always said exactly the same thing: "Dr. Burns, I know you're very busy and I know this is an inopportune time, but would you have a minute to talk to the president?" Although Johnson was no longer in the White House, everyone still called him "the president." Here I was, a young doctor, barely out of training, being asked if I had time to talk to the president.

One night after I had gone to bed and was sound asleep, I got a call: "I know it's late, Dr. Burns, but the president wants to talk to you. He's on his way from the ranch. Where should he meet you?" I said I'd meet him anywhere. We agreed to meet at Luci's house on Macken Street in Tarrytown. I was waiting in my car when the president's car drove up, with his Secret Service guards. It turned out that Luci was gone and her house was locked. I said, "Well, I will just sit in his car." "No," his assistant said, "the president wants to sit in your car." He sat in the passenger seat and I sat in the driver's seat. We talked for maybe an hour and a half as if he had all the time in the world. We talked about a family member who was sick, but mainly we chatted informally. At one point, he said, "This is a shame. I can't believe that the Secret Service can't get into a locked house. I guess they need to go over to the high school and get a couple of kids to get us in."

He would ask a question and then look at me intently, listening to every word I said, as if what I was saying was the most important thing in his life. He asked me what I thought about Medicare, for example, which he had pushed through Congress in 1965, and whether it would affect the way I would take care of his family. He was serious about it. "I guess you probably don't like me very much for passing that Medicare law." I was not expecting that question, stammered around, and finally said, "No, sir, I'm good with the Medicare law." And I was.

He talked at length about Vietnam—how he had agonized over decisions to send troops, how intensive bombing didn't bring the Vietnamese to their knees, and how so much of the American public protested against the war. At one point, I thought he was going to cry. He talked freely while I sat there and listened. In retrospect, I wish I had asked him a couple of questions about the war. I believe he could have cleared up some issues that still nagged at me.

Whenever we talked, I got the impression that he was very open with what he would say to me, surprisingly open. Maybe he was that way with everybody. But he told me things—which I've never told anyone and never will—because I think he knew it would never be revealed. It's been more than forty years since his death in 1973. I feel privileged that he took me into his confidence. Maybe this former leader of the free world just needed someone to listen to him with compassion and without judgment.

Lady Bird Johnson would come to the office if she needed us to arrange an X-ray or test. Other times I would meet her in her apartment above the KLBJ radio/TV station she owned downtown. She was just like her husband, listening carefully to what I said. I never felt that they were taking advantage of me or pressuring me.

Another of my famous patients was Governor Ann Richards. One day in 1991, she called me because she was hoarse and had lost her voice and had an important meeting with the queen of England, who was coming to Austin. She said, "Doctor, I've got to meet the queen at eleven o'clock this morning, and I have to have my voice. What can you do?" I was at Seton Hospital but agreed to meet the governor next door at my office. "I'll wait for you at the front door of the building," I said. She came rushing up with all her security. We all crowded into the elevator, and I pushed the third-floor button to our office. The elevator lurched up about two feet and stalled. We couldn't get out and we couldn't get the door open. It was ten o'clock, only an hour before she was due to meet the queen. I called maintenance. In a few minutes, a man arrived and got the elevator going. We finally got the governor upstairs, I helped restore her voice, and she met the queen on time.

In July 1992, Governor Richards called because she had the same problem. I said, "Well, Governor, I need to take a look at your vocal cords." She said, "There's no way I can get to your office. I'm getting my hair fixed and then I'm getting on a plane and going to New York." I agreed to see her at the beauty shop, which was near Fifteenth Street downtown. I walked in, and instantly the ladies, all in various stages of undress, began scurrying around, putting on towels, and covering themselves up. I told the receptionist my purpose, and she pointed out the governor in the crowded shop. Feeling very self-conscious, I hooked up my headlight, looked at her vocal cords, and told her exactly what to do. "Thanks for giving me my voice back," she said. Without thinking about it, I said, "Governor, the country needs your voice." She looked stunned for a moment. As it turned out, her trip was to the Democratic National Convention, where she served as chair. Afterward, she sent me a big bouquet of flowers with a gracious thank-you note.

Treating people like Governor Richards and the Johnson family, I never knew exactly what was going to happen. I was never totally in control of the situation. But without exception, I found the very wealthy and the very famous to be gracious and pleasant and very appreciative of my making the effort to fit into their demanding schedules.

Governor Richards, Lady Bird Johnson, and President Johnson were the only people I saw on house calls—except for one other individual who stands out in my memory. I received a call in the middle of the night from a woman in a phone booth close to a trailer park near Manor, a few miles east of Austin. She thought her mother was dying and asked if I would come out because her mother wanted to talk to me. I had treated her mother for a deadly cancer at the back of her nose. This cancer is almost always fatal. In spite of radiation treatment and after months of agonizing pain and obstruction, the cancer finally moves into the brain or a carotid artery, and the patient dies. (Her husband had died of the same thing about five years earlier, which is curious because the tumor is rare in the United States.)

I got careful directions to the trailer park and headed out. When I stepped into the tiny trailer house, I looked down and could see through to the ground because one of the boards in the floor was rotten. My patient was obviously close to death, and she really did not want any medical attention. She just wanted to thank me for taking care of her and her husband. We talked for perhaps thirty minutes. Then I got up and left. I got back home around three in the morning. A couple of days later she died. Expressions of gratitude like hers make all the effort of becoming a physician worthwhile.

Singers

When Ernie and I started our practice, Austin had been attracting nationally known musicians to its nightclubs and concert venues for decades. But the 1970s were a turning point. Armadillo World Headquarters opened in 1970 with country and rock shows, Clifford Antone started his jazz/blues club in 1975, and *Austin City Limits* began its award-winning public television run in 1976. By the 1980s, many musicians were migrating to Austin from across the country to launch their careers, and the stage was set for Austin to proclaim itself the "Live Music Capital of the World."

In addition, classical music has always enjoyed a following here, with the Austin Symphony Orchestra (founded in 1911) and the University of Texas School of Music, which invited world-renowned concert artists to join its faculty and perform in public concerts. One 1963 graduate, the pianist James Dick, went on to win international acclaim, including a prize in the Tchaikovsky Competition in Moscow. In 1986, a group of opera enthusiasts founded the city's first professional opera company, the Austin Lyric Opera (now the Austin Opera).

It's not surprising, then, that I treated many musicians. Because one of my principal interests was the larynx, I treated lots of singers when they became hoarse or lost their voices. One of the first was Michael Martin Murphey, a country-and-western singer who hit the big time with his 1975 recording of "Wildfire." To better study his voice, I asked to hear him at his next performance, which happened to be at Armadillo World Headquarters. That night he sang his song "Nobody's Gonna Tell Me How to Play My Music." *OK*, I thought, *I get the message.* Actually, I wouldn't tell him how to sing stylistically, but rather how to care for his vocal cords. Later he dedicated his *Cosmic Cowboy* album to me, and the song "Cosmic Cowboy" became an iconic song of the new country-and-western movement in music. This became important recognition for me in the music world, and I eventually treated a number of country-and-western singers.

With Murphey I realized that Austin was an important center of live music and that no one else was providing adequate medical care to these country-and-western singers. I began studying them intensely, looking for the specific vocal technique causing the problem. I asked Anne Lueck, the speech pathologist working with us, to evaluate their voices. She would listen to them speak and sing and prescribe vocal and breathing exercises to reduce the strain on the larynx.

Eventually, we would treat nearly all the big-name country-and-western singers, and they would call me if they had a problem anywhere in the United States or in the world. In addition, I gave talks on the topic at national medical conferences. I wrote the first article ever written on the medical care of country-and-western singers, and at one time had written every article in the world's literature on the subject. (One article was "Clinical Management of Country and Western Singers," *Journal of Voice* 5, no. 4 [1991]: 349–353.)

I began treating opera singers in the mid-1980s, when I became involved with the Austin Lyric Opera after a visit from Gina Ducloux. She and her husband, Walter Ducloux, an internationally known conductor and opera director, had come to the University of Texas at that time—she to teach voice and he to create the University of Texas Opera Theater. Up to that time, the traditional medical care, even at the Metropolitan Opera in New York, was to have a loose affiliation with a doctor in private practice. Some of the care was excellent and some not so. If opera singers got sick in an unfamiliar town, they would have to take potluck finding a doctor that specialized in the care of professional vocal problems. Opera singers are especially vulnerable because they travel constantly, get exposed to viruses, work strenuous hours, often have no insurance, have high overhead with an apartment back home, and can suddenly get sick just before an important performance. The wrong treatment or advice can wreck a career and financially devastate the singer.

Although the training of opera singers differs markedly from that of country-and-western singers, their problems have much in common. Country-and-western singers begin by singing, usually with no training, in clubs and restaurants, while opera singers typically go through a university program with lots of coaching. But as I discovered, both types of singers develop problems at the same time in their careers. At first they sing alone in a small club or university theater. If they get sick, they take off a few days and get well. As they begin to build a reputation, however, they feel pressured to sing even when sick. The country-and-western singer, for example, has to pay overhead because by now he or she has a band, bookkeeper, publicist, and so forth. The opera singer has rehearsed for weeks, with opening night only a day or two away. Both have people depending on them and financial obligations to meet. So they go ahead and try to sing through it, and that's when they really get into trouble. Additionally, the problem would often arise not from their singing voice but from speaking at a lower pitch. The secret in taking care of either is to figure out exactly which vocal technique is causing the problem and correct it. Anne Lueck and I would do that, and a hundred percent of the singers got well.

I decided to model the care of opera singers after the way the University of Texas managed the medical care of its football team. The team doctor took care of all of the players at no charge to them. I decided to do it the same way with the opera. That is, I would be aligned with the opera but not have a written contract. I would see the opera singers when they came to town to perform and give them an hour's talk about how to care for the voice, what to consider in lifestyle and finances, when to cancel a performance, how to rest their voice, and what kinds of diet and medication were best, for example. The singers, who were here for about a month rehearsing, were free to call me any time day or night and come to the office. They wouldn't wait in the waiting room, but instead would go back to my private office where they wouldn't be exposed to other people who were sick. They did not have to wait for an appointment, and because it was free, they had no inhibition about coming in. They could call me any time for the rest of their careers for any problem or advice, and there was never any charge. It was a revolutionary concept of care for an opera company.

Like the football team doctor who was always on the sidelines during a game, I went to every rehearsal and every performance of the Austin Lyric Opera at Bass Concert Hall on the university campus (where the operas were performed at that time). I also kept meticulous records on the singers who made appointments with me. As a result, we prevented the spread of viruses among them, the singers were healthier and sang better, and fewer singers had to cancel because of illness. The singers loved it because when they do not sing, they do not get paid, despite rehearsing with the company for weeks.

It seems so logical and sensible now, but the first time I presented this method of care at a national meeting, I was met with tremendous derision. The old guard who were taking care of the singers thought it was a horrible idea and let me know in no uncertain terms. But I persisted. I gave several talks on the subject and wrote articles for national journals. Over the years, most opera companies in the United States quietly adopted this method of care as the standard. Some doctors charge; some don't. But the singers have free access to a doctor. I take great satisfaction in having started it, even though I didn't get any credit.

As part of my work with both types of singers, I wrote a thesis, "Acoustical Analysis of the Underlying Voice Differences between Two Groups of Professional Singers: Opera and Country and Western" (*Laryngoscope* 96, no. 5 [May 1986]: 549–554). I was the first person in the world to describe the physics of why these two types of singers sound different when singing the same note. My paper beat out those of researchers in all the nation's medical schools as the most original contribution to the literature that year, an honor unheard of for a doctor in private practice. As a result, I was also invited to join the Triological Society, considered the most prestigious organization for otolaryngologists. (I remain in the society now as a senior fellow.)

Higher Education

Throughout my career, I maintained ties with academia. I believed I had a responsibility to assist in training young people going into medicine or a health field.

For several years after coming to Austin, for example, I served as an adjunct professor at Baylor Medical School, supervising ENT residents at the VA hospital in Houston. I would leave Austin around four o'clock Friday morning, work with residents at the hospital during the day, and drive home on Saturday.

Having patients who needed speech therapy, I realized that the University of Texas could expand its training of speech pathologists. Our audiology consultant, Fred Martin, who was on the university faculty, introduced me to Gene Powers, PhD, who was head of the university clinic and responsible for training speech therapists. I accepted an appointment as an adjunct professor in what is now the Moody College of Communication and lectured on specific vocal problems and medical treatment as well as cancer patients' vocal rehabilitation. I lectured there for many years, a contribution I was happy to make without compensation.

At the same time, I was honored to serve on advisory councils of University of Texas units dealing with history and the arts. I believe it's essential for young people to study the humanities, regardless of the profession they choose, so that they develop critical thinking skills, appreciate diverse cultures, and draw inspiration from the world's art. I owe this belief in large part to my mother's artistic and cultural influence during my childhood.

Consequently, I accepted an invitation more than thirty years ago to serve on the advisory council of the Briscoe Center for American History. I continue to derive great satisfaction from my association with this arm of the University of Texas because of its tremendous research resources in Texas and American history as well as its public service.

In a similar vein, I served for many years on the advisory council of the university's College of Fine Arts, with its fostering of music, opera, painting, dance, photography, and other art forms. As Mirabeau B. Lamar, president of the Republic of Texas, once said: "The cultivated mind is the guardian genius of democracy, and while guided and controlled by virtue, the noblest attribute of man."

Preparing for Retirement

I spent considerable time while I was practicing medicine preparing to retire. I had learned in residency at Baylor that one can practice too long, so I vowed somewhat humorously that the anesthesiologists would never roll their eyes when I came into the operating room. One of my sports heroes, Johnny Unitas, who played for the Baltimore Colts and in my opinion was the greatest quarterback that every lived, played much longer than he should have. It was sad to see him sitting on the bench only to go into the game and throw an interception. I didn't want to do the same thing with surgery. I decided to quit at the top of my skills and abilities and just walk away from it. And I did. I performed my last surgery in 1993 when I was fifty-five years old. (I continued seeing patients in my office for another three years.)

Ernie had retired four years earlier. When he first told me his plans, I fought back tears. It signaled the end of an era. And when I announced I was retiring, Wayne Porter, an anesthesiologist I had operated with many times, asked me to do surgery on his father to restore his hearing on my last day.

Before I left the practice, I studied people who were retired, particularly professionals, such as attorneys and university professors. I discovered that the people who have the most trouble retiring are those who enjoy their profession the most. I noticed that people who didn't particularly like what they did in their professional life could retire happily and successfully. Because I loved what I did so much, I expected to have trouble. Fortunately, I had my family and the ranch to keep me busy, but most important, I had the support of my wife, Toni. And I had intellectual pursuits that proved extremely rewarding. When colleagues later asked for advice about retiring, I would say: "If you really enjoy what you do, be careful about retiring because nothing in retirement will be as satisfying as what you did in your professional life."

But there were also changes that made the practice of medicine a little less satisfying. Insurance and Medicare had become so complex that patients could no longer file their own claims. We began filing claims, which meant hiring more personnel and raising our fees. Toward the end of my practice, I spent several hours a day, after I had finished seeing patients, completing records in compliance with regulations so insurance would pay. As a result, I saw fewer patients and spent a lot less time with them. And I didn't really enjoy doing that. For the first time in my career, I would go home exhausted.

Another change was the risk of lawsuits. I had been one of the busiest ENT doctors in the state and I had never had a lawsuit even filed against me. I had treated tens of thousands of patients through the years and operated on thousands of them, yet none of them sued me. I had seen good colleagues sued for no fault of their own, and in situations in which I thought they did nothing wrong. The suits would drag on for years, so they worried about it every day. My attorney told me that the greatest risk in continuing to practice medicine would be a frivolous lawsuit, not related to fault, that could last for years, with an unpredictable outcome. So I retired early, and I think I retired successfully.

Looking Back

When people ask me what makes me proudest in my career, I say it was seeing patients every day. I enjoyed studying their conditions, making the right diagnoses, and taking care of them in a way that was kind to them. They knew I was always supremely interested in them to the exclusion of everything else. I'm proud that every time I was called for an emergency, I immediately went, no matter the time of day or how tired I was. I am proud that my partners—and many other doctors in town—did the same. None of us ever complained, which made it look deceptively easy.

I'm proud that we took care of children with Down syndrome and others with physical and cognitive disabilities. Growing up with my brother Billy affected my medical practice because I saw firsthand, at a vulnerable age, how casually cruel people could be. Mental illness and cognitive disabilities are tough on a family in a way that no one can really understand unless they've been there. Fortunately, laws were passed, starting in the mid-1970s, that guaranteed civil rights for people with disabilities and equal access to public education for children with disabilities. Ernie and I could have had a silk-stocking practice if we had wanted to, but we chose to treat anyone who walked in the door. I'm proud that we cared for the less fortunate.

Today when I encounter former patients, they tell me how much they appreciated my operating on them or taking care of them or their children. Just recently a woman stopped me in the grocery store and reminded me that I had saved her child's life, when he was only hours old, by doing an emergency surgery on his trachea at Brackenridge Hospital. She wanted to tell me what the grown child was doing now. That happens to me every week or so, and I've been retired now for twenty years. These expressions of gratitude are some of the most satisfying times of my life.

Likewise, I derive special satisfaction when former colleagues express their appreciation. Upon my retirement, for example, the anesthesiologists at Seton presented me with a bronze bust of myself in surgical garb. I am one of only a few physicians they have so honored. Today the bust occupies the most prominent place in my library. It is so meaningful because it was given by those who saw me operate every day for decades; no one else really knows how well I performed in surgery.

Dick Shoberg, an anesthesiologist who often worked with me in surgery, recently said that when physicians gathered in the coffee room, "one often heard that Dr. Burns's surgical team is the 'most efficient and easiest to work with.' The hospital surgery department provided the team, but I believe Paul could have been allocated random choices in personnel and within months would have recreated a team of enviable efficiency and reputation. One should note, however, that given an opportunity to assist a gifted surgeon (or artist, writer, musician, or coach), nearly everyone will give their best effort—a win-win."

One of the greatest compliments of my life was a letter I received a couple of years ago from Debbie Lane, my operating nurse at Seton for many years and one of the most wonderful nurses anywhere that I've ever known. At the end of the letter, she said that the highlight of her life was working with me in the operating room. I attach the greatest significance to that because when you work with someone in the operating room every day and through thousands of operations, they get to know you as almost nobody else does. They see you at the most stressful times when you are making life-or-death decisions, and they know what you decide to do and why you decide. They see when you have to decide whether or not you can help the patient—and occasionally you realize you cannot, and you just have to close down the operation. They are behind the scenes and you each see the other as clearly as I think humanly possible. It's because I respect her so much that I consider it the greatest compliment—and because it was unexpected.

I'm also proud that our clinic took care of everybody regardless of ability to pay. If a cancer patient told me they couldn't pay, I never charged them for the rest of their life. If I talked to the patient's internist or anesthesiologist about the patient's inability to pay, they always, without exception, never charged anything. When I was called to Brackenridge, I don't think I ever charged for anything I did. And when another doctor called me to help, I always came and never sent him or her a bill. I treated patients because it was the right thing to do. And it wasn't any real sacrifice. I did well.

One reason I could afford to care for poor patients is the decision I made early in my career to live modestly. Today I'm still living in the same house that I had built when I came to town in 1969. I've added to it but never moved. I didn't live high on the hog. I didn't belong to exclusive clubs. I didn't do the things that require a lot of money, so I would not have to worry about finances in my practice. Yet I've been able to live comfortably, give my daughters a great education, travel around the world, volunteer my time in the community, and do all the things I've wanted to do.

It's a lesson that is easily lost on successful doctors today. When your lifestyle costs more than your income, you get in trouble. We can see this in every profession. It's not unique to physicians or country-and-western stars or high-tech entrepreneurs. Bill Hewlett, who cofounded Hewlett-Packard, for example, lived modestly even though he was worth billions. He didn't have to prove himself to the rest of the world by conspicuous consumption.

When new partners joined our practice, I stressed the idea of living modestly. "Save every bit of money you can from every paycheck," I advised. "Live modestly, and educate your children. Then you don't have to make any decisions in your life based on financial struggles." It is so incredibly simple, yet most people don't do it.

I feel absolutely fortunate that Ernie and I became partners. He and I spent a lot of time together through all those years, and we got to know each other really well. Today we are as good friends as any two people could ever be. No one understands me better than Ernie, and I understand Ernie as well as any human on earth, except maybe for our wives.

We also shared interests in the community. I served on the boards of the Austin Lyric Opera and the Austin Symphony for many years, and Ernie and his wife, Sarah, gave generous gifts of support to the arts in the community.

I feel blessed to have had a successful career, to follow my calling. In talking to thousands of patients and reflecting on my own experience, I have come to believe that success is rarely a matter of accident but rather the result of hard work, attention to detail, discipline, and sacrifice. Certainly I have worked hard, but I have also had a fair amount of luck. In my practice, I was lucky enough to be in the right place at the right time and with the right people.

Looking Forward

I worry about the future of medicine. Doctors today are no more or no less dedicated than those of my generation. There is no change in their compassion and their desire to help people, to treat the poor, and to help reduce pain and suffering. People go into medicine today for the same reasons I did. It is still a tough profession with tremendous sacrifice and long years of training.

What has changed is the system. When I began practicing, I tried to balance what the patient could afford against what I needed for overhead. I knew if I charged too much the patient would have to go somewhere else or do without care. A successful physician cured the patient and kept the cost affordable.

Today many patients are referred to a group or institution that employs the physician, or to a network of physicians. Rather than choose a doctor who will make the correct diagnosis at the most reasonable cost, the patient goes to whomever is in the medical plan. It's a fundamental change but subtle and complex at the same time.

The physician's responsibility is to make the correct diagnosis and give the correct treatment, as it has always been. Certainly new technology has expanded diagnostic and treatment options, as well as office management tools, but all at a high price. Unfortunately, cost control has been taken from the doctor and distributed over the hospital, insurance, government, business, and all kinds of consultants. As layer upon layer of control has been added, little effort has been made to get input from physicians in private practice.

Today the physician is surrounded by receptionists, nurses, physician assistants, medical technicians, social workers, insurance specialists, Medicare specialists, Medicaid specialists, coding specialists, office managers, accountants, bookkeepers, and attorneys on retainer. They're doing what Ernie and I did with a receptionist and a nurse. I am not advocating that we go back to a simpler time or roll back technology. The tragedy is that the cure rates for the vast number of common illnesses are no better today, but the costs have skyrocketed.

I think all who are working to improve the system are honest people, but they're aiming at different goals. Everyone wants a better system but no one is sure how to do it. I don't have a solution either. I suspect there is no magic bullet. But I believe that how we as a nation deal with our health care system will have far-reaching consequences.

CHAPTER 7

My Enriched Life

The last time I saw my father was in the Brownwood Hospital in 1986. He was dying from lung cancer, a result of smoking all his life. We had never really talked much father-and-son, and now even casual conversation was hard. I talked some about my medical practice—how busy we were, how we were hiring new staff. He listened, nodding his head between labored breaths.

Finally, I said, "I need to get back to Austin. I do surgery tomorrow morning at seven."

Without really thinking, I added, "Thanks, Dad, for making it possible for me to be a doctor. I appreciate all the sacrifices you and Mother made."

He said, "I know you do."

His response took me completely by surprise. As two men who had never shared feelings with each other, we enjoyed a rare moment of mutual respect and appreciation. It's still one of the fondest memories of my life.

ART AND ARTIFACTS

Medicine provided me with a rewarding career, and it inspired and strengthened outside pursuits that have made my life fulfilling. A favorite quote by Goethe comes to mind:

> A man should hear a little music,
> Read a little poetry, and see a fine picture every day of his life, in order

> That worldly cares may not obliterate
> The sense of the beautiful which God
> Has implanted in the human soul.

I have the good fortune of seeing "a fine picture every day" in the art and artifacts I have collected over the years. Rembrandt is a particular favorite. I have some of his etchings, as well as some woodcuts by Albrecht Dürer. I also have a painting by Aert de Gelder, who was the last pupil of Rembrandt and painted in Rembrandt's style. It hangs in our living room, where I see it every day and enjoy it.

Many people like French Impressionist paintings, while others like Mexican murals or Western art. My favorite is seventeenth-century Dutch art. I find it fascinating because it marks a turning point away from the earlier religious and historical painting and toward the realism that began in the 1850s. Whenever I go to an art museum, I always head first to the seventeenth-century Dutch section. I have spent years reading about Rembrandt, Vermeer, and others, studying them, and traveling to museums around the world to see their work.

Dutch art is one of many subjects I have studied in great depth. My pattern is to read about a subject, take trips to see what I have studied, go to conferences to hear the experts, and generally try to learn as much as I can about it. I try to narrow the subject first and then study it in tremendous depth so that I feel that I'm almost as knowledgeable as anybody about it.

Columbus Collection

Early in my medical practice, I began collecting historical documents. At first I collected anything that caught my interest, from rare musical scores to letters written by the signers of the US Declaration of Independence. This was when I realized that I had to narrow my focus if my collection was to be meaningful.

I joined a Civil War club organized by George Lowe, an Austin cardiologist. He had a vast library of books about the war, went to a national meeting at Gettysburg every year—just the most knowledgeable person

I've ever known on the subject. I enjoyed studying the war but realized that it was already thoroughly researched and would not hold my interest. I wanted to dig into a subject that no one knew much about.

That's when I chose to study the exploration of the Western Hemisphere. I put a lot of effort into Lewis and Clark, read their journals many times, and retraced their travels across the western United States. Their maps, as well as those of Zebulon Pike and early Texas explorers, provoked an interest in Christopher Columbus. I tried to read every book I could find on him. I think few books match Samuel Eliot Morison's *Admiral of the Ocean Sea*. Morison, a scholar of maritime history, was one of the first to write a comprehensive history of Columbus. I read it over and over again and kept it out on my desk.

I chose Columbus not just to learn more about the man but also to study navigation, indigenous culture, the spread of disease, and why some explorers succeeded and others failed. I studied him for more than ten years, right up to 1992, the five-hundred-year anniversary of his first voyage to the Americas. A lot of new books about Columbus came out at that time, so it was an exciting time to study him. Of his four voyages, I was especially interested in the third, in which he landed at the island of Trinidad and came within sight of South America (the first European to see the continent).

I spent many vacations retracing his voyages. I believe you really can't understand a historical event unless you've actually been there and seen it. I could never get what Columbus really thought or what he looked at when he first landed in the New World until I had actually been there and done the same thing myself. As an example, my brother Pierce and I went on a small boat and waded ashore exactly where Columbus waded ashore on San Salvador Island in the Bahamas on his first voyage. It opened up a whole new world to me. I found it very emotional to stand on that ground and think, *I'm standing exactly where people walked and died. Their lives changed that day.*

The easiest way to retrace his journeys would be to find a ship that was scheduled to go the way he went. But I was never able to find one that went the whole route. I could follow trip segments, however, such as taking a ship from Spain to the Canary Islands. I also retraced as closely as I could his travels in Spain and Portugal, going down the same road or crossing the same bridge. For example, when Queen Isabella recalled Columbus to tell him she had decided to finance his first voyage, she sent a messenger to find him. The messenger caught up with him at the Bridge of Pinos in Granada. I went down the same road and found the same bridge that he had crossed five centuries ago. Standing on that bridge almost gave me chill bumps.

I was really impressed with Columbus's navigation skills. He was able to sail across the uncharted ocean without any modern equipment. He relied on dead reckoning, in which he used a compass to indicate the course and determined distance by estimating time and speed. After his first voyage, he never missed a port he intended to find.

To get a better feel for early maritime instruments, I bought a sextant (invented about 1730) and took it on all my cruises and travels to see if I could learn to use it. I was never extremely accurate but I could locate my position to within a few miles. The ship's crew was always fascinated that a passenger was following their progress with a sextant. Invariably I was invited to the bridge to see the ship's navigation. This was in the 1980s before satellite navigation. All the huge cruise ships had a sextant in the bridge in case the radios went out, and the captain and navigators were always very good in using the instrument.

As my study progressed, it became clear that Columbus and the other early explorers had a profound effect on the ecology and culture of the Western Hemisphere. Their explorations and search for gold devastated indigenous peoples, like the Aztecs and the Incas. I became so troubled reading about the effects on the natives that sometimes I would go to bed depressed. I decided to move on to something else. I had become as knowledgeable as anyone I knew, and there was not much new to research about him anyway.

Early Texas History Documents

I went back to studying the exploration of the Western Hemisphere, particularly historical documents and maps related to early Texas history. I narrowed my interest to documents and maps that were available to a private collector from just after 1500 to about 1835. In other words, my study included the Stephen F. Austin maps but not those after Texas became a republic in 1836.

When I started collecting Texas maps, few others had taken it up as a hobby. About the time it became popular, I had collected almost every map that included Texas that I could collect. Those I did not have were either not available to a collector or extremely expensive. I would go months and months without finding an important map, and then when I did, it was horribly overpriced. Actually, I developed such a reputation for buying the great maps that all the major map dealers knew me.

A few times I got lucky. Once when my wife, Toni, and I went to a rare-book shop in New York, she was looking through a bin of documents close to the window. She whispered to me, "Paul, he has a Jacob De Cordova map." (She had heard me mention this Jamaican who had settled in Texas in 1839.) "Really?" I said. I looked at it and quickly saw that it was authentic. The price was about $150. *Whoa!* I thought, and bought it on the spot. Later when I sold all my maps, I think this one went for $5,000.

Toni and I went to almost every major map dealer in the world, like Maggs Bros. Ltd. in London and Sotheby's and H. P. Kraus in New York. I would write a letter explaining my interest and ask if they had any maps, and they usually did. If we were in Paris, London, New York, or San Francisco, we would usually go to different dealers and look at their maps and rare books.

Ernie Butler, my medical partner, accused me of just liking to shop. "You are a consummate shopper," he would say, always shopping for maps, historical documents, paintings, and artifacts. There is some truth to that. I did enjoy it.

I was also interested in reference books on cartography. I compiled a listing of all maps ever produced in books and journals, more than a thousand volumes. I had about as good a private collection as any private collector I knew of. All of them were out of print, all of them rare books. It was a great companion collection to my maps collection.

Toward the end of my collecting, I would contact a dealer, and knowing I needed a particular map, he would increase the price. If the item

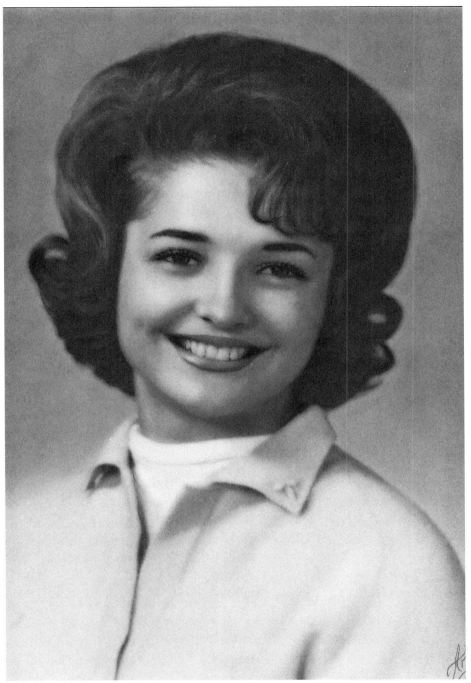

My wife, Toni, whom I married in 1979, participated actively with me in all my projects. (This early portrait of Toni was taken by Harry Annas, the town photographer of Lockhart, whose photographs are part of the Briscoe Center archives.)

was grossly overpriced, I would refuse to buy it. One time, however, I went to Paris to buy a specific map—the first accurate map of the Gulf Coast and the first to mention Texas, drawn by the French cartographer Guillaume de l'Isle in 1718. When I got there, the price was completely out of reason. It was an important addition to my collection, I wanted it, and the dealer knew that. We talked about the price off and on for days. Finally, I paid what he was asking. Afterward I thought, *This isn't fun anymore. I'm not going to do this.* In 1988 I put my collection of 441 maps, books, and documents, mostly on early Texas, up for sale with Dorothy Sloan, a rare-book dealer in Austin.

Although I sold nearly all my collection, I kept a 1504 Reisch map, one of the earliest maps in existence that a private collector can have. I kept my entire Columbus collection (sixty-six volumes) and a pristine first edition of a biography written by his son in about 1530. It is one of the best copies in existence, from the Streeter collection, and I just couldn't let go of that. In addition, I kept everything I had on Magellan, an original first edition of Zebulon Pike's journal, a travel log by George Kendall, and my entire Florence Nightingale collection. I also kept some letters written by two US Army generals—John J. Pershing in World War I and George S. Patton, World War II. They're not great letters at all, but I just liked them.

Looking back, I wish I had kept a first edition of Lewis and Clark's expedition and their journals. It was one of the most beautiful, pristine copies I've ever seen. Although disappointed now that I let it go, I'm pleased that their travels across the western United States inspired my interest in restoring our family ranch to the way it was before many settlers came to Brown County.

Texas Declaration of Independence

Another reason I stopped collecting historical Texas materials was a tremendous increase in forgeries. I had always been very careful with everything I bought. I always researched each item thoroughly, and if I had any questions, I just passed. Interestingly, I never bought a fake

My Texas history collection included a copy of the Texas Declaration of Independence, which proved to be authentic. I later sold it when I sold my collection of rare maps, manuscripts, and books.

or forgery in all my years of collecting. But one purchase in particular scared me.

It started when a man came to my office with a neck ailment. The patient information form he filled out indicated he was Tom Taylor, a rare-book dealer. I told him I was a collector and asked if he had a catalogue. He sent me one, and I asked him to find a broadside of the Texas Declaration of Independence for me. (A broadside is basically a printed poster announcing an event—in this case, that Texas declared its independence from Mexico on March 2, 1836.) Tom found one of the few existing copies at H. P. Kraus in New York. I paid him $33,000; it was the most expensive thing I had bought up to that time.

A few years later he called me at the office. He asked if I would get the document out of my safety deposit box and meet him at the University of Texas. He wanted to compare my copy to the one in the Barker Texas History Collection, which is an absolutely true copy. When we met in the lobby, he looked at mine and quickly said, "Oh, yours is great, yours is great." Then he measured it with his precision ruler, and his face absolutely blanched: mine was the wrong size by a couple of millimeters. He worried whether mine was authentic. I believed Tom was an honest dealer, but I couldn't help feeling worried.

Tom became obsessed with identifying fakes and where they came from. After painstaking detective work, he discovered that in March 1836 not all of the original one thousand broadsides of the declaration had been printed in the same press run. The first one hundred were sent by messenger to the convention delegates, and the remaining nine hundred for general circulation were printed a few days later. My document had been printed in the second batch on a tightened plate, which meant my copy was a tiny bit narrower than the Barker copy. Tom also noted defective letters that were the same on both documents. My copy was authentic—a huge relief!

By the end of 1988, according to an article in *Texas Monthly* (March 1989), Tom had identified more than fifty forgeries, many of which had been sold to universities and historical museums. He himself had to reimburse two purchasers for fakes that (unbeknownst to him) he had sold them. As it turned out, a number of fakes had been sold in a forgery scam that rocked the historical document market.

The scam might have started with no fanfare in the 1960s when several important documents came on the market, many of them undoubtedly stolen. As the documents—and fakes—were traded and sold, prices went up. The business got dirty—and dangerous. One Austin rare-book dealer, Johnny Jenkins, who had sold forgeries but denied knowing they were fake, was found shot in the back of the head under suspicious circumstances near Bastrop in April 1989. His death and the forgeries attracted national attention.

Besides the *Texas Monthly* article, the *New Yorker* published "Knowing Johnny Jenkins" by Calvin Trillin in October 1989. Another article, "Lone Star Fakes" by Lisa Belkin, appeared in the *New York Times Magazine* in December 1989. This second article describes how the authenticity of my copy was verified, and that it was probably the one used to make forgeries.

Tom Taylor published a book, *Texfake: An Account of the Theft and Forgery of Early Texas Printed Documents*, in 1991, and *Antiques Roadshow* devoted its interview segment to the faked declaration in its June 28, 2014, broadcast.

Eventually I sold my copy of the declaration for $75,000, the highest price that I had sold any document. But that doesn't mean I was smart about it, because I have heard that it recently sold for around a million dollars. My experience with the declaration and other Texas documents was one reason that I became more involved with the Barker Texas History Collection, part of the Briscoe Center for American History at the University of Texas.

Ongoing Education Essential to a Full Life

When I was in Blanket Elementary School, Mother and Daddy gave me the book *How to Win Friends and Influence People* by Dale Carnegie. I think it's one of the most important books I've ever read. From this book, I learned to be interested in everyone I met and be honest about it. You never can fake being interested in someone. As a result, I try to figure out what is important to everyone I meet and talk about what interests them and learn from it.

My mother influenced me in a similar way. As a child, I observed that she was always quietly learning something new. It made her interesting to be around. We marveled that she could contribute to conversations, no matter their topics or the turns they took, well into her nineties. She read contemporary books as well as the classics. My sister, Mary Margaret, said Mother is the reason she reads every day.

Being educated and reading widely is essential for making one's life as full as it can be. I'm reminded of what Mahatma Gandhi said: "Live as if you were to die tomorrow. Learn as if you were to live forever." Some of the greatest people I have known were interested in almost everything—the arts, literature, music, science, math, politics, and history. You can't absorb knowledge by osmosis. You can't just read about art in a book; you've got to experience it. You have to go to the great museums of the world. You have to travel the world, broaden yourself, and see other cultures.

Recalling my childhood in Blanket, Texas, I resolved that my daughters would have an interesting and full life, that I would give them every advantage a child could have. When Margaret Ann was about eleven and Laura nine, I began taking them to the world's great cities—New York, London, and Paris. I wanted them to see such things as Vermeer's painting *Young Woman with a Water Pitcher* at the Metropolitan Museum in New York, Rembrandt's self-portrait at the National Gallery in Washington, DC, Egyptian antiquities in the British Museum, and the *Winged Victory* sculpture at the Louvre. When my daughters reached college age, I believe they were as well traveled as any of their peers. When Toni's daughter, Robin, joined our family as a young teen, we also made sure she would travel widely. We took her to New York and London, to the countries of Greece, Egypt, and Israel, and across the Pacific to Hawaii.

As an aside, my daughter Laura and I had a unique experience while she was choosing a college. On a trip to New York to visit colleges there, we stayed at the Carlyle Hotel because it was right across the street from

My wife, Toni, and I took our granddaughter Sarah Spellings as a child on many trips to New York, including this one to the Metropolitan Museum of Art.

My grandsons Paul (*left*) and Henry (*right*) and I may look like the Blues Brothers, but actually we're taking a breather on a hot August day, probably after visiting the San Antonio Zoo when they were boys.

Sotheby's, which was having a sale that I wanted to see at the end of our trip. The only room available was a huge suite of about three bedrooms that must have gone for thousands of dollars a night, way above our means. As I was unpacking and moving clothes to a drawer, I found a small leather pouch about two inches across tied with a string at the top. When I opened it, I found Porsche and Ferrari car keys. In the bottom were loose diamonds, maybe a dozen, small in size. I was astounded! I told Laura, "I don't want any part of this because whoever left these diamonds is coming back to get them."

I called the desk and spoke to security. "Come up to my room. I have found some diamonds." A guard and a manager came quickly. They were obviously confused; this had never happened before, they said.

They put the diamonds in the hotel safe overnight. When I talked to the hotel manager the next morning, he couldn't believe that I didn't want the diamonds. "I know they're stolen so I don't want anything to do with them," I said. He gave them to the police. "If nobody claims them and the police don't want them, they're yours," he said. I didn't think anything more about it.

About a year later I was sitting in the office one afternoon between patients. We were usually quite busy, but this afternoon we had a little lull. I don't know what made me remember those diamonds, but on a lark I called the Carlyle Hotel. I asked to speak to the manager who had been there when we visited. "Oh, yeah," he said, "I remember you well." He had no idea what had happened to the diamonds, but my call stirred his curiosity. About a week later he called. "You won't believe this, but nobody ever claimed those diamonds. I remember promising those to you if nobody claimed them, and so they're yours." He wrote a letter to the police to that effect.

Several months later when Toni and I were in New York, we went to the police headquarters, which was at the end of Manhattan Island in the worst part of town. The building was a huge concrete block, probably from the 1950s, with terrible trash around it. I told the front desk that we were there to pick up some unclaimed items. They took Toni and me to the basement, a huge room with steel bars on all the windows. It was where anyone arrested in New York City would go to pick up their belongings that the police had confiscated for evidence and no longer needed. It was a scary place, and we were obviously out of our element.

After waiting in line for a few minutes, I reached the bulletproof cage, where I spoke into a microphone to a large, burly woman inside. "I'm here because I found some diamonds in a hotel," I said, and showed her the letters from the hotel and the police. She looked at me with a wry smile and said, "Say that again." She laughed. "Sir, I can promise you if that sack had diamonds in it when it came in, it won't have any diamonds in it now, if it's still back there at all." She was gone about fifteen minutes. "I cannot believe this," she said when she came back. "The diamonds are still in the bag." I signed for them, and she passed the bag to me. "Be careful when you leave this building," she warned.

"I'd stick those things in my pocket and get out of this part of town as fast as I could." We did.

Most college visits I made with our daughters had none of this drama, but both girls chose great schools. Their graduate and senior theses are among my most treasured gifts. Margaret Ann graduated with honors from Princeton and went to law school at the University of Texas, where she met her husband, James "Jamie" Spellings. Laura graduated with master's degrees in business and film from the University of Texas at Austin. She and her husband, Phil Rogers, both work in the high-tech industry in Austin. She is a senior manager in organizational development at Advanced Micro Devices (AMD), and he is a chief software architect of the computer server division of Nvidia.

Education is one of two things in our life that Toni and I always said were not budgeted. The other is books. We can spend as much money as either one of us wants on those two things. Our kids' education was expensive but well worth it. Books are a source of knowledge about every subject imaginable, and the first source to which I turn when I want to learn something new or study a subject in depth.

Construction and Restoration

After I started my medical practice, my brother Pierce and I formed a building company, Hill Country Homes. He had worked as a chemical engineer for many years at the Texaco research lab in Austin, but building was his avocation. In our spare time at night and on weekends, we would design and build a house and then sell it. After we finished one, we started another. After a while, we built duplexes and rented them.

This side business became a family project. Pierce, Toni, and I would design the building, Toni would get all the permits, I would arrange the financing, and Pierce would build it. Everybody had a job. We didn't make much money, but we didn't lose money either. It was a diversion, something we all thoroughly enjoyed.

In the early 1980s we bought four buildings on the southwest corner of the old historic square in Lockhart, a small town about thirty miles south of Austin. Our goal was to restore the buildings as much as pos-

Toni, shown here as a baby with her parents, Lillian and Edward Fox, and brother Dick (age six) grew up in Lockhart, where we later restored some buildings on the town square. (Photo by Harry Annas, whose photographs are part of the Briscoe Center archives.)

sible to their original condition. Because Toni had grown up in Lockhart, she saw the project as a way to give back to her hometown. We put tremendous effort and money into restoring the buildings. We added modern heating and air-conditioning, electrical wiring, and plumbing and brought them all up to code, of course, but maintained the original architecture. We consulted with Hadley Sleight, a talented interior designer who worked in Austin for many years. In the years since, many other buildings on the square have been refurbished, and several, including the courthouse, used our colors.

We grew so emotionally attached to our buildings that we didn't want to sell them at first. We rented them out for many years but eventually sold them all. Now every time we drive by them, we feel proud that we were the first to renovate buildings on the square. They're still beautiful buildings and they're restored to much of their original condition.

Retreats

About midway through my practice, in the early 1980s, I developed the habit of taking time off and spending three or four days by myself just thinking about things. Because I found that I couldn't do it at the office, the house, or the ranch, I hit upon the idea of going somewhere that was unfamiliar. I would spend at least three days examining my professional and personal life, including such things as investments, projects, trips, collections, volunteering, and the ranch.

On each topic, I planned what I wanted to do immediately, where I wanted to be in a year, and what my ultimate goal would be over the long term for the rest of my life. I wrote my plans down because I found that if I didn't, the planning did not work. I was never completely rigid with it. If I decided I wanted to do something different between sessions, of course I would change immediately. It's amazing to me how people can spend time doing things they no longer enjoy and not have time for things they do enjoy. So I would review what I had done over the past year, what I had failed to do, and what I needed to modify. It was a retreat—a time to rethink everything and be sure I was heading in the direction I wanted to go.

Thirty years before I retired, for example, I analyzed how much I needed to save every month so I would have enough saved for retirement. People say, "You're so lucky that you had enough saved to retire." Well, it surely was not luck. I found it was a constantly changing target and I needed to continually modify how much I needed to save. It is interesting to go back and read those notes, because I didn't always follow my plan. The plan was constantly changing, but at least there was a plan.

I usually did this thinking in the middle of the winter when my practice was not very busy. Usually I would go to a resort—San Antonio, Santa Fe, and resorts in the Hill Country, for example. One year I went to Hawaii. I found a little bench by the ocean and forced myself to sit there all day with a manila pad and pencil, just thinking about things with nothing else on my mind and not letting my mind wander. I learned by experience that I needed a place like a room in a resort where I could spread out my records, and a nice restaurant so I would not waste time looking for a place to eat.

I went on retreat with an agenda. Before I left, I reviewed all the past notes. I found at times I had set a goal that was no longer important. Then I would go through the same process again. I would write down what I thought I needed to do immediately, over the next year, and long term. I found that five-year and ten-year plans were not practical because I could put off those plans and never get to them. A three-year plan worked better because I could see the deadline and start work on it immediately.

Many times I realized I was headed down the wrong path, and I could reorient myself. The year I went to Hawaii, for example, I was sitting by the ocean and thinking about the home-building business I had with my brother Pierce. I thought about how the national home builder Nash Phillips/Copus was buying land everywhere and building subdivisions. It suddenly dawned on me: *This is a bubble.* I realized the economy was changing and what I was doing was not going to work anymore. I realized the bubble was going to burst, and I needed to get out at the top of the market. I came home and put every piece of real estate I had up for sale. In about six months, the bottom fell out. I watched the fall from the sidelines. I had gotten out of the market in time because I had taken time to think it all through and see the big picture.

Much the same happened two decades later with the dot-com collapse. This time I got help from Van Hoisington, a member of the finance committee of the Austin Lyric Opera. After an opera meeting, we were walking out together and I asked him what he thought of the tech market. I had bought stocks in the 1990s when they were going up, but near the end of 1999 I was worried. He said it was a bubble about to burst and advised me to get out of all tech stocks until the market made some sense. I went home and over the next few weeks sold all of them. That advice saved me financially when so many went bankrupt.

I have suggested going on retreat to many who have asked me for advice. I don't think a single person has ever done it. So maybe it was just something that worked for me but doesn't work for anybody else. But it surely did work for me.

Public Service

My retreats and collections were projects I pursued for my own fulfillment. At the same time, I wanted to give to others, much as my family had done when I was growing up. My experience in Vietnam, however, had made me wary of nonprofits.

When I was invited to become involved with the newly forming Austin Lyric Opera, I gave it careful thought. Was a professional opera company viable in Austin? What were its potential funding sources? What portion of its budget would be spent on overhead? Who were the other people involved? In the end, I was persuaded to join their effort because of the caliber of people involved. Working with them, I believed I could make a positive contribution.

I served on the governing board for nineteen years, beginning when the opera was founded in 1986. I took my role seriously, knowing that board members have ultimate responsibility for the organization's financial condition. The employees produce the operas, and the board makes sure the organization is well managed and accountable.

I started chairing the board in 1996, the year I fully retired from medical practice. As chairman, I relinquished my role as the company's doctor. As a physician, I believed I owed my total allegiance to the singers, and as chairman, to the opera company. The potential for conflict of interest may seem to some like an esoteric concept, but I felt strongly about it.

Chairing the board consumed a lot of my time, which I had not expected. The first couple of years were pleasant, but the economic downturn of 2000–2001 with the dot-com bust hurt the opera as well as the

My wife, Toni, and I attended every opening night performance of the Austin Lyric Opera.

economy. I worked almost full-time at the opera for my last three years as chairman. At one point, I left early from a European vacation trip to participate in the annual planning meeting, a time when we decided what we would do for the whole next year. As chairman, I knew more about the opera than any other board member, and I felt that our decisions could affect whether or not the opera survived.

Many board members supported me in governing the organization. Betty King, the longest-serving secretary of the Texas Senate, was president when I became chairman (she died in 2014). Others were Jeff Kodosky, a cofounder of National Instruments, and his wife, Gail; Ernest Auerbach, a business consultant and author; Wendi Kushner, an arts activist; Alfred King, an investor (he died in 2006); Van Hoisington, the founder of an investment management company; Helen Baxter, a major fund-raiser; and Fred Addy, a CFO of Amoco who retired in 1994.

By 2005 the opera had stabilized financially, which meant I could safely resign as chairman. Plus, it was time for me to pass the chairmanship to someone else, bringing in new blood and allowing me to spend more time at the ranch. I left the board having learned much about the operation of a nonprofit organization, fundraising, introducing children to the arts, and serving the community.

Chairing the board also gave me another opportunity to refine my public speaking abilities. Speaking to groups, large and small, can be difficult for everyone, especially for introverts, which I am. Yet I have had to speak in public many times—at medical conferences, in hospital staff meetings, at award ceremonies, and at large family gatherings. I learned early that to overcome my fear and tendency toward shyness in all these situations, I could carefully prepare what I was going to say. I would practice and revise the speech several times so that I could speak clearly and evenly without mistakes. I planned and practiced even for those occasions when I merely introduced someone to an audience.

Social gatherings—receptions for opera stars and Christmas parties for staff, for example—could have been awkward for me, except that I prepared carefully for those times as well. Before every reception and party, I would get a guest list and memorize the names of those I did not know and find out something about them and their interests so I could visit with them in more depth. I still dislike superficial conversation with comments like "Nice weather we're having" and "What have you been up to?"

Preparation is a habit I had cultivated from my youth, when I memorized the names and faces of my future classmates at Brownwood High School. I believe this habit is yet another example of how intelligence and talent can take you only so far. Success comes with effort and perseverance.

Travel

Toni and I have been privileged to travel to the world's great cities, museums, and libraries, alone and with our daughters, and to travel around the globe in search of rare books and historical documents. More recently, we have had the unexpected pleasure of traveling to distant countries to visit our grandchildren. That's because our son-in-law Jamie Spellings has worked for many years for ExxonMobil, with assignments in London and Bangkok.

Jamie has that rare combination of a brilliant mind that he combines with hard work, perseverance, and study. Bill Powers, the former University of Texas Law School dean and later university president, told me Jamie was one of the smartest students he ever taught in law school. "Jamie would sit in the front row," Powers said, "and every time he raised his hand, I'd think, 'Oh, no. Here comes another perceptive question.'" Jamie could have coasted through life and been highly successful, but he chose to do more. And he's so unassuming about it all. He has always understood our desire to see our grandchildren and welcomed us wholeheartedly. Toni and I visit them every three or four months, no matter where they are in the world. We enjoy not only spending time with the grandchildren but also studying the art and culture of other countries.

One key travel destination for me was Vietnam. In April 1975, President Gerald Ford announced the end of American involvement in that country, and the next year North and South Vietnam were reunited. In June 1995, the United States and Vietnam normalized relations. As I watched events unfold, I knew I desperately wanted to go back to retrace my steps and see what had changed.

I have since been back to Vietnam several times. One time Toni and I took a cruise ship up the Saigon River and docked in the same harbor close to where our troopship had docked in 1965. I sat on deck sipping a soft drink and marveled at how beautiful and how busy the river is now. At our former base camp at Nha Trang, I recognized almost nothing. I recognized the mountains and occasionally a street, but everything else had changed.

On a trip back to Vietnam after the war ended, I returned to the place where I had narrowly escaped an ambush and found this man watering his rice field. Instead of the violence of war, people were going about their lives.

I hired a Vietnamese man about my age to take me out to where I had driven into an ambush. To my surprise, it was a kind of middle-class Vietnamese subdivision. Children were playing in the street, and a man was watering his rice field with a bucket of water on his back, going up and down the rows. I had come as close to being killed there as I've ever come, and now it was harmless. It was people carrying on with their lives, making a living, trying to get through the day.

The main street in Nha Trang is now a quiet part of the downtown. Because of experiences like this, the nightmares that haunted me after my return have ended.

Maybe it helped me understand that everything has changed and I realized that I won't get ordered back to war in Vietnam. There's no war there now. Maybe that's why I rarely have the nightmare anymore.

Taking Care of Family

I heard Mother and Daddy say many times that family members should take care of each other. I understood this to mean those times when someone in the family is struggling or becomes ill or disabled. Mommie Winn, in caring for her brother, and Mother, in caring for Billy, provided excellent role models.

Mother cared for our brother Billy for most of her life. When she was no longer able, my sister, Mary Margaret, who lives in Midland, looked after him. The last thing Mother told me, about a week before she died, was "Take care of Billy." He eventually lived in a state-regulated home and died when he was nearly seventy. He always seemed utterly and completely happy.

Mary Margaret, Pierce, and I—and our families—have always been close. Our families have spent many holidays together, taken trips together, and visited often even though we have lived quite a distance apart. While Mother lived with Mary Margaret, our sister would call us if Mother was having some procedure, and Pierce and I would go out to help. Pierce and I have had several complex businesses together—home building and ranching—and never had any real differences. Today the three of us have lunch almost every day we are at the ranch at the same time. It takes constant care on everyone's part to keep a relationship together. For the last twenty years, the ranch has helped, but we would never have put all the effort into the ranch if we were not close.

As many wise people before me have said, the family is the basic building block of society. Family is where my parents loved and nurtured me as a child. As they aged, our roles reversed and Pierce, Mary Margaret, and I cared for our parents and our brother Billy. Mother, for example, continued to sink into depression from time to time after her electroshock treatments. The first psychiatric drug, Equinil (meprobamate), came out in the mid-1950s, and it smoothed out her depressive episodes somewhat. No one knew at that time that Equinil was addictive, and she got hooked. I became concerned, and after many years, I persuaded her to get off it. Because withdrawal carried the risk of seizures, I brought her to Shoal Creek Psychiatric Hospital in Austin. Withdrawal was difficult, but she managed it somehow and felt much better afterward.

As another example, we had Daddy live with us in Austin while he was undergoing radiation treatment for his cancer. Toni drove him to the radiation clinic, cooked for him, and generally tended his daily needs. She told me later that Daddy, never one to talk much, talked to her candidly about all sorts of things. One of his aphorisms had been "The time you decide to like your in-laws is before you meet them." I hadn't heard that when I married Toni, but her mother, Lillian Fox, would have won my heart and admiration even without my advance decision.

When Toni and I married, her daughter, Robin, joined the Burns family. She appears here with my daughters, Margaret Ann (*left*) and Laura (*right*).

Lillian had not been born into wealth and privilege but was extremely generous with everyone she knew. When Toni was in high school and her friend Gail's mother died unexpectedly, Lillian stayed up late making Gail's pep rally uniform, even though Lillian was the only mother who worked outside the home six days a week.

Lillian and her husband, Edward, opened their doors to people in need. They took in Toni's cousin Kay, for example, when Kay's mother died. They took in Toni and her daughter, Robin, plus their dog and cat, when Toni filed for divorce. They shared what they had without a moment's hesitation.

When my parents said "Take care of family," I believe they meant both the family members I grew up with and those that joined the clan by marriage. If my parents were alive now, I think they might expand "family" to include other people that get intertwined in your daily life, those you come to hold close and depend upon. That would be Miguel Reynosa. We hired him to do odd jobs around the house twenty-five

Robin enjoyed many activities as a teenager, including cheering sports teams at Murchison Junior High School in Austin.

years ago after our friend Pat Koen told us a newly arrived immigrant from Mexico needed more work. Miguel worked so hard and relieved us of so many disagreeable chores that we soon found we couldn't do without him. We eventually met his wife, Norma, and later their son, Michael. We marveled at their sacrifice to send Michael to college and celebrated with them when he earned a degree. We supported Miguel's struggle to shed his immigrant status and shared his pride when he took the oath of citizenship. More recently, he mourned with us when Robin became disabled and has since helped us many times to care for her. Yes, he's family.

We welcomed Robin into family gatherings and took her on trips, including this one to Greece.

Toni's mother, Lillian Fox, shown here at a quilting table with Robin as a teen, generously devoted time and talent to everyone she knew.

One of our family's most memorable trips was a six-day trek in 1990 across the Olympic Peninsula in Washington. We hiked eight to ten miles a day and camped out at night, having carefully planned every detail for the previous six months. *Left to right:* my brother Pierce; his son Todd; me; Pierce Jr.; Laura's friend Betsy Williams; my daughter Laura; Ernie Butler; and his wife, Sarah.

Robin joined the family when Toni and I married. In junior high, Robin Fox was an honor student, a class officer, a cheerleader, and an otherwise typical teenager. But gradually she became emotional and unpredictable. In 1984, five years into our marriage, Toni called me from home one day: "Something's wrong with Robin." That day, Robin was visiting Lillian in Lockhart. Lillian and Kay returned from shopping to find Robin ill and incoherent. Lillian took Robin to a doctor in Lockhart, who advised driving Robin to the Seton ER in Austin, oddly enough, instead of calling an ambulance. Robin couldn't walk, but Lillian managed to put her in the back seat of her car and met Toni and me at Seton.

When we opened the car door, it was obvious that Robin had had a stroke. Her left side was partially paralyzed, and she was semiconscious. I had already called Doug Hudson, a neurologist and good friend, who ordered a CT scan of her brain. I will never forget watching the CT scan scroll across the screen one slice at a time until the blood clot appeared on the screen. Doug said quietly, slowly but with terrible insight, "Oh, no," with agony in his voice. We watched the image appear on the screen and neither of us said another word. Finally, Doug said, "Let's go tell Toni." From that moment, Toni and I knew that our lives and Robin's would never be the same.

Ten days later, Marvin Cressman, a superb neurosurgeon and good friend, did surgery to remove the clot and lessen the pressure on the brain, which helped minimize the problem. Robin was in the hospital for a couple of weeks and then in rehab for months. She had to learn how to sit up, roll over in bed, and walk again. She had to overcome dizziness, double vision, and memory loss. She had to learn how to do all the simple tasks of daily living with the use of only one hand. She is able to live independently but with constant help from us. Toni believes that in her dreams "Robin can run, dance, and wear pretty shoes. She's free."

As a physician, I had seen many times how a single medical incident can change one's life forever. This was true with Robin's stroke. As Toni likes to say, "Life changes in ordinary moments."

CHAPTER 8

Restoring the Ranch

While I was still practicing medicine, I had a few minutes before my next appointment one day to talk to a patient who was CEO of a large corporation and had worked around the globe. I mentioned that my daughter Margaret Ann had recently moved to London with her husband and children, and while I was excited about the opportunity for them, I would miss seeing my grandchildren.

"Do you have any advice for a grandfather whose children are living out of the country?" I asked him.

He thought about it for a minute and then said, "Grandchildren need to have some place that's always home."

When I talked with Toni later, we agreed he was right. Children need stability, a place where they always feel they belong. We decided that the ranch would be the place that was "always home" for our grandchildren. No matter what happened—marriage, career change, move to a different city or country—they could come back to it. The ranch would always be there, and it would never change. We developed it with that purpose in mind, and I think we have succeeded.

FOUNDING THE RANCH

To understand the ranch and our attachment to it, we need to go back to my great-grandfather, Simon Pierce Burns. He was born January 1, 1834, in Logan County, Ohio, the son of Christopher and Rachel Burns. According to family legend, he ran away from home at age twelve, and traveled by wagon train to Texas two years after it became a state. He

Toni and I decided the Burns ranch would be the "always home" for grandchildren. They include Laura's son, Dan Arnold, shown here as a child with me. Now a senior in high school, he lives in Austin and has always loved visiting the ranch.

Margaret Ann's husband, Jamie Spellings, takes his sons, Henry (*front*) and Paul, on a ride on a four-wheeler at the ranch when they were boys.

We named the ranch after Colonel Simon Pierce Burns, my great-grandfather, who founded the ranch with his wife, Sarah, in 1873.

settled in Collin County (northeast of present-day Dallas) and attended school. He married Sarah Ann Gibson (1837–1903) in the mid-1850s.

A short time before the outbreak of the Civil War in 1860, Simon and his family (including three young children) moved to Missouri, where he joined the Missouri Home Guards. He joined the Confederate Army as a private in 1861 and advanced in rank to colonel. According to *Frontier's Generation: The Pioneer History of Brown County with Sidelights on the Surrounding Territory* (1980) by Tevin Clyde Smith, he "saw action at

Oak Hill, Lexington, Missouri, Jenkins Ferry, and Mansfield, Louisiana. After Mansfield, General Sterling Price and other officers recommended him for promotion in rank to Brigadier General." He served in that rank until the war ended, "but referred to himself as Colonel because he never received his commission from the war department in spite of the fact that General E. Kirby Smith, a member of the Army Board, had appointed him to the post of permanent commander of Parson's Brigade."

Sarah Burns, my great-grandmother, managed to raise ten children on the frontier even though she was blind.

After the war, Colonel Burns and his wife lived in Collin County, Texas, where he was elected sheriff in 1866. But he was "soon removed from office by Federal intervention 'as an impediment to reconstruction along with Governor Throckmorton and other state and county officers elected by the people,'" according to Smith's history. Smith believed that statement was made by a US congressman prior to Colonel Burns's death, and was part of a well-earned tribute to his activities in war and peacetime.

In 1873, Colonel Burns arranged for a loan and bought a small tract of state land about fifteen miles north of Brownwood in Brown County on the edge of the frontier. At that time, according to the *Handbook of Texas*, Brownwood consisted of two stores, a log courthouse, and five dwellings. He built a house for his growing family, which by that time included Simon Pierce Burns II, born in 1868 in Collin County, who would become my grandfather. (The homesite is still in our family.)

When they came here, Colonel Burns's wife, Sarah, had become blind. By reconstructing the symptoms, I think she probably had herpes keratitis of the eyes, with bilateral rupture of the globes, because sources described drainage from both eyes and she evidently had no vision. (I have had the same infection in my right eye since I was a child, and fortunately with modern medicine I have been able to save my vision.) Despite the blindness, she reared a total of ten children and lived until she was sixty-six years old.

Colonel Burns worked as a surveyor while reading law in preparation for the bar examination. According to *Something about Brown: A History of Brown County* (1958) by T. R. Havins, the county had no more than 1,200 people in 1876, but "boasted a lawyer for every hundred people. S. P. Burns was both a lawyer and real estate agent and advised anyone holding land scrip that he was in a position to locate vacant, state lands." (A land scrip is a document that entitles a person to acquire a certain portion of public land.)

Colonel Burns practiced law for many years before campaigning for the Texas House of Representatives in 1894. Because of his experience as a sheriff and Confederate general, many people looked to him as a leader. He was elected to the house and served two terms, beginning in 1895, as a Democrat.

While campaigning for the Texas Senate in 1898, he stopped in Granbury, a town ninety-two miles northeast of Brownwood. On April 8, he ate supper in the hotel, said he did not feel well, and retired to his room. He was found dead the next morning from a heart attack. He was returned to the family home and lay in state for a short time before burial at the Heflin Cemetery just east of the ranch. My Aunt Effie Jack, who lived to be 102, remembered buggies lining the road to the cemetery. "It was quite a funeral," she said.

Living on the Frontier's Edge

Colonel Burns was the first of the Burns family to be buried in Heflin Cemetery. Through the years, it has become the final resting place for other relatives, including his wife, Sarah; my parents; my infant brother who died at birth; my brother Billy; my maternal grandparents, T. L. and Mommie Winn; Mommie's brother, Estel Rowland; Mary Margaret's husband, Fred Byrom; another brother-in-law; a cousin, Jerry Towngate; a grandson; and an infant niece.

When I was growing up, our family always reserved the first Sunday in May for Decoration Day, a time for repairing the gravestones, removing weeds, and placing flowers on the graves. The day started with prayers and was followed by a covered-dish meal and a brief speech by a pastor or a chosen family member.

The cemetery dates back to 1876, three years after Colonel Burns founded the ranch. According to a folk story that I think is true, a family heading west in a covered wagon stopped there to bury a child. They dug the grave on a hilltop owned by the Heflin family. The Heflins donated the plot on that hilltop, and it became known as Heflin Cemetery. I do not know if Colonel Burns knew of the child's burial there.

The ranch adjacent to the Burns property belonged to the Small family. Mollie Small (1869–1954), who became my Grandmother Burns, told me that when she was young, Indians camped on the edge of the ranch. She never talked of any raids on the ranch itself, but everyone was afraid of the Indians. They may have been the Penateka Comanche, who roamed the area in the 1800s.

Perhaps a more dangerous frontier threat for the Burns family was outlaws. According to the *Handbook of Texas*, the Brownwood–Fort Worth stage "was robbed five times in two months" in 1875.

My Aunt Effie told a story, later published in *Blanket, Texas, Community History* (1983), about Jim Small and his son John starting a trip home after a "First Monday" trading day at Comanche. While the two spent the night near the Brysonville schoolhouse, two men crept up to their wagon and stole two horses. In the morning, the two thieves showed up by chance at Jim's house asking permission to water their horses at the well. Recognizing the horses, Jim's wife, Matilda, gave permission for watering and even invited them to breakfast, giving one of her daughters time to slip away and notify Colonel Burns at the neighboring ranch. In a true example of neighbor helping neighbor, Colonel Burns came and promptly arrested the men. (The published account ends the story there, with nothing said about whether Jim and son John returned home safely.)

One incident that had elements of a Wild West movie happened to my great-grandfather's eldest son, James (1856–1882). One day in 1882 he was playing poker in a New Mexico bar and drinking too much when the town's deputy sheriff walked in. He and James despised each other. The deputy called him out, they exchanged words, and then the deputy shot him. James died—he was only twenty-six years old. The townsfolk took sides—some believed the deputy was doing his duty; others thought James was shot in cold blood. Later, as the deputy was riding through the middle of town, he fell off his horse and was killed. Although the circumstances were suspicious, no one was arrested.

Cattle rustlers were another problem. Up to the time Colonel Burns bought his land, ranchers in Brown County typically raised longhorn cattle that roamed the open range. Ranchers rounded up cattle once or twice a year, often cooperating with neighbors to brand calves. Rustlers rounded up strays their owners had missed and even resorted to altering brands. But as cattlemen's associations began using inspectors to check brands and law enforcement tightened, rustling declined.

Probably the first cattle drive through the county occurred in 1876, when, according to *Something about Brown* (1976), the Snyder brothers of Williamson County crossed with two herds of 2,500 head. The trail ran northwest on the east side of Pecan Bayou, continued north through Brownwood, and angled northwest to intersect with another trail north of Coleman. This description indicates that it did not go through the Burns ranch.

Because cattlemen got low prices for their tough, scrawny longhorns, they began breeding cows with graded bulls imported from nearby states. (I don't know whether Colonel Burns raised or crossbred longhorns; in later years our family preferred Herefords.) To ensure enough grass for their improved herds and to prevent against encroachment by farmers, large landowners began fencing their land with the newly invented barbed wire. Small landowners who needed water for their herds and nonlandowners who depended on the free range grew resentful. Emotions ran high. The first episode of fence cutting occurred in the spring of 1883 and then spread throughout the surrounding counties. Brown County, in particular, became a hotbed of the fence-cutting wars. Colonel Burns, who favored fencing, was involved in at least one attack by the fence cutters.

In a special legislative session in 1884, lawmakers made fence cutting a felony and the fencing of public land a misdemeanor. Outbreaks of fence cutting still occurred, however, as evidenced by the killing of two fence cutters by Texas Rangers in Brown County in 1886, as noted in the *Handbook of Texas*.

Losing Land in the Depression

After Colonel Burns died in 1898, two of his sons—William "Billy" Burns (1865–1934) and my grandfather, Simon Pierce Burns II (1868–1948)—continued working the ranch. The 1890s were not a good time for agriculture. Farm prices fluctuated and land values fell, causing the Burns family to sell a large part of the ranch to pay debts.

The family pulled out of the economic decline in the early 1900s, and two glorious decades followed. My great-uncle and grandfather developed the ranch into a huge cattle-raising operation, expanding into Comanche County, South Texas, and Kansas. By Brownwood standards, the Burns family was well off. My grandfather, who was regarded as "the boss," was often asked to help family and friends who were financially struggling. His generosity would later prove disastrous.

When my grandfather was in his early twenties, he had his eye on Mollie Small, the daughter of a neighboring rancher. According to family lore, he went to visit her one day and discovered that her father had been abusive. Without a moment's delay, he took her into town and married her. They ended up having five children, one of whom was my father, George Pierce Burns (1901–1986). All five children grew up on the ranch, but only my father would return to help run it.

Only a few years after my parents moved to the ranch to help my grandfather, the whole country sank into the mire of the Great Depression. My grandfather found himself overextended. Bank loans, which he had cosigned for family and friends, came due. He began selling off parts of the ranch to pay debts, and in some cases lost parts through foreclosure.

In one instance, my great-uncle Billy Burns's ranch was foreclosed on and was scheduled to be auctioned off on the courthouse steps. In response, the family arranged a bank loan so they would be able to buy it back at auction. Meanwhile, the judge and one of his friends saw the opportunity to get the ranch. They realized that the loan would allow the family to buy back the ranch if it went at a fair and honest auction. At ten o'clock the morning of the sale, the family waited on the north side of the Brown County Courthouse, where auctions were traditionally held. While the family stood waiting, the judge and his friend slipped out to the other side of the courthouse, and the judge secretly sold the land to the friend for almost nothing. They immediately left town and drove nonstop to Fort Worth. As the family later observed, the buyer didn't care about the land—he never set foot on it. He never planted a seed nor repaired a fence. When he came to Brownwood to arrange a lease, he would rent a room in a hotel to interview ranchers who wanted

My mother's family came to Brownwood from East Texas when she was a child. She is shown here with her father, T. L. Winn (who died when I was four); her mother, Mommie; and her brother Paul.

to lease land. The judge and his friend betrayed us and the public trust, but they were probably not the only ones to succumb to avarice in those hard times. Uncle Billy did not live to see the end of the Depression; he died in 1934.

That same year, my mother had what she described as "the worst day of my life." Government men came to the ranch and shot all the cattle except the milk cows. The government's rationale was that killing cattle would decrease their number, thereby increasing the price. My family had spent decades building a herd, only to see it demolished in one day. The loss was devastating.

My grandparents continued to live in the same house on the ranch until about 1942, when their house caught fire and burned to the ground. Soon afterward my grandfather had a stroke that left him partially paralyzed. He and Grandmother Burns moved to Brownwood, where they could be closer to medical care. He lived until 1948, when he succumbed at age eighty to complications of the stroke. She lived until 1954; she died at age eighty-five from complications of diabetes.

Holding On to the Ranch

It was left to Mother and Daddy to rescue what they could of the ranch. At first we lived in a little house where hired hands used to live. About 1942, early in World War II, the army sold houses in Brownwood to clear the land for building Camp Bowie. Daddy bought one, had it relocated to the ranch, and added two bedrooms for us children. It was about a mile east of the original house on a prominent hill with a beautiful view and some old mesquite trees in the backyard (where Pierce and Reba's house is now). That house transformed our life. A year or so before Mother died, I asked her, "What was the happiest time of your life?" Without hesitation, she said, "When we moved to the new house and the children were young."

After Mother's bout with depression, Daddy bought a house in Brownwood, where they lived until he died in 1986. He would work at his town job all day, go out to the ranch and do chores at night, and then come back to town to sleep. Years later he told me that he never wanted to leave the ranch at night, but he always did. Even though the house at the ranch was fully furnished, my parents never spent another night out there.

When Daddy retired from his town job in 1966, he continued going to the ranch every day to check on things. In 1970, he leased the ranch to a neighbor, which provided income and freed him from having total responsibility for it. He and Mother had held on to those 1,300 acres since the 1940s with determination and backbreaking work. In 1978, our parents were honored by the Texas Department of Agriculture in its Family Heritage Land Program for owning and operating the ranch continuously in the same family for at least a hundred years.

After Daddy died, Mother and Billy moved to Midland to live with Mary Margaret and her husband, Fred Byrom. Mother taught piano at Midland College until she was in her nineties.

Before starting my medical practice, I often brought my family to visit my parents at the ranch. On one visit in the late 1960s, my daughters, Margaret Ann and Laura, rode Daddy's horse.

My mother and father, shown here in 1982, were devoted to each other all their lives. Daddy would die four years later, in 1986, and Mother would live until 2007.

Mother outlived Daddy by more than a decade. We were going to have a big party on her one hundredth birthday on October 15, 2007. She said she was too tired and did not want to have it. She died just before midnight the day before her one hundredth birthday. In my medical practice, I witnessed many deaths but was still unprepared for that of my parents. I realized as I never had before that at the end of a life, love is everything. Our parents were greatly loved, and they taught us to love.

During the whole time Mother lived off the ranch, she had little involvement with it. When she visited, she would walk, pick flowers, or sit in the pickup. She was, after all, a "town girl." Although she loved the ranch, she left it to Daddy and her grown children to manage.

Finding a Purpose for the Ranch

The ranchland on which we had grown up remained leased until 1987, when Pierce took over the management of it. Several years earlier, in 1973, he and Reba, Mary Margaret and Fred, and Toni and I began buying back parcels of the ranch as it had existed before the Depression. Each couple bought separate sections as they came on the market.

Today the ranch consists of six thousand acres, one of the largest ranches in Brown County. The ranch lies in an ecotone, or transition area, where three ecological regions merge. The Rolling Plains sweep down from the north where the tall prairie grasses thrived until the middle 1800s. The Cross Timbers stretch to the east with typical post oak arising from the sandy loam soil. The Hill Country comes up from the south with Edwards limestone capping the mesas and hills.

The ranch is bounded roughly on the north by the mountains, on the west by US Highway 183, and on the south by FM 1467. On the east side is the Muse Wildlife Management Area, owned by the Texas Parks and Wildlife Department. This 1,972-acre area is surrounded on three sides by our ranch. Ironically, this area, even though it was "stolen" from us during the Depression, is now so aligned with the family goals that it is once again a family asset without costing us anything.

As weekend ranchers in addition to our primary occupations, we did what other area ranchers did: we raised cattle. Toni and I wanted to re-

In 2006 Mother celebrated her ninety-ninth birthday surrounded by her grown children. *Left to right:* me, Pierce, Mary Margaret, and Billy.

This stone gate provides entry to the six-thousand-acre Colonel Burns Ranch, one of the largest ranches in Brown County.

BEFORE: When we began buying back the ranch, much of which the family lost in the Depression, the Sunday House sat in shambles.

AFTER: Today the restored Sunday House is my favorite place to read and study when I visit the ranch.

store the ranch, and I naively thought it would be easy. By "restore," I mean returning the ranch to its original condition. We took the customary steps—removed the cattle from the grasslands, decreased our stocking rate, and grazed cattle on rotation. We removed lots of mesquite and cedar (mountain juniper) trees, but we didn't have a real plan for doing it. It was hit or miss. After a few years, we saw some improvement, but I slowly realized our efforts were not going to restore the land the way I had envisioned. We knew the ranch was sick, but we didn't have a diagnosis. Actually, I wasn't capable of making a diagnosis.

That was about thirty years ago. I decided then to stop all work on the ranch, step back, and educate myself. I went to every conference I could find anywhere in the country on range management, ecology, conservation, and wildlife management. I took part in seminars at Texas A&M University and courses in plant identification at the University of Texas. I must have gone to more than a hundred courses to learn about restoration, and I visited many of the best ranches, including the King Ranch in South Texas and David Bamberger's ranch in Blanco County. It soon became apparent that I was making a lot of mistakes—costly mistakes.

In addition, I did something that turned out to be unique. I read every journal I could find—and I owned many of the original texts—in which early explorers described the land before it was settled. The Lewis and Clark and Zebulon Pike expeditions, even though they didn't come to Texas, described the land before the settlers came. Explorers like Randolph Marcy, George Kendall, Jacob De Cordova, and Ferdinand von Roemer described Texas land in great detail, giving us a wealth of information about how the country looked and allowing us to understand how it has changed.

Restoring the ranch meant we had to pick a certain point in time that would represent its "original condition." The reality, of course, is that you can never do that. The climate has changed, the culture has changed, the plants and animals have changed. Actually, any period I might have picked from around thirteen thousand years ago (the earliest evidence of human occupation in North America) to the present would have given me a different picture of how the land looked.

Initially we set the restoration date at 1873 when the ranch was founded. Then I realized we had to go back further because cattle had grazed on the open range for twenty years before that. I considered whether bison herds might have roamed in Brown County, but I doubt they came that far east. Ultimately, I set the benchmark at about the 1840s. I thought that timeframe would be more natural, and it was more appealing to me. It's an esoteric concept, but it influences everything I do on the ranch.

Then I made a fundamental decision: I would not manage the land, as most landowners do, for specific species, such as deer, turkey, or quail, or some economic objective, such as cattle, horses, hunting, or oil and gas drilling. When you do that, you define at the start what the land will look like and which ecosystem will be favored. I wanted to do something entirely different. I wanted to try to bring back the entire ecosystem—soil, water, native plants, and native animals—as close as possible to the way they were in the 1840s.

In my research, I found three seminal events that changed the ranch ecology. The first was the arrival of settlers in the 1800s. Back then, Texas looked like an oasis, and ranchers thought the land could furnish an endless supply of grass. As we know now, that was unreasonable for a county that gets only about twenty-five inches of rain a year. Beginning in the 1870s, early settlers in Central Texas severely overstocked their land with domestic livestock. In fact, the late 1870s and early 1880s had the highest number of cattle ever recorded in Brown County. The cattle selectively consumed tall prairie grasses to the point of extinction. Only the midsize and short grasses remained, and they were sparse.

The second event was the Depression in the 1930s, when ranchers suffered drought, used poor soil conservation practices, and overgrazed because they couldn't sell cattle.

The third event was the 1950s drought, which lasted about seven years on our ranch. Diminished rainfall dried up streams and springs and turned the soil to dust. In 1956 scorching temperatures from late April to late October left the land barren of grass and ground cover. The drought was so bad that the land still hasn't recovered from it.

In studying our ranch, we saw evidence of water runoff, soil erosion,

Restoring the Ranch

Today every member of the Burns family, like the four generations shown here, has a shirt bearing a logo that we had specially designed for the ranch. *Left to right:* my daughter Margaret Ann; her sons, Henry (*top*) and Paul; Mother; and me with Margaret Ann's daughter, Sarah.

and reduced diversity of plants and animals. As a physician, I began to understand that just as I had had to study each patient carefully, I needed to study the ecology carefully. It took me years before I was able to think of the ranch as terribly simple and at the same time infinitely complex. It helped me to think of the ranch as having many illnesses, each of which requires an accurate diagnosis and treatment. As in medicine, the interactions of all the systems are complex, and every treatment may have unintended consequences that can last for decades or even centuries.

In addition, Toni and I chanced upon a philosophical insight for our restoration effort. When we were traveling in England in the mid-1990s, Toni saw a stone carved with the first four lines of William Blake's poem "Auguries of Innocence." She turned to me and said, "This is the ranch."

> To see a World in a Grain of Sand
> And a Heaven in a Wild Flower,
> Hold Infinity in the palm of your hand
> And Eternity in an hour.

We posted a large metal sign bearing those four lines at the western entrance to the ranch. That's what you see when you drive onto the property. When you're on the ranch, you experience those sentiments—seeing bluebonnets in the spring, smelling the earth after a rain, watching a sunrise, hearing the distant yipping of a coyote. Those lines, written maybe two hundred years ago, are so modern. If we could really see and understand "a grain of sand," for example, we would know the universe.

Restoration Practices

In treating the ailments of the ranch, we received excellent advice from professionals. Perhaps the most helpful was Devin Erxleben, a wildlife biologist who runs the Muse Wildlife Management Area. Two others were Scott Anderson, the Brown County Extension agent, and Ricky Marks (who has recently retired), the branch manager for the US Natural Resources Conservation Service in Brownwood. We asked them to evaluate our ranch every year. They have been on the ranch many times and have been invaluable to us.

One of the most important and straightforward restoration practices we used was brush removal, mostly mesquite and cedar. My goal was not to remove all mesquite and cedar but to recreate the old-growth forests of two hundred years ago before humans destroyed them all.

Restoring the Ranch

An old-growth mesquite forest in 1840 would have consisted of 150- to 200-year-old mesquite trees spaced so that their canopies just touch each other and have about a thirty percent canopy cover.

In the 1940s a well-meaning government designed a program to help ranchers and farmers make their land more productive by clear-cutting the mesquite. It was supposed to open up the land so more grass would grow for cattle and sheep. The opposite happened. Mesquites came back with a vengeance.

On our ranch, brush control consisted of three steps. First, I removed all domestic livestock. This step is critical because livestock eat the mesquite beans, pass them through their digestive tract, and deposit the seeds in their manure all over the ranch. In fifteen or twenty years, the mesquite thickets are back and all your work is for nothing. Second, I selectively removed all the young mesquites, leaving only those seventy years old and older. Third, I immediately planted tall prairie grass by hand in all the disturbed areas where I removed trees. Native grass—sideoats grama, switchgrass, big bluestem, little bluestem, Indian grass—will out-compete the mesquite seeds that fall from the trees. I personally walked with the bulldozer operator to point out exactly which trees to remove or leave standing, which is labor intensive—and expensive—but effective.

After twenty years of removing livestock and planting grasses, we have beautiful grass where we once had large areas of bare ground. Each year's grass growth dies, falls down, and covers the ground to form an organic layer on the soil. In addition to mesquite, the ranch has oak, elm, pecan, and walnut trees. Often an old tree will have ten or fifteen species of shrubs and vines underneath. Now we have irregular motts of trees with large, open areas in between, and the older trees have the space to thrive. I have recreated an old-growth forest, making our ranch look different from any other in the county. The greatest compliment I receive is when a visitor says, "It looks like you haven't done anything."

We don't plant improved grasses. A landmark study by the Caesar Kleberg Wildlife Research Institute found that native grass supports significantly more arthropods than improved grass. Without arthropods, the entire wildlife ecosystem is disrupted. Insects, as well as fungi, soil bacteria, birds, and small mammals, live in symbiosis with native grass and wildflowers, feeding off each other in a balance that has evolved over thousands of years. Our motto at the ranch: Butterflies and beetles are as important as deer.

We don't do prescribed burns. It's widely believed that large swatches of prairie and woodlands burned during the centuries when native peoples inhabited the land, but I have not found that to be true. In all my research in early journals, nothing was written about lightning as a significant cause of prairie fire.

Under our land lies the northern and western part of the Trinity Aquifer, where water flows underground from our ranch to Travis County. We are in the aquifer recharge zone. Whereas Austin gets about thirty-five inches of rain a year, we get only twenty-five inches, so every inch of rain is precious to us. When a raindrop falls on bare land, it lands hard, splashes up with bits of debris, and compacts the soil; much of it runs off to lower levels. When the raindrop lands on organic matter, however, the grass, bush, or tree diffuses it, letting it drop gently and infiltrate into the soil rather than run off. With almost one hundred percent organic ground cover, we have effectively stopped erosion. We no longer lose topsoil after every rain. When it rains, we never allow vehicles to drive off the ranch roads into the prairie grass. If we need to cross a grassy area when the soil is wet, we walk. As a result, scientists at Texas A&M have estimated that we have effectively tripled our useable rainfall.

When we stopped runoff, a surprising thing happened: all our ponds, stock tanks, and wet-weather streams went dry. The only ponds that held water were spring fed. All our neighbors' ponds were full, and ours were empty. We had stopped runoff so effectively that no water was running into the ponds. The rainfall was watering the plants and trees, making them lush and green. We had to remind ourselves that there were no ponds or stock tanks in the 1840s—only streams and springs.

Some would argue that we could increase stream flow by removing cedar and mesquite trees, which consume lots of water. Early on we tried that, but water flow in our streams did not change. A study conducted at Texas A&M at San Angelo showed no correlation between stream flow and the removal of mesquite and cedar. Stream flow is so complex that removing cedar and mesquite is not significant.

Spring flow is even more complex. Even though our rainfall was infiltrating into the soil, we saw very little increase in volume in our springs, only a more consistent flow. We plotted our springs on an aerial map, and they seemed to be randomly located. Then we plotted them on a topographical map, and they all occurred at exactly the same elevation, where a layer of clay lies under a layer of sand. That told us that spring flow depends to a large extent on the soil structure below ground.

Water is critical not only for plants but also for wildlife. Many studies show that mammals and birds cannot go farther than a half mile for water. Turkeys, for example, nest within three hundred yards of water. Because our springs were not adequate for wildlife, we drilled twelve water wells all over the ranch. Knowing that animals prefer to drink at ground level, we buried troughs in the ground with the top lip at ground level to simulate a natural pond. We also let one trough slowly overflow to create a mini wetland for insects, bees, and mice.

Besides needing water, wildlife tend to move toward areas where the edge of the open prairie meets the forest. This allows animals feeding in the open prairie to quickly escape to the cover of the trees when threatened—a principle known as the edge effect. The grassy areas between irregular motts of trees provide just that. The bobcats, foxes, and coyotes are free to wander around the ranch. We don't set traps and have no high fences. As a result of all our efforts, native wildlife has returned, including some rare and endangered species.

Like everything on the ranch, nothing happens in isolation. Everything we do has consequences, and our job is to look at the entire plan and decide what is best for the soil, water, air, and biological diversity of plants and animals. Because ecosystems are constantly changing, we don't try to hold the ranch ecosystem static. We do track how it's changing, however.

For thirteen years, we have monitored critical factors: rainfall, temperature (freezing and 100-plus degrees), wildlife census, bird census for certain species, predators and their effects, arthropod conditions, organic ground cover, and soil compaction. We monitor anything that was planted, all soil disturbed, tree removal, and crop planting. Since 2000, following Texas A&M guidelines, we have set up photographic stations all over the ranch. We take pictures in the same places every year to see the progression. As I learned in practicing medicine, documentation is everything.

Restoring native wildlife became easier in 1995 when the Texas Legislature enacted a provision for wildlife valuation of agricultural land. I was the first to apply for the wildlife valuation in Brown County. Over the past twenty years, Pierce and I have worked with the county appraisal office to follow the letter of the law. Appraisal Director Eva Bush and her staff have always been fair and accurate in their dealings with us.

Creating the "Always Home" for Grandchildren

Toni and I struggled for years on how to make the ranch feel as though it belonged to the whole family, even though the ranch has had multiple owners all at the same time—Mother and Daddy; my brother Pierce and his wife, Reba; our sister, Mary Margaret, and her husband, Fred; and Toni and I. The ranch never had a name, so we thought perhaps a name could convey the concept of family ownership. Then one August afternoon, we were hiking the Colonel Bob Trail in the Olympic National Forest in Washington. Seeing a sign that said "Colonel Bob Trail," Toni turned around to me and said, "It's the Colonel Burns Ranch." In that instant, we had a name that integrated the whole family's efforts. The main drawback is that the name recognizes only my great-grandfather, when actually it was my parents who saved the ranch for the family. Certainly Colonel Burns—and his wife, Sarah—started it all, and his name will remind our current and future ranch users that generations of our family have called the ranch home.

Besides the name, we have physical reminders in the ranch buildings. The original home of Colonel Burns's family is gone, but we have taken care to preserve its foundation, cistern, and rockwork. My parents' first house is gone, but the second, and bigger, house acquired during World War II is now home to Pierce and his wife, Reba. It's located at the south entrance.

The ranch provides the perfect holiday gathering place for our family. One Christmas my daughter Laura, her son Dan, and I shared a special moment in front of the traditional tree.

At the western ranch entrance is the house that belongs to Toni and me, the T House, as the grandchildren call it ("T" for Toni). It has a large patio and accommodates our family gatherings. Because we assemble there for holidays like Thanksgiving and Christmas, I have come to believe the ranch has helped bring our family together and keep it together.

A short distance to the east is what we call the Sunday House. When we first came, the roof was gone and its rock walls were falling down. The choice was to let it deteriorate or restore it. (Again, we define "restore" as returning it to its original condition.) We chose to restore it—new roof, rebuilt walls, refurbished front porch. Carved into the rock near the roof is the year 1898. An old windmill stands nearby—nonfunctioning but picturesque.

Mary Margaret and Fred's house stands midway—three miles each way—between the T House on the west and Pierce and Reba's house to the south. It was built in the 1940s and has been restored. Mary Margaret's late husband, Fred, a geologist, rebuilt the rock wall around the house. It was his last project, fittingly undertaken in the months before he died. He did it the way he did all his projects—with care, precision, and permanence. I expect it to last a hundred years.

Another restored house is the Arts and Crafts bungalow in the northeast part of the ranch. Daddy remembers seeing it there when he was a child around 1907. We call it the Spanish Springs House because of a nearby spring that we think the Spanish dug by hand into a cliff wall. That spring has never gone dry in recorded history, not even in the 1950s drought. We don't use this house much because it's isolated in a rocky, wooded area at the end of an unpaved road.

It's so isolated that back in the 1970s when I happened to drive out there, I was astonished to see that someone was living there! No one answered my knock, so I left a note saying that it was my house and they needed to get out. When I talked to the sheriff in town, he suspected who it was. "He's nobody to mess with," the sheriff said, explaining that the squatter was supposed to go back to prison soon. "I'll handle it," the sheriff said, and he did.

Restoration is more expensive than building a new house and requires more frequent and costlier maintenance, but we believe restoration better fits our long-range purpose. The ranch does have a new house, however. Pierce's son Todd and his wife, Liz, have built a house near his dad's at the east entrance, which has a fantastic view of the horizon. Another new house will be built soon by Mary Margaret's daughter Marietta and her husband, Albert Metcalfe. This one overlooks the mountains.

Every house on the ranch has electricity and water (from wells). We have no security lights, and we shield every outdoor light. When you stand on the top of our mountain at night, you can see the edge of our ranch because our ranch is dark. We've also restored a barn and eight water troughs.

Of course, other families owned or worked parts of the ranch in the interval before we bought back most of it. They built homes, which after many years fell into ruin. Altogether the ranch has seven abandoned homesites, some of which have nothing left but a foundation. We have chosen to leave these foundations alone rather than dig them up, because of the cost and historic value. And considering they were once homes where families lived, worked, and raised children, we believe they are places deserving of our respect.

My parents worked hard to keep the ranch. If they could see it today, I think they would be proud to see what we've done with it.

In May 2012 Toni and I were named Lone Star Land Stewards by the Texas Parks and Wildlife Department. Devin Erxleben had nominated us. By recognizing private landowners for excellence in habitat management and wildlife conservation, the department hopes to encourage other landowners to do the same on their property and to educate youth and the public about protecting the state's natural resources. As an award recipient, we have hosted field tours on occasion for students as well as international visitors.

Economic Issues

We have resisted efforts that might result in short-term economic gain. We don't lease the land to deer hunters, for example, because we want to control every aspect of the ranch ecology. We do, however, allow family members to hunt deer during hunting season. Of course, we kill feral hogs because they are not native, they dig up plants by the roots, and they are increasing faster than anyone can get rid of them.

Part of the ranch overlies the Barnett Shale geological formation, which has pockets of oil and gas. But we have chosen not to lease land for drilling because it would destroy what we have worked so hard to achieve.

Several years ago I was approached by a company offering to install wind towers on our ranch. I first saw it as an opportunity for free money, but after studying the prospect, I realized that wind farms are permanent and become obsolete in ten or fifteen years. They end up destroying the land value of smaller ranches surrounding the wind farm. The only ones making money are the wind companies; they get production tax credits. Wind generation of electricity in Brown County would be marginal, and the wind towers would end up inflicting harm over the long term. I have refused to allow wind towers to be built on our ranch, and I have worked hard to keep them out of Brown County.

Our emphasis on restoration has led some to question why we have not placed the ranch in a conservation easement. In studying agreements of this kind, I have become convinced that the restrictions would be too severe to protect the natural resources in the ways we have chosen. What's more, the easement would last in perpetuity, which would eliminate choices our heirs might have in managing the property.

I don't want to restrict their decision-making, because no one can foretell the future. Long ago, I realized that I cannot criticize or judge people for decisions they make about their land use. Previous generations of our family have abused the ranch with overgrazing, for example. Looking back, I realize they did what they had to do to make a living and care for their families. Future generations may look back at us and say something like, "Why in the world did they plant native grass rather than improved grass?" I have concluded that every generation does its best, and I can't criticize past mistakes or tie their hands, because I make errors myself.

Early in the fall we prepare for hunting season by filling deer feeders with corn. We allow hunting only of deer and feral hogs, and only by family members.

I consider it the greatest compliment when ranch visitors tell me, "It looks like you haven't done anything."

Receiving the Lone Star Steward Award from the Texas Parks and Wildlife Department in 2012 allowed us to celebrate our restoration efforts. *Front row, left to right:* my sister-in-law, Reba Burns; my wife, Toni; my sister, Mary Margaret; and my daughter Margaret Ann. *Back row, left to right:* Texas Parks and Wildlife biologist Devin Erxleben; my brother Pierce; me; Toni's daughter, Robin; my daughter Laura; and my brother-in-law, Charles Schwope.

One of the most important things I've learned in the past ten years is there's no one practical way to manage a six-thousand-acre ranch. A ranch that big can have hundreds of different ecological areas, some one or two acres and others ten or more acres in size. Each one must be managed differently, which makes conservation and restoration terribly complicated. In the future, I would advise anyone thinking about restoring a ranch to limit its size to one hundred acres.

The amount of money one can spend on a ranch this size is almost endless. Doing what we're doing is horribly expensive. But we're taking the long-term view. We are planning for decades in the future. Restoration is a long-term process. Some of the land will never recover—surely not in my lifetime—and some will take hundreds of years. We look at the ranch as a multidecade and hundred-year project, an endless endeavor of stopping the erosion, growing native grass, and increasing plant and animal diversity.

The Future of the Ranch

With 1,200 people moving to Texas every day, we can expect the population to be so great that Brown County will be divided up into smaller and smaller pieces. The future of those fragments is not a cow-calf operation, as many ranches have been in the past. I believe the value of our ranch is in its intrinsic beauty, clean water, plant and animal diversity, solitude, and quiet.

Restoring a ranch is much like practicing medicine, except that instead of treating human bodies, we care for the plants, animals, land, and water and gently guide the entire ranch. Restoring a habitat is like helping a sick patient get well.

I am optimistic about our part of Texas. The new landowners, for the most part, really care about the land and want to do the right thing. I think the biggest problem facing ecology today is this: How do we get the wealth of scientific findings from research institutions and public agencies out to landowners? How do we train the next generation of landowners?

One way is to take children to the land when they are young. Teach them to care for wild plants and wild animals, to learn which ones are dangerous, and to live in harmony. Let them see a star cluster through a telescope and the parts of a flower under a microscope. As they learn to care for the most vulnerable plants and animals, they will understand how to take care of the most vulnerable humans.

For our family, the ranch provides a respite from the noise, confusion, and frenzy of daily life. The ranch is 143 miles northwest of Austin, a two-and-a-half-hour drive. You can't just run up to the ranch and run back; you have to plan to be at one place or the other. When I'm on the ranch, I am completely alone, it is absolutely quiet, and I can spend

All is not fun and games at the ranch. It's times like these, when I'm changing a tire in the snow, that I wish I was still practicing medicine.

hours or days there by myself. After days of following a hectic schedule, I find the ranch indescribably peaceful. Every day is different. One day I pull up cedar saplings, and another day I seed grass by hand, scattering it from a pail. The grass may take years to mature, but it changes all the time. We see different flowers, different butterflies, and different birds, yet at the same time, it's all so familiar. Every afternoon, I go to the Sunday House and spend a couple of hours by myself reading or listening to classical music. Every evening an hour before sunset, I drive or walk on a different road and quietly watch the ranch.

    I'm reminded of Jerry Marcontell, who went through every rotation with me in medical school and is still a great friend. He retired after a busy career as an obstetrician in Houston and moved to Rye in the Big Thicket of East Texas. "I never want to be in another committee meeting the rest of my life," he has told me. "I go to Houston only one day a month, and that's to get a haircut." I feel that way about the ranch sometimes when it's quiet.

For our family, the ranch provides a respite from the noise, confusion, and frenzy of daily life. The ranch has given me an opportunity to improve a piece of land in gratitude to past generations and with hope for future generations.

Besides giving me some of the most gratifying experiences of my life, the ranch has given me an opportunity to improve a piece of land in gratitude to past generations and with hope for future generations. The key reason I have put so much effort into the ranch, of course, is that it's where I grew up. It's home to me.

> Generations come and generations go,
> but the earth remains forever.
> ECCLESIASTES 1:4

Acknowledgments

I am indebted to many people who guided me through the writing and publication of this book. In writing a memoir, I am aware that memories fade and the mind can do tricks on the way we remember the past. I have tried to be accurate and have searched my memory over the last few years while I thought about my life.

Unfortunately, I never kept a journal. This would have been especially valuable in recalling my time in Vietnam. I have asked others to read the manuscript and correct any errors as they remember the same events. However, this is the way I remember my life, and if there are any errors, they are mine.

This book would not have been possible without the help and support of my wife, Toni. She encouraged me to continue the project and see it through.

Don Carleton is an inspiration today as he has been for decades. He encouraged and gently guided me in my collections, helped me understand the importance of accurately documenting history, and encouraged me to record my memoirs. I would never have undertaken this project without Don.

Tom Hatfield is a friend and confidant who made telling my story easy. He handled this, as he does everything, with absolute professionalism and insight. In our hours of interviews, his insightful questions made me think of my life as I had never before thought of it.

Barbara Langham took Tom's interviews, and then she and I spent hours and hours talking so she could weave it all together into a story. She has revised and edited the manuscript for more than a year.

My daughters, Margaret Ann Spellings and Laura Burns, read the manuscript and, most important, encouraged me to continue. Robin Fox read and helped me with early manuscripts.

My brother and sister, Pierce and Mary Margaret, helped me remember many details and added their thoughts on what was important. Pierce provided some family pictures.

Lifelong friends Jerry Marcontell and Tommy Coopwood helped me remember details of medical school. They are the only ones of our original group still alive.

I am fortunate to have had Jim Van Straten read the chapter on Vietnam. I did not know Jim until his book, *A Different Face of War*, was published in 2015. He arrived in Vietnam almost exactly the day I left. Amazingly, our experiences were so similar. I have never read anything that brought back memories like his book.

Other than a chance meeting once at a medical conference, I have had no contact with anyone I served with in Vietnam. From the day I flew out of Vietnam, I never saw nor heard from any of my fellow soldiers.

Ernest Butler and Richard Shoberg read the practice chapter. Ernie and I worked together almost every day in the office, and Dick and I spent many days in the operating room.

For the enrichment and the ranch chapters, I relied on family, especially my wife, Toni.

PAUL BURNS, MD
MAY 2017

APPENDIX

Army After-Action Report

22 May 1966

MEMORANDUM FOR RECORD

SUBJECT: Recommendations for Improving Health Care in Vietnam

To: Commanding Officer
        41st Civil Affairs Company
        APO US Forces 96240

I am a captain in the US Army Medical Corps and realize that decisions for "improving health care in Vietnam" are not made by captains. They probably are not made by Medical Corps officers at all. I have been in Vietnam since December 1965 and have spent that time working on the problem of providing health care for the Vietnamese. The 41st Civil Affairs Company has sixteen (16) physicians throughout I, II and III Corps and I have also drawn heavily on their experience. We were the first unit of its kind to be tried in Vietnam and our experience and conclusions should not be wasted or never reported at all. I feel it is my duty to submit a summary of my experiences and recommendations through channels. I know of no one in the US Army who has been more intimately associated with health care at province level and below. As senior medical officer of the seventeen (17) doctors in our company, it was my job to coordinate between them and get their feelings on the problem. Although this report draws heavily on their experience, it is my own, and was not submitted to each doctor before completion, thus it is not a group report.

There is no question that the Vietnamese people need better medical care. We should first clearly decide if our primary aim is to give the Vietnamese better medical care or to achieve a psychological warfare goal through the use of medicine. The methods would be different. The medical officers must be frankly briefed before deployment so that they would know their goal and are able to work effectively toward it. Unfortunately, up to now in Vietnam and especially concerning our company, muddled thinking, by those who should have given us our mission, prevented us from knowing what we should have been doing. Briefings on our mission before we arrived in Vietnam were nonexistent and our briefing upon arrival in Vietnam was reprehensible. I can only condemn this as inexcusable and beg that it not be repeated.

First, I would like to discuss how to give the Vietnamese people better health care. Unfortunately there is no simple, quick, easy cure. Historically, medical care has been an indication of the advancement of a society and has roughly paralleled both the rise and decline of a society. No society in the world as primitive and underdeveloped as Vietnam has a high level of sophistication in their medical care. There is no way the Vietnamese people can provide sophisticated medical care for themselves in sooner than twenty years.

If we want them to have sophisticated medical care quickly, we must provide the doctors for fourteen (14) million Vietnamese people. With the shortage of doctors in the US, and with the additional workload placed on US doctors by medicine, I do not believe it is realistic for us to try to assume medical care for the Vietnamese. Even if we were willing to give them medical care comparable to ours, it would not be successful. Healing the sick is not something that can be passed out like rice or cooking oil. The patient must have enough intelligence and education in the fundamental aspects of medicine to be willing and able to cooperate and follow the therapy regimen. Examples of this lack occur at every sick call. No matter how detailed the instructions are, patients continue to trade pills given them at sick call. Two aspirins are traded for a yellow antibiotic and so on until the patient has a potentially harmful combination. In a study done in New York City in 1960, it was found that in the lower educated classes in New York City, the patients often did not follow the prescribed therapy and would not regularly give the medicine to their children for the full course of treatment. Without education we surely could not expect the Vietnamese people to do better. They want to get well but they don't know what to do and it is not a simple, easy thing to teach them.

If we assume we cannot give them the same level of medical care available in the United States, what are the alternatives? First let us examine the present MEDCAP program, MEDCAP I and MEDCAP II. MEDCAP I was designed early in our commitment here and basically consists of a US medic working through Vietnamese counter-parts to treat the Vietnamese. MEDCAP II was designed for major US units and is to provide more direct medical care and not go through Vietnamese counterparts. First we will assume our objective is to provide medical care for the people, later I will discuss its psychological warfare role. In our MEDCAP programs the medical officer and a medic held sick call in the villages and hamlets. The people all turn out in a pushing and shoving festive mood to see what kind of free "Goodies" the Americans are giving out today. If the team is lucky enough to have a good interpreter, some semblance of order is maintained and each person is given his few seconds with the doctor. All of the medication for MEDCAP comes through ARVN channels and are woefully inadequate. So the doctor dispenses what he has with one eye on the waiting line so he will not run out of medicine. Let me give you one specific example. By listening to a patient's chest and talking to him, tuberculosis is suspected. It cannot be diagnosed, of course, because no laboratory or X-ray is available. The treatment for tuberculosis is one year on isoniazid or another antituberculosis drug. As there is no follow up because a doctor cannot physically visit all of the villages under our control every week, one must give him a year's supply of medication, have him come back to a central dispensary weekly to get a new supply, or give him nothing. More often than not the dilemma is solved by the ARVN supply system, advised by Lt Col Collins Wright because the needed medication is not available. It is not practical to give out a year's supply of a valuable drug because it will be sold to the V.C., lost, or forgotten. It has not proven possible to have a man come in weekly. Also because of the very real danger of developing drug resistant tuberculosis from inadequate treatment, therapy should not be begun unless one is reasonably assured of being able to complete it. Based on all these reasons, usually it is treated with cough syrup. Likewise most other serious diseases cannot be diagnosed and treated. Heart disease, cancer, thyroid disease, parasites, anemia, malaria, and many more are just treated symptomatically. Without a laboratory, X-ray and adequate drugs, a doctor is no more effective than a corpsman. It is a tragic shame that officers in responsible positions continue to permit it to continue.

The reasons why little change has been made needs to be evaluated. I have been amazed at the "Empire Building" that has developed around the MEDCAP medical officers. It seems to be much more impressive for a commander to say "I have so many doctors working for me" than to say "I have so many corpsmen working for me." Another important reason for continuing malutilization of doctors is that too often non-medical personnel make the decisions on what medical personnel should be doing. As far as I can determine, no medical personnel were consulted on the utilization of the seventeen (17) doctors in our company. Then when the recommendations were made by the doctors in our company and the surgeons in our chain of command, still no change has been made. Another reason could be that those in policy-making positions are not interested in true programs as long as it looks good on paper.

Now let us discuss the merit of the MEDCAP program, if their goal is psychological warfare. I believe the program has not been attained here in that we just do not know its effect on the people. No good scientific method has been used to determine if the program is thought to be successful by the people. All too often the attempt at survey is made by the same people who have a vested interest in the program or who wish to please their superiors with an encouraging report. This is no way to get good information, yet literally millions of dollars and hundreds of people's efforts are based on these inaccurate reports. You ask me, could I do better? The answer is no. I am trained in medicine not in statistical analysis of public opinion polls. Because of my training in medicine, I doubt its psychological warfare value. Everyone knows that a sick person knows if he gets well. When we do supposedly "high impact psy-war MEDCAP work" by holding sick call in a relatively unsecure area with no hope of complete long term follow up, there is no way we can treat any seriously or chronically ill people definitively. So what happens? We treat them symptomatically or not at all. Either way they do not get well and they know it. They were seen by an American doctor who examined them [and] [t]hrough an interpreter explained they should leave their home and family to go to some other place for treatment. Then the doctor gives them some pills and leaves. The man gets sicker and it is naïve to believe he blames himself. People are just not cured of real diseases on a village sick call and thus I believe that sick call from village to village by an American possibly does more long lasting harm than good.

What is a good program? If psychological warfare is our objective, I do not believe anyone knows it. It is dangerous to assume that rank or prestige or age mysteriously endows one to be able to decide. Why not set up a good scientific evaluation program?

If better health for the Vietnamese is our objective, the solution must be difficult and long but rewarding. It should be divided into two phases; a short term stopgap measure and a long range plan. Both should remain flexible as no one knows the final solution. Fortunately the short term and long range programs overlap and augment each other.

There should basically be two education plans; one to train more Vietnamese doctors and one to train other health workers. The increased training of Vietnamese doctors is a long range goal that will require about six or seven years to produce the first class of doctors. I do not profess to know anything about how this should be done. However, it must be done in Vietnam or the Vietnamese doctors will not want to return here to practice. Also the length of service of the American teacher at the medical schools should be at least one year. If it is not possible to recruit civilian doctors to do this, then US Army doctors should be used.

The training of the other medical personnel, nurses, district health workers, midwives, hamlet health workers, etc., should be as decentralized as possible. People should be recruited from the village to which they plan to return and trained in their province or corps area. This will not remove them too far from their home and it will be easier to get them back to their village to work. A large percentage of doctors and nurses who are trained in the United States will not be content to come back here to work.

The MILPHAP teams should be relied heavily upon to train personnel to work at district level and below. Our ultimate goal should be to train the Vietnamese to be able to assume responsibility for their own health care. If deployed wisely, there are enough US doctors in Vietnam now to provide temporary medical care for the Vietnamese people and to train doctors, nurses and health workers. However it cannot be accomplished if our present mistakes are continued.

The concept of the MEDCAP program must be reevaluated. A US doctor and medic holding sick call in a village may sound good in the newspapers and in a units report but is a tragic, inexcusable waste. The US doctors must be at some fixed, semipermanent or permanent location. He must have adequate supplies and equipment for performing minor surgery and treating war wounds. The correct approach should be for a medic or health worker to screen the mass of patients and to refer the seriously ill or complicated patients to a US doctor centrally located. All too often the MEDCAP program results in an American doctor finding a seriously ill or complicated case in a village and, having no diagnostic equipment available, he cannot care for him. It is hard for non-medical personnel to realize that a doctor in a village with no diagnostic equipment is no better than a well-trained corpsman. He can only pass out pills. It is an effective way to negate a physician's training and reduce him to a corpsman.

A physician working above should have as a minimum of equipment the Medical Instrument and Supply Set, Dispensary, Field, C6545-919-1500; Surgical Instrument and Supply Set, Individual, C6545-927-4960; Surgical Instrument and Supply Set, Combat, C6545-927-4200; Refrigerator, Mechanical, Biological, 4110-707-2550; Field X-ray; Laboratory Set and Microscope. The doctor should be supplied through US supply channels as the ARVN medical supply system has not functioned adequately. This doctor would serve as a referral center for US medics,

ARVN medics, village, hamlet and district health workers and Vietnamese doctors. The US doctor's function would be to treat the seriously ill and to diagnose the complicated cases. He could be located in any populated area, but should not compete with a MILPHAP team.

MILPHAP teams are usually located in province capitals and have a similar function but with greater capabilities. They augment the province hospital and serve as a referral and treatment center for the province. An equally important function should be to train medical personnel for the villages, hamlets and districts in the province. As MILPHAP teams are provided for each province, individual doctors with adequate supplies and equipment will be used in other heavily populated areas. But should be provided at province level first.

It should be kept in mind that MILPHAP teams and individual US doctors will be replaced by Vietnamese doctors trained at Saigon and Hue. In the meantime the MILPHAP teams will be training personnel for use in the provinces. It should take a minimum of six to seven years before Vietnam can begin to provide its own medical care.

George P. Burns
Captain, MC
Public Health Officer

Sources and Methodology

I met Paul Burns through Tom Hatfield, with whom I had worked when he was dean of continuing education at the University of Texas at Austin in the 1980s. Tom said he had conducted oral interviews with Paul that could make a significant contribution to the oral history archives of the Briscoe Center. Paul had lived "an extraordinary life," Tom said. I was intrigued.

I was given transcripts and electronic files of the seven interviews Tom had done with Paul between November 6, 2012, and February 27, 2013. I met Paul and his wife, Toni, in August 2016 in their home. For the next twelve months, we had conversations that elaborated his personal recollections from the transcripts and reawakened memories.

Paul supplied virtually all the information about his medical training and practice. He also shared copies of various talks he had given at family gatherings, particularly those at Heflin Cemetery, where several family members are buried. These talks provided anecdotes that illuminated incidents in his life as well as insight into his strong moral and family values. Genealogical information from research done by the Burns family not only verified biographical facts but also enhanced our conversations about ancestors and the family ranch.

Seeing parallels between his ancestors' experiences and events in Texas history, I consulted the *Handbook of Texas Online* for information about such topics as Brown County, Brownwood, cattle ranching, and fence cutting. I also went to the Texas State Library and Archives, where I found sources on Brown County and the Burns family, notably the following:

Allen, Estill Franklin. *Blanket, Texas, Community History*. Blanket, TX: Sims Office Machines for Blanket History Committee, 1983.

Havins, T. R. *Something about Brown: A History of Brown County*. Brownwood, TX: Banner Printing Co, 1958.

Smith, Tevin Clyde. *Frontier's Generation: The Pioneer History of Brown County with Sidelights on the Surrounding Territory*. T. C. Smith, 1980.

Paul's experiences in collecting early Texas documents, particularly references to forged copies of the Texas Declaration of Independence, led me to the following magazine articles:

Belkin, Lisa. "Lone Star Fakes." *New York Times Magazine*, December 1989.

Curtis, Greg. "Forgery Texas Style." *Texas Monthly*, March 1989.

Trillin, Calvin. "Knowing Johnny Jenkins." *New Yorker*, October 1989.

John Anderson, a retired archivist at the Texas State Library, referred us to a book, *Texfake: An Account of the Theft and Forgery of Early Texas Printed Documents*, which was written and published in 1991 by W. Thomas Taylor, as well as to a June 28, 2014, broadcast of *Antiques Roadshow* in which the interview portion featured the forgeries of the Texas Declaration of Independence.

In talking about the Colonel Burns Ranch, Paul directed me to an online video produced by the Texas Parks and Wildlife Department when he and Toni were named Lone Star Stewards for their restoration efforts. The video allowed me to visually experience the place his family has called home for generations. I drew additional information about the ranch restoration from a speech he gave April 7, 2017, to the UT Forum, an adult enrichment program at the University of Texas at Austin.

I am especially indebted to Tom Hatfield, not only for inviting me to undertake this project, but also for suggesting the title, reviewing the final manuscript, and offering continuing advice and support.

BARBARA A. LANGHAM
MAY 2017

Index

Locators in italics indicate photographs

A

accreditation standards, changes in, 94–96
Addy, Fred, 168
Advanced Micro Devices (AMD), 162
advertising taboo, 113
advice: from Alford on practice, 116; for others, 142, 145, 166, 206; second opinions, 101, 126
after-action report, 85, 213–219
air-conditioning, 71
alcohol, abstaining from, 116
alcoholic patients, 132
Alford, Bobby: advice on practice, 116; as instructor, *95, 97*, 103, 108; offering faculty position, 109
Allen, Julia, 128
allergy shots, 6
"Always Home," 178, 200, 202–203
ambush: fear of, 73; revisiting, 170, *170*; training for, 51; in Vietnam, 74–75
amphibious landings, 54–55, 69–71, *70*
amphitheater, surgery in, 102
anatomy, 36, 125–126
Anderson, Scott, 196
anencephalic baby, 48–49
anesthesia and anesthesiologists: appendectomy at sea, 63–64; cocaine, 115; epidural, 46–47; importance of, 126, 128; machine, 63–65. *see also* surgical team
Antiques Roadshow, 157
antiwar sentiment, 90
Antone, Clifford, 137
appendectomy at sea, 63–65
Apple II Plus, 114–115
Armadillo World Headquarters, 137

Army After-Action Report, 85, 213–219
army service. *see* Civil Affairs Program; Medical Corps; Vietnam War
Arnold, Dan (grandson), *179, 201*
art and artifacts, 148–149, 158
Ascension Health, 130
Askew, Bob, 124
asphyxia, 64–65
asthma: childhood, 3–4, 6; and Margaret Ann, 106; and smoking, 50; and Vietnam, 56
athletics, 10, 26
atomic bombs, 45
audiology, 118, 132
Auerbach, Ernest, 168
Austin: annual rainfall, 198; decision to practice in, 110; and live music, 137; living in, 115; meeting with area doctors, 112–113; as premier surgeon in, 105, 124; student council workshop, 9
Austin, Stephen F., 154
Austin City Limits, 137
Austin Ear, Nose, and Throat Clinic: advice for partners, 145; audiology, 118, 132; bookkeeping software, 114; Burns and Butler as partners, 111–112; on call for ER, 115–116; and Dehan's active duty service, 119; and Down syndrome patients, 131–132; efficiency of, 120–124; expansion of, 118–120; fees and payments, 112, 114, 115, 145; formation of, 111–113; meeting Austin area doctors, 112–113; meeting wives of staff, 120; nurses, 114, 120–121; office equipment, 112, 114; partners in, 111–112, 118–120; patient referrals, 115; philosophy of practice, 112, 145;

profit-sharing plan, 120; routine of, 121–122; staff of, 114, 115; success of, 117, 129; theft of drugs, 115; treating singers, 137–140. *see also* medicine, practice of; patients; surgeons and surgery

Austin Lyric Opera: attendance at, 139, 167; board members of, 167–168; board service, 2, 146, 166–168; founding of, 137; Hoisington and, 165; lessons from, 168; and Tobey, 119; treating singers, 138–140

Austin Symphony, 146

authenticating documents, 156–157

autopsy of dogs, 41

B

babies, delivery of, 46–49, 79–80

baby, anencephalic, 48–49

Bahamas, 150

Bailey Square Surgical Center, 124–125

Baker, Jerry, 2, *117, 125*, 128–129

Bamberger, David, 193

Bamberger ranch, 193

Baptists, 6, 14–15, 77–78

barbed wire, 185

barn, restored, 203

Barnett Shale geological formation, 204

Bass Concert Hall, 139

Bastrop federal penitentiary, 131

Baxter, Helen, 168

Baylor College of Medicine: adjunct professor for, 140; and Alford, 97; application and acceptance to, 33–34; and Ben Taub Hospital, 35, 97–100, 103; Burns on impact of residency, 109; and calling for help, 94, 95–96; clinical research, 106; competition and pressure at, 40, 41–43, 106–107; confidence in training, 106; developing judgment, 95–96; difficulty and standards at, 36, 106–107; dissection, 36, 126; dogs and research, 40–41; ENT rotation, 46, 103–105; ER rotation, 35, 98–100; exams at, 41; faculty of, 36, *95*, 105–106, 107; financial challenges, 36, 106–107; as first year resident, 94–95; as fourth year resident, 104–105; friends, *35*, 39, 92, *95*; general surgery rotation, 97–98, 100–102; graduating class, 42; hospital shifts, 36; as medical student, 34–36, 39–40; memories of, 97, 107; and nightmares, 92, 93; rarity of praise, 99; referring patients to, 126; residency, 87–88, 93–109; responsibility for patients, 94; Vietnam and, 87–88, 92, 93. *see also* internship, medical

beauty shop, 135–136

beef, in diet, 18, 20, 37

beepers, 104–105

Ben Taub Hospital: charity clinics at, 103; Christmas at, 98–99; and ER rotation, 35, 97–100; general surgery rotation, 100; largest ER in world, 98; observing surgery at, 110; opening of, 34–35

Big Bend National Park, 28

billing, computerized, 114

birds and water, 199

Blake, William, 196

Blanket, 20–25

Blanket Baptist Church, 14, 15

Blanket Elementary School, 20–25, *23, 25*

Blanket State Bank, 15

blindness, 181, 182

boats on Saigon River, 66–67

bookkeeping software, 114

books, 2, 162

BOQ barracks, 47

boredom, 47–48, 62, 65

Brackenridge Hospital, 115–116, 128, 145

Braniff Airways flight, 90

Bridge of Pinos, 151

Briscoe Center for American History, 141, 157

bronchoscopes, 115

Brown County Livestock Show, 22

Brownwood: Camp Bowie, 19; in 1873, 182; grandparents' move to, 18; high school at, 25–27; move to, 9; and Vietnam, 90–91; visits to, 37; during World War II, 44–45

Brownwood High School, 25–27, 168

Brownwood Hospital, 148

Brownwood Rotary Club, 91

Brownwood School Board, 26–27

brush removal, 196–197

bubbles, economic, 165–166

Buckley, Wayne, 104

building restoration, 162–164

Burns, Billy: burial of, 183; and Burns's medical practice, 131–132, 143; family caring for, 6–8, 171, 188; image of, *24*; and Mary Margaret, 131, 188; with Mother, *191*; sleeping in

Index

parents' room, 19; in state-regulated home, 171–172
Burns, Christopher, 178
Burns, George Paul. *see* Burns, Paul
Burns, George Pierce (Daddy): athletics and, 26; and Billy, 6–8, 19; and Burns's asthma attacks, 6; Burns's last visit with, 148; character of, 10; and children's education, 20, 23, 25, 30–31, 32; and church, 14; draft notice, 45; education of, 10; and Family Heritage Land Program, 188; horseback riding, 14; images of, *11, 12, 24, 189*; lending career, 13, 188; loss of child, 4; parents of, 186; and radiation treatments, 172; and ranch, 14, 188, 203; as role model, 10–15; stroke, 187–188; on taking care of family, 171; and value of education, 10, 15–16; and value of money, 15; and Vietnam, 56–57, *59*, 91; whistling, 18; and wife, 9, 10, 18; work ethic of, 13
Burns, James, 184
Burns, Laura (daughter): birth of, 38–39; and Burns's return from Vietnam, 90; college visits, 158, 160–161; education of, 162; with family, *38, 173, 176, 201, 206*; impact of residency on, 106–107; playing with, 39; vising ranch as child, *189*
Burns, Liz, 203
Burns, Margaret Ann. *see* Spellings, Margaret Ann Burns (daughter)
Burns, Mary Margaret. *see* Byrom, Mary Margaret Burns (sister)
Burns, Mollie Small (grandmother), *17*, 183–184, 186, 187–188
Burns, Ona Louise Winn (Mother): and Burns, 13, 15–16, 141, 171; caring for Billy, 6–8, 171; and continuing to learn, 158; death of, 190; depression of, 8–9, 172, 188; education of, 10; and education of children, 20, 23, 25, 30–31, 32; electroshock treatment, 9; and Family Heritage Land Program, 188; happiest time of life, 188; and husband, 9, 10, 18; images of, *5, 8, 24, 187, 189*; judging men by wives, 45, 120; on Laura, 38; living with Mary Margaret, 188; loss of child, 4; and Margaret Ann, 37; on 99th birthday, *191*; as pianist, 10, 23; piano lessons, 8, 27, 188; on pregnancy with Billy, 7; and ranch, 10, 188, 190, 203; as role model, 10–15; and Sunday dinner, 14–15; on taking care of family, 171; as "town girl," 10, 190; value of education, 10, 15–16; and Vietnam, 56–57, *59*; and wind at ranch, 18; work ethic of, 13

Burns, Paul: birth of, 6, *20*; childhood (*see* childhood); education of (*see* education); career (*see* Austin Ear, Nose, and Throat Clinic; patients; surgeons and surgery); abstaining from alcohol, 116; as adjunct professor, 140–141; album dedicated to, 137; and art, 149; asthma of, 4, 6, 50, 56; on big classes, 31–32; calling of, 2, 3–9, 42–43, 109; care for hands and eyes, 117; on choosing professional practice, 109; as collector, 148–152, 154–158, 160–162; competitiveness of, 25–26, 29, 30, 40; computer, 114–115; conflict with Guilford, 103–104; and conservation laryngeal surgery, 105, 124; and delivering babies, 47; ear and nose surgery, 97–98; eyesight, 26, 117, 182; family (*see* family; individual family members); first marriage of, 36, 37, 38, 59, 100; friends (*see* friends and friendships); on future of medicine, 146–147; and Hill Country Homes, 162–164; impact of Vietnam War on, 83–85, 92; as infant, *12*; last moments with Daddy, 148; and LBJ, 133–135; and learning to save, 15; lessons from military training, 52–53, 121; living modestly, 145; and Lone Star Land Steward award, 203, *206*; on medical career, 143–146; medical school (*see* Baylor College of Medicine); memorizing of names, 26, 168; military service (*see* Civil Affairs Program; Medical Corps; Vietnam War); on "minor" surgery, 126; on morality, 24, 84; naps, 122; nightmares and flashbacks, 60, 91–92, 93, 107, 171; and nonprofits, 77–78, 166; and parents' deaths, 190; on parents' resilience, 4; part time jobs, 27, 33, 53, 106; and patients (*see* patients); on perception of time, 3; philosophy of, 2–3; "Plan B," lack of, 42–43; as president of Seton medical staff, *123*, 130–131; public service, 166–168; ranch restoration (*see* Colonel Burns Ranch); relationship with siblings, 172; reputation of, 99, 105, 107, 124; retirement of, 2, 108, 141–143, *208*; retreats for reflection, 164–166; seasickness, 63; and second opinions, 101, 126; on self-evaluation, 104; serenity after surgery, 129; and shopping, 154; on success, 3, 146; talks on treating singers, 138; travel, 169–171; value of military service, 44, 56; on Vietnam, 92; Vietnam War (*see* Civil Affairs Program; Medical Corps; Vietnam War); visualization before surgeries, 107–108, 125

Burns, Pierce (brother): in Austin, 110; and building homes, 162; as business partner, 162–164, 172; childhood of, 6–7, 13, 19; dislike of riding, 14; education of, 23, 28; with family, *109, 176, 191, 206*; and football, 26; Hill Country Homes, 162–164; navy service, 9; in Pasadena, 38; relationship with, 172; and restoration of ranch, 188, 190, 200; travel with Burns, 150

Burns, Pierce Jr. (nephew), 38, *38, 109, 176*

burns, prescribed, 198

Burns, Rachel, 178

Burns, Reba, *109,* 188, 190, 200, *206*

Burns, Sarah Ann Gibson, 180, 181, *181,* 182, 183

Burns, Simon Pierce (great-grandfather): Civil War service, 180–181; and fences, 185; image of, *180*; and outlaws, 184; political career, 182–183; as sheriff, 182, 184; as surveyor, 182; travel to Texas, 178

Burns, Simon Pierce II (grandfather): birth of, 182; and family ranch, 185–186; generosity of, 186; image of, *17*; marriage of, 186; stroke, 16, 18

Burns, Todd, *109, 176,* 203

Burns, Toni Fox: and Burns, 123, 142, *167*; and Burns's map collection, 154; caring for Daddy, 172; cruise up Saigon River, 169; and diamonds, 161–162; divorce of, 173; Hill Country Homes, 162; images of, *153, 159, 163*; on life changing, 177; and Lockhart, 163; Lone Star Land Steward Award, 203, *206*; naming of ranch, 200; ranch as "always home," 178, 200; and ranch restoration, 190, 193, 196; and Robin's stroke, 176, 177

Burns, William "Billy" (great-uncle), 185–186, 186–187

bus, school, 20, 22

Bush, Eva, 200

bust, bronze, 144

Butler, Ernest "Ernie": and Austin Lyric Opera and Austin Symphony, 146; as bookkeeper, 114; on Burns liking to shop, 154; Burns on, 145–146; computer, 114–115; and ear, 111–112, 124–125; images of, *110, 122, 176*; as partner, 110–112, 120; profit-sharing plan, 120; retirement of, 142; as surgeon, 110, 124–125; and unpredictable nurse, 121

Butler, Sarah, 146, *176*

Byrom, Fred: burial site of, 183; with family, *34*; and mother-in-law, 188; and ranch, 190, 202

Byrom, Marietta. *see* Metcalfe, Marietta Byrom

Byrom, Mary Margaret Burns (sister): bedroom for, 19; and Billy, 131, 171; on Burns's medical school, 42–43; childhood, 6–7, 9, 13, *24*; college education, 29; with family, *34*; house on ranch, 202; and Mother, 9, 172, 188, *191*; on reading every day, 158; receiving Lone Star Steward Award, *206*; relationship with, 172

Byrom, Paul (nephew), *34*

C

cadaver, dissection of, 36

Caesar Kleberg Wildlife Research Institute, 197–198

calls received daily, 121

calves, 14, 15

Camp Bowie, 19, 44–45

Camp Bullis, 51

Camp Hale, 54

Camp Pendleton, 54–55

cancer: Daddy's, 148, 172; head and neck, 105, 124, 132; linked to smoking and heart disease, 50; and mustard gas, 6; patients with, 113, 126, 132–133; and second opinions, 126; of Uncle Estel, 6, 9

capture, risk of, 47–48

career. *see* Austin Ear, Nose, and Throat Clinic; patients; surgeons and surgery

Carlyle Hotel, 158, 160–161

Carnegie, Dale, 157

cars: carpooling, 37; Chevy coupe, 1947, 28; drive to Washington, 43; Ford pickup, 13, *24,* 28; jeeps, army, 52, 54, 72–73, 74–75, *79*

cartography, 154. *see also* map collection

case presentations, medical, 42

casualties, during training, 54

Catholic nuns, 116

Index

cattle: calves, 14, 15; "Charlie," 22; and family ranch, 190, 193; Hereford, 185; impact on land, 190, 193; longhorn, 185; and mesquite beans, 197; milk cows, 18; overstocking of, 194; and rustlers, 184–185; slaughter by government, 187; and tall prairie grasses, 194
cattle drives, 185
cattlemen's associations, 185
cattle rustlers, 184–185
Cecil, Jim, 35
cedar trees, 196–197, 198–199
Central Intelligence Agency (CIA), 58–59
chairs, practicing sutures on, 102
charity clinics, 103
charts, patient, 96, 113, 114
Chevrolet, 43
Chevy coupe, 1947, 28
chicken, in diet, 18
childhood: Blanket Elementary, 20–25, 21; Brownwood High School, 25–27, 27; chores, 13–14; drought of 1950s, 14, 194; electricity, 16, 19–20; elementary school valedictorian, 25; enjoyment of learning, 25; fires waiting for school bus, 20, 22; growing up on, 15–20; homes, 16, 19, 21; house fire, 16, 18, 187; junior class president, 26; memorization of names, 25–26; reading *Compton's Encyclopedia*, 24; refrigeration, 18, 20; summer jobs on, 13; telephone, 20; windmill and water, 14
children: as patients, 1–2, 131–132, 143; teaching to value land, 207; Vietnamese children, 73. *see also* Burns, Laura (daughter); Spellings, Margaret Ann (daughter)
Chisos Basin, 28
cholera and cholera wards, 75, 76, 78–79
Christmas: asthma attack, 3; at Ben Taub hospital, 98–99; in childhood, 3, 15; Laura's birth, 38; in Vietnam, 68–69, 69–71; visit home, 37
citizenship oath, 174
Civil Affairs Program: after-action report, 85, 213–219; Burns's perspective on, 65–66, 80; cholera epidemic, 78–79; disillusionment with, 81; failure of, 82–83; idealism in, 72; lack of equipment, 61, 72, 80; lack of information, 47; mandate and mission of, 47, 58, 72; and Steger's evaluation, 81–82;

supplies for, 72. *see also* Medical Corps; Vietnam War
civilians, 86–87
Civil War, 180–181
Civil War club, 149–150
class size, 31–32
Clausewitz, Carl von, 61
clear-cutting, 197
clinic. *see* Austin Ear, Nose, and Throat Clinic
clinics, charity, 103
cocaine, 115
cocktail party, 80–81
Coggin Avenue Baptist church, 14
cold, 54
Cole, Ruth, 26
Coleman Production Credit Association, 13
colleagues: Baker, 2, 117, 125, 128–129; Butler, 111–112, 145–146; clinic partners, 111–112, 118–120; Lane, 1, 117, 128, 144–145; recognition from, 144–145; surgical team, 2, 116, 117, 128–129, 144–145; surgical technicians, 128–129. *see also* friends and friendships
collections: Columbus, 149–151; early Texas History, 151–152, 154–157; Florence Nightingale, 154; historical documents, 149–151, 154–157, 155; letters, 154; paintings, 149
College of Fine Arts, University of Texas, 141
Collin County, 182
Colonel Bob Trail, 200
Colonel Burns Ranch, 191, 209; abandoned homesites, 203; as "Always Home," 178, 200, 202–203; annual evaluation of restoration, 196; boundaries of, 190; buying back land, 190; changes to land, 193–196; childhood on, 184; conservation easement, 204; Daddy and, 14, 188, 203; diagnosing problems, 193; ecological regions of, 190, 206; economic issues in restoration, 203–204, 206–207; electricity, 16, 19–20, 203; and family, 172, 179, 202; first home, 16; foundation of original home, 200; future of, 207–209; and Great Depression, 185–188, 194; heritage of, 200; hunting on, 203–204; learning about restoration, 193; leased to others, 188, 190; loss of land, 185, 186–187; managing for species, 194; Mother and, 10, 188, 190, 203; multiple owners of, 200; naming of, 200; natural appearance of, 205;

"new house," 19, *21*, 188, 200; "original condition," 193–194; original purchase of land, 182; practice of, 196–200; purpose for, 190, 193–196; refrigeration, 18, 20; as respite from daily life, 207–208; restoration as retirement project, 142; restoration compared to practicing medicine, 195–196, 207; restoration cost, 202–203, 206–207; restoration date, 194; restoration plan and inspiration, 190, 193, 196, 207, 209; security lights, 203; size adding complexity, 206; summer jobs on, 13; Sunday House, *192*, 202, 208; telephone, 20; T House, 202; windmill and water, 14
Colt Automatic Pistol, 1911, 71–72
Columbus, Christopher, 150–151, 154
Columbus collection, 149–151
Comanche High School, 10
commander, South Vietnamese, 78–79
commission date, 65
committees, 130–131
complications, surgical, 115, 128, 129
Compton's Encyclopedia, 24
computers, 114–115
Confederate Army, 180–181
conferences, medical, 106, 138
Connolly, Patrick, *110*, 120
conservation easement, 204
conservation laryngeal surgery, 105, 124
cookstove, wood-burning, 16
Cooley, Denton, *35*, 101
Coopwood, Tommy, 34, *35*, 39, 40–41, 42, 124
corporations, medicine and, 113
Cosmic Cowboy (album), 137
"Cosmic Cowboy" (song), 137
cost control and medicine, 147
country-western singers, 137–138
cows, milking of, 18
Cressman, Marvin, 177
cruise ships, 151
CT scans, 115, 177
cure rates, 147
curve, grading, 31
cystic fibrosis, 40

D

Daddy. *see* Burns, George Pierce (Daddy)
Dairy Queen, 28
"Danny Boy," 69–70
Daughters of Charity of St. Vincent de Paul, 116
deaf patients, 132
dealers of hearing aids, 118
DeBakey, Michael, 35, 40–41, 42, 102
Decoration Day, 183
De Cordova, Jacob, 152, 193
deer feeders, *205*
Dehan, Chris, *110*, 119
de l'Isle, Guillaume, 154
dental work, 47–48
depression: of Mother, 8–9, 172, 188
depth charges, 68, 69
desegregation, 26–27
details, surgical, 101–102
diamonds, 158, 160–162
Dick, James, 137
Dickie, Ray, 95
diet: beef, 18, 20, 37; childhood, 16, 18; during medical school, 37; on ship, 62–63, 68; vegetables, 16, 18, 62–63, 68
dinner, Sunday, 14–15
disabilities, treating children with, 131–132, 143
disease in Vietnam, 75
dissection and anatomy, 36, 126
doctors: and Burns's treatment for singers, 140; committees governing, 130; *vs.* hospital authority, 130–131; Mennonite, 77; referring, 112–113; responsibility of, 146–147; second opinions, 101, 126; taboo against advertising, 113; Vietnamese, 75–78
dogs, as test subjects, 40–41
dot-com collapse, 165–166, 166–167
Downing, Gail, 128
Down syndrome, 7–8, 131–132, 143
draft, military, 45
driver's license, 28
drought, 1950s, 14, 194
drugs, recreational, 115
Ducloux, Gina, 138
Ducloux, Walter, 138
Dutch art, seventeenth-century, 149

E

ear, nose, and throat (ENT) specialty, 46, 93–109. *see also* Austin Ear, Nose, and Throat Clinic

Index

ear surgery, 97–98
ecology and native grasses, 197–198
economy, 165–166, 166–167
ecosystems, 194, 199–200
ecotone, ranch in, 190
Eden, David, 128
edge effect, 199
education: academic challenges, 32; Baylor College of Medicine, 34–43, 93–109, *95*; birthdate and start of school, 20; Blanket Elementary, 20–25, *21*; Brownwood High School, 25–27, *27*; Burns on residency, 94–96, 97, 109; concerns over success, 25–26; confidence in, 50; culmination of medical education, 108–109; elementary school valedictorian, 25; enjoyment of learning, 25, 35–36; ENT specialty, 93–109, 94; importance of, 28–29, 162; importance to parents, 15–16, 20, 23, 25, 30–31, 32; internship and residency requirements, 45; Madigan Hospital internship, 43, 46–50; medical school applications, 33–34; medical student, 34–43, *35*; observing great surgeons, 102; ongoing education, 157–158, 160–162; of parents, 10; as professor, 140, 141; reading *Compton's Encyclopedia*, 24; research project with dogs, 40–41; residency, 93–109, *95*; University of Texas, 28–33
efficiency and minimum staff, 115
electricity, at ranch, 16, 19–20, 203
electric shock treatments, 9
emergency room rotation, 35, 97, 98–100
emergency rooms and private practice, 115–116
ENT conference, Mexico, 106
ENT (ear, nose, and throat) specialty, 46, 93–109. *see also* Austin Ear, Nose, and Throat Clinic
epidural anesthesia, 46–47, 63–64
Equinil (meprobamate), 172
equipment, medical: and civil affairs program, 61, 72, 80; diagnostic, 115; investing in, 112; used in tonsillectomy, 127
equipment, office, 112, 114
erosion, soil, 194–195, 198, 199–200
Erxleben, Devin, 196, 203, *206*
Eskew, Jim, 119, 120
examination of patients, 48
exams, medical school, 41

executive committee, 130–131
explorers and exploration, 151
ExxonMobil, 169
eye chart, memorization of, 26
eyes and eyesight, 26, 117, 182

F

Fabion, Darrell, 128
face-lifts, 124
facial plastic surgery, 97–98, 105
family: caring for, 171–177; caring for Billy, 6–8, 171, 188; first marriage of, 36, 37, 38, 59, 100; influence on Burns, 9, 112, 141; influence on patient treatment, 9; last moments with Daddy, 148; and medical school, 36–38; and parents' deaths, 190; protecting Burns from distractions, 123–124; and return from Vietnam, 90; support of, 2, 36–37, 42–43, 106–107, 142; visits home to, 38. *see also* parents; individual family members
Family Heritage Land Program, 188
Farmall tractor, 13
fatigue and residency, 96
Federal Land Bank, 13
fees, medical, 112, 114, 115, 145
fence cutting, 185
fences and fencing, 1, 13, 185, 199
field tours, 203
Fifth Mechanized Infantry Division, 51–53
fires: and grandparents' house, 16, 187; prairie, 198; waiting for school bus, 20, 22
fireside chats, 19
First Air Cavalry, 57, 62, 70, 86, 88
"First Monday" trading day, 184
flashbacks, 60, 92. *see also* post-traumatic stress disorder (PTSD)
floor, dirt, 23
Florence Nightingale collection, 154
flying in uniform, 90
food, fresh, 68
football, 32–33, 106, 139–140
Ford, Gerald, 169
Ford pickup, 13, *24*, 28
foreclosures and Great Depression, 186–187
forests, old-growth, 196–197
forgeries, 154, 156–157
Fort Carson, 51
Fort Gordon, 47–48, 56, 58–59

Fort Worth psychiatric hospital, 9
Fort Lewis, 43, 44, 46–50
Fort Sam Houston, 50–53
Forty-First Civil Affairs Company, 47, 69–71. *see also* Medical Corps
4-H project, 22
Fox, Dick, *163*
Fox, Edward, *163*, 173
Fox, Kay: cousin, 173; and Robin's stroke, 176
Fox, Lillian, *163*, 172–173, *175*, 176
Fox, Robin: as cheerleader, *174*; with family, *173*, *175*, *206*; living with grandparents, 173; stroke and disability of, 174, 176–177; support for Burns, 123; traveling with, 158, *175*
free-fire zones, 84
free range, 185
French class, 32
friends and friendships: army Medical Corps, 50–51, 55; elementary school, 23; high school, 26, 27, 28; Marcontell, *35*, 37, 39, 40–41, 208; medical school, 39; Minear, 27, 31; residency, 96–97, 107; Shoberg, 1, 113, 128, 130, 144. *see also* Butler, Ernest "Ernie"; colleagues
frontal sinus surgery, 124
frontier life, 183–185

G

Gandhi, Mahatma, 158
garage, 19
Gelder, Aert de, 149
Gibson, Sarah Ann. *see* Burns, Sarah Ann Gibson
gift, Christmas, 3
glasses, eye, 26
Goethe, Johann Wolfgang von, 148–149
gonorrhea, 68
government slaughter of cattle, 187
grand rounds, 94
grasses, native, 197–198
Grayson, Richard "Dick," *95*, 96
Great Depression, 10, 185–188, 194
Great Society program, 82
guesses, educated, 42
Guilford, Fred, 103–104
Gunthrie, Janet, 128
gynecology/obstetrics rotation, 48–49

H

habitat management, 203
Handbook of Texas, 182
hands, care for, 117
Haug, Scott, 118
Hawaii, 165
Hayes, Tracy, 26
health care system: Burns on future of, 146–147; change to hospitalists, 96; cost of, 147; hospital authority *vs.* doctors, 130–131; information gap, 96; insurance changes, 142, 147; medical records, 96, 113, 114; Medicare, 134, 142
hearing aids, 118
heart disease, 50
heart surgery, 99
heat, 71
Heatter, Gabriel, 45
Heflin Cemetery, 183
Heflin family, 183
hemilaryngectomy, 105
Hermann Hospital, 34
herpes keratitis of the eyes, 182
Hewlett, Bill, 145
Hill Country Homes, 162–164
Hilsabeck, John, 128, 131
historic documents, 149–151, 154–157
history, understanding of, 150
hitchhiking, 33
hogs, 18, 204
Hoisington, Van, 165–166, 168
Holiday Inn marquee, 90, *91*
holidays at ranch, 202
Holy Cross Hospital, 116
Hopkins, David, 128
Horwitz, Melton "Buddy," *95*, 96
hospitals: Ben Taub Hospital, 34–35, 97–100, 103; Brackenridge Hospital, 115–116, 128, 145; *vs.* doctors' authority, 130–131; Fort Worth psychiatric hospital, 9; Hermann Hospital, 34; Holy Cross Hospital, 116; and hospitalists, 96; Madigan General Hospital, 43, 46–49, *47*; MASH unit, 72; MD Anderson Cancer Center, 34; medical school and residency, 34–35, 36, 97–100, 100–101, 108; Memorial Sloan Kettering, 126; Methodist Hospital, 34, 36; Pueblo mental hospital, 53; racial integration in hospitals, 116; role

Index

of, 130; Seton Hospital, 116, 128, 130–131, 176–177; Shoal Creek Psychiatric Hospital, 172; St. David's hospital, 116; St. Luke's Episcopal Hospital, 34, 100–101, 108; surgical privileges at, 130; surgical team, 2, 116, *117*, 128–129, 144–145; Texas Children's Hospital, 34; VA Hospital, Houston, 35, 103, 140; Vietnamese, 75–78, *76*, 85
house calls, 136
houses: boarding soldiers, 45; first home, 16; grandparents', 16, 187; Hill Country Homes, 162–164; during medical school, 37–38; "new house," 19, *21*, 188, 200; Sunday House, *192*, 202, 208; T House, 202
housing bubble, 165
Houston: during medical school, 37–38; moving family to, 93; surgeons in, 102; traffic, 110; VA Hospital, 35, 103, 140. *see also* Baylor College of Medicine
Howard Payne College, 10, 26, 28, 29
Hubbs, Clark, 32
Hudson, Doug, 177
Huff, Leta Lu, 33
humidity, 71
hunting, 203–204
hunting of people, 84

I

Ia Drang Valley, 62
ice, 18–19
impetigo, 73
Indians, 183–184
infantry, 66–69
information gap and medical records, 96
in-laws, Daddy on, 172
institutions for disabled children, 6–8
insurance: changes in, 142, 147; Medicare, 134, 142; opera singers and, 138; patients and, 112, 114
internal medicine, 77
internship, medical: confidence after, 50; obstetrics/gynecology rotation, 46–49; personal impact of, 49–50; selection of, 43, 45–46. *see also* Baylor College of Medicine
interpreters, 72
interrogations, 83–84

J

Jack, Effie, 183, 184
jail, call from, 132–133
jeeps, army, 52, 54, 72–73, 74–75, *79*
Jenkins, Johnny, 157
jobs, part time: Palace Drug, 27, 33; at Pueblo mental hospital, 53; during residency, 106
Johnson, Lady Bird, 135
Johnson, Luci Baines, 133
Johnson, Lyndon B.: decision not to run for reelection, 103; and Great Society program, 82; and night troop movements, 59; relationship with, 133–135; sworn in as president, 50; and Vietnam War, 55, 59, 103, 134
Johnson, Ronald, 106
Johnson, Tom, 133–134
Jones, Lamar, 124
judge and land theft, 186–187
judgment, development of, 95–96
Junger, Sebastian, 92

K

Kendall, George, 154, 193
Kennedy, Dabney, 33
Kennedy, John F., 50
kerosene lamps, 16, 20
King, Alfred, 168
King, Betty, 167–168
King Ranch, 193
knots, surgical, 102
Kodosky, Gail, 168
Kodosky, Jeff, 168
Koen, Pat, 174
Kraus, H. P., 154, 156
Kushner, Wendi, 168

L

lab tests and lab work, 39–40, 115
Lamar, Mirabeau B., 141
lambs, 14
Lamppin, Doug, 95
land management, 194
landowners, new, 207
land scrips, 182
Lane, Debbie, 1, *117*, 128, 144–145
laryngectomy, supraglottic, 105
larynx: interest in, 137

laundry day, 10
lawsuits, medical, 142–143
Leatherwood, Elaine, 118
letters: collection of, 154; from Debbie Lane, 144–145; from Vietnamese mother, 86, *87*
Levin, Ralph: and Baptist mission, 77–78; friendship with, 51–52; math problems as activity, 65; meeting after war, 85; meeting with Steger, 80–81; and professor, 58
Lewis and Clark expedition, 150, 193
life planning, 164–165
lifestyle, 145
lights, security, 203
Lineback, Carl, 46
Litel, Jerry, 39
literature, classic, 23
livestock, 14, 197. *see also* cattle
loans and lending, 13, 37, 186
Lockhart, 162–164
Lone Star Steward Award, 188, 203, *206*
Longhorns (football team), 32–33
Love Field, 90
Lowe, George, 149–150
Lubrizol Corporation, 38
luck, in Vietnam, 84
Lueck, Anne, 124, 138, 139
Lyric Theatre, 45

M

MACV (Military Assistance Command, Vietnam), 72
Madigan General Hospital, 43, 46–49, *47*
Magellan collection, 154
Maggs Brs. Ltd, 154
magnetic resonance imaging (MRI), 115
Main Library, 31
malpractice suits, 129
mammals and water, 199
map dealers, 152, 154
maps, rare, 2, 151–152, 154
maps, topographical, 199
Marcontell, Jerry, *35*, 37, 39, 40–41, 208
Marcy, Randolph, 193
marines, training with, 54–55
Marks, Ricky, 196
Martin, Fred, 118, 141
MASH (Mobile Army Surgical Hospital) unit, 72

math problems, 65
Mayo Clinic, 126
McFarlane, Joe, 119
McFarlane, John, *119*, 119
McMaster H. R., 82
MD Anderson Cancer Center, 34, 126
mechanized infantry division attack, 54
Medical Corps : advantages of internship with, 43; amphibious landing, 69–71; basic training, 44, 50–53; battalion surgeon, 52–55; discharge from, 89–90; Doctor *vs.* Captain, 48; enlistment, 44; Fifth Mechanized Infantry Division, 51–53; Forty-First Civil Affairs Company, 47, 69–71; impact on medical practice, 52–53, 121; internship at Madigan General Hospital, 43, 46–49, *47*; loss of medical skills, 93; mechanized infantry division attack, 54; principle of service, 44, 56; rank, 44, 65–66. *see also* Civil Affairs Program; Vietnam; Vietnam War
Medical Park Tower, 111
medical practice. *see* Austin Ear, Nose, and Throat Clinic; patients; surgeons and surgery
medical school. *see* Baylor College of Medicine
Medicare, 134, 142
medications, recording of, 77
medicine, practice of: accreditation standards, 94–96; Burns on future of, 146–147; changes in, 96, 113, 142; cost control, 147; hospitalists, 96; hospital *vs.* doctor authority, 130–131; information gap, 96; insurance changes, 142, 147; medical records, 96, 113, 114; Medicare, 134, 142
Memorial Sloan Kettering, 126
memories, personal nature of, 49–50
memorization of names, 26, 168
mesquite trees, 196–197, 198–199
metal chair, patient impaled by, 99–100
Metcalfe, Albert, 203
Metcalfe, Marietta Byrom (niece), *34*, 203
Methodist Hospital, 34, 36
Metropolitan Opera, New York, 138
Mexico City, 106
microscope, surgical, 125
Midland College, 188
midwives, Vietnamese, 79–80
Military Assistance Command,

Index

Vietnam (MACV), 72
military service: principle of, 44, 56. *see* Civil Affairs Program; Medical Corps; Vietnam War
Minear, Johnny, 27, 31
missionaries, Baptist, 77–78
Missouri Home Guards, 180–181
Mobile Army Surgical Hospital (MASH) unit, 72
money: army wages, 43, 45–46, 47; living modestly, 145; medical school and residency, 36, 37, 106; as motivating factor, 2; retreats and planning, 164; value of, 15; wages at Palace Drug, 28
Moody College of Communication, 141
morality, 24
morality in war, 84
Morgan, Boyd, 119–120
Mother. *see* Burns, Ona Louise Winn (Mother)
mother, Vietnamese, 86, *87*
mountain ski training, 54
MRI (magnetic resonance imaging), 115
Murphey, Michael Martin, 137
Muse Wildlife Management Area, 190, 196
music: in Austin, 137; *Cosmic Cowboy* (album), 137; country-western singers, 137–138; Mother and, 10, 13, 15, 23, 188; opera companies and singers, 139–140
mustard gas, 6

N

Nail, Ben, 95
names, memorization of, 26, 168
naps, 122
Nash Phillips/Copus, 165
National Honor Society, 26
Native Americans, 183–184
navigation, 150, 151
navy, 9, 63
Neely, Gail, 95, 96, 97
neurosurgery, 97, 98
New Yorker, 157
New York Times Magazine, 157
Nha Trang, 69–71, 77–78, 169, *171*
Nightingale, Florence, 154
nightmares, recurring, 91–92, 93, 171. *see also* post-traumatic stress disorder (PTSD)
night movements, military, 59

1911 Automatic Colt Pistol, 71–72
Nixon, Richard, 103
nonprofits, suspicion of, 77–78, 166
nose surgery, 97–98, 105, 124
nuns, Catholic, 77, 130–131
nurses: Allen, 128; at clinic, 120–121; Lane, 1, *117*, 128, 144–145; surgical, 128; Vietnamese, 77
Nvidia, 162

O

obstetrics/gynecology rotation, 48–49
Odom, Dwight, 35
officers' dining room, 62
Ogura, Joseph, 105
oil, 204
Olympic National Forest, 200
Olympic Peninsula, 176
on call, 104–105, 115–116
opera companies and singers, 139–140
opinions, medical, 126
"original condition" of ranch, 193–194
otolaryngology (ENT), 45, 93–109. *see also* Austin Ear, Nose, and Throat Clinic
otoplasties, 97–98, 124
outlaws, 184
Owens School District, 20

P

pagers, 104–105
Painter, T. S., 32
paintings, collected, 149
palace, missionary, 77–78
Palace Drug, 27, 33
parade, military, 45
parents: commitment to care for Billy, 6–8; education of, 10; and education of children, 20, 23, 25, 30–31, 32; holding onto the ranch, 188, 203; loss of child, 4; as role models, 10–15; on taking care of family, 171; value of education, 10, 15–16; and Vietnam, 56–57, 59. *see also* Burns, George Pierce (Daddy); Burns, Ona Louise Winn (Mother)
Paris, 154
Parks, Peggy, 26
Parson's Brigade, 181
patients: alcoholics, 132; anesthesia, 46–47; appendectomy at sea, 63–65; bargaining with, 132–133; Burns's reflection on, 143;

call from jail, 132–133; with cancer, 113, 126, 132–133; children, 1–2, 131–132; of clinic, 117, 131–136; complications, 115, 128, 129; country and western singers, 137–138; deaf, 132; and delays, 121; with Down syndrome, 131–132, 143; ER record for, 98–99; examination of, 48; family of, 2; family's influence on treatment, 9; first, 113–114; focus on, 122–123; frankness with, 49, 126; gratitude of, 2, 136, 143–144; gunshot victims, 98–99; house calls to, 136; impaled by metal chair, 99–100; and insurance, 112, 138, 142; Johnson family, 133–135; last surgery, 142; mother of anencephalic baby, 48–49; obligation to, 112; obstetrics, 46–48; opera singers, 138–140; prisoners, 117, 131; and residency, 94; Richards, 135–136; Taylor, 156; in Vietnam, 78–80; wealthy and famous, 136
Patton, George S., 154
peace, after surgery, 129
Pearl Harbor bombing, 44
pediatrics specialist, 120
peer pressure, 94
people, interest in, 157–158
Pershing, John J., 154
personal connections and referrals, 112–113
PET scans, 115
Phi Beta Kappa, 32, 39
philosophy of practice, 111, 112
phones. *see* telephones and telephone calls
photographic stations, 200
physicians. *see* doctors
physics, freshman, 30
piano, 10, 13, 15, 23, 188
Pike, Zebulon, 150, 154, 193
Pike expedition, 193
pistol, 71–72
pitch, speaking, 139
"Plan B," lack of, 42–43
plane, cargo, 88–89
planning, 130, 164–165
Pleiku, 88–89
police headquarters, New York, 161–162
polio, 40
ponds and runoff, 198
pop songs, American, 88
Porter, Wayne, 128, 142
postholes, digging of, 13

post-traumatic stress disorder (PTSD): of doctors in Vietnam, 84; flashbacks, 60, 92; impact of friendships on, 107; nightmares, 91–92, 93, 171; and revisiting Vietnam, 171
poverty, 23
Powers, Bill, 169
Powers, Gene, 141
practice, medical. *see* Austin Ear, Nose, and Throat Clinic; patients; surgeons and surgery
prairie fires, 198
prairie grasses, tall, 194, 197
praise, rarity of, 99
preparation, 26, 107–108, 125, 168
prescribed burns, 198
president, junior class, 26
president of Seton medical staff, 123, 130–131
Preston, Leroy, 26
Price, Sterling, 181
Princeton University, 162
professor, adjunct, 140–141
profiteering, war, 78
profit-sharing plan, 120
prosection, 126
public service, 166–168
public speaking, 91, 168
Pueblo mental hospital, 53

R

rabies cases, 75
racial integration in hospitals, 116
radiation treatments, 172
radio, 19, 45
rain and rainfall, 71, 198, 199–200
ranch, family. *see* Colonel Burns Ranch
ranching, 10, 13–14. *see also* cattle; Colonel Burns Ranch
rank, privileges and disadvantages of, 65–66
real estate bubble, 165
records, medical, 96, 113, 114
referring physicians, 112–113
refrigeration, 18, 20
rehearsal, mental, 107–108, 125
Reid, Isla, 22
Reisch map, 1504, 154
Rembrandt painting, 149
reputation, 99, 105, 107, 124
research, clinical, 40–41, 106

Index

reserves, military, 119
residency, medical: and Alford, 97; and Ben Taub Hospital, 97–100, 103; and calling for help, 94, 95–96; clinical research, 106; confidence in training, 106; developing judgment, 95–96; difficult of, 106–107; ENT rotation, 103–105; ER rotation, 98–100; faculty of, 95, 105–106, 107; financial challenges, 106–107; first year, 94–95; fourth year, 104–105; friends, 92, 95; general surgery rotation, 97–98, 100–102; impact of, 109; memories of, 97, 107; and nightmares, 92, 93; rarity of praise, 99; responsibility for patients, 94; and Vietnam, 87–88, 92, 93. *see also* Baylor College of Medicine; internship, medical
responsibility, 51, 94–96
resting, after lunch, 24
retirement, 108, 141–143, *142*, 164
retreats, personal, 164–166
Reynosa, Michael, 174
Reynosa, Miguel, 173–174
Reynosa, Norma, 174
R. F. Hardin High School, 27
rhinoplasties, 97–98, 105, 124
rice field, *170*
Rice University, 106
Richards, Ann, 135–136
Richardson, Sharon, 118
riding, horseback, 14
Roberts Hall, 31
Roemer, Ferdinand von, 193
Rogers, Laura. *see* Burns, Laura
Rogers, Phil, 162
Rosedale, Ray, 46
Rosenberg, Jack, *95*, 96, 97
Rotary Club, 91
rounds, 94, 98
Rowland, Estel, 6, 183
Royal, Darrell, 33
runoff and grasses, 198
Rural Electrification Act, 19–20
rustlers, cattle, 184–185

S

Saigon, 68, 86–88
Saigon River, 66–69, 169
San Antonio, 50–53
scheduling problems, 86–87
Schwope, Charles, *206*
screwworms, 14
seasickness, 62, 63
second opinions, 101, 126
Secret Service, 134
segregation in hospitals, 116
serenity after surgery, 129
sergeants, 52–53
Sessions, Roy, *95*, 105
Seton Hospital: and Allen, 128; anesthesiologists at, 128; executive committee, 130–131; medical staff of, 130; president of medical staff, *123*, 130–131; and Robin's stroke, 176–177; and Sister Mary Rose, 130–131; surgical practice at, 116; surgical team, 2, 116, *117*, 128–129, 144–145
sextant, 151
Seybold, William, 101, 126
sheep, 14
shell shock, 84
Shoal Creek Psychiatric Hospital, 172
Shoberg, Dick: on Burns's surgical team, 144; calling for help, 1; at Seton Hospital, 128, 130; on taboo against advertising, 113
shoes, 22, 23
showers, 71
sick call: mountain ski training, 54; in Vietnam, 72–75, *76*, 79, *81*
Silvas, Peggy, 128
singers: country-western, 137–138; opera, 138–140
singing, physics of, 140
Singletary, Otis, 32
Sister Mary Rose, 130–131
skin infections, 73, *74*
sky, comfort of, 69
Sleight, Hadley, 163–164
Sloan, Dorothy, 154
Small, Jim, 184
Small, John, 184
Small, Matilda, 184
Small, Mollie. *see* Burns, Mollie Small
small-group and solo practitioners, 113
Smith, E. Kirby, 181
Smith, Larry, 63–65
smoking, 50, 132
Snell, Colonel, 52, 53, 54

Snyder brothers, 185
soda jerk, 27
soil structure and spring flow, 199
soldiers, 44, 45, 83, 84
Sotheby's, 154
Southern Baptist Convention, 78
Southwestern Medical School, 33
Spangler, Richard, 39, 41
Spanish Springs House, 202
Special Forces camp ambush, 74–75
Spellings, Henry, *160, 179, 195*
Spellings, James "Jamie," 162, 169, *179*
Spellings, Margaret Ann Burns (daughter): asthma, 106; birth of, 36–37; education of, 162; with family, 38, *38, 173, 195, 206*; and family ranch, *189*; and father's return from Vietnam, 90; living out of country, 178; time with father, 39, 106–107
Spellings, Paul, *160, 179, 195*
Spellings, Sarah, *159, 195*
spinal anesthesia, 46–47, 63–64. *see also* anesthesia and anesthesiologists
sports, 10, 26
spring flow, 199
St. David's hospital, 116
Steger, Byron, 80–82
Stewart, Mary Lou, 121
St. Luke's Episcopal Hospital, 34, 100–101, 108
stock tanks, 198
Stratton, Cary, 95
stream flow management, 198–199
streams, wet-weather, 198
STRIKE unit, 51
stroke: Daddy's, 187–188; grandfather's, 16, 18; Robin's, 176–177
student council, 26
success: Burns on, 3, 146; family's faith in, 42–43
summers, college break, 33
Sunday House, *192,* 202, 208
Sundays, childhood, 14–15
supraglottic laryngectomy, 105
surgeon, battalion, 52–55. *see also* Medical Corps
surgeons and surgery: and anatomical knowledge, 125–126; appendectomy at sea, 63–65; arriving early for surgery, 124; cancer, 119; children and throat surgery, 1–2; compared to symphony, 129; complications and survival rates, 115, 128, 129; conservation laryngeal, 105, 124; cosmetic, 124; ear, 97–98, 124–125; emergency, 144; facial plastic, 97–98, 105; final, 142; hospitals, 116, 124; importance of studying details, 101; mental rehearsal, 125; minor surgery, 126; observing, 102; outpatient, 124–125; reconstructive, 105; during residency, 97–102; retirement of, 108, 141–142; rhinoplasties, 97–98, 105, 124; thyroid, 124; tonsillectomy, *127;* visualization of procedures, 107–108, 125. *see also* Austin Ear, Nose, and Throat Clinic
surgical team: Baker, 2, *117, 125,* 128–129; connection with, 144–145; in early practice, 116; lessons from military, 52–53; at Seton Hospital, 116, *117,* 128–129, 144–145. *see also* anesthesia and anesthesiologists; technicians, surgical
survival rates, 115, 128, 129
sutures, practicing on chairs, 102
swimmer's ear, 114
symphony, surgery as, 129

T

Taylor, Tom, 156–157
technicians, surgical, 128–129. *see also* surgical team
technology, medical, 146–147
Teel, Karen, 42
telegram, *59,* 59–60
telephones and telephone calls: and being on call, 104–105, 115–116; long distance, 33; from patient in jail, 132–133; portable, 114; at ranch, 20; from Vietnam, 87–88
tennis, 26
"tent city," 71
Tenth Mountain Division, 53
Terry, Luther, 50
testing, animal, 40–41
Texaco research lab, 162
Texas A&M University, 193, 198–199, 200
Texas Army National Guard, 44–45
Texas Children's Hospital, 34, 100–101
Texas Declaration of Independence, 154–157, *155*
Texas Department of Agriculture, 188
Texas House of Representatives, 182

Index

Texas Institute for Rehabilitation and Research, 40
Texas legislature, 182–183, 185, 200
Texas Medical Center, 34–35, 100–101. *see also* Baylor College of Medicine
Texas Medical Center Library, 34
Texas Parks and Wildlife Department, 190, 203
Texas School for the Deaf, 132
Texas Tech University, 31
thesis, 140
Thirty-Sixth Infantry Division, 45
Thorn, Milner, 128
T House, 202
three-year plan, 165
throat surgery, child's, 1–2
Throckmorton, governor, 182
thyroid surgery, 124
titles in Medical Corps, 48
Tobey, David, 119
toilet, indoor, 19
tonsillectomy, *127*
torture, 83–84
Towngate, Jerry, 183
toy and asthma attack, 3
track, 26
traffic, 110
Trans-Olympic Expedition, 1990, *176*
Trans-Texas Airways, 47
traps for wildlife, 199
trauma medicine, 93
travel, 150–151, 158, 169–171
traveling in uniform, 90
Trinidad, 150
Triological Society, 140
troughs, buried, 199
tuberculosis, 73
tumor, brain, 121
Turpin, Luci Baines Johnson, 133
Tyler, Carmen, 118
typhoon, 63

U

uniforms, 63, 90
Unitas, Johnny, 141–142
University of Texas: on advisory councils, 141; application to medical school, 33; bachelor's degree, 33; classes and instructors at, 30, 31–32, 193; and copy of Texas Declaration of Independence, 156; first walk across campus, 29; football games, 32–33; Laura at, 162; and parents' ambition, 28; physics class, 30; and restoration of ranch, 193; School of Music, 137; and speech pathologists training, 141; as student at, 30–34
University of Texas Medical Branch, Galveston, 33
University of Texas Opera Theater, 138
USS *General LeRoy Eltinge*: accommodations and food, 62–63; appendectomy at sea, 63–65; boredom and math problems, 65; service history of, 61–62
US surgeon general, 50

V

VA Hospital, Houston, 35, 103, 140
Vail, 54
Valbonna, Carlos, 40
valedictorian, eighth grade, 25
vegetables: and family ranch, 16, 18; and USS *General LeRoy Eltinge*, 62–63, 68
Vietcong: entering villages at night, 74; knowledge of American movements, 83; price on American doctor's heads, 56–57; sapper attack, 71; targeting departing soldiers, 85; villagers selling medications to, 73
Vietnam: ambush site, 74–75, 170, *170*; Baptist mission in, 77–78, 166; capture risk, 47–48; cholera epidemic, 75, *76*, 78–79; departure from, 85–89; doctors and hospitals, 75–78, *76*, 85; heat, 71; life in, 71–72; medical care in, 65–66, 75–78; revisiting, 169–171. *see also* Medical Corps; Vietnam War
Vietnamese: doctors, 77; expectations of, 73–74; harassment of, 83; interrogation of prisoners, 83–84; as people, 83; selling medications, 73; and sick call, 72–75, *76*
Vietnam War: ambush, 73, 74–75, 170, *170*; ambush training, 51; Army After-Action Report, 85, 213–219; Burns's feelings on, 82–83; choice to serve, 56; "Danny Boy," 70; departure for, 56–57, 59–60; distance of, 51; effect on families, 90; focus on numbers and efficiency, 82; foreboding, 48; free-fire zones, 84; harassment of Vietnamese girls, 83; impact on doctors, 84–85; interrogation of prisoners, 83–84; and Johnson, 55,

59, 103, 134; lack of direction in, 82; life in jungle, 71–72; loss of medical skills, 93; medical equipment, 61, 72, 80; in news, 55; nightmares from, 91–92, 93, 171; opposition to, 90; orders for, 56–60; as ranking doctor, 65–66; reluctance to discuss, 92; return home, 85–89, 90, 91, *91*; Saigon River, 65–69; sick call, 72–75, *76, 79, 81*; Steger's visit, 80–82; USS *General LeRoy Eltinge*, 61–65, *67*. see also Civil Affairs Program; Medical Corps
viruses, 138, 139–140
VisiCalc, 114
visualization, 107–108, 125
vocal function, 124
vocal problems, 138–139
vocal technique, 137–138
voice, caring for, 139
voice, loss of, 135–136
Vung Tau, 65, 69

W

wages: in army, 43, 45–46, 47; at Palace Drug, 28
Wang computer, 114, 115
war, as club, 92
war, psychological, 75, 82–83
water and water management: and 1950s drought, 14; buried troughs, 199; luxury of hot, 19; runoff, 194–195; stream flow management, 198–199; trenches for garden, 16; wet-weather streams, 198; and wildlife, 199; windmill, 14, 16, 202
Weaver, Allen, *95*, 96–97
Weber, Sam, *95*, 96
wells, 199
Western Hemisphere, 150, 151
wetland, creating of, 199
Wiggins, Major, 65

wildlife and wildlife conservation, 197–198, 199–200, 203
wildlife valuation, 200
Williams, Betsy, *176*
wind, 18
wind charger, 19
windmill, 14, 16, 202
wind towers, 204
Winegar, Brad, *110*, 119
Winn, Mary Etta "Mommie": and Billy's birth, 7; burial site of, 183; and Burns, 3, 6, 26, 112; caring for brother, 171; Christmas dinners, 15; and Mother's depression, 9; photos of, *4, 5, 24, 187*; reading Bible stories, 24; religious faith of, 6; renting rooms to soldiers, 45
Winn, Ona Louise. see Burns, Ona Louise Winn (Mother)
Winn, Paul (uncle), *5,* 37, *187*
Winn, Rowland, 28
Winn, T. L., 183, *187*
Winn Pharmacy, 37
wives and character of men, 45, 47–48, 120
Wooten, Angela, 118
work, 10–15
World War I, 6
World War II, 13, 19, 44–45
worms, stomach, 14
Wright, Bill, 105
Wucher, Gay, 118

X

X-rays, 48–49, 98, 115
Xylocaine, 115

Y

Yaneke, Johan, *95*
yard work, 117
Yellow Pages, doctors in, 113
Youngblood, John, 115